The Lively Credentials of God

The Lively Credentials of God

KENNETH CRAGG

DARTON · LONGMAN + TODD

First published in 1995 by
Darton, Longman and Todd Ltd
1 Spencer Court
140–142 Wandsworth High Street
London SW18 4JJ

ISBN 0–232–52128–X

A catalogue record for this book is available
from the British Library

Phototypeset by Intype, London
Printed and bound in Great Britain by
Page Bros, Norwich

Contents

	Preface	vii
1	Divine Credentials Sought	1
2	Conjectured	18
3	Queried	35
4	Anticipated	52
5	Presented	71
6	Comprehended	88
7	Enscriptured	108
8	Credalised	128
9	Hazarded in the Church	145
10	Suspected and Neglected	164
11	On Many Counts Discounted	182
12	Finding Credentials Divine	200
	Notes	219
	Post Scripta	243
	Index	245

Preface

THERE cannot be intelligent enquiry without the presence of meaning. Any significant question assumes that answer is needed and is conceivably available. Otherwise no interrogation would suggest itself, no query could arise. It follows that doubt cannot be totally inclusive. There is no mapping without territory, no climbing in the absence of mountains.

The more comprehensive the question the more crucial the answer. Hence the concern of this book with the credentials of God. The notion that we need to ask about them may surprise a pious believer. It is anxiety to the wistful sceptic and folly to the hardened secular soul. That God might *need* to be answerable to humankind might be a near blasphemous idea to the traditionally godly: it must be urgently desirable to the weary and the heavy-laden.

But – either way – what could, what would, divine credentials be? For the way we think to identify what they are may beg the questions they should satisfy.

In all our transactions and relationships we require documentation. 'Get it in writing,' we say, aware that things said and heard may be denied, misheard, distorted or disowned. 'Bring a testimonial' says the interviewer to a prospective employee. 'By these presents' runs the legal script. 'Here to affirming, we have affixed our episcopal seal this day of our Lord . . .' run 'Holy Orders' at ordination. Everywhere there is the rubric: 'Have it in writing.'

How, then, might God be credentialled and what could the 'writing' be? Note 'credentials' are not 'guarantee'. The latter does not ride with faith. What, we are asking, can be identified as credentialling God for intelligent, honest and dependable trust? The human scenario, rightly measured, must set the terms. Shakespeare's Sonnet 66 has that scenario well.

> '. . . needy something trimm'd in jollity,
> And purest faith unhappily foresworn,

And gilded honour shamefully misplac'd,
And maiden virtue rudely strumpeted,
And right perfection wrongfully disgrac'ed . . .
And art made tongue-tied by authority,
And folly, doctor-like, controlling skill,
And simple truth miscall'd simplicity,
And captive good attending captain ill . . .'

The poet's realism about us humans is where we have to start concerning God. The sound credentials of God will need more than the sweet beauty of Grasmere, though this they will incorporate. It is where the oppressed spirit registers protest and despair that we must locate the concerns of faith. Cartography of the ocean deeps has no use for a few fathoms line.

All in all it looks like the kind of world where only wounded hands will offer divine credentials. The divine element in human experience, as Plato knew, is persuasive not coercive. Christianity deepens that insight into persuasive and redemptive. What we can perceive to be *over* us in law and ethics, we may discover *with* us in grace and forgiveness and so *through* us in the human transactions of all four.

It would seem that we have a situation in which the transcendent is the vulnerable, where sovereignty is a story of risk and the Infinite is Self-finited, a world, in brief, where God could well be crucified. If indeed it were so with the divine, then history must have contained that abiding truth of things in a drama, in time and place, where its meaning was discernibly enshrined. The clues would then be in that event, its quality and sequel, the reception it received in a community of conviction that learned to identify its evidence as 'the Lord's doing, marvellous in our eyes.'

We should then know what the old Biblical writers called 'the place of the Name', the locale which, as history and event, gave us 'in writing' the credentials we find for our seeking. It is these that the chapters here aim to understand and to have understood – the Christian credentials of God.

KENNETH CRAGG
Oxford, 1995

1 Divine Credentials Sought

i

'I WOULD not have known what to make of the world if it had not been for the French Revolution,' wrote Thomas Carlyle to a friend.[1] He made it the theme of a massive telling in volumes of historical fervour and imagination phrased in his own arduous prose. For he saw in the French Revolution a reassuring vindication of an ethic at the core of time, a principle of nemesis on political tyranny and corruption, a spontaneous vindication of the human meaning. William Wordsworth had shared the same exuberance about

> France standing on top of golden hours
> And human nature seeming born again.[2]

Both poet and historian were disproved and knew themselves so when the thrust of revolution brutally devoured its own authors and issued into the imperalism of Napoleon.

'I would not know what to make of the world but for the cross of Christ' might well be the *cri de coeur* that constitutes being Christian, provided we take that open secret at the heart of things with all the implications of its antecedents and its sequel as faith perceives them. That would be to anticipate. There is much ground to cover, much interrogation to allow, before we can with integrity think to know what we 'make of the world' and where. For the moment we simply note the human impulse to seek (playing on words as we do) the inclusive clue, the point where we might be bold to identify what must contain all else, the key to perplexity and the warranty of hope.

Perhaps no such criterion exists. Maybe any faith there could be is merely stuttering with metaphors. Perhaps we should only and ever-more interrogate and never conclude. Edwin Muir has the idea exactly:

I would rather have the problems themselves, for – from the awareness of their vastness – I get some sort of living experience, some
sense of communion, of being in the whole in some way, whereas
from the explanations I should get only comfort and re-assurance
and a sense of safety which I know is not genuine.[3]

A frequent note in the current critique of believers reproves and resists
what it sees as no more than the desire to be consoled. There is point
in the warning. Even so, it needs a warning in reverse. Joy might still be
the categorical imperative in our existence, in which case we should
be wary of the cult of sceptical masochism, making a pretence of
despair.

Either way, we are here. We are free to think the fact absurd but
we could not even make that judgement without reference to some
meaning. Meaninglessness is disproved by the very will to suspect it.
For the more we suspect meaninglessness the more we circumscribe
within our private selves the limits of reality, and even there it will
intrude upon our wilful isolation from it. To relate is to realise – the
more open the one the more ample the other, ample both as mystery
and as wonder, as discovery and demand.

It follows that 'being in the whole' sets for us the question of God. It
makes the question of God paramount round all other searchings of
the mind and yearnings of the heart. Or, if 'God' seems here for some
too equivocal a word, let us say 'the transcendent', the counterpart to
that within us which keeps venturing to understand, the referent which
is somehow there to leave meaning in our very inquietude and misgiving. However distracted we may be with the perplexity of our affairs, our
ironies and our frustrations, we cannot be those for whom everything
matters except everything, the whole to which we must return the
parts. For different parts, familial, social, economic, academic, artistic,
aesthetic and political, are all inter-wholes elsewhere, and as the
embrace widens we sense the 'one' that for ever remains and belongs
with these 'connections'. All the significant questions we raise in our
mind because of life transcend (while they incorporate) our own
immediacy. There is thus religious dimension in the very feasibility of
sciences, the celebration of arts and the pulses of society. Life leaves
us no final option of neutrality. It is insistent that values must be
identified and pursued. Perversities have their occasions and their
consequences no less than righteousness and love. 'O what a quench-
less feud is this,' cried Herman Melville, 'that Time hath with the sons
of men.' Decisions belong in a hierarchy that tends towards an absolute
by which relatives can be known to be such. That necessity can be made
sharply imperative as in some forms of the Muslim cry: Allahu akbar,
'Greater is God.' Yet such abrupt custody of the demand, 'Let God be
God,' may fail to realise that the custody itself may forget its true role
and sit on God's throne as its own. For the religious institution is never
the transcendent. To know that 'God is greater' holds the hope of a true
subordination of all else to the only sovereignty that truly relativises

the false claims and claimants. In all our studies here we are bound over to the will to understand how, and where, it is that God is God, doing so in the fullest awareness we can reach of what it is that humanity is human. The two must always interfuse if divine credibility is the theme. It is that fact alone which makes it legitimate to speak at all of divine credentials.

ii

At first glance, and perhaps throughout for some religions, it would seem inappropriate to hold the transcendent to any sort of liability of our requiring or desiring. Shall the clay say to the potter: 'Why hast thou made me thus?' How can that to which, or to whom, all else is subject be itself subject to scrutiny or assessment from the realm over which sovereignty presides? Our thoughts of God need definition and elucidation throughout these chapters, but can we well begin with some notion of divine accountability of which we are judges? Must not all be arbitrary, absolute, immune from all interrogation? To call the transcendent into question might seem to imply that 'it' ceases to transcend, being liable to criteria somehow above and beyond it – of which, ironically, humans are presuming to be masters.

There have been faiths that held aloof from any and all interrogation of God. It is possible to think of some malevolence which has deliberately poisoned life in the world and no cause for our demur. In the burden of unravelling the Shoah, Elie Wiesel is ready to credit God with evil.[4] Or, seeing the transcendent as incorrigibly inscrutable, others have wanted to be rid of God as the only way of holding on to their own liability. 'You were quite right when you cut out the character of God. He only distracts us from our own responsibility.'[5] That might well be true of *some* characterisations of God. To see that is to concede that characterisations indeed differ. There is, then, no escape from assessing them and we are left to realise that an indifferent transcendent makes for a contradiction in terms. 'Shall not the judge of all the earth do (and be) right?'

Islam perhaps of all semitic faiths has been most ready to enthrone the unquestionable as power, to understand the divine as beyond interrogation. Nevertheless, the Qur'ān acknowledges Allah as accepting to be obligated. It is legitimate, in proper context, to say 'God ought . . .'[6] The most notable occasion is in Sura 4:165, where the vital 'sending' of messengers to humankind is read as the discharge of a duty for lack of which Allah must be found in default. For it describes their being sent as ensuring that 'there is no case (or argument) against Him seeing they were sent'. The clear implication is that for lack of their being sent, Allah would have failed the test of the 'ought' that was upon Him. For, in that event of divine dereliction of duty, humankind would have been left to grope in the dark of ignorance with no occasion for a right *islām*.

There are other theists who would want to take this insight further,

believing that what it takes God to be God – *vis-á-vis* what humankind is
– must mean, for law's own sake, something more than law. If so,
divine relation to the world must be not only legal and hortatory but
redemptive. That larger sense of things divine and human will be with
us throughout these chapters. For it belongs with God as Messianically-
divine and divinely-Messianic. Can we leave the Questioner of all else
alone unquestioned? If nature and history, for all their vagaries, are
truly supportive of the human enterprise – the case we have yet to
explore – and, being supportive, also hospitable, then it is impossible
to think of unrelated transcendence or of sovereignty as sublime
immunity.

Human identity, for all its limits, is an experience of autonomy. It
tells of an entrustment in which we have been 'let be' – not in the sense
of abandonment but of privilege and mutuality. Circumscribed our
powers may be, but they are our own and assume our engagement with
the onus of their nature. And purposiveness left to our own human
competence suggests a magnanimity that sets its ends only in our
freedoms. A transcendence that waits for partnership takes the risk of
our withholding it. By the deepest measures of our humanity we are led
to the perception of the vulnerability of God. The infinite in being such
is Self-finited.

Some sense that, even if it were not so, it ought to be, seems to arise
from the agony of the author of Job – surely among the most anguished
of all searchers for divine credentials. 'O that I knew where I might find
Him' is a cry that knows itself authentic in the very urgency of its
despair. At the outset it is said that Job did not 'charge God foolishly'.
When his travail deepened the implication became clear that God
could, and should, 'be charged wisely', that is, responsibly. So much is
evident from the feeble measure of credentials his 'friends' adopted,
with their trite philosophy of due requital and omnipotent will, in their
attempt to counter Job's own insistent confidence in transcendent
justice, his appeal to a sovereignty on which worship might lay honest
claim. To be sure, the conclusion of the drama can be read in overwhelming terms of divine power that seems to leave credential-seeking
futile. Modern technology would not find their challenge overwhelming
in the least.[7] Even in submission, however, the towering figure of the
man from the land of Oz remains in all literature a supreme seeker and
framer of the tests by which God might be credible. No Christian
believing can leave him repenting 'in dust and ashes' nor think to 'see
God' with the same cowed and timorous eyes. Job's final image belies
the book's conclusion. We can hardly be content with divine greatness
that leaves Job greater than God.

The deeper clues *we* have to guide us lay outside his ken. For a while
we had better stay with the advocacies of his 'friends'. For much of the
puzzle about divine credentials is the case-making and the clamour of
those who think they have them in possession. In a crisis of near despair
the psalmist cried: 'O God, say something on your own behalf' (Ps.
74:22 - 'plead thine own cause'). Credentials for God tend to be pro-

nouncements of custodians. There is much 'taking of the Name in vain' – a situation which only underlines the need to perceive where the credentials, not the custodians, could be speaking for themselves. Partisanship distorts or confuses what supposedly it has in trust. 'The Son of man', we remember, was 'betrayed with a kiss.'

If credentials are to be dependably 'God's', we shall need to have ground for a faith that they have been self-given. That necessity can only deepen the question of criteria. It must also mean that their being truly found will turn on their being rightly sought. For they are not placarded in the form of overwhelming evidence that would leave no room for our honest perception or our glad discovery. But can such perception and discovery be truly ours so that each and all have responsibility for their response? Will not many be caught in circumstances of poverty, pain or mental privation which will preclude their real capacity for any venture of faith? Or will not the sheer dimensions of mystery and meaning send them back timidly or languidly to the consolations of established authority, the burden of faith being too heavy for any individual decision?

If so, we shall be back with the counterparts of Job's 'friends', the professionals about God, the God-sponsors, who will undertake the God question for us. That issue will recur throughout these pages – the dilemma of personal liability for the all-important decisions of faith and yet the necessary role of counsel, common concern, institutionalised experience and shared enquiry, since none begin *de novo* and 'no man liveth to himself'. Yet the several 'theologies' that might serve us – though subject to a proper scrutiny – may want to override it in the confidence of their tradition and the prestige of their canons, as these are patterned into creed and structured into rituals which the uncritical may all too easily adopt as sacrosanct and inviolate.

Submitting, if we do, too readily, we play into the hands of our authorities and ignore the temptations they undergo precisely by being proprietors of divine things. For, as such, they acquire repute and dignity and succumb to self-interest as though somehow they have become masters of the themes they once had only as servants. We have to leave room for the suspicion that they have identified 'the name of the Lord' with their own placing of it. When the psalmist pleaded with God to 'maintain His own cause', he assumed it must coincide with his 'own cause', 'the heathen being come into His [his] sanctuary' (Ps. 74:3). Religions and theologies thus become possessive of their own versions of faith. So doing, they generate a claim on loyalty which becomes a loyalty to loyalty, a demand to abide with an orthodoxy which has come to represent inviolable things of God. The situation may then resemble that of orchestras, theology in the place of music, in Thomas Beecham's reputed comment: 'The English may not like music, but they absolutely love the noise it makes.' His might be a wry verdict on centuries of believing – Jewish, Christian, Muslim and all else. In our age of secularity many have come to despise or deplore 'the noise it makes' – a fact which then renders it more difficult for each and all to have ears and mind for the music of truth and faith or to appreciate what the harmonies are, or whether they are only discords.

iii

Crucial to all the foregoing are the concept and the claim of 'revelation'. Most faiths prize the thought of divine disclosures, mediations of meaning that hold the referents by which to know where the answers are. The fact that these differ so widely while being comparably assertive only makes discernment the more problematic for those who may be minded, and able, for it. What, we might ask, of the credentials of credentials, the proof of the worthiness to be received, as claimed by the documents where all worthiness resides? Scriptures, in most faiths, have acquired, and long enjoyed, a status assumed to exempt them from any dubiety so that the contents are *ipso facto* truth. Fidelity is then expected to be entirely receptive. The formula, 'This is the word of the Lord', even said incongruously after some command about massacre or, as in Qoheleth, a most bewildering expression of futility,[8] ends all question. Almost at the outset the Qur'ān announces itself as 'a Book wherein there is nothing dubious' (Sura 2, 2). When in Hebrew Torah and *Tanakh* 'God spoke to Moses saying . . .' or 'The word of the Lord came to Elijah,' we may not stay to ask: 'How did he know?'

In a necessary sense, though differing widely in its degree and rationale, all Scriptures require engagement with their content. 'Fundamentalism' in the strictest form would be that of anyone consulting a telephone directory. Being purely informational and statistical, it can be taken as the given truth (barring misprint). Plainly, sacred texts can never be that way. The wise reader always has to relate intelligently, asking whence they came, why they happened, how they work – whether as narrative, metaphor, allegory, poem, argument or sermon. What layers of meaning might they comprise, immediate in time and place of origin, or ultimate in due perspective? The Qur'ān distinguishes between verses that are 'categorical' and others that are 'allegorical' (Sura 3:7), but leaves with the reader the task of identifying both. Elsewhere, it has an enigmatic passage about questioning:

> When My servants question you [Muhammad] concerning Me, in truth I am near. I answer the call of the suppliant who cries to Me. So let them hearken to Me: let them believe in Me that they may be rightly led. (Sura 2:186)

Clearly questions belong and one can be 'wrongly led', but 'belief' is requisite. The verb in the first sentence is about 'interrogation' – being addressed to Muhammad about Allah. That might be taken for theological enquiry. Yet the second verb seems to be about 'answering' prayer. How should 'I am near' be understood? Is there a divine sympathy with puzzled readers?

Comparable situations of reader tutelage by text are familiar enough in the houses of Torah study in Judaism. Chapter 7 below will broach the vexed issues of being scriptured, and scripturising, in Christianity. Wherever things divine are textualised the onus persists on every readership as to how it should align with what is read. It is clear that the text is entirely at the mercy of such aligning, since it can never interpret itself. Believers may well talk of 'understanding the Qur'ān by the Qur'ān' or of holding a fully 'biblical theology', but the crucial decisions will still be theirs. Scriptures cannot rise from the page and countermand what readers say they find.

It is this disconcerting fact which makes resort to, care for, and reliance on, Scriptures more complex and responsible than these are often thought to be. It does not simplify the task of pursuing divine credentials, the more so if there are those among the faithful who think they can short-circuit the equation. Time also is part of that teasing situation. For Scriptures are 'canonical', closed, sealed, final, being the last word in an unrepeatable category. If there is 'yet more light to break forth' from them, they will not say what it is. Believers must find it out, which might seem to make 'breaking forth' an odd turn of phrase. God's scriptured credentials, then, can be no simple blueprint we need do no more than cite as if meaning were verbatim.

There is a further problematic many have sensed in the concept of 'revelation', aside from that of its entrustment into document and text. It has to do with a certain paradox. 'Revelation' needs to be, and is, acknowledged as such. We are meant to believe that we have it. Recognition has waited on its claim and purport. This may imply that we have known what we should be looking for by our very ability to realise that we have received it. If, however, we have known what to look for, did we really need it? Or, conversely, if it were addressing us in total ignorance, how were we to identify it doing so? The issue, of course, is not insoluble: it means that truth has to be self-authenticating, intrinsic to, and for, the situations it addresses.

The sharp issues about authority, the relation of reason to revelation, or the concepts of 'natural' and 'special' revelation can perhaps best be handled under the analogy of a river – springs and tiny streams in the hills and tidal flow into and above the estuary. The latter only flows up the banks and channels afforded by the former, which, for their part, merge into the tidal current. The two have a converging destiny. The tiny, tentative, flowing sources, sensing a destiny beyond their own attainment, would then symbolise the queries and intimations of the rational mind, the questing ventures of intellectual courage. For such courage, by its own nature, must necessarily resist suspicions of its own futility. Confronted by riddles it may well feel itself to be, yet that very fact can properly only stimulate it to deeper encounter with what vexes it. It may then find itself ready, without humiliation or duress, to realise the relevance of revelation, conjoining and confirming its proper dignity. If so, then revelation, for its part, will more truly deserve its mandate to illuminate, precisely by enlisting, not countermanding or dismissing, the mental quality of its recipients. As we shall find ample occasion later to insist, neither reason nor revelation will deserve attention if they do not stay realistically close to the human predicament as an honest realism about sin and evil knows it to be.

iv

Revelation presupposes something intervening in history. It must have the category of 'event,' whether in terms of prophetic call like that of Amos and Jeremiah in the biblical tradition and of Muhammad in the Qur'ānic, or in terms inread in happenings like the Exodus, the Exile, the battle of Badr,[9] or the person, ministry and death of Jesus as the Christ.

Some modern thought is liable to reject any sense of divine intervention in history, presumably because it conflicts with the 'laws' of nature or implies something fickle, arbitrary or spontaneous in the, supposedly, self-sufficient and unchanging transcendent. Thus, for example, Maurice Wiles writes: 'The idea of supernatural divine intervention was a natural category of thought and faith in a way that is no longer true.'[10] It would follow that the Christian faith in the Incarnation has to be seen as appropriate only to an earlier age when humanity thought in such 'advent' terms.

It would seem to follow, then, that up-to-date thinking must opt for a divine absentee or at least for a transcendent seen as incapable of doing other than transcend. It must follow, again, that we are sent back to the perennial contradiction of a sovereignty that can never exert what sovereignty supposedly means. Reservations will be right if we are thinking of the merely capricious or haphazard. Divine interventions, if we credit them, must carry credentials close to issues urgently human and worthily divine, but that such credentials are viable and discernible must surely be part of faith in any transcendent at all.

Moreover, the problem of divine 'intrusions' dissolves if we see that it is incurred by the very nature of time. If we are positing an eternal/temporal relation then a point in time will be crucial. What is meant into time will enlist time into its meaning. Its 'substance' will have 'accidence', not in the old philosophic sense of 'matter', but in the requisites of where and when as the theme of who and whence and whither. In the old haunting Hebraic phrase, there will be 'a place for the Name'. That its identity may be misread, argued, queried, may well happen – that whole theme is our present care. That identity in time and place can never 'happen' would make the transcendent either indifferent or absurd. That, either way, would 'untranscend' it. Faith must mean history, unless – impossibly – we are to go out of this world and out of ourselves. If 'emmanuel' – in some sense – is not right about God, all else is vacuous.[11]

V

That 'God with us' formula as a vital clue is also a deep pitfall. We can best pursue our sense of divine credentials being scrutinised and assessed if we turn now to study the ways in which they might be falsified. Doing so will be a significant part of our positive task. It is natural to our human scene that conjectures or convictions about God should have had, almost invariably (we might say inescapably) frames of reference that are tribal, territorial, racial and so, in turn, proprietorial. Rituals, Scriptures, theologies, by these denominators of earthly experience, would seem to be instinctive to our humanness. For ancestry, heredity, locale and memory are elemental forms of life and being. Birth, habitat, community of breed and place, and the history these celebrate, cherish and commemorate, determine in every people the awareness, in some form, of transcendent reference. Being Jewish, as the Hebrew Bible enshrines it, is the most signal, but by no means the unique, expression of peoplehood religiously received. There was, and is, nothing naturally exceptional about the rain that falls on Canaan, the waters from the snows of Hermon, the migrations across Jordan, or the patriarchs who symbolise the story.

Inasmuch as all identities possess territories, shape cultures, nurture offspring, revere tombs, fear death and dream dreams, all in their diversity recruit symbols, make ritual, hallow sites and enshrine worship. Their sense of what transcends only slowly escapes the constraints of their own awareness of themselves. Given wider perspectives it still competes with what, perhaps idyllically, Wordsworth called

> Those mysteries of being which have made
> And shall continue evermore to make
> Of the whole human race one brotherhood.[12]

If, as in the biblical, Christian tradition, one particular expression of a people's register of the transcendent and themselves is seen to have been the vehicle of a universal divine fulfilment, one clear fact must follow, namely, that all other aspirations belong in that fulfilment. We have already seen how revelation needs 'minute particulars'. Where it has found and fulfilled them they will remain neither 'minute' nor exclusive. Discussion to come in Chapter 5, around the divinely Messianic, will address this point more fully.

A sense of privacy, or privilege, or exceptionality, obtaining between the divine and our human societies, was for long natural and instinctive in varied cultures. Isolations of geography made it so, corroborated by racial enmities and the sheer competitiveness of human interests, fortunes and conflicts. 'The Lord of this house', as it was in Mecca in the birth-throes of Islam, echoes round the human story in countless sanctuaries of divine-human encounter induced by hope and fear, the vagaries of nature and the passions of time. When, in the narrative of Exodus 24:9–11, Moses and seventy elders went up the mountain and 'they saw the God of Israel', the nexus of 'He and they' is evident in the divine title. When, later, we learn of 'the Lord of hosts' the phrase is more likely to mean the armed 'hosts' of Joshua and other heroes than the starry 'hosts' of the night sky over all the human lands.

How might the sanctities of Sinai compare with Jomo Kenyatta's Kere-Nyaga, or Mount Kenya? He writes:

> The mountain of brightness is believed by the Gikuyu to be Ngai's resting-place, and in their prayers they turn towards Kere-Nyaga and, with their hands raised towards it, they offer their sacrifices, taking the mountain to be the holy earthly dwelling-place of Ngai . . . literally, 'descending and resting or dwelling place of God'.[13]

Earlier, quoting his own teacher, Kenyatta explains: 'All words which express religious beliefs, moral values or specific technical or ritual proceedings, can only be rendered by reference to the social organis-ation of the tribe, their beliefs, practices, education and economics.'[14] Anthropology yields parallel evidence from the vast diversity of such tribal, territorial reference for the divine. It follows that the divine credentials we are seeking must belong radically with all that is implicit in such corporate, endlessly multiple, patterns of such human refer-ence. It follows, also that they will be falsified if they are still bonded unilaterally with the interests, the perceptions, the traditions, of *any* racial context, if these are not opened out to that universal possession and participation which alone is compatible with the unity of God. 'The grace of God' is, indeed, 'manifold' and in need of 'good stewards' who will possess how manifold it is (1 Pet. 4:10). As such, however, it will not offer credentials essentially contracted to some, by dint of birth or place or culture, as conditions which, by their nature, are denied to others. Credentials manifestly cease to be such if there is that about them which withholds them from universal recognition or acceptance. They cannot be in the coded language of private privilege or admit of the paradox of an only people's other people.

That necessity is not only a corollary of the unity of the transcendent. It must also follow from the realisation, across human history, of how far the name of God has been invoked to sanction racial self-esteem and warrant martial strife. Religions have a tragic history of abetting discords and conflicts, adding dimensions of pseudo-holiness to the passions of competition over territory or the honour of clan and nation. Sacred Scriptures themselves have been recruited to those ends – if they have not initially required them. The Bible, or its users, have not been the least of offenders in this context. Writing in *Voices from the Margin*, Robert Allen Warrior, an Amerindian Christian, explains his difficulties with the Book of Joshua which provided the perfect cue for the white conquest and possession of his country, historically achieved on the same grounds of 'the name of God' and the dispossession of 'the heathen'. Thinking of Egyptians and the hapless Canaanites, he writes:

Yahweh the deliverer became Yahweh the conqueror. The obvious characters in the story for Native Americans to identify with were the Canaanites, the people who already lived in the promised land. As a member of the Osage nation of American Indians who stands in solidarity with other tribal people around the world, I read the Exodus stories with Canaanite eyes.

He goes on to add how Israel in Canaan was divinely empowered to 'build a society where the evils done [to Canaanites] have no place [i.e., no recognition] . . . The indigenes are to be destroyed.'[15] Clearly, the Biblical – indeed, the Semitic – faiths, if not others, have much to do dissociating the credentials of God from all that, unpurged of race and pride, would render them null and void. 'Let God be God' has to be retrieved from all that, otherwise, would privatise a universal sovereignty purloined to racial ends. Perhaps we should even ask whether the fitting credentials are fitted to belong in any entrustment at all? Darkly to conclude so forgets 'the God of patience'.

vi

Akin to the falsifying racial and territorial prepossessions in theology and faith is the sense of being 'proprietor to truth', which goes too often with the institutionalising of religion in cult, creed and ritual.[16] Divine credentials will be found involved with the pretensions of their purveyors. These have often been seen as inherently competitive. The truth of one must imply or argue the untruth of another. That situation has been a factor in the rise of an impatient secularity, turning away from things divine in a distaste for the controversies of believers. Secularity, however, is itself in no way free from pretension. Liberalism (vague term as it is) may contrive its own fundamentalism.

The contemporary concern for 'dialogue', limited as its circles are, has made some aware of the need for self-interrogation and for reconsidering their inhospitality to others. It goes without saying that divine credentials must be liberated from the bigotry, the hardness of heart, the atrophy of love, which too often have beset them. The 'we' and the 'us' of spiritual identity must be ready to have and to claim only servant status when they speak of 'ours' concerning God.

That necessity in the care of God's credentials needs, however, to be vigilant. For the will to be inclusive may obscure issues requiring to be broached. Tolerance has to be robust about its limits as well as generous about its range. It is hard to have honest reservations about what has traditionally defined ourselves. It is no less hard to maintain firm, and gentle, conviction where reservations have no place. Examples of the former might well lie for Christians (as we shall see in Chapter 8) in the mind and terms of the Council of Chalcedon or in some approaches to St John's Gospel.[17] For Judaism they may lie in the inferiorisation of the 'Gentiles' consequent on 'chosen' status. For Islam there remain the open questions about *Allahu akbar* and whether suffering love is within the range of the 'greatness' meant, and about the propriety of force in the constraints within belief. The liabilities of some Buddhists for a possible 'double-crossing' of 'the good intention' (if such it be) behind creation will call for concern in Chapter 11.

The liabilities here must belong, in every case, with the faiths concerned, even if wise interrelations may assist. The only point here is that they belong also in a common business with divine credentials. These deserve insistent reverence and sustained humility. If, as will be argued here, Christians believe they have, in Jesus as the Christ, an epitome of what divine credentials need to be, adequate as a self-disclosing of God in convincing relevance to our human case, that sense of things must hold itself ready at all times for the utmost ministry to, and converse with, whatever makes other faiths sceptical or hesitant about the criteria. The situation, properly undertaken, must engage all and sundry in authentic realism about humankind and what we might discern as measures of transcendence. Only so will witness be commensurate with its own meaning. If it is only 'the pure in heart who see God' it will only be they who can report their 'seeing'.

vii

For this whole context there remains the question: What fields of interest are divine credentials expected to satisfy? It will suffice here to ponder three: the miraculous, the speculative and the liberationist. There has long been an instinct in religion to yearn for the kind of certitude which may be induced in certain moods by what is taken to be sheer overwhelming miracle, some arbitrary demonstration of the otherwise inexplicable which may be supposed to constitute stunning, incontrovertible evidence – this being, precisely, what we need to have. For others, theology is required to keep in step with philosophy and probe truth for its puzzlement rather than for its wonder. Others again, not least in this century, have called on theology to stay close to the issues and tasks of political liberation, recruiting faith's texts and traditions for light on injustice and oppression and resources to overcome them. On this third view, speculative theology is no more than an escape mechanism, a tactic of neglect, if not evasion, in view of the despairs of travailing societies.

All three will bear on what credentials about God must comprise. The first need not detail us long. For credulity can never equate with faith, unless it can be educated into it. Nor can magic belong with the kingdom of heaven. Merely fortuitous miracle clues no mysteries, redeems no lives, penetrates no despairs. It always leaves the haunting question of why it befell here and was withheld there. It shows no reason for its whims and vagaries. It degrades the dignity of human intelligence and relies only on the extraneous element of marvel to have its way. In a Christian context we have only to ponder the narrative of Jesus in the wilderness to know that casually 'turning stones into bread', or descending brazenly from the Temple's pinnacle supposedly to land unscathed among astonished spectators, have no part in 'the ways of God'.

Robert Browning puts the point with characteristic force:

> . . . there needs no second proof with good
> Gained for our flesh from any earthly source.
>
> . . . . .
>
> So faith grew making void more miracles
> Because too much: they would compel, not help.[18]

The more extraneously compelling, the less morally and spiritually authentic are the elements of faith. That which breeds perplexity cannot well underwrite faith.

'Extraneous' is a deliberate word here. For the reader may well be wondering: Are there not 'signs and wonders' in the New Testament, in the Gospels and in Acts? What are we to say of what seems their centrality in the Fourth Gospel? We need discernment here. It has been supposed by some expositors that 'signs and wonders' were relevant at a different time and temper than ours in human culture, a time when hearts were capable of being impressed that way, a concession to human imagination as it may have been.

That, at most, is only part of the story. If divine credentials have their ground and index in the Christhood of Jesus they must stand integrally in all that Christhood was in word and action, quality and meaning, for its own sake and by its own significance. As such, however, its mediation into faith-telling may well be 'signified' in what, for 'wonder,' is seen to derive from, and be consonant with, the meaning of the whole. But those 'signifyings' will in no way be mere magic or marvel achieving anything in isolation, or by their sole warrant, as means to faith. On the contrary, they will stand only for the way they 'tell' the inner sense which will for ever be the thing that has credentials for the heart and mind. Thus we have the birth narratives only because we have the Incarnation, the empty tomb in knowledge of the risen Christ. We must be clear which underwrites the other and beware lest we reverse them. The theme will recur when, in Chapters 5 and 6, we take up the fact of *ex eventu* formulation around Jesus as the Christ. All begins in Galilee not at Chalcedon, in Gethsemane and only thence with vacant grave-clothes. To understand one 'who for us and our salvation came down from heaven' and who 'is seated at the right hand of majesty on high', we essentially confess that divine credentials were traced, and are for evermore traceable, in the one who 'came preaching', 'loved to the end', and 'under Pontius Pilate was crucified, dead and buried'. The birth and tomb narratives, enclosing Jesus in his story, belong with his being, from eternity to eternity, the Christ of faith. It is 'significance' which 'signifies' and is, thereby, 'signified'.

Postponing further reflection, the present concern is to know that the divine credentials are responsive to where our deepest needs of mind and heart belong, needs more fitted to the crown of thorns than to some magic wand. 'Our faith does not stand in the wisdom (or the credulity) of men, but in the power of God.' That power is not one to cajole belief, but to love to the uttermost and be known in doing so.

viii

If living faith puts magic away, what of speculative mind? Christian theology has had its *Summa Theologica* and *Summa Contra Gentiles*, its system-builders, its conciliar debates, Judaism and Islam less so in their instinct to concentrate on law and doing, rather than on formulae of thought. Theology, to be sure, can never desert its frontier with philosophy nor fail to relate its hopes to reasons and its meanings to intelligence. To 'love the Lord with all the mind' is part of 'the first and great Commandment'. The intellectual liabilities of what we take to be divine credentials can await Chapters 2 and 3 as a prelude to the logic which will find them narrowing, or perhaps gathering, into the search for what can be identified as the divine *qua* Messianic.

For those two chapters have to do with nature where credentials may be 'conjectured' and history where they are desperately 'queried'. It will be there that the intellectual liabilities of theism are most rigorously at issue. A poet might blissfully say:

> Thou hast set a throne on the soil of our earth
> Whereon a man can see the heart of God,

— but not every man. Many would find nature equivocal, moody, blithely beneficent and inscrutably mysterious by turns and, therefore, an ambiguous credential of whatever, in fact, or only possibly, transcended her. And there was history. One could not honestly ignore in the earthly stage of human things what had desperately ensued in the drama humanity enacted there. Creation might have been benign in its intentions but were these well entrusted to the human custody that had so evidently compromised if not appalled them? To discern 'the heart of God' in the natural order would certainly tax the speculative intelligence and, by the same token, require it to kneel as well as explore, to come with awe as well as law. If the mind of theology needed due note of the sciences, it could never rightly think that they were all.

Deferring to two succeeding chapters these large areas of God's being credentialled, there remains here the aspect of the case from history we now identify as 'liberation'. The instinct, then, around what needs 'proving' about God is the urgent concern for freedom over against tyranny, for justice in situations of oppression, for due righting of the enormous wrongs within society and between nations. A theology that is *only* discursive, only occupied with rituals and dogmas for definition and exposition, connives with the evils it ignores or neglects. There is no neutrality. Not to engage against is to side with all that must offend any deity worthy of credence or worship. Indeed, to worship God, as it were, merely for God's own sake, is to betray whatever 'God' might be.

For, in the absence of a passion for 'righteousness', all else is vain. The 'God' of merely speculative interest is an 'idol', a figment of imagination erected by a false religion. 'Righteousness', in this context, must be read as 'rightingness', vigorous, inexorable and ever vigilant. The Hebrew prophets can well be invoked in this case. 'Bring no more vain oblations,' cried Isaiah; 'cease to do evil; Learn to do well' (1:13, 16, 17). 'Let righteousness roll down like a mighty stream' was the demand of Amos (5:24). These are imperatives fit to be translated into any and every idiom in human tragedies of time and place. It is no accident that theologies of liberation are also frequently theologies of national identity. These have multiplied widely this century, so that 'water-buffalo theology', 'Papuan theology', 'theologies of Hindustan', the Caribbean, Sioux-land, Amazonia and the like, recruit locale and culture in the bid to belong, justly, equally, politically, with 'the family of man', perceived as willed diversity from God. Such ardent affirmations of identity, in the givens of history, situate themselves in the struggle against the legacies of imperialism and the ongoing wrongs of economic disadvantage and exploitation. It is, then, mandatory that the divine credentials should be known and sifted by their relevance to these canons of what is crucial to their recognition. All this is no more than the always critical question about 'letting God be God', taking passionate form from 'unaccommodated man', of whom many theologies 'have ta'en too little care'.[19] Perhaps they never will nor care how far they do not.

The Hebrew 'exodus' from Egypt is the most frequently invoked of all biblical analogues for liberation theology. It has entered far into Negro folklore and music and belongs with scores of wistful scenarios for local, national aspiration theologically perceived. It is the supreme metaphor, the Pharaohs on every hand, and Moses with the arm over the Red Sea, for release of the oppressed and retribution of the oppressor. Perhaps also, however, the 'exodus' is what might give pause, as well as cause, for a liberation theology. It was, after all, succeeded by a wilderness of wandering and it could not incorporate its enemy.[20] This is not to argue it is pointless. On the contrary, its legitimacy is authentic. 'Let my people go' will always speak the demand of redemption.

Nevertheless, in the biblical case, as earlier noted by our Osago 'Indian', exodus had as its destiny gross injustice for the Canaanites. There was not only Moses at the Red Sea, there was Joshua, his 'young man', over Jordan. Where 'the young' take the liberation will always be in question. Where and how is 'the promised land' will always need an answer. For 'liberation' is never an end in itself, the more not so if the categories are only political and economic. We have to say that 'it costs more to redeem their souls' (Ps. 49:8) if – as the psalmist implies – we have things eternal in view. We shall hope to see in Chapter 5 how such thoughts bear on the criteria of what is fully and duly Messianic, since these in turn are crucial to the credentials of God. There is, no doubt, much more than this to liberation theology, but not germane to our present search.

ix

If some justice has been done in the foregoing to what might be right, and what false, trails in quest of divine credentials, to the obligations constituted by revelation and Scriptures, and to criteria sufficient for the whole venture and its propriety, there would seem to remain two concluding observations. The one has to do with the nature of 'fact', the other with the evident interplay of theme and comprehension.

What we say is 'transcendent' is always with us and among us in the 'contingent'. In *The Opposing Self*, the literary critic, Lionel Trilling, observes about Leo Tolstoy's novel *Anna Karenina*:

> The human spirit is always at the mercy of the actual and the trivial [in] . . . our passionate sense that these are of the greatest importance – though we are certain that they are not of final import- ance. Let us not deceive ourselves . . . to comprehend uncon- ditioned spirit is not so very hard, but there is no knowledge rarer than the understanding of spirit as it exists in the inescapable conditions which the actual and trivial make for it.[21]

We are therefore all too prone to take 'immediacy' as being tantamount to reality. We are then liable to be unduly constricted over what we take to be the nature of 'facts'. We enquire whether this or that can be 'literally' true as if 'literal' was the one and only adjective that could apply to 'fact'. 'Acid is needed to bite into an etcher's plate.'[22] Similarly, a lively sense of mystery and wonder is imperative if 'fact' is to have its full contours. If we circumscribe it to the visible, the tangible, the scientific, the physically demonstrable, we plainly impoverish the whole experience of our humanness.

Do we not too readily trot out the phrase, 'as a matter of fact', and not pause to wonder what is, or might be, the 'matter' in 'fact'? Are there not truths of fiction? Does the sun, in truth, rise, do horizons, in fact, recede? Experientially – yes! Cosmically – no. One cannot have music without time, but is music merely letting time pass? Is the 'fact' of the symphony a two-hour duration and uncounted breves and semibreves and quavers? Blessedly, there *can* be a literalness of the most apt eloquence, as in 'My ending is despair unless I be relieved by prayer,'[23] otherwise, the more 'literal', or 'bare', a 'fact' the less it signifies. Was there a tourist at the Grand Canyon who remarked: 'Something's happened here,' or, 'Look what the river did'? If so, he spoke well, but how much did he say as compared with 'A panoramic eternity of geological time'?

Throughout any quest for divine credentials we shall have to guard against the foreshortening of perception which confines us pathetically (or it may be proudly) to the 'bare' and the 'literal'. There is no proper repose away from the truth. If, as Aristotle supposedly said, one 'should think as a mortal', the advice must take due stock of the reach of mortality. We must know metaphor for what it is, and can be, and beware of the sad reductionisms of mere science.

Doing so wisely will in no way disparage either the senses or the sciences. It will simply allow them their true dimensions. These thoughts have conveyed us to our final point, namely, that if there is an imparting from the godward side it will be reciprocal on our side to an enabling. Truth is never placarded like some arrogant hoarding. Nor are its ways taken in passivity. Our desire for divine criteria will always be responding to their accessibility but this, in turn, will defer to our concern to find the how and where. If, as the loved Hebraic phrase has it, there is 'the place' and 'the Name', we shall have, by the same token, 'to come to know' and 'to know to come'. Where the finding is is only where the seeking comes, if we are ever to discover as

> Too bright for our infirm delight
> The truth's superb surprise.

2 Conjectured

. . . every side my glance was bent
O'er the grandeur and the beauty lavished through the whole ascent.
Ledge by ledge outbroke new marvels, now minute and now
immense,
Earth's most exquisite disclosure, heaven's own God in evidence,
And no berry in its hiding, no blue space in its outspread
Pleaded to escape my footsteps.[1]

AUTHENTIC, one might allow, for Robert Browning and the Alps, but
the real world is more than he and they. We are not all well endowed
with vivid mind and ample leisure for the mountains. There is much
death, too, down those awesome peaks. There are berries that poison
and blue spaces that mock our tribulation till 'the curious stars' look
down upon human reason making what bargains it can with man's
insanity.[2]

Yet, the poet insists, will 'you bar me from assuming earth to be a
pupil's place'? Are there not 'exquisite disclosures'? May we not think
them 'heaven's own God in evidence'? Nature around us has always
been a source of glad conjecture about the transcendent – nature in its
order, its hospitality, its intimations of mystery and grace. To be sure,
these are ambivalent. Yet we do not have ambiguity if we decry what
alone makes it such, failing to keep the faith-negating in due balance
with the faith-suggesting. Two of our most lyrical poets of nature-love
in the English tongue, Walt Whitman and Robert Frost, had keenly
known and registered the tragic in their human stories, yet it had not
denied for them their salutation of glad mystery in woods and waters.[3]
Theology has the right instinct in keeping close to nature and the poets.
Browning, too, was carrying the pain of sharp bereavement into the
Alpine climb he had often made in company with the one he mourned.[4]

It would be false to credit his poetic strain to any blithe immunity from the verdicts of adversity.

At all events, in conjecturing about divine credentials we begin with ourselves, each our own *persona*, housed in this mortal flesh, ushered by birth into an intriguing, bewildering context in which we practise an inalienable autonomy and find the whence and whither of things and people responsive to our private being. No Buddhist could object that the point of departure is mistaken, for it is the point of all return. We, after all, are at the heart of what we must define, the crux and incidence of all we must conjecture, where nature is at once our discovery, our experience and our empire. 'Why', Thomas Hardy asked himself in his diary in old age, '. . . should a man's mind have been thrown into such close, sad, sensational, inexplicable relations with such a precarious object as his own body?'[5] The adjectives were characteristic. 'Sensational', among them, would need to be read in the strict sense of what sensibly transpires, whether or not it be untoward or newsworthy. For those senses are the fount and fund of all we comprehend, given that mind and reason have them for a school.

Some two and a half centuries earlier another poet, Andrew Marvell, had written his 'Dialogue between the Soul and Body'. The Soul asks:

> O, who shall from this dungeon raise
> A soul enslaved so many ways?
> With bolts of bones, that fettered stands
> In feet and manacled in hands.
> . . . . .
> A soul hung up, as 'twere, in chains
> Of nerves and arteries and veins.
> . . . . .
> What magic could me thus confine
> Within another's grief to pine?
> . . . . .
> And all my care itself employs
> That to preserve, which me destroys.

Body, for its part, complains

> O, who shall me deliver whole
> From bonds of this tyrannic soul?
> Which, stretched upright, impales me so,
> That mine own precipice I go;
> . . . . .
> Has made me live to let me die.
> A body that could never rest,
> Since this ill spirit it possessed.
> . . . . .
> What but a soul could have the wit
> To build me up for sin so fit?[6]

Querulous friends, no doubt, yet lifelong, inseparable ones. It can hardly be doubted that their partnership is actual, an experienced reality, a microcosm commanding a personal 'dominion', that, however loaded by circumstance, heredity, chance, or choice, is, nevertheless, the 'mine' in which we delve through all the seams of meaning and experience belonging to its deeps – or levels. We have to start with personhood, with the 'me' that joins to 'us' and 'ours', to scenes and tasks and destinies to which our days are lent that we may borrow their significance. In the 'bone-bound island' of the self we learn all we know, flesh being where there is an

> . . . inmost, ultimate council of judgement,
> Palace of decrees,
> Where the high senses hold their spiritual state,
> Sued by earth's embassies,
> And sign, approve, accept, conceive, create.[7]

When, surveying his situation under the imagery of sheep, pasture and shadow, the psalmist concluded: 'I shall always be in the house of the Lord,'[8] he was expressing, in poetic terms, the most intimate meaning of the biblical doctrine of creation. He was registering a creaturehood for which the entire context was a realm of divine hospitality where the very landscape was a 'table spread' and his selfhood was nourished, watered and renewed. He was confidently conjecturing divine credentials in the awareness of his own self-dimensions.

ii

The theme of 'natural theology' has, from time to time, been discounted in Christian faith-perceptions. Every biblical consideration, not to say our inner awareness, requires that it be reinstated firmly. The argument has sometimes been that the whole weight might be given to 'special revelation', to 'history' as the vital sphere of divine Self-disclosure. There have been those for whom 'God in Christ' is so emphatic that it needs no partnerships from other evidences of the divine. Apart from excluding rich relevance (both for faith and for doubt), this stance does less than justice to the historical theology for which it stands exclusively. Unless, in some sense, all things have a sacramental significance, nothing could. If we are to hold with Incarnation, and 'the Word made flesh', it must be only because the physical order already carries that potential.

It is important in this context, as it will be throughout, to have an adjectival as well as a nounal theology. Many of the tortuous things about Creeds and the councils phrasing them could have been relieved, as Chapter 8 will argue, if the point had been taken. One can understand adjectives like 'divine' and 'human' interpenetrating more readily than nouns like 'Son' and 'substance', 'Person' and 'Nature'. 'Hypostasising', though we need to take its point, can unduly complicate what we need to understand.[9] We must have what we can call 'natural' if we are ever to comprehend what we claim as 'spiritual'. That is not only so about Incarnation and the sacraments: it belongs necessarily, also, for the very sake of these, with our understanding of creation as the setting of divine credentials.

Faith in creation is not speculation about a 'start', but rather conviction about an 'intention'. As Kant knew, there are many antinomies about 'space and time'. We need 'time' to originate 'time', and we know we cannot look at 'the other side of the sky'. These insolubles, however, about a 'when' and a 'how' need not deprive us of the 'here-we-are-ness' about all that is – the givenness of being in, and therefore at, the world. Conceding all the mysteries attending on cosmology, we can undertake the 'why' that is more cogent than the 'how' and 'when'. Just as the word 'end' has the twin meanings of 'finis' (about duration) and 'purpose' (about aim or goal), so 'In the beginning God . . .' concerns initiative, not 'origin' but intention-there-should-be, or (better) 'origin' as intention. We can hardly deny that all there is has been 'let be', and we humankind within it, 'thinking what we can do with what there is' and manifoldly doing it in culture, nurture, cities, farms, techniques and arts and sciences.[10]

Seen in this way, faith about creation will not be excluding the cosmologists, astronomers and physicists but only embracing them in the manifold of being human in the given context on the edges of reality. All practitioners in the art of exploring what is there, and what there is, can hardly doubt the 'me' in the me-aning, or – if they do – it will still be there in the very negligence. As George Herbert has it:

> Man is all symettrie,
> Full of proportions, one limbe to another
> And all to all the world besides.
> Each part may call the furthest brother,
> For head with foot hath private amitie
> And both with winds and tides.[11]

Each person's body is a part of the universe possessed *totaliter*; while that universe in its totality each possesses *partialiter*. Gregory of Nyssa, among the classical Christian theologians, drew out the significance of human erectness, as Muslims do when that same stance opens and ends Islamic *salāt* before and after the symbol of prostration: 'Man stands upright reaching towards the sky and with his eyes raised aloft. This posture fits him for command and signifies his royal power.'[12] With such royalty the human is the only animal that truly laughs and weeps. God's credible credentials cannot be exempted from those twin tokens of our human consciousness.

The world, then, by its nature as reciprocal to ours, is undeniably a place of human being and becoming. Its Creator, if we can allow ourselves to consider that concept, has clearly bestowed an endowment with an intention of a character thereby circumscribing itself, running a risk, opening out a liability to the human 'other', being, in short, 'the God of patience'. We find ourselves possessing the latch-key to the universe in that reach of it where we play 'a pupil's part', indeed a lover's part, a poet's part, a peasant's part, an artist's part, a builder's part and if, in all these, no doubt a sufferer's part, and (the suffering not being uniquely ours) a partner's part in knowing it. Thanks to body, we are in the mind's fields of discovery, the soul's fields of expression. In a sort of *Benedicite Omnia Opera Domini* we are invited into mutual celebration and congratulation. Nature makes us instrumentalists of its entire significance.

It is important to insist that this sense of things is not to be appalled by sheer immensity or nullified by realisation of 'infinite spaces' and vast unimaginable vistas of endlessness. The psalmist's question, 'What is man?' is never properly to be asked in terms of puny irrelevance or, worse, in the presence of awesome emptiness that could never have been envisaged to stage recorded time. On the contrary, it was an exclamation of undaunted surprise at being so 'highly regarded' – indeed, with a regard that made the boundless context only the more tributary to the surprise. The furious energies at the core of enormous mysteries multiplying billions of stars at inconceivable distances might be thought to engulf this human realm in utter pointlessness as never a credible intentionality on the fringes of infinite waste and wantonness.

Even so, that register of what unnerves is, nevertheless, ours. The universe does not 'know' its vastness, nor Everest its height, nor the oceans their depth. That cannot minimise meaning which has already maximised the quest of it. All fear of belittlement is awareness enlarged. Not only so. It is legitimate in pondering earth's exceptionality to ponder also how fortuitously it was so and wonder whether fortuitous is the right word.[13] We can, with John Milton, conjecture 'every star perhaps a world of destined habitation', if so, only another wonder in no way cancelling ours. We shall still need that poet's lovely vision of the divine 'compasses':

> He took the golden compasses, prepared
> In God's eternal store, to circumscribe
> This universe and all created things.
> One foot He centred and the other turned
> Round through the vast profundity obscure
> And said: 'Thus far extend thy bounds,
> This be thy just circumference, O world.'
> And earth self-balanced on her centre hung.[14]

In our conjecture of such divine craftsmanship initiating what we now experience, human minds have always been puzzled about *ex nihilo*, 'out of nothing', another of those antinomies. It is important, however, to realise that creation can be thought of as 'taking the nothing-ness away'. The Spanish poet Antonio Machado has the point well:

The great feat of having wrested a world out of nothing is no greater than that . . . of having wrested 'nothing' out of the world. Reflect on that . . . It is time that we broadened our questions like the broadening of a sail, if we are ever to make for the open seas of contemplation.[15]

iii

Taking the nothingness away has left 'us' in possession of a dependable domain, a realm of being that requires and invites response that is responsible. Beset by enigmas it must remain, but they are all within its liberties. All obtains because the threat of nothingness is held at bay. 'Change and decay in all around I see', yet what undergoes them nevertheless itself abides because of 'Thou who changest not'. We can take this point readily if we understand how Genesis I requires us so to do. There are, in verse 2, three detached clauses leading up to the main verb: 'and God said: "Let there be . . ." ' namely: 'When God began to create . . . the earth being unformed and void and darkness upon the face of the deep . . .' The 'void' is chaos, primeval disorder. The restraining word holds them back to give occasion for the ordered world. It is part of the meaning of creation that the word never fails its ordering will so that that on which our humanity utterly depends is reliably sustained and the Eternal does not 'weary of mankind'. Nothingness is dependably nonplussed: as it were, 'no-mored'. Human opportunity is ever 'more and more' through time and meaning. By natural history human history comes. It is in the latter that divine credentials are most at issue (see Chapter 3). For that very reason we must let the former sustain us all it can.

It is, of course, the poets who most signally persuade us. John Keats was sure of 'the holiness of the heart's affections'. 'Simple sense', thought Thomas Traherne, 'is lord of all created excellence'. His poems and *Centuries of Meditation* are in no doubt that

> The heaven's were an oracle and spoke
> Divinity: the earth did undertake
> The office of a priest.

His was supremely 'a theology of the senses', where 'all his care was to be sensible of God's mercies' and so 'to behave himself as the friend of God in the universe'.

> Everywhere and in all things thou must meet His love. This the law of nature commands, and it is thy glory that thou art fitted for it. His love unto thee is the law and measure of thine unto Him, His love unto all others the law and obligation of thine unto all.

Only when that happened were the senses purified in their proper employment. Perhaps his most famous passage runs:

You never enjoy the world aright till the sea itself floweth in your veins, till you are clothed with the heavens and crowned with the stars: and perceive yourself to be the sole heir of the whole world, and more so, because men are in it who are everyone sole heirs as well as you. Till you can sing and rejoice and delight in God as misers do in gold and kings in sceptres, you never enjoy the world.[16]

In his different idiom, William Wordsworth was no less priestly:

> In such access of mind, in such high hour
> Of visitation from the living God
> Thought was not: in enjoyment it expired.
> No thanks he breathed, he proffered no request,
> Rapt into still communion that transcends
> The imperfect offices of prayer and praise,
> His mind was a thanksgiving to the power
> That made him: it was blessedness and love.[17]

The artist Vincent Van Gogh was of like mind: 'I always think that the way to know God is to love many things . . . but to love them with a lofty and serious intimate sympathy, with strength, with intelligence.'[18]

The impulse in all such reverence towards the world of nature in the cognisance of the senses and the meditations of the soul is to find credentials about a panoramic meaning that compels crude ego-hood into humility and gratitude, yet sweetly confirms that ego-hood received as the one, inalienable recipient made percipient by powers and faculties entirely suited (and surely meant) for such awareness. When Thomas Hardy wrote his poem: 'The Impercipient', it was sub-titled: 'At a Cathedral Service':

> That with this bright believing band
>   I have no claim to be,
> That faiths by which my comrades stand
>   Seem fantasies to me,
> And mirage mists their shining Land,
>   Is a strange destiny.

There would be times, but not all times, when he would hold 'comrades' Traherne and Wordsworth likewise deceived. For he had a lively sense of nature cruelly bleak, harsh and inimical. His poetic exceptions are all the more precious, and he wanted to be remembered as 'a man who noticed such things.'[19]

Before, however, we come to what might give pause to conceding, rapturously or otherwise, the natural realm as divinely credentialling, there is a caveat to be made. It may be reached by reference to Richard Jefferies and his *The Story of My Heart*. He wrote a lyrical prose in rapt surrender to the world of nature, yet he remained firmly resistant to any divine significance in his experience.

I was utterly alone with the sun and the earth. Lying down on the grass, I spoke in my soul to the earth, the sun, the air and the distant sea far beyond sight . . . I turned to the blue heaven over, gazing into its depth, inhaling its exquisite colour and sweetness. The rich blue of the unattainable flower of the sky drew my soul toward it and there it rested, for pure colour is rest of heart. By all these I prayed: I felt an emotion of the soul beyond all definition: prayer is a puny thing to it and the word is a rude sign to the feeling, but I know no other . . . Touching the crumble of earth, the blade of grass, the thyme flower, breathing the earth-encircling air . . . I prayed that I might touch to the unutterable existence.[20]

While he breathes and lives wonder, Jefferies resists credentials. There is something of the same yielding into a nature of the senses in Albert Camus and his ardent celebration of sea and sun and sand finding, as it were, an authorless text, a music that needs no attribution. Is there an ignoring in this shape of knowing, a wonder sufficient to itself? Believers should be gentle in their responding. Yet may there not be, about some aestheticism, an evasion as well as an enlargement of what belongs in selfhood? We cannot well be 'one with nature' only in terms of beauty, mystery or passionate imbuement with its charm and splendour. 'Nature-participation', as Wordsworth was careful to insist, must always return us to other dimensions of our selfhood, lest the very desire that takes us there abstracts us from the life it enriches, where nature is more than the beautiful, the sensuously enthralling, and its credentials, therefore, more demandingly in question. One may well press one's human frame on to the good earth, lying prone upon the sweet turf of the Wiltshire Downs and, holding one's gaze on a fleecy cloud in motion above, sense the turning of the planet in one's very limbs. So doing, one may stretch out a reaching arm and let the sunlight light a glow behind one's fingernails and so yield oneself to the embrace of vastness. The experience, however, must yield again to the dimensions of existence it has for the time renounced. The self imbued with awe and beauty must return, invested into mundane things and the traffic of a world of folk and claim.

Richard Jefferies called his response to such experience 'prayer', because he knew no other word. He did not mean 'prayer' as theological. It sufficed that beauty, through surrender, told 'the story of his heart'. For others, with a kindred awareness of what the senses tell, mood or mystery require not so much an absence, or an irrelevance, of God but rather an implicit accusation. Among these others Thomas Hardy must be a notable and ardently articulate example. Some of the aspects of the kind of reproach of the divine his stories and his poems breathe come more directly into Chapter 3. For he was a very pointed querist of theology. When, however, he pressed his vision of a world free of all human consciousness he only wryly showed how fundamental the gift was. It was as if he sought to resolve all that oppressed by deploring the only factor capable of knowing it. Thus, even in wistful negation, he was still registering the place where credentials, whether for rejection or acceptance, have to be, namely with the human in the world, and the world in the human. His dream of 'nescience' was 'wide awake':

> A time there was – as one may guess
> And as, indeed, earth's testimonies tell –
> Before the birth of consciousness
> When all went well.
>
> But the disease of feeling germed,
> And primal rightness took the tinct of wrong:
> Ere nescience shall be reaffirmed
> How long, how long?[21]

The very language here betrays him – unless he has his tongue in his cheek, which, with Hardy, we must scout. For what 'testimonies' can 'tell' without minds and words? And how is it 'known' that all went well 'before the birth of consciousness'? 'Primal rightness' could only be the absence of any criteria of either 'wrong' or 'right'. Hardy has established, if only ironically, the point which is here at the heart of all else – how to make sense of being human in an intelligible and credible world, inasmuch as evacuating those two descriptives would take us out of it and end all pros and cons in oblivion. Whether or not credentials are divine there is no escape, in mere enigma, from the necessity to weigh the case for them.

iv

Thomas Hardy and all his fellow puzzlers at nature and the human scene rightly urge the vagaries and enmities they register in the natural order (and disorder) they experience. It will not do to stay only with the Trahernes and the Wordsworths of this world. To affirm a wondrous hospitality in our experience, and salute it with celebration as lyrically credentialling a divine beneficence that meant it so, is not to ignore the harsh inhospitality our situation also tells. Grasmere is not the world. There are torrid and there are arid wastes, bare and battered islands and deadly swamps, climates and catastrophes with their tragic toll of fear and pain and disease. The nature that is supportive is also hostile; her moods are savage as well as serene.

No divine credentialling can stand in facile philosophies about pain as warning, or the compensating 'values' in adversity, or the crude fatalism that elides the problem. Man's inhumanity will concern us when we come to history in the next chapter. Here it is 'natural' evil which is, and must remain, our burden. It is no wise theology which ignores or minimises those aspects of natural 'reality' that (registers of human will and liability apart) must be acknowledged either malign or incompetent. We must recognise that it is oddly obstinate or disingenuous to hold together power, wisdom and love as unambiguously credited with the world we know. Inscrutable power might have to be allowed its role, but hardly in any sort of league with love or wisdom. The issue, badly stated, between a will that would but could not, or a power that could and willed not, is familiar and trite enough, and many in resignation or anger are content to leave it there. Then any search for credentials is surrendered.

It would seem to follow that the whole question will have to be 'contained' within a frame of reference which, on other grounds, would afford us sufficient warrant for 'containing' it, without illusions or evasions or palliatives, because those grounds had generated a confidence that they are worthy of the role. It is precisely this that we shall explore in later chapters. For, in Christian experience, it has to do with things Messianic about God, with where and how they might be understood and found, with reasons why they might outweigh what otherwise might require of us an honest atheism.

Deferring that whole case, it is necessary here to add one further consideration about 'natural' evils, namely that they come within the undoubted consciousness, conscience and at least partial competence, of humankind. Inimical, daunting, vexing they remain, but they do not cancel, or immobilise, or atrophy, the human will and spirit. Some of those, like Albert Camus, who have most grimly concluded absurdity as the logic of life, have nevertheless commended a courage that outfaces it. There is always a 'thesis' of human energy to counter the harsh and sharp 'antitheses' of mortal experience. What we most deplore, and accuse, and have need and case to do so, we still administer, assess, and answer from within the humanness we have and share. Whatever we undergo fortuitously, we undergo personally – and, often, vicariously. Adversity does not eliminate identity: it requires it. It is not, finally, what happens, but rather our reaction to what happens, that decides its character and its interpretation.

This sense of the abiding significance of being human, even amid what most calls it into travail about what humanness is, continues to leave ground for our underlying conjecture about God. Could there not be a supreme dignity in our being willed this way? The argument is far removed from the old facile 'proofs' – cosmological, teleological or ontological – for the existence of God. We are not hingeing divine credentials on argument from design, invoking the rainfall cycle of wind over seas bearing clouds that hit cold mountains and precipitate waters to feed the streams that, via the rivers, replenish the seas. Nor are we citing the endless adaptations of animals and vegetation to their habitats. For all these could be no more than mechanical contrivances of nature's own ingenuity or necessity, arguing no transcendental significance. The same, however, could not be said about human accounts of all the resulting 'mechanisms' as a plain arena of endeavour, enterprise and fulfilment, even in spite of the vagaries, as well as via the feasibilities.

Similarly, we are not relying on the perfect being necessarily existing, however deep our sense of Anselm of Canterbury as a saint and thinker. For such ontology is highly cerebral, of little persuasiveness to the sufferer and vulnerable, as Kant showed, to the charge of reason arguing beyond where the evidentiality of sense-experience could properly take it.[22] 'Existence' anyway must be a curious category to ponder about, allegedly, the source of all existence. Credential is a sounder word, taking us beyond mere 'whether' to 'by what tests?' At best, Anselm might persuade us of an ingenuity that needed surer canons drawn from where we are.

To think this way is not to retreat from old traditional citadels of theism: rather, it is to advance to where theism is at once more crucial and more robust, namely in the human meaning honestly wrestling with what refuses to be facile or complacent in its own search or conniving with the mere will to be assured. Our being rigorous about divine credentials has to be part of their being credentials at all. That duty, itself evidence of good faith, will be the best part of having faith 'good'. As such it will be its own evidence about the integrity that love of God requires. For how we reach them participates in what the credentials are.

Yet not by wishful thinking, on repudiating which, and the capacity to do so, the whole case rests. As St Augustine said about 'the bread and wine': 'It is the mystery of ourselves that we receive,' whenever, from within the realities of our own human awareness, we enquire about the transcendent explicitly and implicitly known within it. Conversely, atheism will be a sceptical understanding of ourselves.[23]

V

In thinking so, are we not perhaps ignoring the possibility that what is transcendent may be itself discordant, or morally indifferent? Greek religion thought and feared that the gods themselves were wilful and at odds, merely mirroring human enmities and passions and, indeed, conniving with these as theatres of their rivalries or protégés. More darkly still, we may enthrone an ultimate dichotomy from which we can await no justice and plead no necessary truth or love. The great Muslim poet, Jalal al-Din Rumi in his *Mathnawi* put the point with stark equanimity:

> He is the source of evil as thou sayest,
> Yet evil hurts Him not. To make that evil
> Denotes in Him perfection. Hear from me
> A parable. The heavenly artists paint
> Beautiful shapes and ugly. In one picture
> The loveliest woman in the land of Egypt
> Gazing on youthful Joseph amorously.
> And lo! another scene by the same hand
> Hell-fire and Iblis with his hideous crew.
> Both master-works created for good ends
> To show His perfect wisdom and confound
> The sceptics who deny His mastery.

Could He not make evil He would lack skill.
Therefore He fashions infidel alike
And Muslim true that both may bear witness
To Him, and worship one Almighty God.[24]

Despite the Muslim source, something has obviously happened here to the Islamic doctrine of the unity of God. For here is a 'unity' ethically divided against itself. Or, if we say the principle of unity is grounded in power alone, sheer arbitrariness leaves it at war with itself. Such final dualism also decries, indeed devastates, what is supposedly the righteous norm for human *islām*, or obedience. Job knew well enough that he could not rightly conclude himself better than God – which was his only ground for believing, against the grain of his admonishing 'friends', that there must be, about God, an ultimate righteousness, however elusive its ways. A right theology will always be reciprocal to a true humanism.

That dictum can be seen to be the more true when we take due account of how devious our response to natural evils can be, how far our human capacities mingle either with the other, so that good bears company with ill, and wrong with virtue. It is futile to suppose evils as 'arising accidentally just as a carpenter's work produces shavings and sawdust'.[25] Could it ever be seen so, truly knowing the workings of the self? The full theme of human wrongness belongs elsewhere. The immediate point is to stress that a sort of 'dualism' frequent in the actual incidence of human experience, as our moral attitudes transact it, warrants no speculative dualism in our sense of the transcendent. A right humility may indeed harbour a wrong pride, a genuine logic conceal a false motive, a spiritual purpose hide an unholy ambition. The complexities are legion. Nor can our private fortunes be isolated from common woes. For 'none of us stands outside humanity's black collective shadow',[26] and all of us stand inside legacies of a wrongful past that survive into present wrongs. To know this, however, is not to enthrone some heavenly duplicity. For only by reference to transcendent truth are these situations known for what they are. Her vagaries apart, the neutrality of nature makes ethics possible.

Things being such, it must follow that human selfhood is no rule-of-thumb business but rather a steady crisis of ethical perception responding in a *will* to the good, in constant alertness to its reading of the world and the demands of inward honesty. Doubtless we may succumb to habit, sloth, boredom and a bland conformity. Social conditioning or cynical weariness may overbear the will. Truly seen, however, the art of humanness has to be discerned by analogy, say, with navigation where what has to be overcome – winds, tides, currents, calms – has to be made to serve what needs to be attained. The critical will always characterise the normal. For norms have to be creative. 'Deep calls to deep,' as the psalmist knew (42:7). We can perhaps think the more wonderingly about a transcendent that willed it so, making potential tenacity, courage, caringness and liability, or even magnanimity, so ultimate a dimension of what we are assumed and invited to be. It is not simply that such a Creator tolerates us but is vulnerable at our hands as the condition of ever being vindicated in our integrity. We have thus to reckon with the kind of responsibility it must be that has made us so responsible. The human dignity must be seen to be a corollary of divine generosity. The personal, social and moral significance that is ours, for all its hazards and perplexities, commends us to a divinely counterparting sovereignty and such a sovereignty to us.

Nor is the case disqualified by the consideration, never far from mind, that this esteeming of selfhood proves in actuality a highly élitist version, tragically beyond the vistas of innumerable folk whose lives are constricted by poverty, conflict, brevity and pain. Not so, for two reasons. These privations – if duly registered for what they are – are only significant if we hold on to some sense of the true vocation they desperately contravene. If those privations were all that was ever meant to be, then logically they are no more privations. Furthermore, there is more, much more, than such logic. What is desperately at odds with the human becomes an urgent part of what that human meaning demands of any and all who have a capacity to relieve and redeem it. That sense of things, too, would be forfeit if there were no vision – the 'vision without which the people perish' (Prov. 29:18).

vi

There are two other themes in the natural order about this interplay between divine condescending into human responding and responsibility, namely our sexuality and our dying. The former, of course, covers our own arriving by collusion (apt word?) of our parents and, in turn, our own place in the sequence of procreating trust. In the mystery, physical and spiritual, of copulation we learn the deepest secret of divine empowerment in us and so of our enablement within the truth that 'God does not weary of mankind.' If we cannot sense the wonder here we are unlikely to record it anywhere. For is there a greater self-surrendering, self-imparting, self-discovering, than in the true trans-actions of human sexuality? Perhaps that is why, *corruptio optimi pessima*, we deprave them in the tawdry, casual, mundane and commercial. Travestied sexuality is the sordid distortion of a divine economy of benediction and a human prerogative of grace.

Rightly received, the sexual gift hallows an entire giving and receiving. Desire knows itself to be properly possessive in the will to be worthily possessed. Love binds by setting free our deepest capacity for otherness as the fulfilment of inward being. It sets us in the debt-incurring, debt-paying of the generations. It invites us to find in vow and pledge the keystone that ties into one the limbs of the marital arch which then holds up a domestic world where childhood can grow securely under auspices that gently interpret the world and welcome its new initiates. For better measure, it conditions its parental meanings with emotions of delight and wonder that carry its transactions beyond procreative action to sacramental hallowing in the depths of personality. Here we are having to do with God in 'the pupil's part' of mutuality, told in the time of embrace and kindled therefrom for all else in the sharedness of mortality. In true sexuality, flesh interprets spirit and spirit engages flesh, to make either know their double benediction.

Again, we may demur. Sex, we must concede, when it is merely 'had' (as the jargon goes), proves to be all too readily perverted, abused, prostituted and destroyed. One of the most haunting phrases in the Gospel is that 'the Son of man [was] betrayed with a kiss' (Matt. 26:48; Mark 14:44; Luke 22:48) – and many of the sons and daughters of men likewise – the 'kiss' of sordid lust or casual transience, flouting joy and degrading personality to commodity. An ultimate nemesis of satiety waits upon whatever lends the physical organs to lascivious ends: not only so, the entail of disorderly sexuality lives in blighted homes, deprived childhood, psychic turmoil and, through all, a prejudice of society at large with legacies passing far into the turning years.

From this, however, we may not conclude only an urge to witness to ideals involving no more than an onus to reproach and censure of what defies them. Right sexual meanings and a vision for the care of them, they being divinely entrusted to our freedom, make repair of their violation inseparable from their truth. We can, if we will, detect something of transcendent compassion in the necessity always to hold together the spiritually right and the redemptively possible. There is no salvation in what merely deplores. For to deplore can readily go on to despise and soundness in judgement give way to hardness of heart. It is well to remember how, in the Gospel, the broken box of precious, fragrant oil had (presumably) been purchased by 'the wages of sin'. Pious calculations of 'this waste' failed to register how Mary's gesture was retrieving the 'waste' of her own past in having, trading and unbridling sex.

There has always to be, as Ezra Pound phrased it, a task of 'maintaining antisepsis.' That, however, must always belong with the great positives of soul and body which sexuality releases and fulfills.

> 'Tis a place of wonder
> Where these have been, meet 'tis, the ground is holy.[27]

Seeing it so, in being male and female in these realms, each hallows the body *qua* person and person *qua* spirit. Our sexuality is then a kind of priesthood in which the possession of the physical, where we most consciously and passionately transact it, and know ourselves in doing so, learns the holiness of personality. Perhaps we also learn that something about us and beyond us is credentialled there.

vii

Sexuality is in our disposing, dying is not. Having, in this chapter from the outset, made selfhood *qua* guesthood central to our conjectures, what do we say of its demise, of the end of the tie between soul and body? If the form of our personhood is where divine credentials can be read, what of its forfeiture at death? For death ends the only shape in which hitherto we have known ourselves, perhaps the only shape in which a self can conceivably be known. Does our bereavement from others, our bereavement from ourselves, void all our case in the void it leaves?

Conjecturing from the realm of nature allows us no clear answer. We have to wait for other frames of reference through later chapters. In mortal experience we have known that death was always awaiting us. Our years, being a steady addition sum, are, by the same token, a steady subtraction sum – subtraction from an always unknown quantity. Life is lived with 'the sense of an ending'. Is it, however, of *an* ending, or *the* ending? Mortal experience cannot contain 'the undiscovered country'. We have to say with Shakespeare's Feeble: 'By my troth, I care not: a man can die but once. We owe God a death . . . An't be my destiny, so.'[28] We can, of course, disregard the fact. It has been noted, for example, that in all his voluminous writing Karl Marx only once mentioned death – in his youth around 1844. The mystery of death is perhaps sometimes (if rarely) thought on in the will to procreate. When, in *Paradise Lost*, Eve ponders a wilful childlessness, Milton has Adam seeing it as 'reluctance against God'.[29] Death haunts thought in the precariousness of desire among the living. Wherever love is, there is apprehension for its jeopardy as being mortal:

Thou among the wastes of time must go,
. . . . .
     And nothing 'gainst Time's scythe can make defence.
. . . . .
That time will come and take my love away.
     This thought is as a death which cannot choose
     But weep to have that which it fears to lose.[30]

So it is that death seems to many the supreme disqualifying of any reassuring credentials about God. Funerals, at best, can be embarrassing when, as John Betjeman has it, 'nobody knows quite what to say';[31] or, at worst, they can be desperately anguished, with voids where meanings were.

There is little help in the reflection that there is no dust that has not been alive, or that death 'coming to all equally, makes all equal when it comes'.[32] Some may find stimulus in curiosity, seeing not 'the last enemy' but new adventure. Yet the sharp enmity remains if we value at all what death seemingly decries in wastage of the body's exquisite beauty, the atrophy of its finely crafted faculties, its final destination into dust or ash.

We can, of course, fall back on a philosophic nonchalance and tell ourselves that anyway we have merely been experiencing a lull before a nullity. Or perhaps a philosophic apologetic that notes how what makes all things contingent is that which makes any thing possible. The limits

of time and tenure that circumscribe us are the ones that admit of all
the occasions we enjoy. Should we complain about what terminates if
it has itself been what nevertheless availed? A will for endlessness
is evidently futile and maybe also egoistical. Perhaps we can find
perspectives that make death 'the true best friend of mankind'. If so, it
will likely be in what most detracts from life – its frailties of limb or
mind, its wearying decay, its slow forfeiture of all that was its legitimate
pride.

Bereavement may well be overcome by renewed immersion in life,
taking revenge, as it were, on all that we resent and must accuse. Thus
John Bright, solaced by his friend Richard Cobden on the death of his
sweetheart wife less that two years after their marriage: 'Until she
became mine,' he wrote, 'I did not know that mortality ever was the
abode of so much that was pure and lovely.' As his wife still lay a cold
corpse in the bedroom, Cobden said to Bright:

> There are thousands of homes in England at this moment where
> wives, mothers and children are dying of hunger. Now when the first
> paroxysm of your grief is past . . . come with me and we will never
> rest till the Corn Law is repealed.[33]

Bright, in his own words, 'accepted the invitation'. But surely it would
be odd to conclude that some Creator could, or should, contrive it so
that way. And there are so many would-be things that death makes
definitive only when it is too late.

It will be wise to leave our perplexities until we may know better how
to read them in the light of Christ – since that is where we are proposing,
in due course, to think the light may be. Then we may find that the
inevitable necessity to forego ourselves, which physical death exacts of
all of us, may be both parable and occasion of that willingness to 'be
not our own' which, by association with the Cross of Jesus, has ever
since been the principle of self-discovery and self-possession. Death
perpetually underlines the egocentric situation and, in physical terms,
finally undoes it. So it may represent to us, in life, the spiritual truth
that 'to lose is to find', making that truth at the same time our vocation.
Meanwhile, the question stays.

viii

In all the foregoing we have found strong intimations checked by
formidable dissuasives about credentials duly transcendent. Nature
can only ambiguously offer entrancing beauty and puzzling riddles of
innocence, suffering and mercy belied. Ambivalence there cannot be
idly ignored or honestly denied, either way. We have to carry forward
what Paul called *ainigmata* in its mirror to the more exacting arena of
human history. There moral inter-human evil is a far more agonising
mystery than the evils which explode from the crust of the earth or
surge from raging waters or doom our flesh to terminal disease.

It might seem that both realms come together in the story of Jacob as we have it in Genesis 32:22–32. He is about to ford the river Jabbok to encounter his long-estranged brother Esau. The river doubtless alerts him to impending crisis – a crisis which comprises his whole story, his low cunning, his tricks with flocks, his gathering progeny of wives and sons, his scarred memories, his gains and pains. He is confronted with himself, and nature has connived with all his selfhood has done through it.

We are at a loss, at this remoteness from the time and mind of the record. Scholars call what happened vaguely 'a theophany', concealing in a word (as scholars often do) a mystery they fail to resolve. 'There wrestled a man with Jacob until the ascending of the morning.' He gets a new name which suggests he is victorious, but only by becoming also, now, a cripple. We can read it as the saga of a self. All the elements are there which we have been pondering – a personal identity, a name, competence, action, response, crisis, destiny: Jacob doing what men do with what there is, with heredity, relationship, a brother, family, exile, wandering, gaining and now, finally, the reckoning. The story, while remaining enigmatic, conveys us from this chapter to the next, from the doings and beings of our selfhood in the natural order to our selfhood where accountability comes home in history.

Charles Wesley felt he knew – reading with Christian lens – what 'theophany' should mean:

> I need not tell Thee who I am.
> My misery and sin declare.
> Thyself hast called me by my name,
> Look on Thy hands and read it there.
> But who, I ask Thee, who art Thou?
> Tell me Thy Name, and tell me now.[34]

The hands were those of One crucified. 'Tell me now' speaks an urgency that has to wait.

3 Queried

THAT 'God is the denial of denials' has often been a wisdom of the mystics with their own elusive meanings about a 'knowing of the unknowable'. Oddly, though, their saying could also be read in two other quite contrasted ways. It often seems to sceptics that believers are endlessly capable of finding reasons for not conceding that God has failed them. To be sure, prayers seem to go unanswered: to hold that 'God is love' appears steadily more incredible by an outsider's logic. Riddles persist, but resolute believing goes on persuading itself that somehow, somewhere, riddles they will cease to be. Such spirits are perhaps rarer now than once they were, but that religion has a resilient 'will to believe' seems not in doubt. Piety can be a resourceful apologist for God. Neutrality or agnosticism suspect that faith has no warrant outside its own earnestness, creating only what it wants to be true. It has too ready a will and too scant a critique for God's credentials.

The thought of 'denying denials', however, can be taken in a quite opposite sense. It may mean undertaking, from a deep, conscious despair, the obligation of 'good faith', reading that term as denoting not a pious disregarding of perplexity in the interests of solace, but a firm encounter with the liabilities. 'Denial of denials' will not, then, be from instincts of fear or simple piety but rather from authentic honesty, an honesty which knows that it has much undenying to attain. It may even find that some aspects of the other 'simplicity of heart' will prove appropriate but not its mere doggedness, its hindering fear. Or, put differently, 'the will to believe' will want to have mind in close company and alert consent. To have it so is the duty of this chapter, passing – as we now do – from conjecturing about the divine from experience in the order of nature to the tense querying of the divine through the actualities of human history.

That creation as a theatre for history could well have been concluded at the start an incredible folly on the part of God is suggested in no less a source than the Qur'ān and Muslim exegesis. Sura 2:30 tells of a 'denial of denial' in the very counsels of heaven. It has God in the heavenly conclave informing the angels: 'We are appointing [setting] a vicegerent in the earth.' The privileged recipient of this high dignity is 'man', Adam, to whom the angels are bidden to prostrate themselves, in due acknowledgement both of the divine intention and of the human status it confers. The angels unanimously demur. They urge that the creature man is no fit being for such 'dominion' over nature, being fickle, vain and liable to blood-shedding – surely a very wise angelic warning. The Lord, however, tells the angels, enigmatically: 'I know what you know not,' and renews the command to prostrate, and – so doing – to recognise some ultimate, if still incredible, divine wisdom. Reluctantly, it would seem, they all submit and prostrate to Adam – except Iblis, Diabolos, in Arabic Al-Shaitan, who persists in his defiance of God and his disavowal of the human. He thus becomes what his name means: 'the adversary,' 'the lie-giver' to the human meaning, 'the overthrower' of divine design.

It is vital to realise what this 'myth' within creation indicates about history as the arena which puts at issue a wise, conscious intention on the part of God. It makes of history a crisis about humanity entailing, by its very shape, a radical query about God. In human being divine sanity is at stake. For it becomes 'the arch-denier's' satanic business to distort and disorder the human thing to demonstrate to God His folly in the 'dominion' He rashly bestowed. In turn, it becomes the human calling to resist satanic temptation and 'give the lie to the satanic liar', and thus to vindicate the divine wisdom. Only a right discharge of the human dignity will 'put God in the right'. Doing so is both the theme of history and the crux of being human. God will then indeed be 'the denial of denials'.

The heart of all our queries is whether it is, can or ever will be so? 'The only form of worship is to be,' wrote D.H. Lawrence. He had his own intention in the words.[1] We suspect that the sentence is unfinished - to be what? Is he suggesting some self-idolatry? Perhaps, yet his form of words, no doubt unwittingly, captures what human 'dominion' means under a divine sovereignty. It is to acknowledge and to fulfil what we are in the intention by which we have been 'let be'. That takes us to what, inclusively, humanity has made of history, how history has sifted the human meaning. Is it a theme we can ever comprise or comprehend in a theology? There has at least to be a will to do so. The task of a right theology is none other than the business of being fully human. If 'the denial of denials' is in any way a definition of God, it has to be the vocation of man.

ii

We have that vocation in other terms if we recall the language already familiar to us in Hebraic tradition about 'the place and the Name'. 'The place' is now the whole locale of earthly geography as the stage of human history and the human drama. In the biblical tradition 'place' always included 'time'. Whether 'theophany', or exodus, or entry into land, or temple-founding, it was event that gave place significance. Happening hallowed locality, locality memorialised happening. We find that this same pattern is written large across the whole human story.

Here we encounter the first deep query about the divine sovereignty and the human situation. For around what happens in place and time, upon the good earth and through the human generations, there runs a third dimension – people-possession. If, by the first two (geography and history), the divine is present as transcendent intention, by the third it is strangely particularised and privatised. Every 'here' means 'us-here', every 'then' an 'us-then'. Things divine are partialised by things human, and the factors that make it so are in the very shape of creation. They belong inseparably with the natural order. We come, we humans, in tribes, races, cultures. We have cherished ancestries and occupy distinctive habitats. These our several climates and territories diversify and make unequal. Blood and memory, nurture and story, will be 'the name of the place'.

Nevertheless, all these in their diversity faith sees as one human experience and one divine patterning. It is with these common yet competitive, or contrasting, denominators that we have been 'let be' – we suppose divinely. If we accept geography and history (what we do in what there is) as index to the human meaning under God, how can they be exclusified at such great cost in suffering and tragedy? Yet, given the way creation has it, how can they not be? Is there something awry with the whole economy of God?

It seems to be right to ask why the transcendent should have made divine register among us thus inherently divisive. Has creation somehow contrived a frustration at its heart by the very diversification of that human 'dominion' by tribes, territories, memories and enmities? The question might be ruled out, as earlier we ruled out Thomas Hardy's musings about some world 'before [sentient] life', as being totally unreal. Even so it goes on recurring, the more so when we are thinking, not merely of human consciousness, but of human conflict: 'There would be no absolute loss if every human being perished tomorrow . . . Don't you find it a beautiful clean thought, a world empty of people, just uninterrupted grass and a hare sitting up?'[2] Who would then be registering the absence of man or knowing either grass or hare? Yet perhaps 'man is the mistake of creation'. Being never able to assert that 'nothing' is preferable to 'something', man we *must* reassert, yet when we do so we restore the problem he sets as to God and the wisdom of the way creation is.

For it has been precisely these constituents of creation's times and places, parcelled out among human collectives with all their puzzling differentials, that have been institutionalised in the patterns and prejudices of religion. Collectives of people and power, identified by place and race, have vested their natural identities in sanctions of creed and cult and code and community, making religion in turn a diversified expression of the universal. Religious pluralism thus requires puzzling interrogation of the way creation is. For it has taken over, often in mutual antagonism, what has to be understood as unitive – if creation really meant a human meaning intended to be singular.

Writing in a concern for 'high' Christian perception of the sacramental, the Roman Catholic theologian Von Hugel argued:

> If man's spirit is awakened by contact with the things of sense and if his consciousness of the Eternal and the Omnipresent is aroused and, in the long run, sustained only by the aid of happenings in time and space, then the historical, institutional and sacramental must be allowed a necessary position and function in the full religious life.[3]

The case here is exactly that of the previous chapter, where 'things of sense' and 'happenings in time and space' were known as central to a natural theology, being where personhood belongs. The case, however, is much more inclusive than a plea for ornate Masses, colourful rituals and sacerdotal agencies. For 'sacramental' read 'economic, social and political' and what 'happenings in space and time' and 'things of sense' require means all these institutionalised in collectives where human diversity makes them competitively religious and religiously self-warranting. While parties to the whole, they take the whole into parties. That dark paradox has harshly vexed the human story. Religious pluralism shapes into the first of what has to be queried about the ways of God.

Not all its aspects are intended or appropriate here. We stay with the question why creaturehood was made, left, devised, or otherwise allowed to be this way. The worship that should constrain us evokes enmities, passions and conflicts, which, being collectivised, make transcendent reference sadly partisan. Is there a right clue to Muhammad in thinking that he saw the way to reconcile tribal disunity and strife by eliminating, in the doctrine of divine Tawhid, or 'unity,' the sanctions that disunity had in the patronage of plural deities and idol-lords? If so, he attained it only in collectivising that unity in Islam alone, making Islam only another, if impressive, institution of separate divine/human interrelating.

The way creation is poses what in this context we have to ponder. It seems to give religion need of vested interest in the three ingredients that belong with being ourselves in the here and now: our tribe, there and then, our kind; our locale; our history. In finding God we are unable to escape from our empirical selves. The issue obtains through all faith-diversity. It deepens when we realise that Hebrew Scriptures bear much responsibility for legitimating and arrogating to their people alone this nexus between the inclusive divine and the particular human. That issue we can defer to Chapter 4. The immediate point is to know what tragic reason the patient earth for 'place', and history as 'time', have to deplore what humans have been in their tenancy and their story. Can religious relevance only avail in the partisan shape hitherto required by identity and territory, by the personal plural pronouns of peoplehood?

iii

That it has long centred there we cannot deny. Examples are legion from every sphere of faith, every response to habitat. An idyllic one from D. H. Lawrence may suffice.

> The Brangwens had lived for generations on the Marsh Farm. . . . Two miles away a church-tower stood on a hill, the houses of the little country town climbing up to it. Whenever one of the Brangwens in the fields lifted his head from his work, he saw the church-tower in the empty sky, so that as he turned again to the horizontal land he was aware of something standing above him and beyond him.[4]

A like scenario can be multiplied a myriad times with equal nostalgia. Minarets, pagodas, temples, totem-poles or other skyward things give voice to transcendent meanings across every local horizontal. Should creation, or creaturehood, have made the meanings partisan?

To be sure, humanity is not as local as it used to be, nor yet so heavenward-minded. Yet mobility and secularity have not altered the passions with which identity itself can be asserted in quasi-religious forms. Mobility may only serve to make them the more sharp by educating inequalities in all that differentiates. Secularity keeps the gaze downward but only at the cost of forfeiting perspective that, if better mediated, might still redeem the passions. When human collectives are secularised they still trade the absolutes of state, or nation, or profit, or culture. Nor is technology salvation. For while it massively multiplies resources, contrivances, solutions and amenities, it no less massively multiplies menaces and leaves them more crucially in human hands.

So it is that any faith in divine sovereignty in terms of wisdom, power or love has to reach, if it can, some 'denial of these denials' of all three. 'The name of the place' has so often been aggression, zenophobia, competition, tension over *lebensraum*. These, when rampant, stir passions 'right in their own eyes', making clamour, anger, slaughter, 'rightful' and evil things expedient. Let one passing image suffice, the more eloquent coming from Robert Browning who could at times persuade himself that 'man is made in sympathy with man', but has captured the contrary in the mob-scene in *Sordello*.

> . . . Not a face
> But wrath made livid, for among them were
> Death's staunchest purveyors, such as have in care
> To feast him. Fear had long since taken root
> In every breast and now these crushed its fruit —
> The ripe hate, like wine, to note the way

> It worked while each grew drunk. Men, grave and gay
> Stood, with shut eyelids, rocking to and fro,
> Letting the silent luxury trickle slow
> About the hollows where a heart should be.[5]

'Where a heart should be' across the human story is, or ought to be, the onus on each and every religious faith. They have so long and so far allied themselves with either 'the ripe hate' or the 'shut eyelids'. Their not 'denying those denials' of sovereign good or grimly abetting them puts everything into question, and makes a wise transcendent the more hard to trace.

It would be trite to argue that religious diversity might be read as an invitation to compete in goodness, like rivals in a market. Interrogation must go deeper and probe into what seduces humankind into wrong in ways that are the more subtle for being religious. The issues present in the diversity of religions and their institutional vested interest as hierarchies of doctrine, office, tradition or ritual, have to be taken into the responsibility of each for their own character. Dialogue may help them to self-honesty but answer can only be from within. It will require of them a repudiation of coercion and a making relative, in openness to all humanity, of those elements which, differentiating human race and place, have no proper mandate to be absolute. How answer might be from Christian mind and conscience must be had in Chapters 5–8.

iv

Querying divine credentials thus far by reference to creaturehood and the religions, we have incurred sharp issues about politics and power. Long ago Thomas Hobbes gave us the case for consigning all that menaces the hope of any human well-being to 'Leviathan', to an all-powerful State. The human wisdom in so doing, provided that the surrender is absolute, more than outweigh – he thought – in protection and security the forfeiture of personal liberty. Only so was life not 'nasty, brutish and short'. By his lights, Niccolò Machiavelli had already demonstrated how necessarily crafty, subtle, conscienceless, political power would need to be.

What emerges here, when we bring into the domain of history the sort of faith we have conjectured in Chapter 2 by reference to nature, is that faith about God must wrestle with the uneasy relation between power and conscience and the ironies that attend on law. There seems to be a constant compromise of the best in the cause of staving off the worst. The peace of society is void without some coercive restraint of the will to violence. That necessity was long ago recognised when 'ancient law' willed to absorb all 'private' 'peaces', personal 'laws-unto-themselves', into some 'king's peace', which undertook what justice might be feasible. Society has to be acknowledged in some sense to be such and equipped with sinews to make its writ run, safeguarding via citizenship and democracy a modicum of private freedom.

Yet that process, if not often precarious, is attended by what power exacts of justice and love as the price of its pursuit. The dictum that power corrupts and that absolute power corrupts absolutely is familiar enough. But if we are wanting to affirm that the world is congruent with divine goodness we have much explaining on hand when we survey history, when we register the coarsening of character, the cheapening of life, which wait upon the necessities of statehood and the conflicts, within and without, which it entails.

If we ask, for example, whether politics can repent or whether states can forgive, the denials that they do or can which come at once to mind can hardly be denied. There has to be a realism about things political and economic – or perhaps a likely cynicism about the rules of the game – if we are to retain the ideals by which to judge them. That will still more be so if what we have in mind is the vindication of God.

Conscience has to undertake a steady perception of things critical on every hand, not merely for its 'peace', but for its integrity, its very right to either. Yet it must know that only a partial rightness is attainable, only a modicum of justice, of goodness, or of love. Moreover, it is evident that reason is no final guarantor of truth, no honest broker in the social scene. On the contrary, minds espouse interests, arguments serve motives and investments decide issues. Hope of an honest mind cannot be had without the goodness of the will – a condition which itself must turn on the honesty of the mind. Even criteria, norms, values, standards are – increasingly, it seems, in the present climate – assigned to social factors merely using them to legitimate conventional establishments. Ideologies are seen as no more than vested interests, disguised as 'right', by endowing them with universal sanction the better to secure and perpetuate sectional advantage. The very notion of any 'credentials' anywhere, whether concerning God, or man, or truth, or love, surrenders to sheer confusion, and reciprocal suspicions descend on all exchange of meanings. Sincerity then becomes no more than the capacity to be self-deceived. Not believing in belief overtakes all confidence in ascertainable significance, and the human autonomy itself is undermined. Rationality itself becomes a dubious entity.

Other aspects of this contemporary style of doubt about the very capacity of humans 'to mean' with genuine 'truth' will come later. The immediate need is to reflect on its implications about any 'sovereignty of good'.[6] One might conclude that any such sovereignty had been incredibly inept in not having ethics explicit, free of such strenuous quality that lays such exacting onus upon us about ever being 'genuine'. Or, contrastedly, one might wonder whether sovereignty had not been incredibly trustful and large-souled, making the human and the moral so far a challenge. It had certainly allowed satanic wiles a generous scope. The way things human are, in relation to any authentic righteousness, compels us to query what theology should think.

Must it not follow that how the meaning of God bears on the human will is what really matters? It seems clear that any divine relation to humanity must be more than juridical, merely enjoining and requiting, given that the deepest moral issues turn on what searches the will. The stakes are often inexplicit, or – if explicit, like 'Love your neighbour' – leave to our responsibility the interpretation of the range and intention, even the very meaning involved. We are not browbeaten by some naked will on high: we find ourselves left with a liberating onus to discern and attain what good demands.

V

Another criterion which points to the same conclusion is present in the very nature of law itself. Law and the penalties it wields are the necessary form of power exercised for the ordering of society and the restraining of evil in care for the common good. Furthermore, law bears crucial witness to the human dignity. Without its constraints, its prescripts and its vigilance (answerable as these are to right perceptions of that dignity), we would be wretched and anarchic. Law, however, for all its majesty, suffers curious frustrations. For, while it regulates, it can rarely retrieve. Where it adjudicates it also concedes defeat. It presides over human failures, retributes to warn others, resolves issues only in part. It comes only into action when the evils exist and when its preventive, regulative, positive writ has failed. Legists will always have to face the dilemmas they create in being what they are.

Offences are committed, rapes are perpetrated, wrongs are inflicted, victims are made and law-violaters brutalised by their deeds. Law intervenes – legitimately, and urgently so – for it must deal decisively, deterringly, visibly, with what defies it. Otherwise its authority wanes and withers. Yet, at its intervening, the wrongs, the contraventions, already exist. At best they can only be partially halted. Much of their entail in tragedy enmity, exploitation, suffering, suspicion and inter-human despair, persists in terms that law is powerless to overcome. The case, doubtless, would be worse were law absent or effete, and wrong met no restraint and evil no challenge. Some measure of repair is possible. Damages can be assessed and extracted, libels legally undone, and rights re-established. These items of repair, however, will always be limited and will apply least to the most heinous deeds. It has always been a matter of deep irony that whereas victims of slander may be recompensed by active law, victims of murder cannot. Part of the moral plea for immortality has always been that without it death closes all accounts as surviving rape, or assault, or theft – happily – does not.

These are not the only paradoxes pointing to the partiality in legal perceptions of reality. For law, whatever its sphere, has that about it which somehow provokes defiance. Paul knew this puzzling feature well in his own self-discovery. So also did the master in Islam of soul-analysis, Al-Ghazali.[7] 'A law of sin is in my members ... that when I would do good evil is present with me' (Rom. 7:23, 21). So 'by the law is the knowledge of sin', inasmuch as the fact of being commanded, required, warned, enjoined, will stimulate the will to defiance. To be sure, this is no case for regretting that law exists: rather, it is the perverse tribute of our human automony to its own reality. Autonomy would be impossible in a lawless world: it has to be pursued in a lawful one. Seeing that the will must at one and the same time both preside and consent, the tension is inevitable and ever-present. It belongs with our dignity – and our crisis – that it should be so.

Hence the situation in which we find ourselves of having to acknowledge with Paul that 'while I would do good evil is present with me'. (Rom. 7:21). Even the martyr knows that this is so,[8] and every alert penitent. Self-abnegation can excite self-congratulation, humility a subtle pride and righteousness a very unrighteous zeal. In identifying hypocrisy we frequently practise it. There are recesses of evil which law can never reach or identify, still less control or reform. In all this the question of theology can never be far away. It seems at least clear that purely legal concepts of divine purpose and power can never suffice in a world where the legal, for all its 'legitimacy', is never the final or the ultimate. Even jurisprudence in earthly terms has conceded the concept of 'equity' and higher prerogative. Theologically, we have surely to 'let God be God' in terms that go beyond divine law-Giver, law-Enforcer, law-Sufficer. We shall need to return to the thought in later chapters about the divine as Messiah-Sufferer.

For, clearly, law has ends which law cannot and does not reach – the ends of having humans 'pure in heart', 'walking in newness of life'. It doubtless intends 'the good life', 'the good will', 'the just society', yet its witness to what these might mean does not attain them. Its quandaries are many, beyond those we have already pondered. Among them is the degree to which law and 'the right' entail all the problems of reproach, of censure and condemnation – in a word, the necessity to judge. These may themselves impede, as well as ignore, the possibility of redemption. Principles of right and just may be upheld but often only at the price of new possibilities of the right and the just. Necessary ethical discrimination generates treacherous psychic superiority that readily confirms the inferiorised either in their guilt or, more likely, in a sort of defiant satisfaction. Defiance can then take on a certain glamour or excitement, and pride doubtless. The core issue will then not only be confused but also distorted into a new confrontation between propriety and contrariety, or even between idealism and heroism. All readers of *Paradise Lost* know the pains John Milton had in not making Satan a more splendid, admirable figure than the Almighty Himself. Many think he did not succeed. 'Who durst defy the Omnipotent to arms', and the cry, 'Better to reign in Hell than serve in Heaven' could make even evil attractive.[9] The Muslim Qur'ān is always warning against suspicious thoughts and 'surmisings' against God's truth.[10] Satan will always turn them in his favour, wanting – as he does – to 'deny God's denials'.

Once again we find things conducing us to ask whether God can be other than vulnerable in the situations where what would seem to be His righteous ends are set in such disconcertingly human complexities, making them the more at risk precisely in being so precariously staked. Are we led to think of the divine as 'almost a brooding presence, the presence of a God virtually at the mercy of His world'?[11] Answer will have to wait.

vi

Rarely in modern literature have the puzzles that ethics, power and law present to theology been more incisively probed than by Albert Camus, especially in The Fall and The Rebel. Like labyrinthine city streets, the self-deceptions of 'the judge-penitent' in The Fall turn back upon themselves. In his capacity as 'judge' by profession, he is self-empowered to bring all and sundry into the court of his censuring mind. When drastic compromise of self-esteem is incurred by his failure to rescue a drowning prostitute from the river in Paris, the awareness of guilt finds him still congratulating the self that has it. He recovers his ability to look down on others by finding his very penitence commendable. He then disqualifies all, by suspecting seriousness in anything. He is at once a scandal and a trophy to himself. Or, conversely, there is 'no giving of absolution and no blessing'.[12] Yet the writer somehow senses that reality at issue is not so godlessly dismissed. His hero knows that

> that cry which had sounded over the Seine behind me years before had never ceased, carried by the river to the waters of the Channel, to travel throughout the world, across the limitless expanse of the ocean, and that it had waited for me until the day I had encountered it. I realised likewise that it would continue to await me on seas and rivers everywhere, in short where lies the bitter water of my baptism.[13]

Because it had universal meaning, it stayed for him as a person. Perhaps the divine sovereignty is not so vulnerable after all – or differently so, with resources of its own. Humanity still demands meanings for itself where despair most oppresses. Perhaps that fact is where divine credentials are in hand. If, with Camus, we can love life while lacking the meaning of life we give the meaning room to overtake us.

Meanwhile, Albert Camus has radically explored the deviousness of what in the human has to engage the divine. He portrays the cowardice of the cynic, the cheating in facile believing, the easy drift to amorality (as in The Stranger)[14] and the 'reverse side' that all vices and virtues possess. Do we not have intimations of a divine sovereignty in the very experience of flouting it? If so, both forbearance and ultimacy must be its hallmarks.

Camus's The Rebel,[15] with equally penetrating clarity, explores the moral paradoxes of political power. When the prophet wrote of his people's story as 'vexing God's Holy Spirit' (Isa. 63:10), his words chime strangely with what Camus sees to be something about reality which holds nemesis for all philosophies of power that overreach themselves. They provoke their own defeat. They do violence to what gives them warrant. They fight against themselves. *The Rebel* is eloquent of the way in which revolt, revolution, make their will absolute and so, in the end, merely change the name of the evil. The victors at the fall of the Bastille passed via the Jacobins to the imperialism of Napoleon. The casting out of demons became itself demonic. The liberator Prometheus becomes himself another Caesar, victim to what is perceived to be his own necessity. The absolute that is needed for dethroning the tyrant becomes itself enthroned in tyranny.

Many matters theological at once follow. Whence and what is this principle of nemesis? Is not the will to be absolute thereby required to acknowledge that it cannot be? Can it achieve if minded to do so? What should be said of the enormous human cost in tragedy and suffering entailed in the whole circuitous sequence? Could not a divine wisdom de-absolutise the making right of wrongs in less costly ways? The yearning Camus feels acutely about the last question only conveys him towards a negation of all but private courage, living without transcendence. Almond trees will still blossom[16] and the skies glow in summer sun. He is only *not* nihilist in the sense that incomprehensibility can, by the individual, be endowed with positive value in defiance of all logic. With approval he quotes Vincent Van Gogh: 'I believe more and more that God must not be judged on this earth. It is one of His sketches that has turned out badly.'[17] Asking 'Who looked at the olive trees on the way to the Cross?' he accepts art, and the will to art, as learning to do without God by oneself creating a world, whether in pen or brush or chisel. Yet will not these 'creations' be part of 'judging' the divine on earth? And where, anyway, are 'the other sketches' known? We might recall the rhyme about Beethoven and Michelangelo:

One made the surging sea of tone subservient to his rod,
The other from the womb of stone raised children unto God,

and find it significant for divine credentials that they could do so.

Vincent Van Gogh was in good philosophic company when he conjectured in creation a 'sketch which turned out badly'. With his artist's and erstwhile preacher's anguish[18] and the ardent questionings his landscapes told, he had some reason. Not so the suave and elegant Scottish academic David Hume, who offered the world the utmost in empiricism, deeming the knowable no more than a stream of isolated, serial perceptions which could credibly sustain no experiencing self within them, except in similar terms of percipient flux. To be sure he did not 'live' this 'faith'. None could. He readily regaled the world with a history and essays which purported to address both mind and memory. It might have seemed wiser to arrive at a philosophy one could live by rather than merely indulge one's wits and earn a reputation. We may thus duly gauge his suggestions about divine ineptness when he has his 'Philo' say:

Look around this universe. What an immense profusion of beings,

animated and organised, sensible and active! You admire this pro-
digious variety and fecundity. But inspect a little more narrowly
these living existences, the only beings worth regarding. How hostile
and destructive to each other! How insufficient all of them for their
own happiness! How contemptible or odious to the spectator! The
whole presents nothing but the idea of a blind nature, impregnated
by a great vivifying principle, and pouring forth from her lap, without
discernment or parental care, her maimed and abortive children.[19]

The whole passage, replete with evident contradictions, puts itself in
urgent need of 'the denial of denials'. 'Inspecting narrowly' is hardly
likely to register, even *qua* doubt, the width of things and their
'immense, organised and animated profusion'. At least the great bung-
ler was not niggardly. How will 'maimed and abortive' ride with 'pro-
digious fecundity'? Are 'the only beings worth regarding' Hume's own
fellow Scots? 'Spectators' may see only the 'contemptible and odious':
participants will see the endearing, the lovely and the holy and will be,
in turn, endeared. As is one's sort of desire, so is one's sort of search.[20]
What 'the whole presents' cannot be left to the scorners, if only that
intelligent doubt may be the more intelligent.

It is necessary to deal thus roundly with the Humes of this world
whose verdicts help to shape the theme of paradox but, lacking – or
decrying – both sides of it, only destroy it. It is time to ask what sort of
clues we have been in the way of in all the foregoing. We seem to have
been discovering meanings, entrustments, obligations and liabilities,
hints and intimations, worthy, by their mystery and their claims, to be
thought 'divine'. They correspond, both as magnanimity and crisis, to
experiences in nature and society, that are worthy to be received as the
truth of being 'human'. We stay for the present with these adjectives.
For to characterise the 'divine' and the 'human' and to think of their
inter-definition eases, without evading, what nounal language incurs.

It is almost as if we have been led by our effort after inter-definition
to a God who could be crucified. Hints only, to be sure, and the thought
is too startling to come easily. Yet clearly, in the slow drama of history,
through our existential situations in selves and societies, we discern a
presence of infinite patience, principled and resilient, almost self-
effacing, yet never abandoning a purpose pursued within our freedoms,
incredibly generous in how it risks the purpose in the freedoms, yet
credibly faithful to the conjunction between them.

The familiar dilemma ordinary humans have, as well as more subtly
articulate philosophers, concerning 'omnipotence', hinges on the
apparent mutually excluding concepts of 'power' and 'love'. Either
divine 'love' would but cannot, or divine 'power' can but does not.
Either love is, effectively, powerless, or power is necessarily loveless. Is
there no way to 'the denial of either denial', that both may be credentialled? Only if we think of God as One whose only omnipotence is love.
Perhaps there is a divine *kenosis* in the whole scheme of things[21] – and a
human humility reciprocal to it identifies its meaning more readily than

the modernist scouting of significant selfhood, of Humean empiricism, or Nietzschean arrogance, ever could.

Certainly God conditions His power precisely in making room for us, For humanity is pivotal in whatever the 'right' and the 'holy' and the 'true' are meant to be. If their authority is His their arena is ours. We need, in that light, to think no longer of God in terms of arbitrary power and will – unless we wish to take ourselves out of this world. Cannot our whole situation, both of grandeur and despair, in active cognisance of all its dimensions, be read as 'a means of grace'? Too often, our demand for a divine omnipotence and, therefore, our quarrel with what then proves adversarial to our perceptions, rest on wanting our 'rights'. Sensing all that 'graces' us in being here makes for a very different theology, having grounds in a different awareness of ourselves. To think then of 'love' as definitive of God will not be a difficult, perhaps impossible, calculation of rationality, but the form of our communion with experience as sufficiently inviting us to read it in those terms. If and when we do so, two great and confirmatory consequences follow. To know our humanity so 'graced' by divine love must extend to all. It can never be private to one land, one people, one culture. It makes humankind itself one community. Being so graced becomes the sure logic of inter-human relationships in the same terms. To have seen divine/human inter-definition so is to be enabled and energised for our own perceptions and exchanges by its light.[22]

vii

Have we not been asking throughout this chapter: 'What is the referent when we use the word God?' Language can often quite fail meaning, not least when words are familiar or have such room within themselves. It is a wise theology that never allows the word 'God' to have the indefinite 'a' – even in order to say, for example: 'The God of the Bible is a God of mercy.[23] That indeed is true but does not avoid saying what is untrue, if we conclude (as the construction allows us to conclude) that 'a God of mercy' is selective rather than descriptive. There is no other 'God' *not* of mercy', from whom 'this one' is distinguished, though the attribution of 'mercy' is authentic. If we want to speak of 'a god' or 'gods' – as we may – we are referring to idols, pseudo-deities, who do not exist except as figments of imagination or as hypotheses for purposes of what needs to be denied about God as God alone – as in the phrase just used about 'a God of mercy' where the purpose was to exclude the hypothesis of 'a God of malign indifference'. Theologians need to be sound grammarians.

The point here, however, is not merely a right grammar. We are not using the word 'God' as of an object among objects, whether 'out there' or 'down there' or 'up there'. The referent is in the relation. 'God' is whom we reach in the realities of awe, wonder, hope, need, communion and acceptance of being us-humans. We reach God through what we must deny – hatred, fear, distrust, self-love, ill will, mere 'rights', and claims. For these, in contravening our humanity, also terminate the inter-definition where the divine clues belong.[24]

At once it may be asked: Does not this theology imperil transcendence? Must there not be that which is 'out there', a sovereign 'beyond' which may never be known in human relatedness? No, we do not imperil transcendence: all we imperil is an absolute absentee. That transcendence transcends is clearly explicit in the term. We are not left thinking the transcending non-relational. For to 'transcend' outside all relevance to humankind is not only to cease to mean in our sort of world. It is also to deny the sort of world it is. Whatever transcends – as we must concede it may – unrelatedly to us-humans cannot do so otherwise than congruently with what the pro-human relevance confers and requires. Why not? the speculative sceptic asks. Answer: because that human relevance has given us the right to acknowledge that things divine are human-relational. As Deuteronomy finely puts it (29:29): 'There are things hidden, and they belong unto the Lord our God, but what is revealed belongs to us and our children.'[25] The authenticity of whom we seek as the referent of our humanness is such, by that very humanness, as to assure us that it is not cancelled out by what, of mystery and beyondness, our experience does not and cannot contain or comprehend.

Were it not so, the futility of any faith would be negating mystery itself. The clue of inter-definition is therefore central. It belongs with all that may be thought discernible and accessible about God. Further, it sees and affirms that 'divine' and 'indifferent' are a contradiction in terms. An indifferent 'godness' would never be known or discerned as such. Sovereignty neutralised or absconding is thereby vacuous. In emotions of despair we may well conclude a divine 'absentee'. No living faith has ever escaped that experience. Indeed, it belongs truly in what faith can, nevertheless, comprehend. The very idea of 'absence' requires what 'presence' needs to mean. 'O that I knew where I might find Him' is not a cry that has 'finding' inconceivable. One cannot be urgent about 'where' and hopeless about 'whether'.

Whoever it was who said, 'I accept the universe,' may well be thought a fool. He had no other option. Yet there is a 'givenness' about all that is and about ourselves within it. Do not the sciences speak of 'data'? Receiving is reciprocal to givenness. As we have seen, it suggests guesthood and invites courtesy. But it suggests so much else that seems like outrage, malignity, folly, injustice, perversity and shame. Histories are laden with guilt. Times gone bequeath legacies of enmity and wrong that replicate in times that follow. There is what rhymes with hospitality and gratitude but these mourn with what desolates and appals. Unless sold incomprehensibly on divine arbitrary will as absolute and inscrutable – in which case we go out of the world – faith can only opt to identify the divinely caring as being where doubt has to be resolved. Were we to resolve doubt the other way by enthroning the callous as the divine we would be denying the clue of our own humanness. The caring and the callous cannot be alternatives concerning God if the word 'God' is to 'mean' at all. Faith has to belong precisely where doubt most presses – not by wishful thinking but by opting to believe that what most fully defines our humanity by that same token warrants correlative love to God and love in God. It may well be that divine credentials exact this kind of travail in their very wisdom, leaving us the vocation of faith through the very stresses of legitimate doubt. So doing, they invite to an assent which knows its own mind and has taken its own risk. If so it be, all who have known the trust and adventure of inter-human love will recognise the likeness. For love gives either party the prerogative of 'proving true', in sustained experience of how it does. Can it be less so in the theology of faith, the divine-human relatedness in daily life? The atheism that, presumably, thinks not has, by the same token, forfeited the deepest wealth and wonder of its own humanity.

viii

If faith, in this way, needs honestly to concentrate its mind where doubt most presses, it will be well to end this chapter and anticipate the next by reflecting on the fear of vacancy or callousness where the divine is supposed to be. The distress that cries, 'There is nothing there,' is all too common a human anguish. An empty heaven (though a contradiction in terms) is all too readily supposed when life here seems empty of hope or compassion. Literature, not least contemporary literature, is full of this theme. 'Waiting for a Godot' who never arrives has been the stock in trade of more than Samuel Beckett. It was ironic 'comfort' when staged in Sarajevo.

Astronomers too have given the poets the same theme.

> How cold the vacancies
> When the phantoms are gone and the shaken realist
> First sees reality.[26]

In his *Lucretius* Tennyson muses on

> The lucid interspacer of world and world
> Where never creeps a cloud . . .
> Nor sound of human sorrow mounts to mar
> Their sacred everlasting calm.[27]

Were it so, we would be better defying such transcendence after the manner of Albert Camus, than deploring it. But does the divine indeed withdraw from all human involvement? If so, how does it avail to transcend? For there is no transcendence that merely comprises all space in some nebulous neutrality – not seeing that worlds exist and this human earth among them. We cannot even posit an empty heaven without first emptying our earth.

Our saying so, however, will be pretentious if God has not justified that logic. We cannot trust as being from God and truly about Him what has only human enterprise or reason to underwrite it. Hence our insistence throughout on inter-definition human and divine. No relation can be unilateral, or it ceases to relate. Keeping the human side in place, the saying in the Gospel that 'With God all things are possible' cannot mean that anything is possible in some chaotic sense – not if we hold with any divine unity. The Gospel is surely inviting us to contemplate the 'possibility' from Him of 'the Word made flesh' and of divine love crucified. For such things, otherwise, might be excluded from our thoughts as incongruous or merely wistful.

But is the 'possible' ever actual? If so, where and how? If transcendence is to 'mean', answer there must be. All the foregoing in this and previous chapters puts us in the way of it but quest it remains. Let us conclude here with the intriguing story in Acts about Paul on the Areopagus in Athens (Acts 17:16–31). He is with the philosophers whom he commends for their solicitous (if also dilettante) concern about religion. He takes a text from an inscription on a wayside altar noted on his way to the rendezvous: 'To an unknown god.' The Greek read Agnosto Theo. We might almost translate: 'A god for agnostics.'

It would seem that Greek religion feared lest gods took umbrage about being ignored by worshippers who were uncertain of their existence or their relevance. They, nevertheless, for all their failure to communicate, expected to be recognised. Hence the inscription to 'a god to whom we apologise for not having identified'. The text was a prudent insurance policy. 'An unknown god' is a phrase with many arguable meanings. It must not be mistaken as implying the 'unknowable' of the gnostic sects. In the light of Paul's following discourse about rightly reading the natural order, it may be that, as a Christian, he is underlining the fact that 'God' is 'unknown' to them by virtue of their superstition. Or they have made God 'an unknown God' by their pagan inattention to His 'signs'.

Given, however, Paul's evident will to communicate, it is likelier by far that he is highlighting for them their curious situation of registering an obligation to a god who takes no cognisance of them by being content to be anonymous. Such altars as theirs were more likely to be in the plural to 'gods unknown', perhaps in Athenian tribute to gods in Africa or indeed anywhere outside Athenian ken. The sources tell of altars raised in time of plague, at points of sheep sacrifice to avert it, which read: 'To the appropriate gods.'

We might then translate Agnosto Theo: 'to the god whom it may concern'. The human not knowing is then reciprocal to the god's indifference. The worshipper is vaguely concerned, the god blandly unconcerned, except about being slighted, albeit unwittingly. All is a far remove from what Paul goes on to tell of 'unknownness' taken away in the Gospel's measure of how deep divine 'concern' had reached, how appropriately to yearning.

'To the appropriate god' echoes to us from Greek usage and from Luke's narrative to carry our case from 'conjecture' and 'query', from the tentative and the enigmatic, to learn in more known and explicit terms where anticipation might find sure and decisive grounds. Like Paul, we have in the foregoing been deferential to where we have to start. Even the pagan altar searched out of its own perplexity for a theology that was 'appropriate'. We can do no less. But where is the God who is appropriate to all that being God must mean for the divine in sovereignty and humankind in fully human expectation?

4 Anticipated

i

> There is, as every schoolboy knows in this scientific age, a very close
> chemical relation between coal and diamonds. It is the reason, I
> believe, why some people allude to coal as 'black diamonds'. Both
> these commodities represent wealth: but coal is a much less port-
> able form of property. There is, from that point of view, a deplorable
> lack of concentration in coal.[1]

MOST schoolboys know, too, that there is a debt to carbon in both coal
and diamonds, arguably an apt analogy for one humanity, differentiated
from biblical times into Jewry and 'the Gentiles'. What has characterised
the former has been an intense focus of concentration, an insupport-
able form of spiritual property, often-times too precious to be borne,
namely the covenantal state of 'chosen-peoplehood.' There is a wealth,
as we have insisted, about *all* peoplehood, all tribal tenancy of territory,
all corporate sense of memory and history. There have been exoduses
and entries in all directions, the same sagas of mobile identities across
the earth and down the centuries. Judaic self-understanding has somehow proved unique, a diamond form of human carbon.

We have carried forward from the previous chapters a tentative sense
of divine credentials discernible in the inter-definition of the divine and
the human. Discernible but in no way proven. Believing that 'with God
all things are possible' except divine irrelevance – creation and history
being what, as humans, we find them to be – we look for where that
relevance may be discovered by the urgent test of its adequate liability
to the creation and *for* the eventualities of history. It was argued that 'a
Creator who keeps faith' cannot only be in originating or legislating
relation to the human situation.

It is this, the inclusively human, side of any inter-definition of divine
and human which – quite apart from themes biblical faith has made

traditional – points any seeker towards something like what Jewry called 'the Messianic hope'. In the broadest terms this Messianic hope was the anticipation of 'something' big enough to be acknowledged God's and full enough to answer to the human crisis as known in Jewish terms. That such hope had its origin and anticipation among Jews derives from the 'diamond quality' of 'concentration' mysteriously at work in the 'carbon' of their humanity.

This means recognising a human instrumentality within divine-human involvement. The particularity is inevitable. It will 'choose' time and place and means, and this may presuppose 'elect' people. We noted in Chapter 1 that if there is to be revelation it must be in a time and via a mediation in which the human must share. Inclusive ends are not compromised by selective means, provided that the means know, and let it be, so. The purpose in this chapter is to carry our earlier surmises and soundings into the context of Hebrew tradition to discover whether 'conjecture' and 'query' have prospect of satisfaction through the shape that Judaic self-awareness gave to the distinctive Messianic theme. Hence the title: 'Anticipated', a sort of reconnoitre looking for the traces to lead the quest further.

ii

It would be unfair to characterise the other people of the ancient Near East, the contemporaries of the early 'tribes of Israel', by any 'deplorable lack of concentration'. Israelites themselves were debtors to them. Egyptians, certainly, concentrated monumentally on the mystery of death. Even so, 'the children of Israel' did arrive to inter-identify themselves and God with unique intensity and assurance. They came to see themselves as the 'privilege' of Yahweh and Yahweh as the 'privilege' of them, an inter-definition of 'God and His people' of 'people and their God'. How it came to be so is a long, complex and controversial story. As we saw earlier, the physical, historical ingredients were common human property. It is what Israel did with them that gave the Hebrew tradition its theological apartness. Might it then be right, as the Bible assumes, that we should take things Hebraic as a kind of divine pilot scheme with humanity, a sort of test-case in which issues ultimately relevant to all would be made explicit in sharp particularity?

If so, scholars and historians are faced with enormous problems concerning the scriptural documentation where the elements of that test-case are embodied. Indeed, the narration and biblical presentation of it constitute, in large part, the event itself. It is not simply what did happen, or may have happened, which signifies but that record and interpretation saw it so.

It will be well to explore this situation first because it entails critical responsibilities which, even if there were any competence here to pursue them, would take us far into the margins of what we are about in divine credentials. But it will be part of any credentials that the situation be broadly understood. There has undoubtedly been much mythicisation of history in the Hexateuch concerning Exodus, Sinai and the conquest, with 'covenant' as the central concept. We have to acknowledge a 'tradition' that has emerged through factors that must remain in part irrecoverable. We cannot intelligently ask for *all* the 'bare facts' about Abraham or Moses or the Judges or even David. The 'facts' have been 'storied' in memory and the original 'event' quality imaged into how it has been received and memorialised as the defining heritage of its possessors. By the criterion of factuality as scientific procedures might investigate it, we would have to posit elaboration, even falsification. It must always be recognised that pious lies cannot satisfy history nor ever rightly underwrite theology. Yet, never losing sight of that principle, it has also to be recognised that significant history is never mere bare factuality. There is always what happened meant in the incidence, and the retrospect, of the experience of it. Meaning is always mediated through possession and interpretation.

Then how things are received as having been becomes in turn a fact in history. The emergence of event, via reception, into tradition is evidence with a legitimate claim to reckoning. We will need to return, in Chapter 9, to aspects of this situation so that the instinct that talks of 'getting down to the facts' will have no occasion to feel ignored. Meanwhile, if the Bible invites us to acknowledge 'acts of God', it will be necessary that we find them such only in the interplay of event, memory and mythicisation, understanding that third term in no pejorative sense but as what happens in *all* communal, long-range, 'digest' of history. One might say that the Hexateuch and the Hebrew writings constitute Israel's memory of 'its story with the Lord'. 'The historical efficacy of the event often consists in the experiences which those involved gained from it and the way in which they interpreted those experiences for their historical existence.'[2] This claim, which we shall have to clarify as we proceed, is not to leave critical research with nothing to do: it is to indicate that history is never mere data, just as music is never mere sounds.

Were it not so familiar to Bible readers, there would seem something quite incredible about Jewish self-interpretation. Consider the following and wonder if it is not either the ultimate in spiritual *hubris* and pretension, or compelling mystery:

> Ask now of the days that are past, which were before thee, since the day that God created man upon the earth, and ask from the one side of heaven unto the other, whether there hath been any such thing as this great thing or hath been heard like it?
>
> Did ever people hear the word of God speaking out of the midst of the fire, as thou hast heard, and live? Or hath God assayed to go and take him a nation from the midst of another nation, by temptations, by signs, and by wonders, and by war, and by a mighty hand and a stretched out arm, and by great terrors, according to all that the Lord your God did for you in Egypt before your eyes?
>
> Unto thee it was shown thou might know that the Lord he is God:

there is none else beside him. Out of heaven he made thee to hear his voice that he might instruct thee. Upon earth he showed thee his great fire and thou heardest his voice out of the midst of the fire. Because he loved thy fathers, therefore he chose their seed after them and brought thee out in his sight with his mighty power out of Egypt, to drive out nations from before thee, greater and mightier than thou, to bring thee in and to give thee their land for an inheritance as it is this day.

Know, therefore, this day and consider it in thine heart that the Lord he is God in heaven above and upon the earth beneath: there is none else.

It is the Deuteronomist (4:32–39) writing in the middle of the seventh century before Christ when, during the reign of Josiah, the 'second law' was promulgated. His book marks a watershed in the Judaic story. Familiarity may well leave readers with no adequate urge to ask: Whence came this grandiose conviction, this totally self-absorbed assurance, this unilateral annexation of God by one people and of one people by God, so that comparison not with, but against, all other peoples and their histories is their central designation of themselves?

In searching for the reasons the force of the question must be allowed to register. The language, being particularist and tribal, nevertheless begins with creation and is aware, for contrast's sake, with a diversity of other tribes and peoples. Its perspective starts with 'the day that God created *man* [humankind] upon the earth'. It celebrates 'the God in heaven above and on the earth beneath'. That is, or ought to be, a confession giving pause to tribalism. Monotheism cannot well be privately believed. Creation is not partially contrived. This is the world, of all of us. It is history which dominates the Deuteronomist, the history of exodus and entry, of driving out and settling in. History, however, as it happened to the tribes of Israel, cannot be isolated from histories made plural by peoples in whose other stories the Jewish happenings transpired. One cannot be aware of land-possession, forcibly, and be unaware of the corresponding dispossession inflicted. No histories are lived in self-enclosure.

There are clear signs that the Deuteronomist, in his long romanticising retrospect, is well aware of this. The indications are that it may well have been reflection on a whole panorama of violent transitions between peoples in a flux of habitats which lay behind the conviction that a special destiny had marked the Jewish share in them. In Deuteronomy 2:21–22 he writes:

Giants [*Zamzummim*] dwelt [in the land of the Ammonites] in old time, a people great and many and tall as the Anakims, but the Lord destroyed them before them and they succeeded them and dwelt in their stead. As he did to the children of Esau who dwelt in Seir, when he destroyed the Horims from before them, and they succeeded to them, and dwelt in their stead even to this day.

Such historical sequences spelt great fear, making the juncture of tribe and territory always potentially precarious with retributors, under divine aegis, suffering retribution by and by. In the prophetic period, as we must see, that sense of insecurity posed by great empires may well have induced from earliest times the Jewish feeling for the stakes they must comprehend in their covenant with Yahweh. Even when they were confessing Yahweh as 'the Lord of the heavens and the earth' they came to be retaining Him as their own patron by the very sovereignty that had universal disposal of history.

Earlier, the writer in Judges 11:24 sees divinity in terms of sheer tribalism. His chronicle describes Israel's expulsion of the Amorites as done by Yahweh for His own people's sake, and then, confident that this is final, tells the Amorites: 'Possess what Chemosh thy God gives thee to possess.' 'All that Yahweh our God gave us as we came forward is ours.' Unless this is satirical, it concedes that other gods fight for other peoples and implant them in lands. Yahweh is still one among many in like phenomena of history. He happens to be a more successful fighter.

This awareness, however, of divinely sanctioned mutations of people in places, of places for people, instils perpetual insecurity, actual or potential. It throws client peoples back existentially on the prowess of their sponsor and so, in turn, on the steadfastness of their allegiance to him, so that – in the haunting phrase of later Messianic hope – 'every man [in Israel] sits under his vine and under his fig-tree, none making them afraid'. For the knowledge that one's predecessors have evicted others, given history's ever-present chronicles of retaliation, brings home the fear that eviction can happen in reverse. When later long-range exile supervenes vital reassessments have to be made about the nature of covenanted protection. But that is to anticipate.

We are still in search of the clue to the uniquely Jewish shape of historical particularity. Its physical factors are in no way unique. Creation posits one humankind. Histories under god-auspices belong everywhere. Lands and peoples are evermore conjoined. We are looking for the logic of Messianic hope in the fabric of Judaic covenant. Beyond Deuteronomy we have its measures again in striking vehemence if we ponder Psalm 2. Any untutored reader, like the Ethiopian in Acts 8, could well be totally at a loss to understand the psalm's incredible bravado. A petty Judean kingdom sings what is perhaps a coronation hymn for its own insignificant rulers and calls upon all other potentates to 'kiss the son lest he be angry'. Overall divine sovereignty is affirmed but in incongruous linkage with a negligible rule that, nevertheless, visualises ruling the nations. These are enjoined to do it homage ('kissing the feet,' cf. Psalm 72:9) 'lest he [it] be angry and they perish'. It ('he') had no conceivable means to make good the demand or implement the 'perishing'. There was never a historical situation to warrant this pretension. The nations who threatened Israel's existence and flouted divine dominion in doing so were dominant and destined to remain so – the Scythians, Assyrians, Babylonians, Persians, of this world. What 'fetters' (v.3) can Jewry lay upon these conspiring magnates of the earth? The psalm indulges in a complete reversal of reality, a powerful satire of defiance, as if what its people most had reason to fear and had indeed experienced (depending on when we date the psalm) was actually the lot of those who made them victims. The real Judaic exile was in no way 'a futile plot vainly hatched'. The Lord almighty can laugh at the perpetrators because He has 'an anointed king in Zion', his own inviolate favourite. The psalm has his subjects feeling about them like a peasant dashing his hapless pitcher into fragments. How do we read it? Is it all wishful thinking, self-persuasion, pointless hyperbole? Is 'the anointed', the Messiah (v.2) on whom all this hangs and who is the protagonist of the equation, a figure capable of the imagined role? If so, how? And by what sort of association with Yahweh?

iii

Allusion in Psalm 2 is to the memorialised figure and repute of David whose seizure of Jerusalem, the city with the highlands the first comers under Joshua and his successors never attained, united the northern and the southern areas of Palestine, Shechem and Hebron, into one kingdom. His vision of the Temple created, under Solomon, a single shrine where Jewish 'men ought to worship', and gave a principle of unity, liturgy and legend that evoked the poetry and the soul of his people, confirming in new and powerful idiom the community in Abraham and Moses. There is no doubt that the emotions focussed in 'the holy city', as the peak of 'the holy land', contributed strongly to the history writing about all that had preceded David. Thus the twin aspects of the Davidic achievement, both in fact and legend, namely the royal and the priestly, came to serve as central themes in the identity of Messiah, 'son of David'. Hebrew memory conjured from the Davidic past a paradigm for his story's future.

With the twin institutions in being, monarchy and priesthood, and with their aura having presided over the narrating of the long antecedent history in terms that have greatly simplified and idealised its complexities, was not all arguably in place, a destiny attained, the people of God manifestly so in the land of divine promise? Why need any 'Messianism' arise? The only necessity was to perpetuate the Davidic pattern which Yahweh, according to the telling the chronicler makes of the Temple's inauguration, was pledged and bound to do. 'There shall never lack a son to sit on the throne of thy kingdom' (Jer. 33:17). With the aura that gathered around him as wistfulness later saw it, Solomon seemed to be that one.

Sadly, Solomon himself contrived to set in train the decline of the monarchy from that high peak and, through dark and sordid ups and downs of royal quality and fortune, decline became chronic, issuing into the two exiles, first of the northern kingdom in 722 and then of the Judean in 597. Those vicissitudes were surrounded constantly by the menace of great and conflicting powers, with their centres on the Nile, the Tigris or the Orontes.

Trailing their menacing battalions along the coastal lowlands, they necessitated subtle diplomatic manoeuvres on the part of the Hebrew kingdoms to ward off their powers, or tempted them into precarious alliances that seldom gave long reprieve from the insecurities of the highland capital. Geography might have in part secluded it, but politics required unremitting vigilance and an astuteness that was often wanting.

A fascinating consequence of the rooted sense of being a divinely singular people – though after Solomon, two 'kingdoms' – emerges in this scenario. While conquest, settlement and establishment belonged in the pre-Davidic story, the Hebrew mind was able to locate evil always in the Canaanites, the Philistines, the 'heathen' in the land. Despite the real debts owing to all non-Hebraic factors in the scene,[3] a 'chosen' logic could always turn reproach outwards to these unwanted pagans. The 'other peoples' of the land provided a sort of alibi to relieve the Hebrew conscience of any self-reproach, except at times in terms of having imitated their idolatries. Others were the *bêtes noires*, the culpable, the fit for reproach. Where evil could be thus externalised, the 'chosen' could be exonerated. 'The Philistines be upon thee, Samson,' makes the Jewish hero magnificent. David against 'this uncircumcised Philistine' – giant though he be – impresses as the youthful hero whose heroics are the 'covenant' in full assurance, as the sequel showed both in the hero's career and the immediate fleeing of the enemy hosts.

A far more sombre and self-critical mood came when the fluctuating and embattled monarchy(ies) was face to face with then worldpowers. History moved on. The sanctions of conquest gave way to the purposes and the pains of power and its preservation. 'Thorns in the flesh' were replaced by burdens of state. Israel/Judea were then more prestigious and more vulnerable, with more to lose. A parallel change emerged in the rise of Hebrew prophethood – in its full implications surely among the most significant of all religious attainments, as well as being the living parent of Messianic hope and the deepest evidence of what differentiates Jewry among the nations.

The Philistines, and others, as the *bêtes noires* of Hebrew self-esteem, give way to an interiorising of the sense of evil. In the jeopardy that looms at the hands of great powers, it is Israel/Jewry that comes to be arraigned. Those powers, at times, are prophetically perceived as instruments in the hands of Yahweh to requite His own people. Prophets, then, can even be pilloried as 'traitors' by those unminded for rebuke. It is as if self-patronage indulged under 'covenant' has become self-accusation by the same logic. It could be claimed by the Deuteronomist that such liability had always been the case, but it was only the great writing prophets who made it so in fact. So there came a great indictment of the nation, voices urging that only 'righteousness before God' mattered. Hebrews had rarely thought so when they were only dealing with the Philistines. Much of that old spirit persisted under the prophets and, indeed, made their task and their travail all the sharper. It is in this context we must trace the emergence of the Messianic theme and the deepest clues to what it must comprise.

Any such tracing has much ground to cover first. We might begin pursuing it by noting, in the development just summarised, an aspect of profound significance. It has to do with the moral dimension and the holy. The two might be subsumed under 'the righteous', but there lies the problem. With the emergence of the Jerusalem Temple with its priesthood and the sacrificial system of which the wilderness wanderings were innocent, the category of the holy comes to be central. It then happens that the holy takes up, even usurps, the criteria of the ethical. It can then readily become itself unethical and be unaware of its metamorphosis into wrong. It is intriguing how little there is in the Hebrew Scriptures about 'conscience'. When David is rebuked over Bathsheba it is Nathan's intervention and not David's prior conscience that turns him to repentance. Presumably, royal prerogative – and in this case symbolically priestly prerogative – gave him licence until Nathan's story set the whole in the simple ethical terms of the ordinary man.

The story is symptomatic of how prophethood had to moralise the holy in far more inclusive ways, seeing that in the priestly world of daily ritual and animal holocaust liturgies so readily sacrilised the ethical and, so doing, often left it no longer rigorously ethical at all. Hence the urgent calls of Amos and his kind against the crimes of the sacrosanct, the violations of justice in the complacence of rituals. Or the cry of Isaiah: 'Bring no more vain oblations . . . cease to do evil, learn to do well' (1:13, 16, 17). These voices could even extol the wilderness for its lack of such sacral indulgences in the sin of sanctuaries. At times, when these champions of a true integrity became too much for the holy mind, folk cried out against them: 'Cause the Holy One of Israel to cease from before us' (Isaiah 30:11). Uncongenial truths that disturb traditional minds must be suppressed. Ironically, 'the Holy One of Israel' is at once the plea and the victim. He is named in the demand to have no more of Him. Then the divorce between the holy and the ethical is complete. We will have reason to locate later a deeply Messianic clue in this situation the great prophets bring to light.

There is nothing wrong with 'the idea of the holy', that is, about giving ethical righteousness the aura, sanction and 'mystery' that ritual acts and 'holy places' can provide. The tragedy comes when these become themselves the essence, instead of the vehicle, of what alone hallows and sanctifies, namely the moral obedience to God. When the one usurps the authority, even the very meaning, of the other, then a travesty of 'righteousness' occurs. Such travesty was the deepest burden of the prophetic protest against the Temple and all its ways. A signal example, costly to him in sorrow and persecution, was that of Jeremiah in the Temple scene, where he satirised the bland assurance of unrighteous priests crying: 'The temple of the Lord, the temple of the

Lord are these' (Jer. 7:4). 'Lying words' he called them, leading to
the false concept of 'inviolability' for 'Holy places'.

The displacement of the ethical by the holy has been a dark feature
of some forms of present Zionism. It is often said that the truth of any
cause is validated or found fraudulent by the way in which it confronts
the Jewish people.

The dictum would be right if it meant that the way Jews are treated is
a touchstone of the moral character of those concerned. The same
would be true of any people. It is clearly treacherous if it means that
the test of righteousness is saluting as 'good' whatever benefits Israelis.
There are notions holding that residence alone in 'the land' sanctifies
such residents, just as wilful absence desecrates the absentee. These
dicta are held to be true without reference to the moral behaviour
within 'the land' of the returnees or to the consequences for the 'other'
occupants. 'Holy inviolability' will always be at odds, in any faith, with
ethical integrity. Thanks to the prophets, Hebraic tradition has been
keenly aware of the snare of false sanctity. The Messianic relevance of
that divine truth is implicit in the whole biblical story.

We can perhaps usefully anticipate Chapter 5, without losing the
present thread, by turning in this context to the parable of the vineyard
in the first three New Testament Gospels. It has, of course, its origin in
Isaiah 5:1–7, where the theme is the 'wild grapes' it produced, despite
the owner's hopeful purpose in its planting. There is no mention then
of 'husbandmen'. The people themselves and their doings are the
unworthy farm. In the New Testament parable it is the tenants as would-
be displacers of the Lord who are meant.[4] It is no longer a blight of the
fruit but a defiance of the ownership. The moral has deepened from a
sorry, disappointing yield and a long story of unrighteousness to a wilful
dereliction of vocation itself. We shall return to the point in Chapter 5,
for it is crucial to Jesus' interpretation of what he experienced in the
course of his ministry.

Something analogous, however, is implicit in the burden of many of
the Hebrew prophets. It can be reached if we reflect on the paradox
present in oath-taking. For covenant is vow and vow is a sort of oath.
The paradox is that accepting to be 'on oath' may imply that one is not
liable to honesty otherwise. Oaths in that way imply a devaluing of
ordinary speaking or promising. Then oaths can have the effect
of absolving one of the need to be generally truthful. That miasma can
then in turn effect one's sense of liability when under oath itself and
the intention to deceive which might accompany taking one. Vows can
underwrite indeed serve, the intention to dishonour them. There is then
religious perjury.

It is this very deviousness, applied to covenant itself, which some
prophets seem to have in mind when they accuse Israel of perverting
their status to their own ends, and of dishonouring what it requires of
them by using what they are, to withhold what they should bring. The
conditionality of the covenant was always a kind of paradox. On the one
hand, it had been made irrevocable by decree of Yahweh who would

evermore 'be their God and they His people'. On the other, it necessarily turned on the people's loyalty to its claims and meaning. The central paradox here lay at the heart both of the urgency of prophethood and the ground of its mission. Israel had 'to be what it was'. Yet status could be, and was, received and read as proxy for fulfilment. What was by covenant, in some sense, inherently 'holy' stayed falsely confident of perpetual inviolability, however 'unholy' it became. So the prophets. Hence, in turn, the different perceptions of the vineyard in Jesus' citation from Isaiah 5.

iv

Prophethood lived with this paradox and the burden it laid upon spirit and word through all its representatives between Amos and Jeremiah. Meanwhile, Israel/Judea's several great power scourges continued their threatening vicissitudes, requiring crippling vassalage interspersed with relative calm under stronger or more fortunate Jewish kings. External history and that perennial issue about covenant gave the prophets their characteristic themes of doom, requital, renewal and restoration. Beginning with Amos and remarkably so with Zephaniah, the author of the Hebrew strains of Dies Irae,[5] came the concept of 'the day of the Lord'. Those who thought, self-patronisingly, that 'the day' could only be light and victory, were told that it would be dark and dire before it could ever spell triumph and security. Both ways, 'the day of the Lord' meant anticipating a future in which the present would be transformed. The sense of dire endings presaged a sense of coming beginnings in which covenantal truth would prevail over covenanted people-compromise. The new world would be called in to retrieve the guilt and afflictions of the old.

It was clear on all hands that this futurism must have an attaining aegis, a leadership through which divine action would accomplish earthly ends, on the holy soil and for the holy people. This, in all its varied accents and surmisings, was the core of Messianic hope, the need for some 'anointed one' to actualise the expectation. The word Mashiach simply took from the anointing ritual of kings and priests the idea of consecration to an end. The term indicated a place for an answer and an answer fitted to the 'where' and 'when' and 'how' for which history and faith awaited it. 'Let God arise' in the agency of 'the Lord's anointed'.

It is vital to realise that the Messianic task necessarily belonged with all the presupposition of its own matrix. It had to do with covenant and covenant's people. It would spell national liberation essentially, though this might be romanticised for the inclusion of outsiders too, as notably in Psalm 72.[6] It would only become essentially all-people-centred in New Testament terms, as a shared redemption responding, not to Hebrew despair, but to 'the sin of the world'. Messiah, as seen in the yearnings of prophethood, was instinctively bound over into a Hebrew self-understanding.

Nevertheless, prophethood itself yielded a clue which could ultimately, via Jesus and the church-event in sequel to his Cross, afford a Messianic frame of reference to transcend the one that first defined its confines within Jewry. The clue lay in the tragic suffering which so often overtook prophetic vocation. Such suffering derived, inevitably, from the nature of the prophetic encounter with the paradox of covenant already studied. Too often the constituency resisted prophetic ministries of truth. It disliked being reminded of the ambivalence of trusting in 'chosenness'. It resented the revelation that heathen powers were truly agents of divine requital of its sins. It denied the charges levelled against the compromises and injustices of the social order, the exactions of their economies and the corruptions at their sacrifices. In those terms they 'wanted no more of the Lord God of Israel', preferring their own lived version of His supposed favouritism or His satisfaction with them as they saw themselves to be.

In turn 'they wanted no more' of those meddlesome nuisance factors in their story, those warners of legitimately impending dooms supposedly visited on legitimately indicted priests and people. They derided the likes of Hosea telling them, 'You are not My people,' as coming from a Yahweh who had pledged the contrary for ever. They taunted Amos as a rustic better occupied picking sycamore fruit in far-away Tekoa than annoying the pride of Samaria. Wanting 'smooth things', they figuratively all but 'crucified' Jeremiah, a country boy who wanted but never found relief from an ever more burdensome, entirely unsought, ministry, and finally they carried him down into captivity in Egypt.[7] Harsh prophetic experience was simply the desperate underside of the outwardly ornate and proudful tapestry of covenant and election. Prophethood was at once the deepest witness to the inner integrity of covenant on God's side and the surest measure of its faultlines on the human.

From this whole situation there emerged, as surely the most final vindication of what God was about in covenanting with Jewry, the figure of 'the suffering servant'. In some way which is perhaps too sacred, as well as too mysterious, to define, there came via prophetic tragedy the image of a witness to the righteousness of God in ways that went beyond word alone into personality and character, where the burden of words was transmuted through suffering into the very passion of truth against wrong. When prophethood maintained its indictment of evil to the point of 'bearing' it in pain and grief, evil was thereby denied both excuse and triumph. Being neither condoned nor palliated, wrong found its match. The tragic could disclose the redemptive. The impact of a *suffering* fidelity could persuade and convert as no other factor could. It embraced evildoers themselves in its wide compassion, on the sole condition of their penitent recognition of its meaning. It did not have to avenge and so perpetuate wrong, nor did it have to acquiesce as if wrong had no point. Like the arch bearing weight, it also overcame weight, creating the 'space' of forgiveness – a forgiveness which was legitimate and viable only by having been righteous and costly.

The 'servant songs' in Isaiah 42,50,52 and 53 have long been a puzzle for biblical scholars. This has not prevented them from being preludes to gospel. It seems reasonable to see them as arising, if not serially then certainly conceptually, from what actually transpired in prophetic tribulation and fidelity. Jeremiah certainly was 'led like a lamb to the slaughter', and the psalmist (at least in Psalms 22 and 69) had strange anticipations in suffering of what happened to Jesus of Nazareth.[8] To ruminate on what threatened and then was inflicted on Jesus at the climax, and as the response, to his ministry is to realise how closely the parallels belong. Whether they did so consciously within what we will need to call his Messianic mind will concern us in the next chapter.

v

There is little firm evidence that Messianic anticipation realised the clue latent in suffering prophethood prior to the post-crucifixion insight about Jesus that gave birth to the early Church. There is much impressive evidence to the contrary. Jewry, despite universal yearnings and aspirations, continued to keep its expectations of Messiah within the national identity which had fathered them. But, given that people-confinement, they had followed a sound instinct in believing that creation should be 'faithful', and that, being faithful, a fallen broken history (which their wisdom acknowledged) required of a sovereign Creator some adequate retrieval of its vast miscarriage. It was the genius of their greatest prophets to have known that miscarriage as it truly was. This was the supreme honesty of the covenant confession. To be, to have been. and to remain, the privileged of humans, the pilot project of a divine ends, the exemplification of what all identities might ultimately be taught to be, was, by the same token, to be the seed-plot of Messianic hope. The credentials of God in that whole chequered story might be enigmatic, obscure and patiently cumulative, but they were not illegible, thanks to the prophets.

After the ultimate bitterness of Judean exile to Babylon in 597 BC the implanting of the alien people or unworthy remnants on the holy soil, and the loss of the Temple rituals, Messianic hope had to find what comfort it could. In some hearts, as evident in the 70-year calculus, it took longer perspectives and had to wait with what trust it could on eventualities yet to be revealed. It had (as some now see it) to settle for an immediate pragmatism, accepting to farm and fend in exile and allow a certain vague futurism to supervene, tending towards the eschatological, or end-time, strain which would be its hallmark centuries later. Hope struggled to retain its tenacity while more and more approximate about its realisation. When Cyrus, 'in his first year as king of Persia' (Ezra 1:1), permitted and encouraged the return of some Jews (as they come to be described) to Jerusalem, he could be hailed, by the Isaiah of 45:1, as himself 'the Lord's Messiah'. So far had Hebraic hope come necessarily to turn on the mood of pagan powers.

In 'the day of small things' that followed, as interpreted by the contemporary prophet Haggai at the time of the forlorn rebuilding in Jerusalem at 520, the aura of David and the promised unfailing Davidic line was never out of mind. Jeremiah (23:5–6 and 33:14–18) and Ezekiel (34:20–31) had so affirmed, while Amos 9: 11–12 (which some see as an oracle appended to his scroll but belonging to exilic times) stressed a rebuilding of 'the fallen booth of David'. The psalmists of the exile had likewise sung of the eternity of David's dynasty (cf. 89:3–4, 20–37). The soul of a bewildered people still yearned for the *redivivus* that most legendarily enshrined the *sacro egoismo* as their divine gift, however tenuous its historical prospects.

In the immediacies of Haggai's brief prophetic tenure came the even briefer, and more enigmatic, figure of Zerubbabel, described in Haggai 2:20–23, as 'governor of Judah', Yahweh's 'chosen servant', whom Yahweh will 'wear as His signet ring'. (The 'Messiah' term is not used but one term does not monopolise the meaning.) Haggai was bidden to announce him in terms like those of Psalm 2, calculated – were they circumstantially viable – to strike terror into the hearts of 'heathen realms'. This same Zerubbabel disappeared completely from the scene and was not heard of again. Royal 'signets' – earlier snatched from the hand of the hapless Jehoichin (Jer. 22:24 as exile began) – symbolised the entire trust and commission of Yahweh, conferred legal authority, and were tokens of sovereign identity. Clearly Zerubbabel was being hailed as a new David. The passage, Haggai's last oracle, may well confirm the conjecture that *all* Judea's monarchs were in some sense 'Messianic potential', explaining why so many royal 'coronation' psalms salute accessions in such celebratory terms. Psalm 72 has already been noted. As a retrospective psalmody of history, Psalm 105 even throws back the aura of 'anointing' on to the old patriarchs who never received that ritual. It sees their wanderings as 'guests of God' proleptically part of the David royalty to which they would lead. 'Touch not My annointed and do my prophets (*sic*) no harm'[9](105:15). They were, in turn, the 'fathers' of the vision of hope Zerubbabel and Haggai found so painfully elusive. There could be no clearer witness to the total integration, not only of history and hope, but of being Hebraic and 'having' Messiah.

A measure of the sad miscarriage of the hopes placed in Zerubbabel by Haggai may perhaps be found in the oracle comprising Zechariah 6:9–11, where it seems that the name of 'Joshua the high priest' has been substituted for that of Zerubbabel in the bestowing of 'a crown of gold and silver'. It is clear that a royal figure was meant (v.13), and all the other details fit Zerubbabel. Did the alteration – if such it be – derive from some scribe disappointed by the demise, perhaps the murder(?) of Zerubbabel, or should it be read as a portent of the concept of a Messiah from the priesthood, or perhaps a joint Messiahship suited to a people who were all 'kings and priests'?

Either way, the Messianic dimensions of the period of Nehemiah and Ezra were parlous enough. The returnees had strained relations with the people whose forebears had remained and also with the Samaritans. Deep psychic and historical factors lay behind these frustrations in which the most ardent contributed to their own disquiet. They had only limited autonomy. 'Sword and trowel' were the order of the day for Nehemiah's builders. The economy was poor and conditions adverse. The Persian period left its mark on the fabric of a Judaism beginning to be expressed in the perspectives we find in the Chronicler and several post-exilic psalms, a 'Judaism' for which that word itself had begun to connote a sacrilised literature, Holy writings now set to be formalised as 'Scriptures' down from the long centuries of their parturition in legend, sage, story and song. That development would come to have profound significance for Messianic meanings and for the staying power of all things Judaic when prospects Messianic faltered, faded or finally receded into pure futurism.

vi

The Messianic theme in the long Greek period down to Pompey and the Roman/Herodian era in the last pre-Christian centuries might be thought to have wearied and wavered. The Book of Daniel has its diaspora stories of faithful exiles of Babylonian times demonstrating fidelity to their Hebraic loyalty sanctioned by divine interventions on their behalf – all a pointed heartening of spirit for the tribulations of the second century BC to which the writer belonged. Those stories in the first six chapters of the composite Book of Daniel (unique in the Bible, apart from pieces in Ezra, to be written partly in Aramaic) are followed by visions and oracles concerning the fate of heathen powers – these for the guidance and solace of the sufferers of persecutions and 'abominations' under Antiochus Epiphanes. In this context there emerges the puzzling figure of 'the Son of Man', coming to 'the Ancient of Days'. (7:13f.) and receiving from Him 'sovereignty, glory and kingly power'. This 'one like a human being coming with the clouds of heaven' ('Son of Man') passed into New Testament vocabulary to be, at length, the exacting theme of nineteenth- and twentieth-century New Testament scholarship.

What must be clear for our present purposes is that the Messianic hope, amid the beasts and horns and visions of the writer-seer, has passed into apocalyptic terms and, so doing, has become both more remote and more ambivalent. Some of the old Davidic features remain, of kingly prowess and efficient power, but the perspectives are vaster, the ambitions wider and the whole grandly futurist. The theme is moving into eschatology which, by the paradox of time and tribulation, brings the greater comfort in being the less immediate. The logic of figures like Daniel and his companions in those diaspora stories, with their comeliness, their talent for dreams and interpretation as a road to high places, and their exemplification of a steadfastness reciprocal to that of Yahweh Himself, suggests – maybe unconsciously – that any 'hope of Messiah' must lie with a whole people approximating to that image, in a sort of *imitatio Danielis*. That thought comes later into view intermittently, especially in the exaltation of Torah after Jerusalem's fall. For, while Torah was co-equal with God 'in His bosom', 'Messiah' was not so conceived. The formula 'the Name of the Messiah' came into currency as a circumlocution, implying a 'hiddenness' about Messiah. If, as the proverb had it, 'hope deferred makes the heart sick' (13:12), that formula might well confirm ambivalence.

The difficulty about a whole people being their own Messiah, keeping true Sabbaths and fulfilling an entire Torah, lay in the fact that their not doing so was the reason why Messiah there had to be. Possibly a 'remnant' of the people, eminently true, could avail for the wayward generality. What, however – as it almost seemed to Jeremiah – if such quality was found only in the single, solitary, commonly hounded prophet? Could any Messiah fulfil the role for a people with no mind to let him do so? Was the very notion heading into impasse as a thing impracticable? Yet to conclude so would be to abandon all core faith in the meaning of creation and the divine fidelity of covenant.

Is this the context in which to understand the apparent quiescence of the Messianic concept in the ventures of the Maccabees during their spirited but brief successes in the Hasmonean dynasty? Here, it might seem, was David redivivus, martial leaders reaffirming Judaic power in liberation and recovered liturgy. The songs which Luke would borrow with keen imagination to convey the paradox of the Christ nativity belonged in origin, not only with Hannah in the birth of Samuel, but to those heroes of Maccabean triumph whose mothers sang them. Then truly 'the mighty were put down from their thrones' and 'great things were done'.[10]

It seems strange, then, that the Maccabean princes do not seem to have been hailed in Messianic terms. Could it be that nationality had become a mission in itself? Political struggle led into zealotism and, when martyrs were made the cult of them, became, in turn, a warrant for the self-sufficiency of conflict per se. In so far as this is so, that suffering does not redeem beyond the terms of its own militarism. Even if, and when, it has succeeded, there is still a vacant place for a larger answer. However, the absence of clear association of Judas Maccabeus with any Messianic fulfilment might be due to his being of the priestly not the Davidic line. More than that technicality, the fact that his feats proved only a temporary relief robbed them of final Messianic relevance.

Time with its post facto disproofs was, of course, the besetting puzzlement of hope itself. In retrospect, we can see experiences of frustration giving rise, in Messianism, to three distinct Hebraic reactions in the period around the genesis of the Christian Church.

The first was a retreat into complex apocalypticism retreating also into the desert to await the intervention and striving to earn it by a rigorous obedience to some 'teacher of righteousness', leaving the wrongful world, meanwhile, to languish in its defilement. Let Messiah's task wait till Messiah made it final. The second was to be, if not his, then the nation's zealots, to hasten Messiah's tardiness and ensure via ardour that he did not fail or further postpone his due time. The third was to begin to suspect that Messiah never 'came' because he was always to be awaited. Historians can identify all three in the period that extended from the onset of Roman power, through Herod and his successors, and the several procurators down to, and beyond, the fall of Jerusalem. The third was to develop in full articulation under diaspora conditions, in more recent centuries and must be explored below. The inter-testamental writings are eloquent of the first and second. Both could show charismatic features, as for example if an ecstatic 'prophet' should announce the coming of the bearer of the hidden name, thought to be awaiting such designation and by being so attested was carrying, in fact or in mystique, the Davidic credentials.

There was always at the heart of the issue the crucial question as to the relation between Yahweh Himself and His Messiah. That issue was to come to be the heart of Christian theology. It was implicit, where it was not explicit, in all Hebraic belief. When Zephaniah, for example, said 'the King of Israel shall be Lord in thy midst, thou shalt see no evil evermore', what did he mean by 'the Lord being King', and how?[11] Messiah would be somehow 'proxy' for God but only in a sense understood as all the time *within* the sovereignty of God, just as politics distinguishes between what legislates and what executes a political will thus seen to be single. In that way the Messianic question was the theological question. What – on earth – was most proper to Yahweh?

A God of power unilaterally related to one people left the Psalms of Solomon, for example, in no doubt, or the Similitudes of Enoch. There Yahweh's Messiah was a supernatural being, ruling on earth, purging Jerusalem, judging Israel and expelling all strangers from their midst. In some passages he had access to esoteric mysteries, with power to raise the dead, and stood in the immediate presence of God.[12] Antagonism to 'Gentiles' in such versions may stem from Jewish bitterness over foreign oppression.

Beyond capitulation to the Romans after the Jewish War and the dire events on Masada, the mount of zealot defiance in 73 CE, Messianic hope could not extinguish itself like the suiciding defenders. For its faith in inviolability was not symbolised by some impregnable fortress. But the reckonings were no less shattering. With the forfeiture of the Temple, especially after the failure of Bar Kochba's revolt in 132–3 CE underlined how final that forfeiture proved to be, the mind of Judaism sought refuge in the centrality of Torah and the synagogue, in obedient *Halakhah*, or faithful law-abiding, as the ultimate form of co-operation, in covenant, with the hidden ways of God. History, however, must surely remain *sub specie Messias*, cherishing even in its inscrutability the concept-symbol of a divine fidelity. Messiah could never be 'in forfeit' but nor could be always 'at hand'. In Talmudic Judaism conjecturing or calculating a time tended to dismay. Eschatology was not for calendar calculus. The one viable element in hope was repentance. 'Akivah, grass will be growing in thy cheeks but the Son of David will not yet have come.'[13] Hope had to apply the logic of past history in which – perhaps – Messianic 'fact' had already happened symbolically. To cling to that memory was the only way to yearn aright. Thus, perhaps, Messianic – if transitory – realities had been known 'by the hand of Moses', or Joshua or the good king Hezekiah, in mortal terms, to be sure, but indicative of how some 'eternal' counterpart might contrive the deliverance. Meanwhile, fidelity must faithfully anticipate without panic or despair. There were deep implications for Christian Messianism here, in that Jesus via Cross and Resurrection could be acknowledged as the divinely meant and final counterparting of early precedents.

It was in this way that Joseph, too, with his saga of suffering and sovereignty, could be a kind of paradigmatic Messiah – an emblem, in what once had been, of what might yet be, when the true Messiah was finally 'unhidden'. It was in this way that the thought even of 'a suffering Messiah' was not impossible for the Talmud.[14]

From time to time through the long centuries, spasms of Messianic excitement spread through Jewish communities, the most spectacular being that of Sabbatai Svi (1626–76).[15] Their tragic failure could only contribute ultimately to a contrasted quietism, taking many forms. Some were tempted to the idea of a people immolated by 'Gentile' adversity and by that very status meriting whatever Messiah could contrive. Israel was thus fulfilling her side of the covenant by very patience. It was comfort to hold that divine intervention was not meant to be intelligible, or discernible, in secular history's causes and effects. One could not speculate about 'the hand of God' except in mysteries.

By total contrast, some diaspora thinking in the nineteenth century came to read improved, post-Enlightment conditions of Jewry as incorporating the Messianic hope, inasmuch as Jews were now free to fulfil themselves within German, or other, nationalism. The Messianic could marry with 'the idea of progress', and trust itself to a new age of tolerance in which Jewish destiny would actively translate its meaning into visible terms without forfeiting the covenanted identity. The problem here was that in Torah, Talmud and Yeshiva, sacred Jewish 'study' could never secularise. The historian Simon Dubnow, however, found himself very ready to secularise Jewish identity and see its vocation in terms of other liberation movements like those in Mazzini's Italy or in line with the ideas of Auguste Comte. Judaism would be like 'a state within a state', internally and spiritually autonomous anywhere. When Enlightenment hopes failed, that philosophy pointed directly to the 'solution' perceived in political Zionism. Since our present context has to do with Messianic Judaic 'anticipation' in its discernible bearing on 'the credentials of God', it need not obligate itself here to delve into the vexing question as to how political Zionism and its culmination in the State and securing of Israel have been, or could never be, read in Messianic terms.[16]

vii

That there was a splendour in the Messianic theme is clear. Hebrew tradition had taught the world to have 'an expectation' and to have it 'from the Lord'. *Expectans expectavi*, cried the psalmist (40:1). Messianic hope turned his cry into the plural: 'Our expectation is from Him.' Doing so they were realistically believing in the meaning of creation and connecting that belief honestly with the burden of history. Not to hold the human tragedy to be the arena where God would need to be in responsible Lordship would be to cease to believe. It would be to 'take His Name *as* vain'. Not 'to hope in the Lord' would be a sort of cosmic blasphemy; not to have reason to hope would make the blasphemy legitimate. There is no point to theism in a world left 'on its own'. If God *is*, He must be 'let be', consistently with what waits for Him. So much even the absurdists have seen: only they have concluded there is neither Messiah nor God. Wrong in the negation, they were right in the association. The Messianic hope was Jewry's great tutorial of the world in the theme of a God whose Name is Lord. Messianic anticipation is inseparable from the meaning of faith. It is in that quality that its abiding significance belongs.

It was, however, compromised by its confinement to one people. For, generous as its capacity for universality may intermittently have been, its particularity was always emphatic and was, indeed, for ever perpetuated by the paradox that its privacy was the eternal condition of its wider relevance. It might signify to, but could never embrace, all and sundry. As we have seen, and as most religions have to exemplify, what has universal ends may well need to move from selective means, as well as by them, in order to equalise the resulting truth and grace. Given the unity of God, a divine Messiah who avails differently for the few from the many becomes a contradiction in terms. We have to ask whether the de-privatising which the Christian faith gave to hope was the right transforming logic of the hope itself. The authentic shape of a privilege that faithfully awaits Messiah, as God's credentialling, cannot well remain the same privilege in receiving him – unless he is himself a private Messiah. In that event he makes good no creation and satisfies no history. If the world is not his arena, Messiah's God is not Lord of all.

The following chapter must take up the duties in this conclusion. There are two other concluding points concerning Messianic hope and how we should think of the inter-involvement, divine and human, in history. The one has to do with what is often called 'concreteness'. In the Hebraic mind it will not suffice as something qualitative, a principle only exemplifying what redemption might require. The Messianic task must be seen as concrete and physical. One of the foremost Jewish analysts writes on this theme:

> The Jews . . . saw no spiritual progress in a messianic conception
> that admittedly abdicated from the sphere of history and denied that
> redemption was a public act, manifest on this earth in soul and

body. They prided themselves on their refusal to betray their ideal and distrusted a spirituality whose redemption was not realised on earth as in heaven.[17]

Martin Buber also insists on this 'down-to-earth-ness'. The emphasis has been used in many quarters, by diverse minds, to 'require' Zionism as politically, actually, physically making real what could never be merely a dream.[18] The Messianic task, this insists, is quantitative, identifiable as measured whether in a state or a society or an earthly *utopia Hebraica*.

Given how human history – not to say human nature – are, this sense of things Messianic has given rise to the transformation of Messiahship into hope alone. To require evidence of the tangible in the terms just quoted is to realise that history never yields it. So, paradoxically, Messiah must be transmuted into what the same author calls 'perpetual futurism'.[19] Messiah must be an achiever: an achiever he can never be. What has, by its own dimensions, to be actualised, actualised can never be. For such thinkers, the 'idea of Messiah' (as it thus becomes) is, in effect, a posture of fidelity towards God which has learned not to look for occurrence in history, lest hope, being turned into sight, has nothing more to hope for. In short, if one is to have a future from God one must forego the illusion that we have already had from Him any definitive 'past'. Jewry, of, course never thought this way about the exodus – a past event which could for ever underwrite a confidence for the future. With Messiah it is seen to be different. Jews, according to recent theorists, do not want, or have, 'a failed eschatology', a theme of alleged Messianic actuality which subsequent events necessarily disprove.[20] Holocaust thinking has grimly insisted on the certainty that 'the world is *not* redeemed'. Only illusion (or stupidity) could ever think it was. All faith can do is to believe without seeing or, if need be, in spite of all one sees.

There is spiritual heroism here but it might seem that, in its light, the whole Messianic theme is vacuous. We are left with God and no Messiah when having Messianic responsibility was (we thought) at the heart of what being God must mean. As for vacuity, we must return to the point in Chapter 11.

The whole case, which reaches far into Jewish-Christian relations, could be resolved if we allowed ourselves to see the Messianic reality as qualitative, occurring truly as a pattern of redemption, but being eminently renewable (thanks to its actuality) by those who understood it as event. It would then be indeed a past with the energy to warrant a present and a future. We need not then fear it would ever be outdated, overtaken by time, or disqualified because subsequent events disproved or cancelled its reality. How a qualitative Messiah might be understood and recognised is the task of Chapter 5, carrying now forward to it the same grateful mandate Hebrews believed they had for believing realistically in God.

5 Presented

i

'THESE presents' are familiar, if archaic, words still used in formal legal documents. 'What we have here', they intend to say. 'Presents' are not in this case gifts, they are credentials, evidences, formulated, legible and here and now produced. The usage simply pluralises an adjective and lets it be a noun, reinforced by the demonstrative 'these'. This time, this place, is where you have them.

Christian faith was born and continued in the conviction that, in the event of Jesus as the Christ, divine, 'these presents' were submitted to history and the world. The credentials of God were presented to humankind. Divine/human inter-involvement which – as we have argued – is inseparable from the truth of either had come to decisive definition, the text of which was present in that time and place as 'Word made flesh', historical and perceptible, offering its authenticity to intelligent recognition.

About 'these presents' there was both a patient deference and a firm authority. The two were mutually congenial. As we must see in two succeeding chapters, meaning meant interacted with meaning perceived. With truth and love it could not be otherwise. Comprehension could celebrate discovery only because revelation contrived that it should be that way. That God 'commends' was how it was that Christians came to be 'persuaded'.[1] There are no press-gangs in the kingdom of heaven. Mind and heart in us have a door where there knocks the hand that serves the mind and heart of God.

Credentials are nothing if not for inspection. Large tasks of scholarship and study are necessary in reckoning with the Christian claim. We have to carry forward the concerns remitted from previous chapters. Central among them are the implications from the Hebrew experience of Messianic waiting. If that faithful hope was truly father to all Christian thought we have to learn patiently from the crises of understanding through which it passed as the last chapter examined them, not least the anguish about whether Messiah was ever really a viable expectation and, if so, how? Can we 'with assays of bias/By indirections find directions out'?[2] reading beyond the slant the originating tradition gave to Messianic hope and, so doing, finding our way to the qualitative, inclusive Christ-Jesus? If so, it must always be with a debt of love, knowing that there could be no rewriting of Messiah had he never once been written in Judaic expectation. The rewriting, anyway, was that of Jesus with his own 'assays of bias'. He had only been Messiah by first redrawing all the criteria, yet a truly 'Jewish Jesus'.

That Christians owe their being to Jesus being the Christ is evident from their very name. 'Christianity' as a denoting of their faith derives in turn from them. There can be no mistaking that it is constituted by the Christhood of Jesus incorporating, to be sure, the ethics of a 'sermon on the mount', but embracing the whole significance of a personality and a story through life, ministry and death, transacting in human time and place the will that tells the character of God.

Taking that naming of the first Christians as rightly the key, it must follow that the Christhood of Jesus is where our perception both of him and them has to concentrate. It may be well, therefore, to have always in mind Ho Christos, 'the Christ'. The personal name was 'Jesus', 'the Christ' was the quality, the office, the achievement. It is true that the definite article is often elided and it is thought that Christos, without it, becomes a personal name. This has caused much confusion. Thus a recent exegete of the Fourth Gospel writes: 'Paul appears to have little interest in Messiahship as such. The title of Messiah has been so devalued . . . that it appears there mostly as part of a proper name.'[3] Quite the contrary: proper name status, far from diminishing the significance, shows how central it was. 'Jesus Christ Lord', 'Christ Jesus Lord', 'The Lord Jesus Christ' – these were the interchangeable 'confessions' throughout the Epistles, in any order. Ho was omitted from Kurios in that very first of credal beginnings: Iesus Kurios – 'Jesus (is) Lord.' It is precisely the frequent absence of the Ho with Christos that requires us to realise how intimate had become the meaning of its presence in the mind. There are other examples in the ancient world of titles becoming names. If Christhood is where New Testament meanings focus as the factual source of Christology, the urgent question follows: In what did Christhood consist?

ii

Remembering there are those who consider that the Messianic theme is not the clue-thread to the story of Jesus we might, nevertheless, begin by asking why Judas betrayed his Master 'with a kiss'. We found the phrase a haunting one in Chapter 1. Embracing with double kissing on both cheeks was, and is, Palestinian custom between males. Thus far, there would be nothing remarkable about it. But, according to Matthew 26:48 and Mark 14:44, Judas had made the gesture a sign to the soldiers so that, in the darkness and a potential scuffle, they would be in no doubt about their quarry. It was important, also, to ensure a rapid, as well as a right, arrest leaving no chance for resisters to intervene. In the event, the 'kiss' proved the deep irony of an encounter in which acceptance of it signified an unbroken will to friendship, an abjuration of hostility.

On Judas' part it would seem that the irony lay deeper still. There remains much mystery about his motives. The weighing of them has been affected by much natural, though not Christian, resentment about the crucifixion. The charge about him being merely a thief (John 12:6) reflects this and is surely superficial. The 'thirty pieces of silver' were only a retaining fee on their part once he had committed himself to the chief priests. His purpose was far other than monetary. In any case 'betrayal' is hardly the exact word for what he did. The term *paradidomai* means 'a handing over'.[4] The 'treachery' was in the surrender – we might almost say the forfeiture – of a hope. It was only in being acutely disappointed about Jesus that Judas became a recusant. What had been his impulse anyway as a recruit? Surely, in some sense, Messianic. Gradually he had become disillusioned. If only Jesus would come to grips with a vigorous Messianic leadership and consecrate those incredible powers of mass appeal, that joyous popular eloquence, that superb charisma, to the real business of national liberation, what might not have been achieved. Instead that last straw, that mawkish acceptance of a former prostitute's extravagant devotion. No true Messiah could ever be, or avail, that way. Judas resolved to throw in his hand. Then deliberate malice may have set in to ease the pain of the treachery Jesus himself had committed against his – Judas' – dearest hopes.

Why should he stay longer with Messianic delusion in Jesus' form of it? Let indignant anger explode into emphatic repudiation. Or could it even have been that Judas hoped and schemed somehow to force Jesus' hand by confronting him, at long last, there in Gethsemane, with a situation from which, by dire necessity, he would have to break out into defensive – and then aggressive – action if all was not to be lost? If so, his subsequent remorse would tell how bitterly he immediately realised that this was the darkest miscalculation of all, the final proof that Jesus had never been Judas' sort of Messiah. Suicide then became his only and tragic option. If we have, this way, read Judas rightly, it is clear how the Cross – as an event before it was a doctrine – had to do essentially with the Messianic theme. In defining the Messianic, the antecedents had desperately contended over it.

iii

Indeed, latent or only half articulate with other disciples, they had been contending all the time. There are many ways in which to try to assess the significance of the brief ministry of Jesus. Whichever course we follow we must always be alert to where others want to start. When J. R.

Seeley published his great work on the ethics of Jesus, the title *Ecce Homo* seemed to place it squarely in the Passion, yet the gist, broadly, was the moral power and beauty of the teaching.[5] It will be wisest if we seek to hold all the elements together, having for a symbol the single robe in which Jesus the teacher appeared before Pilate.

We shall be doing do, emphatically – for better reassurance in a complex field – if we focus on antagonism to Jesus as a key to the whole. We will not immediately invoke 'the suffering servant' but simply note, and weigh, how Jesus encountered what all 'messengers', prophets, teachers meet in the human world. We must disown any 'anti-Semitism' here, however sceptical those may be who suspect it everywhere. There was, and is, no unilateral, or bilateral, opprobrium concerning Jews and Romans in what later the Fourth Gospel came to call 'the sin of the world'. What happened to Jesus in his time and place was only symptomatic of the way our humanity is – the humanity we all share.

'He suffered', says the Epistle to the Hebrews, 'the contradiction of sinners against himself' (12:3). The source is late, but the theme is there almost from the beginning. Readers of Epistles had a feel for the fact because they too were in affliction. Yet it was not only as sufferers themselves that they had their sense of Jesus the sufferer. They knew their antecedents and where to locate their own experience. In 12:3, the writer is telling of the *auctor et consummator*, 'the originator and perfecter of faith', that is, of the thing believed and the quality of believing. He invited his readers to 'consider him'.

His word *analogizomai*, not found elsewhere in the New Testament, means to 'analogise' or 'to estimate carefully', 'point by point', so that all the implications are honestly sifted. This is, truly, what all readers should be doing with the Gospel. The thing to be 'considered' is *antilogia*, i.e. 'words against . . .' – the very term used in verbal form, in John 19:12, when Jesus is falsely charged with 'speaking against Caesar'. The Epistle to the Hebrews clearly has the Passion narrative in view, and makes the meaning quite dramatic with the phrase, 'all those sinners', 'all that hostility' such as we all know of. This is the force of the Greek. The writer is well aware of the joint agencies in the crucifixion (cf. Mark 14:41, 'the hands of sinners'). He is alert also to the double meaning. For in acting 'against him' – Jesus – they were 'against themselves', flouting the truth of their own being as human and Hebraic.[6]

In locating the vital clue to Jesus and Messiahship in this sharp context, we are, of course, in line with entire prophetic experience and of human sinning against the light. In its own odd ritual context, Numbers 16:38 tells of 'sinners against their own souls'. Proverbs 8:36 and Jude 10 have the same idea. We have seen this as the truth about Judas. The *antilogia* that defies God, denies man, and the Cross is where 'the sin of the world' reveals itself in both meanings. We noted in Chapter 4 the descending spiral of the issue between the Lord of the vineyard and the husbandmen in the parable in which they become ever more perverse towards him and he ever more vulnerable to them.[7]

Let not the reader think that this is a melancholy reading, as if we have forgotten the glad exuberance of the Galilean preaching, or have ignored the ripples of gentle amusement that flowed around the hillside at the wit and irony of Jesus' parables. To be sure, 'the common people heard him gladly'. That – for the authorities – was part of the problem. In Jesus we must never separate the teacher from the sufferer: they belong in one. We are in no way saying crudely with D. H. Lawrence: 'Man has done his worst and crucified his God. Men will always crucify their God, given the opportunity. Christ proved that by giving them the opportunity.'[8] That foolish verdict would eliminate all that was vital, open and joyous in the ministry of Jesus. Could there be any 'opportunity to crucify' discernible in the Beatitudes? Was occasion given for it in the strangely moving invitation Matthew sets at the end of his Chapter 11: 'Come unto me . . . take my yoke . . . learn of me. I am meek and lowly of heart and ye will find rest unto your souls.'? Who would quarrel with the kingdom of God in those terms? The truth is that the gathering hostility Jesus faced stemmed from the very terms of his appeal. It is this quality of the story that makes it so comprehensively explicit of the divine/human situation. We have to appreciate how the controversy was joined, how it deepened towards its final climax.

That word 'controversy' was familiar enough under the old Hebraic order and had much to do with the role of Moses as seen by the Deuteronomist and of kingship by the Chronicler moderating between men. But Hosea (4:1; 12:2), Micah (6:2) and Jeremiah (25:31) knew that there was a sharp 'controversy' between Yahweh and His people. Jesus, in effect, renewed it by the terms in which he read the relationship.

It is important in all our study of the Gospels and their sequel to realise that the Christology with which they were written was not there in the outset – except as latent and awaiting realisation. The Christology of 'Sonship' identity, 'coming from the Father', 'the only begotten Son given', are all *ex eventu*, a comprehension (to be reviewed in the following chapter) which found itself in words only in the aftermath of the history where it had been implicit and throughout unknown. 'Jesus came preaching.' 'Is not this the carpenter?' men asked. Experience among disciples and the listening crowds had to do with a presence, a personality, a voice, a mind, a face, and a charisma. No one listened to him consciously because they heard he had been virgin-born or that eastern Magi had visited his cradle. He was himself, teaching, healing, itinerating, his own sole and sufficient credential. When, later, it could be understood and said that 'the Word' had been 'made flesh', with 'glory to behold', it was in retrospect to enfleshed days and deeds and words by which alone their origin was known.

The point is vital for the meaning of Incarnation itself. Postponing how 'comprehending' came until the next chapter, our concern in context is with how and why Jesus, in his Christhood, came to be crucified, the story being the key to the divine/human inter-meaning in which Messiahship belonged.

iv

The answer might be that it was all a ghastly tragedy, that Jesus was the hapless victim of a fortuitous set of circumstances where ecclesiastical (Jewish) and political (Roman) factors stumbled into his elimination. Weighed against the vagaries and risks of their sort of world, there and then, we should think it all merely incidental and in no way – otherwise – significant. Or, Jesus himself invited, even instigated, that sort of fate by a blundering zealotry, an ill-contrived nationalist fervour too naïve, or desperate, to bring anything to pass. Jesus came to be crucified because he was an upstart, a nuisance, an embarrassment, an enigma. Conjectures may be as numerous as those who make them.

None of them could survive an intelligent reading of the New Testament. None of them have reckoned with the significance of the sequel in the Church. Nor – as being behind both these – would they contain the actual experience of the disciples. Though Peter, James and John and the others followed Jesus in only partial, though growing, awareness of him, the interrelationship between them and him has to be acknowledged as the seed-plot of all the later Christology.[9] What had happened for them and to them because of him alone accounts for what, by and by, became the faith of the Christian community. It was the idea of the kingdom he proclaimed which they confessed later when they saw him as the image of its actualisation. It came to be so only on either side of the crucifixion, the Cross in its antecedents and its sequel. We have to understand the Passion as the end if we are to know it also as the beginning, as where the faith *of* Jesus climaxed and the faith *about* Jesus was fully derived.

Let us linger for our start around Matthew 11:28–30. It is a strangely wonderful fragment. How should we appreciate it? The preceding verses have a very Johannine ring. 'All things are delivered to me of my Father.' 'All things', indeed, are here – mysteriously inter-involved with God in his own person, keenly responsive to human 'ladenness', perceptive about what 'rest' has to be and confident about its being 'found', and all a 'learning' of which he is present as example. All is characterised as 'my yoke'.

What images that last word conjured up in Jewish minds. There was the yoke of the covenant and the law, the harness the people carried in partnership with Yahweh. More frequently in the histories there was the yoke of rapacious kings, the yokes by which the prophets symbolised the retribution of sins in the burden of exile. Jesus recruits the contrast to tell the 'lightness' and the 'ease' of the yoke he offers. The Hebraic associations are unmistakeable but they are given a transformation. All seems to turn somehow on himself, yet his assumptions about that inter-fact derive wholly from his sense of God. When, in Luke 15:1, he is challenged about his attitude and authority, he replies with parables that have to do with how *God* acts, namely like the shepherd, the housewife and the father in the three stories. That is how it always was with him. The meanings which he makes so central to his message, and thus to his own significance, belong with his reading of 'his Father' and the fellowship it mediates – a fellowship which can be shared by word and action, by preaching and parable.

It has been suggested that if we translate back into Aramaic Jesus' reported parables, or *meschalim*, their poetic, strophic quality is readily identified – a fact which must have contributed largely to their being remembered.[10] The Jesus of the Christian tradition is in no way at risk by steady, and proper, reminders that he was 'Jesus the Jew'. It is the shape of his Jewishness which is at issue. For he emphatically transfigured basic, crucial concepts in his heritage. His Gospel concerned a loving, forgiving Father of whom he would consistently use the formula: 'One there is who knows,' 'One there is who forgives,' 'One there is who numbers your hairs.' That 'a certain man' had two sons, or went down from Jerusalem, did not require him to be a Jew nor limit the relevance to a chosen people. The old Yahweh covenant theme found a different currency in an open grace, which, more than exacting requital on the erring, could bring them into penitent acceptance, on the sole condition of faith. There was a divine love to all, whether just or unjust, which tempered righteousness with mercy.

His imagery of 'new wine bursting old skins' filled his own ministry. By associating with sinners he pointed away from preoccupations with 'enemies' of Israel and their elimination and towards sheer human redemption and retrieval from sin. Such 'learning from him' had to do with the *emathen-epathen* play on words between teaching and suffering which a later writer was able to make.[11] For 'the sight of the people moving him to pity' (Matt. 9:36) yielded the setting of all that he said to them. The teaching and the empathy were one.

We can discern that situation in all he had to say about meats and cleansing of vessels and washing of hands. To differentiate pollution from without and pollution from within is to look beyond purity legislation and beyond the privacies of privilege to which it relates. The possibility of 'making meats clean' entails the possibility of having all peoples 'holy'. Those perspectives, however, were more than uncongenial to the custodians of the cleansing tradition. They were threatening to religious vested interest.

Similarly, Jesus' observance of the Sabbath in synagogue worship yet his readiness to have it overridden by criteria of compassion, even his unawareness of any feasible Sabbath-breaking in the latter, alienated the rigorists, as did what seemed to them his assumption of personal authority. There was nothing remotely 'rabbinic' about his stance. Rabbis gathered neophytes around a sacred text where the mind of Moses had been enshrined to yield an 'oral law' only by strict canons of exegesis scrupulously mastered by those who had once been neophytes themselves. This was in sharp contrast to the 'But I say unto you . . .' with which he deliberately revised what 'Moses wrote'.

It is clear that such revision was in the interests of discerning personal conscience, rather than routine conformity to a written code. A rule of thumb regime of mind had to give way to a certain rule of heart.

The focus had to be on the inner motive that underlay the outward deed. Intention could be present in lust, or hate, or greed, without the committing, and would be the culpable reality, inasmuch as the deed might be restrained by fear or reputation. In the matter of almsgiving, likewise, Jesus was alert to the pitfalls of self-congratulation, enjoining the sort of secrecy which would obviate self-advertisement. 'The Father saw in secret,' and that should suffice. Rewards being post-mortal, they could not serve favourable comparison in the here and now. The demands of the ethical should always countermand the claims of what – without them – became the merely holy. A 'gift to the altar' should be held over if there was first some reparation or reconciliation to be made.

There is no need to claim entire originality for many of these ruling notes in Jesus' teaching. Contemporary Judaism was in no way incapable of such insights into the vagaries of the religious mind, the temptations of the institution. What differed might be called 'action in character', and the clarity, courage and penetration with which Jesus held to his course. The contention that developed was not only because he was innovative but because he was thoroughly and consistently so, with a verve and a liberty that brought vision and hope to those who heard, and doing so with a range of public that could crowd lake-shores and throng the hillsides. When, later, the evangelists liked to write of 'multitudes' were they perhaps recalling how the old tradition used the word of all Israel at the foothills of Sinai. Matthew came to preface his collection of 'the sermon on the mount' by setting the scene by analogy with Moses on 'the holy mount' minus the fire and thunder.

Those same writers seem clearly taken by the likeness and difference between Jesus and the Baptist. There was nothing in the sharpest tones of John the Baptist more searching than the Jesus sayings Matthew gathered into his Chapter 23. Both were capable of using and meaning a ringing: 'Woe to you . . .' With Jesus, however, the inexorable demands of righteousness were tempered by hope and promise. Jesus withdrew into the wilderness only to pray and ponder. He taught where crowds mingled in Temple courts, in streets and highways, in fields and villages. In total contrast to John in this quality, he could be accused of consorting dubiously with those whom severity must condemn. If the axe was 'laid at the root of the trees', they might also be fructified by patient expectation such as John might have been minded to discount. Jesus had a ministry which made Zaccheus the tax-gatherer intrigued to meet him. Was it so via hearsay about parables? It was skill as well as charm that could make of a Samaritan a parabolic saint.

Throughout, in ruminating thus, we are measuring in the ministry the sources of hostility and its incipient disavowal of Jesus. We may take its measure also in his choice of disciples. Galileans, and especially Nazarenes, were considered unimpressive in Jerusalem. That may have been an accident of Jesus' origins. For the first 'Christian' movement was very much a local, even a family, affair. How among those fishermen, did Matthew co-exist with Simon the Zealot, the latter probably not the only Zealot in the group? Was such ambiguous choosing Jesus' way at once of recruiting, yet neutralising, what lay behind Judaic nationalism? 'The kingdom of heaven' had much to do with, though not by, the 'men of violence'. They could perhaps be taught to subdue their passion to the ways of grace and admit to that ambition the fellowship of recovered hirelings of Rome. Opposition to Jesus, as we must see, came not only from his being the sort of Messiah he finally was, but from his *not* being the sort of Messiah so many awaited – those whose sense of things Messianic centred on Rome and Caesar. There was no ring of political belligerence about a teacher who could greet hated Roman forced pack-carriage by commending two miles rather than the mandatory one.

At the heart of Jesus' whole delineation of 'the kingdom of heaven' was his constant sense of its being the response of an ethical human autonomy to the nature of God. The precepts that characterised it were at once law and liberty. They came imperatively from the sovereignty that made the world but did so affirmatively of the dignity it had bestowed. Homely analogies, lively anecdotes, from the familiar scene of homes and farms, merchants and housewives, could capture its simplicity in showing its inclusive claims.

V

The Gospels as we have them read retrospectively and we have yet to take account of what that may mean for the scrutiny of their portrayal. Yet there is no need to doubt the deep realism of the teaching, caring situation in which Jesus moved, nor the warm popular enthusiasm its course engendered in the Galilean mode. Yet, for all the gladness of the enthusiasts and the appeal of the Beatitudes, his was no success story. We have instead a brooding sense of gathering storm, of impending crisis. Popularity found an anticlimax in a climax of rejection. That it should have proved so is the story's supreme commentary on human nature in the human scene. The two main locales of the ministry are the symbols of the contradiction. The dark shadow of Jerusalem fell across the sunlit fields beside the lake. Joining them, as John 4:4 strangely has it, 'he must needs go through Samaria'. There was for Jesus an inner compulsion to fulfil the logic of his teaching by readiness for whatever its reception might entail. Only so would he be consistent with its meaning. Increasingly this pointed to encounter with Jerusalem and a prospect of suffering. It seems he came to read this as 'the cup which my Father has given me'. Those words are perhaps the fullest summary of the Messianic theme.

Great and reverent care is needed when we seek to enter into the self-consciousness of Jesus and his being of Messianic mind. It would be stupid, on our part, to ask: Did he think that he was 'Messiah'? if, by the question, we meant some abstract notion or idle surmise. It could only be an existential question, rooted in a living situation with issues turning on decision. It would be still more foolish were we to think to ask: Did he believe that he was God? For, posed in that form, about a human self, the question is meaningless or nonsensical. For God is in heaven and his Lordship is never usurped, except deludedly by the insane or one drunk with power like Tamerlane – conditions we could never posit of one so warmly human, so truly God-aware, so ardently alive to fellow mortals as Jesus of Nazareth.

We will be close to what came to be understood as incarnation if, as earlier our plea was, we stay with adjectives and ask: Did Jesus sense a divine role shaping in his human experience? Was there that of God and in God which was making him its human means whereby he in his decision would be, as it were, the fulcrum of divine action? If the answer was Yes, then we know the meaning of his being, in truth, divine. It is in the translation of his Jesus name: 'Yahweh saves'. He is the 'Emmanuel' in whom and through whom 'God is with, and for, us.' He did not think, pretentiously, that he was 'God', as if heaven had become untenanted: he knew himself meant for 'oneness with the Father' in all that the vocation unfolded before him.

What is often called, especially in reference to Mark's Gospel, 'the Messianic secret'.[12] belongs in this same context. We need to understand Messianic consciousness within the experience of 'Sonship' and both in the practical immediacies of a living situation which the Fourth Gospel, by long hindsight, could formulate in the words: 'For crisis am I come into the world' (9:39). 'Are you the Messiah,' would be a question neither intelligently to ask nor significantly to answer in some vacuum of pretension or hypothetical conjecture. 'Messiah' meant an identity in the throes of a self-awareness moving within an interpretation of events and only finding itself in response to them. Jesus could 'be' Messiah only in first transforming what 'being Messiah' meant. The Messianic 'secret', therefore, was not some cryptic mystery kept under deliberate disguise or tantalising enigmatism but a discipline of vocation patiently finding its way. What the way demanded was being steadily delineated by 'the contradiction of sinners', by the deep antagonism to his teaching as the central circumstance of his whole ministry.

Before we trace this inner crisis further there is a parenthesis to make concerning the charisma which belonged with that ministry.[13] The deeds of healing and works of compassion which marked its course could so easily have been read as Messianic evidence or, if not, they could have been recruited to launch a pseudo-Messianic enthusiasm and set rebellion, uprising, mob excitement, or whatever else Messianism might embrace, on its passionate way. That Jesus never instigated or permitted such devisings is eloquent enough.[14] The fact that this 'man of many mercies' was made 'a man of sorrows' underscores how perverse is the world of our humanity. It is of one piece with the antagonism to his teaching. As such it only sharpens what the situation entailed within his own experience. Clearly, Messianic realism would have on hand more than turning stones into bread or distributing charismatic largesse across beds of physical pain and mortal infirmity.

It is right, surely, to understand Jesus' ministry as proceeding steadily into these preoccupations, an evident 'learning to suffer' as the inner consistency of its own meaning, brought home by its actual course. We can sense the logic happening in the exchanges between Jesus and the disciples at Caesarea Philippi recorded alike by Matthew (16:13–23,) Mark (8:27–33) and Luke (9:18–22). They have withdrawn temporarily from normal scenes. There is crisis in the air. Jesus is clearly weighing what it means. He asks the disciples about how the public sees him. This is not, of course, omniscience pretending to enquire, nor self-esteem wanting itself confirmed. It has to do with whether Messianic destiny is presenting itself and, if so, in what terms. The answers are conjectural. Jesus consults the disciples more directly: 'What do you say?'

Should we not understand here a human search for the divine mind? Peter could use the Christ word while being far – as the sequel proved – from the Christ mind. The disciples were at a loss, and would remain so until the end, about the identity they were identifying. Confessing *who* he was, they had no comprehension *how*. The exchanges seem to have confirmed Jesus in the pain of that ambiguity as it became vividly unambiguous to him. 'The Son of Man must suffer.' 'We are going up to Jerusalem.' The criterion was in the phrase Jesus used in now decisive rejection of Peter's frame of reference. 'You do not think like God thinks.' It is there we have the active meaning of the divinity of Jesus.[15] Only beyond the Cross would the disciples, by then apostles, be able to say: 'We have the mind of Christ,' and to know it for the index in history of 'the mind of God'.

Given a Messiahship, in this sense *in via*, 'on the way', in no way merely nominal or formal, but operative and vital, it would have been idle folly to 'blaze the name abroad'. It would be the loyalty of such inner conflict to shun acclaim and avoid the popular (and vapid) conclusions that could only confuse. One cannot publicly announce what one has first radically to redefine. There was every reason for the so-called 'Markan secret' in the all too open-to-falsity of the Messianic task.

vi

Faith must always be alert and careful in its case-making about Jesus, the logic it reads in his ministry and the bond it perceives between that logic and his own mind. In that carefulness it is here concluded that a perceived vocation of suffering presents itself to Jesus in all that follows from the Caesarea Philippi encounter. So at least the Gospels saw and showed. The sequel might be described as the self-consistency of the ministry in the context of the antagonism it increasingly experienced. Running through all was simply the nature of his interest in mankind – realistic, incisive, compassionate and unfailing.

> . . . Only I discern –
> Infinite passion, and the pain
> Of finite hearts that yearn.[16]

How could hearers, enemies, disciples, Jews, Samaritans, priests and publicans, be abandoned without treachery to everything since Galilee, betraying is own sentness and the Father's mind?

It is this movement both forward and inward which we have to understand. It would be out of character to think it some sheer fatedness, some martyr complex. Still more out of character to think it some dire conspiracy to force the hand of God in apocalyptic intervention when all else seemed lost. Temptation in the desert had thought of that and found no warrant for it in any 'It is written.' Judas, we surmised earlier, had perhaps intended a plotted version of the same idea.[17] That was not the sort of Gethsemane into which Jesus came. But come he did, which is the climax – and the credentialling – we have to understand.

To have taught as Jesus did was to have staked divine intentions for humanity and to have grounded them in the dignity of free response. They were not of a kind, or content, that could be compelled. When their appeal plainly elicited a reaction of rejection the stakes remained, becoming only more crucial. They could not be forfeit. The reaction only served to vindicate them as authentic while threatening them as unwanted. The fidelity that had brought the appeal of the word would have to undertake the travail presented to it by the world as the impact of the word revealed that world to be. Suffering would be the word's ultimate insignia.

There was precedent enough in the suffering tradition of the greatest biblical prophethood. That it was significant for Jesus is inseparable from this reading of the climax in his story. Conversely, those who wish to reject the precedent as having any relevance have to interpret differently what eventuated, attributing the association to the evangelists.[18]

Truth can neither relinquish its meaning nor renounce its mission. When adversity bids it do both, suffering is the only option. So much loyal prophethood knew and exemplified. That was the long burden of the man Jeremiah. It finds expression in the 'servant' passages in Isaiah 42, 50 and 53. Echoes of these pass, according to the Gospels, through the mind and speech of Jesus. Mark 9:12 runs: 'How does it stand written of the Son of man that he shall suffer and be set at nought?' 'Set at nought' is, word for word, the text of Isaiah 53:3, 'we noughted [thought nothing of] him'. We have here a verbal citation. Moreover, the contextual atmosphere of fear and surmise is the same. And there is that haunting word 'ransom' and life being given, captivity on behalf of liberation. Most telling of all was the imagery of 'the lamb' – not from Passover (merely animal) but from prophet (Jer. 11:19).

Nor were these moulds into which Jesus might fit the pattern of his own obedience mere abstract formulae. How could they be in that intense situation? They both guided and enabled vocation. The figure of 'the servant', so elusive yet so luminous, was no avenger, no tyrant, no contriver. His identity lay in a readiness to hold the truth of his meaning against all odds and, so doing, deny the victory to wrong and enable an open future of forgiveness and hope.

The final narratives which so dominate the Gospels see Jesus translating that paradigm into the terms of his own passion. There is the resolve for Jerusalem, the capital of High Priest and Roman procurator. Seclusion in Galilee could well have spelled immunity, or why not remoter parts beyond Caesarea Philippi? 'It cannot be that a prophet should perish out of Jerusalem,' breathes a note of very conscious irony. What, in Jesus' terms, it meant to be Messiah could not shirk or shun 'the city of David'. Let the issues be joined where they most insistently belonged.

Then came 'the cleansing of the Temple', an event puzzling enough to generate every kind of exegetical conjecture. In part so out of character, as being public, forcible, even imperious. Should it not be seen as the very quintessence of the Beatitudes, indeed of all the teaching – 'the terrible meekness' demanding the ethical as the crux of 'the holy', a 'hunger for righteousness' requiring to oust the merchandising that cluttered the courts where 'all nations' were allowable? All the priorities of clean hearts, reconciliation prior to ritual, of inward motive over external form, were present in the action, epitomising an entire mission.

Through the final week broods the aura of the Passover. Some have even detected traces of an early Christian liturgy in the sequences of the Markan story.[19] Psalms 22 and 69 would then have been in mind with their echoes writing themselves into the very texture of the narrative. However that may be, the theme is suffering, voluntary, climatic and emancipatory. The passion story has its archetype in an ancient memory of divine deliverance. It would seem to have been Jesus' intention that the event of Gethsemane and beyond should for ever dominate the consciousness of the future it would inaugurate.[20]

Is that how we should understand the Upper Room? So familiar are the taking, the breaking and the sharing of the bread, the hallowing of the wine, that it is well to pause over 'This . . . in remembrance.' Surely he, and all that comradeship and mystery stretching back to Galilee, were unforgettable? Why any sacrament recalling them? And what could be meant by 'this is my body' with the speaker, in person, there saying it? And what of some 'covenant' in his 'blood'? The fishing, the itinerating, the listening – could they, the disciples present, ever become oblivious of these? It must surely have been, not memory *per se*, but rather the theme of memory, not whether (in case of forgetfulness) but how, the matter and the manner of the never forgotten.

Jesus did not plan to be remembered, like Demosthenes, for eloquence.[21] The theme will recur in Chapter 9 in the context of ministry with priesthood. There, and here, we see his dying, not to the exclusion of his teaching but as the crown of it. And his death was to be in *anamnesis* around bread and wine, not in mourning as of tragedy but as the principle of on-going life, the perpetual patterning of Messianic community, living by its light and power. How 'he took and blessed and broke and gave' would always remain the sweetest recall of what had transpired among the crowds in Galilee, joined abidingly with what was being transacted in his death, and thus becoming the symbol of their unity. On all occasions they had to 'take and eat', to make their own the logic of the mystery and the onus of community within it, theirs and his. These were credentials of a divine hospitality, of its nature and its cost. And it could use locations borrowed both from nature and a friend, a hillside and a guest-chamber.

All these measures of vocation in the final week of Jesus' encounter with Jerusalem intensified in Gethsemane. Why did he enter there at all or linger so long, in the knowledge that plans for his arrest were made, their activation imminent? Escape could have been readily contrived down into the desert and across to Moab. The time he spent so long in prayer, while dazed but dogged disciples struggled hard to stay awake, he might well have passed in effective evasion of the end. 'Father, save me from this hour' (John 12:27, transposing Gethsemane with the enquiry of the Greeks) did not mean: 'Keep me from going into it' as a cry for voidance, but rather: 'Bring me forth from it.' The prayer, echoing that in the Synoptics, is about the issue not the experience.

The Muslim writer Kamil Husain, in his *City of Wrong*,[22] imagined an urgent debate among the disciples after Jesus' arrest in which they considered armed measures of intervention for his rescue. Impracticable it was, but affording some anguished compensation to themselves for their failure in the garden. They were divided, some adamant that Jesus would never have wished it in the light of their every recollection. Others were urgent that, if so, they should override him and rescue him in spite of himself. They agreed to get a message to him and abide by the answer he sent. It was that they should have no such thoughts of rescue. What was afoot was in better hands than theirs. In his extra-canonical imagination Kamil Husain understood his Jesus well.

There followed the 'trial' and that strange exchange – according to the Fourth Gospel – between Jesus and Pilate about 'kingship'. All the meanings of the whole are there in heightened intensity. The procurator's brusque opening was: 'King of the Jews, I understand?' Patient self-possession and unfailing perception marked the reply, which seemed to be no answer – for the question needed first to be clarified. 'Pilate, the word "king" you used, are you using it as a Roman would, or quoting from another, reported context?' Pilate, impatiently, abandoned the crucial word and asked bluntly: 'What have you done?' Jesus, returning to the 'king' word, explained that had it meant, in context, what Pilate assumed, his prisoner would never have arrived there without a fight. 'My kingdom', Jesus added, 'is not that sort.' 'So you are a king, then?' Pilate retorted in soldiery exasperation, leaving Jesus one final opportunity to end the confusions around the 'king' word.

That drama epitomised all the stakes, being about credentials. The prisoner, in his very being one, bent the whole dire occasion to his truth, the truth that explains both his quality and his fate. It was not Jesus who embroiled the ecclesiastics with the politician. They negotiated their own intrigues and passions. Cunning, cajolery, bribery, undisguised scorn only set the stage for the ultimate, Judaeo-Roman presentation of 'the suffering servant'. What possibilities for histrionics, demagoguery, subterfuge or panic Jesus majestically ignored. 'A cup my Father has given me' was what he let us see there when Pilate cried: 'Behold the man.'

So we pass, finally, to 'the place called Calvary, where they crucified him, on either side one, and Jesus in the midst'. When the evangelists report of 'the Son of Man' that 'he had nowhere to lay his head', one of them (John 19:30) uses the same verb of Jesus, in death, 'laying his head'. The Cross was one with the whole story. Taunts coined the gibe that – given omnipotence – all was somehow still reversible. Messiahship – in other terms – could even yet be proved by 'coming down from the Cross', a mockery sometimes renewed by the deriders of the Church's faith. Celsus, as quoted by Origen, observed:

If Jesus really wanted to show divine power, he ought to have appeared to the very men who treated him despitefully, and to the man who condemned him, and to everyone everywhere. . . . He ought, in order to display his divinity, to have disappeared suddenly from the Cross. . . . He ought to have called all men clearly to the light and taught them why he came down.[23]

His divinity was not of that sort. The 'clear light' was in his readiness to be there, how and why he came there and all that having been there brought in its train.

vii

How, so darkly tragic, so singular in its incidence, could this be the presentation of divine credentials? The thought that it could be seems utterly incredible. Can it be that by such victimisation we come to God? Can he be thought Messiah who either cannot, or will not, save himself? Can such a scene of human pathos be the heart of divine grace?

Incredibly, it happened so. The event which might be thought the very dereliction of hope became hope's very birthplace. The two incredibles belong in one – the passion of Jesus and the emergence of the Church. It is in their unison that we understand the Resurrection. Through deep travail, and with dramatic confidence, a community was born out of total desolation to identify 'the mind of this Messiah' as 'the mind of God' and to read the Cross as where they knew it so. Within a mere quarter century, New Testament Epistles had already set down that comprehension in passages like Philippians 2:5–11 and 2 Corinthians 5:16–22, perceiving how 'the ultimate dimension of the glory of God lay . . . in that activity which created its own passion.'[24] That sequel has to be traced in Chapter 6, which must ponder the pilgrimage of mind that brought faith through to it.

The need here, in prelude to the apostles' 'comprehending', is to ask why divine credentials could ever take – or have – the form of Jesus crucified. For credentials, in any context, are for the sake of verification, given and received. Any answer must recognise what its dimensions are, namely, can history, things human, things divine, be so radically brought together in an event so local, so singular, so 'once-for-all', so repeatable in Roman time and place, so charged with eternity? We are asking about its incidence, its import and its imprimatur, the evidence it offers for our credence.

As for history, death, as Samuel Johnson observed, 'concentrates the mind wonderfully'. The Cross of Jesus truly concentrates a vast universal in an intense particular. Many have disqualified the Christian reading on that ground. Crosses littered the hillsides around Jerusalem. They were a very ordinary, mundane method of death. It cannot be that so much should turn on an event so commonplace. Christians have concentrated their minds too avidly around a single crucifixion. They have grossly overloaded what any one event can signify. Rome, if not Pilate, thought nothing more of it.

That, of course, is to reckon without the factors which gave import to the 'incidental', considerations human and divine. But, before we come to these, is it not fair to ponder how inclusive the particular may be? We had the point in an earlier chapter, namely that all religions entail concentrations of significance in – otherwise – minute places and occasions, whether a merchant in a Meccan cave, a prince under the Bho Tree, or a Moses among bulrushes. Does not the theatre epitomise the world's stage and tell it in an hourglass? Is it not the genius of ritual – Christian or other – to tell meaning in memory, to 'present' the past as still 'a here-and-now'? Do we not concede that moments of celebration can capture time across the centuries, rehearsing 'there' and 'then' and 'thus' so that, like characters impressed into the clay, they yield credentials for our knowing? If we would paint a scene do we not require a canvas on which it may be set? In drama, music, the poem, the metaphor, the parable, there is always the necessity of the immediate for the relevant, the fabric for the theme. Meaning finds itself in words only by finding words for itself. If the Cross of Jesus represents an intense focus of significance it is one with all significant history in doing so in a place, at a time, with a name. People have thought there are many Calvaries but only by virtue of the only one there was.

On what, in retrospect, did the Cross of Jesus concentrate the mind? Three realities in one: it measured and enshrined the wrongness of the world, it defined what Messiahship takes, and revealed how in filial consciousness Jesus transacted what was there in the mind of God. It suffices to ponder these briefly, leaving to the following chapter how they came to register in the understanding of the Church.

We have seen how the Cross was the climax of a long and steadily deepening controversy. Its elements have already been traced. Jesus was accepting the consequences of his own version of 'the kingdom of God'. What disallowed that version was disclosed, by its reaction, as symptomatic of our common human pride and sin. The Cross admits no sanguine complacence about our human condition. It identifies what needs forgiveness in that it mirrors our perversity. It tells how collective vested interest magnifies the selfishness of selves, how selves conspire with collective passions, suppressing their own private conscience. It has in Pilate the uneasy cunning of office, in priests the scruples of holiness and the preservation of power, in the crowd the fickle capacity for wayward manipulation and callous clamour. All these are 'the sins of the world'. The Cross, as it were, gathers them into itself as the scenario of all human history, not quantitatively as some vast aggregate which history, in time, could not admit, but qualitatively as being the dimensions of this, about us all, which needs and awaits that 'Father, forgive . . .' in which Jesus died. The grace is as universal as the indictment is inclusive.

As the climax and logic of the whole ministry the Cross thus portrays and defines what the Messianic fact must undertake. By this perspective all other measures of being Messiah – political, eschatological, popular, zealot, or 'pure-land' holy – are seen to be awry, unrealistic, ill-conceived, as remedies that have not perceived the disease, like bridges too short for the width of the river. The credentials of Messiah had to be – and be presented – in terms responsive to the full truth about us. Thus the Cross only fulfilled the Messianic hope by radically transforming it. What the course of Jesus' story had indicated, its climax confirmed. That 'the Son of man would suffer' was the corollary of *who* in vocation he was and of *how* the world itself proved what he needed to be.

What history concentrated and Messianic meaning achieved had its motive and meaning in the being of God. 'God was in Christ reconciling the world' would soon become the great formula, but only so because 'Christ was in God'. This mutuality of what transpired in the filial obedience of Jesus and what belonged with 'the mind of God' is what faith means in 'the Father and the Son'. The way to the Cross was, for Jesus, a perception and fulfilling of 'the Father's will'. This is altogether clear in the narrative where the Church housed the event, in the 'Father forgive . . .', the 'Father into Thy hands . . .', that told the Cross from within. 'As Thou wilt . . .', 'the cup Thou hast given . . .', disclose what the sovereignty was that willed to be verified by credentials such as these. For the Church to have known them for what they were was benediction only second to the wonder of their divine presenting.

6 Comprehended

i

'THE mark appearing on Cain's brow and the wound in Christ's side.'[1] The poet Edwin Muir found himself wondering what connection there might be. What might 'the mark of Cain' have to do with the wounds of Jesus? By its very strangeness the thought required to be explored. The Bible sees fratricide hard on the heels of the fall of humankind. It was the first murder – a brother's. Human eyes had never seen a corpse before. 'Am I my brother's keeper?' was Cain's astonished cry as he saw for the first time the awful fragility of human flesh, the fearful lifelessness of Abel's lovely frame and red blood staining the good earth. Everything had been violated in a single deed.

The grim story in both Biblical and Qur'ānic faith gives rise to a ruling principle: 'He who saves one human life it will be as if he had saved an entire world and he who destroys one human life it will be as if he had destroyed the entire world.'[2] Single death is universal death. Universalised, the logic of Cain's deed means that any other Abels may be his victims too. And fratricide, if Abels will it so, becomes reciprocal. Hence the 'mark of Cain'. For, by the law of his own anger, he is himself a universal prey. He has become an 'outlaw' in the sense that human life cannot survive in his sort of world. With every man's hand against him he needs protection – protection from the replication of his own murdering. He is branded by the sign of his own deed as a plea for the non-retaliation he had done to death in the person of his brother. His own life would depend on others suspending the principle of his own sin.

There we reach the wounds of Jesus and, in them, the 'comprehending' by which the Church came into being in sequel to Gethsemane and the Resurrection. We have not been misled in opening this chapter at Genesis 4:1–15. For those wounds came to be identified as where a divine encounter with human enmity had 'saved a whole world' in the quality of vicarious love. The Christian Church was born in the realisation that what happened at the Cross incorporated all mankind in a guilt which had met a response of patient endurance in love. So doing – only so doing – it had sufficed to break the fatal sequence of wrong and liberate from evil.[3] The Church further concluded that this had happened in, and because, God was Himself this way. That by which and for which the worlds were made was a transcendence capable of undertaking the redemption of humanity in terms of the one supreme law of that human unity, namely that, if all were 'destroying' in the one, in the one – this one, the Christ of that transcendent sovereignty – all could read the secret of their 'saving'.

That this realisation was the very making of the New Testament, as both a faith and its document, is our present study. It will be useful, however, to preface it by some reflection on things vicarious.

ii

The term goes to the heart of Christian theology. It is also central to our experience of life. When that wise women, Abigail, pleaded with her king, David, concerning her foolish husband, Nabal, she spoke of 'being bound in the bundle of life' (1 Samuel 25:29). That is how we all are, mutually tied into circumstance, reciprocally, if not always comparably, vulnerable to each other. Our debts begin in our mothers' wombs. All of us are variously suffered for, all in some sense 'on sufferance' in the social scene. The situation is much less so when the incidence is that of physical evil. To watch by a terminal cancer-sufferer or look down from an aircraft on a drought-stricken landscape makes us want to be 'bearers' of the trial. But we cannot be: alleviators is all we can aspire to be.

With moral evil, humanly devised and inflicted, it is otherwise. When others suffer from our own contriving that they should, when we are angry, violent Cains, when we play the cad, withhold affection, practise dishonesty, pervert relationships, then inevitably others suffer, are deprived by us, depraved because of us. They suffer because of what we are. Being, or not being, 'brothers' keepers' ramifies endlessly through homes, families, societies and nations. Where there is a guilt on us there are consequences upon others. Life on all hands is dominated by this vicarious quality, inflicting and being inflicted, hurting and being hurt, exploiting and being exploited. Behaviour that mutilates others in body, mind or heart, incriminates the mutilator. Society is a perpetual bruising by the bruisers of the bruised, and has, therefore, also to be a perpetual crucible of vicarious involvement.[4]

It is also clear that what we do with each other gathers momentum. Just as motion breeds motion, so evil accelerates. Evils do not just die, or wind up in inertia like streams lost in desert sands. They need an active forgivingness in which to be absorbed and spent. If they are ever to be 'borne away' they have to be borne. This is not to say that no resistance should ever be offered or that no 'legal damages' are ever in order. There are many situations in which restraining evil is urgent and authentic, though they must be rightly discerned and handled. What, however, restitution, restraint, recompense, can achieve is mostly partial, after the fact, and leaving the deepest dimensions of the fact untouched. Law may mitigate consequences but rarely fully overcome them. For it is not in law's power to be fully redemptive. There remains a sense, in every real situation, where 'what is done cannot be undone'.

Not 'undone', that is, as a deed which is there, never to be unperpetrated. In its effects it may be partially undone, in its character, never – unless by forgivingness which truly can, and will, unperpetrate it in its relatedness to victims and to sufferers. Then the *status quo ante* can be restored – and not merely restored but enhanced and enriched by the fact of what the restoration cost. This is what is meant by 'vicarious'. To forgive is always to suffer seeing that forgiveness foregoes the satisfaction of 'having one's own back'. When the father in Jesus' story of the wayward son takes the pain of the situation for what it is, he does not break relationship. Nor does he resent, retreat into sullenness, swear repudiation or vow retaliation and revenge. He continues to remain a father, changed, indeed, by the burden of the situation but blessedly unchanged in sustained love. That, strangely, is what the son assumes when resolving to return 'to his father'. Had the father in fact taken any of those unloving ways, what 'return' could there have been? No father 'returnable to' would exist. Since he continues to love, and stay 'vicarious', the past can begin to be undone. But continuance in love is continuance in pain. Only in his 'bearing it' is the evil 'borne away'. The robe and the ring, the shoes and the feast come only from the broken heart.[5] What is not borne by the wronged is never borne away from the wrongdoer.

Nor can this heart-truth of things Christian be rightly read in any static way. For wrong is cumulative, aggrandising, self-accentuating. History shows us how. People are envious, bigoted, fanatical, apathetic, perverse, because – back near or far in time – they have been worsted, embittered, beguiled and warped.

> In ancient shadows and twilights
> Where childhood had strayed
> The world's great sorrows were born
> Or its heroes were made.
> In the lost boyhood of Judas
> Christ was betrayed.[6]

Those are always the stark alternatives. Either we transcend what otherwise distorts us, or we succumb to what otherwise might be our saving. The issue, however, will largely turn on how little or how far those in whose reactions our destinies lie have been vicariously for us or vindictively, conspiratorially, against us, or have simply not known whether or how to care.

Yeats's lines about his native Ireland take the meaning raw and well.

Out of Ireland have I come.
Great hatred, little room,
Maimed us at the start,
I bear from my mother's womb
A fanatic heart.[7]

History will not let us honestly deny the centrality of the vicarious in the human situation. Christianity learned at the Cross to see how central, likewise, it had to be in the heart of God. What could be adequately Messianic by this reckoning with the world would constitute a once-for-all expression of it and, thereby, an energising release into its replication. It is time to explore how in their very birth-throes as the Church, the heirs of Jesus' Resurrection discerned and knew it so.

iii

The previous chapter's theme of 'controversy', Christ's with the time and place, and these with Christ, will have set us on our way. There can be no doubt where the Gospels concentrate their story, dominated as they are by 'the sense of an ending'. 'This Jesus whom you crucified . . . Lord of glory' (Acts 4:10 *et al.*) was how Luke, the narrator, understood apostolic preaching on the lips of Simon Peter, a man himself transformed by what he told. The same theme runs through the several Letters of Paul, dominates the Johannine literature and finds its expression in the distinctive accents of the First Epistle of Peter and the Letter to the Hebrews. The New Testament is unanimous in its unfailing identification of the significance of Jesus in the climax of his suffering. It is unanimous also in seeing the climax as integral to the whole ministry, and further in reading both as the ground and theme of his 'glory'. When, later, the Creed was content with the word 'suffered' (under Pontius Pilate) as the sufficient reference for the incarnate Lord to preface his being 'crucified, dead and buried', it simply gave credal form to the perception that shaped the Four Gospels and controlled the Epistles.

It is fair to say that what Jesus presented was what they comprehended and that there was a deep congruence between them. What scholarship owes to that claim must be attempted in Chapter 7. The mutuality between the mind of Jesus and the mind of the Church is our present concern. What was there to comprehend from the one was the principle of vicarious love. That same principle was at the heart of all that comprehension by the other came to acknowledge and receive. The Gospels and the Epistles witness, by their very existence, to the fact of a Christ-minded Church. We have to say that *if* they had it wrong, he had it wrong also, and that, further, *if* they are to be trusted about him then we have what he entrusted to them.

Before coming to the trauma through which they passed on their way beyond Calvary to this comprehension, it will be well to plot our onward course from the theme of vicarious love we have taken as the central clue. Doing so, we must take up the dependent notion of 'justification' which has so prominent a place in the Epistles, notably in Romans, Galatians and – in its different idiom – Hebrews. In the language of John 1:29 and 1 John 2:2, the Cross was seen as a cosmic symbol of forgivingness. The evil done there had the inclusiveness latent in the logic of every expression of human malignity as noted in 'the law of Cain' with which we began. The Cross demonstrated what sin is and does, what sin, universalised, means. There, as Paul told his Galatians (3:1), it was 'placarded' for all to see. But, demonstrating as it did, the Cross was in no way merely demonstrative. It availed to enable 'justification'. How so? we must urgently ask, for the term, and the thought, have been much confused or obscured by excessively legal analogies that do them little justice.

At first sight, it must seem that the Cross, far from justifying, can only – and truly – incriminate. That, in truth, is part, as we must see, of how it justifies. We saw earlier in respect of Cain the need to suspend the principle of his own sin. We saw how evil is implicitly cumulative, retaliatory, vindictive, reciprocal – enmity to enmity, wrong to wrong, gossip to gossip, crime to crime, sin to sin. There is always what, in some legal language, is called 'the entail'.[8] Situations where, as we noted in Chapter 3, evil encounters are 'managed' by restraining, reimbursing, damage-awarding, apologising and the like are, to be sure, a matter of 'so far so good', but they are rarely the most deep or heinous of wrongs and they seldom, if ever, achieve any *status quo ante*. In the haunting words of Psalm 49:8, 'It cost more to redeem their souls.'[9]

The Christian sense of being 'justified by faith' means this 'more' whether or not it carries the psalmist with it. The phrase initially in prophets like Habakkuk had to do with the 'fidelity' in which the (already) 'just man' held to his integrity against all odds, refusing to compromise the truth of his word. By so doing he ensured that 'good was not overcome of evil'. He might even suffer and die, as did Jeremiah, but thanks to his faithfulness, wrong was not condoned, left unchallenged or conceded as 'right' simply because it had power or honour or popularity. By his suffering the just man ensured that the truth had a future. He lived in and by his fidelity and so, with him, did righteousness and hope.

Paul in the New Testament does at first seemingly strange things with this principle of the 'just living by fidelity'. Indeed, he turns it on its head. The 'faith' Paul has in mind is not the fidelity of the righteous in well-doing: it is an act of trust by those who know themselves unrighteous. It is not a faithfulness exemplified but a faith *about* another, about an event, about a comprehension of that other in that event. Paul moves from 'the faith *of* Jesus' (which has many resemblances to that of suffering 'faith-ones') to faith *concerning* Jesus. We might well ask with Nicodemus: 'How can these things be?' (John 3:9).

Let us answer by a question in negative form: How can unrighteousness be undone? If there is an answer it will take us to 'justification'. Surely answer lies in the will of the wronged to be vicarious, by the non-entailing of evil. In Jesus' 'Father, forgive them,' the Church came to comprehend such a will and related it, by its reading of the Cross, inclusively to 'the sin of the world'. It was able, therefore, to believe an inclusive vicariousness responsive to representative human wrongness as Jesus' death comprised them both.

In such terms, and in such terms only, 'our unrighteousness was being undone', no more held against us as by an unrelenting law, no more held within an inexorable logic of insistent entail. By our deep acceptance of the costliness for the 'other', 'this Christ in this God', we could be ' justified', i.e. freed from what, otherwise, would be the due implications of our wrongness in estrangement, penalty, accentuation into further guilt. All these had been halted in the vicarious love that had borne − and borne away[10] − what otherwise would have been that sequence. In the consummation of penitence and pardon, evil had met its match and all that law had meant, had intended and had darkly failed to attain, had been accomplished by means beyond law's reach or grasp. God remained alike 'just and justifier'. So much more wonderfully than 'the mark of Cain', the wounds of Jesus − only thanks to the way he bore them − suspended the principle of the world's sin. The principle by which evil renews itself by momentum of its own logic gives way to the principle by which vicarious love halts it in its tracks. To comprehend and yield to the second is to be redeemed from the first. In such comprehending and yielding the Church knew itself defined and warranted.

iv

Before we underline how radical this comprehension was by tracing its expression in New Testament language, it will be well to sift whether it might have been mistakenly arrived at by a community moved, not in terms of comprehending divine vicariousness in Christ, but out of other constraints. The integrity of faith requires to be open to the sort of 'yes but' intelligent scepticism might suggest. The positive case will be reinforced if we have to conclude that no credible alternative exists.

We have, of course, to deal with a Jewish decision from within Semitic mind. There were no 'Gentiles' among the first apostles. Moreover, precisely in being wholly Jewish they were wholly shattered. Gethsemane and the sequence had been totally devastating. 'All forsook . . . and fled.' Only women, it seems, witnessed the crucifixion. Only they, with help from the Arimathean, Joseph, came to the tomb with spices and ointment. We have, therefore, to realise that their comprehension of the Cross of Jesus as 'presentation' of the credentials of God came, and came only, from the depths of desolation and despair. Had the disciples been present at the dying of Jesus they would have heard the taunts about 'coming down' from the Cross, about someone so manifestly *not* Messiah in being so wretchedly unable 'to save himself'. The taunts would have chimed with their own worst agonies of hopes destroyed. There was, for added remorse, their own distraught, bewildered abandonment of Jesus in the garden. Why had he denied them the only heroism they could understand? Why had they deserted him by the only treachery remaining to their cowardice? Brooding over all was the awful 'curse' upon those 'hung on a tree'.

The faith *about* Jesus grew mysteriously from within this terrible forfeiture of all faith *in* him. There belongs the deep paradox of Easter, yet so puzzling. It has been conjectured that the nascent faith was somehow a desperate devising of wishful compensation. Were there not traditions in martyrology of heroes whose tragic demise wistful admiration could not tolerate, insisting that they had survived their immolation? Perhaps the very depth of tragedy can generate a blind refusal to concede its actuality. Perhaps; but not for long and not in terms of New Testament conviction around Jesus, where it becomes clear that the Gospels telescope events with dramatic licence around the tomb on Easter Day. We are not allowed to go down where the disciples went into the anguish of their own Gethsemane, of Peter's bitter tears and Thomas's lonely vigil in the 'dark night of his soul'. The Passion/Resurrection narratives, we must remember, are drama through the eyes of faith's own retrospect. If the triumphalism seems immediate, 'seems' will be the right word, especially if we recall Semitic tradition about 'the third day'.

But if comprehending grew like a dawn rather than broke like a thunderclap it had all the authority of a new day. The disciples' agony was not of the sort that could generate its own solace by contriving to disbelieve the fact. All the narratives indicate that the fact was taken, in all its overwhelming starkness. Given all the yearnings Messianic – and their lights – it could not be otherwise. Until things Messianic had been understood to be 'cruciform' in their very nature, the Cross must have remained anathema to all hope of them. Until that equation had been understood the Cross could have given rise to no illusions of artificial solace. When it was, there was no place for them. The Messiah, for whose death illusion could only have falsely and vainly compensated, had incorporated death itself into his own evidences.

Nor, surely, as some have surmised, could it have been by sheer power of imagination that the primitive Christian community could have hailed the dead Jesus as the risen Christ. The juncture of the two words in the first embryo of final Creed, 'Jesus . . . Christ', is eloquent enough. Messianic definition, on any terms but those of Jesus in his dying, was decisively and for ever negated by his having died on a cross at all. Messianic definition – on Jesus' terms – had been decisively and for ever achieved by his dying as he did. No power of imagination on the part of stricken disciples could have conjured into being the Christian conviction. What did so was a light of recognition that 'this Jesus' was 'the Christ', the only Christ there could be if, as the Cross showed, the un-entailing of evil, through the love that suffered it, was effectively 'the righteousness of God' in 'the justification of 'whosoever wills to come' and find it so. So to perceive, however hesitantly at the first, left the disciples stricken no longer, but in debt to the world with a remembered past and an open future of good news. 'This Jesus' in being 'this Christ' was truly Lord.

V

Locating the comprehending of the divine credentials in their Jesus-presentation as belonging in this way so squarely with the Cross,[11] do we disesteem the Resurrection? Not at all, but we require ourselves to understand the Resurrection wisely. We can only rightly reach the crown of the Mount of Olives from the garden at its foot. For resurrection was not some extraneous miracle that carried all else by its sheer incredibility, as a sort of compelling of faith. It is not as a marvel that it conduces us to faith but only as an index to what we must recognise in the Cross. It is there we discover what credentialled divine power, namely the love we find divine in encounter with a wrongness in which all of us are mirrored.

One careful way to do this is to return to the New Testament but reversing the sequence from Gospels to Epistles, so that we start with the Letters to the Churches and let them be our lens on the Gospels. This, after all, does justice to history. For it was out of the world of the Epistles that the process-formation of the Gospels came. Those Letters in Christian nurture via self-definition give us the primitive Church more clearly in its growth into full awareness – the awareness which necessitated the documentation of its memoried origin which the Gospels afford. What this 'Epistle perspective' involves will be deferred in detail to the following chapter. It will suffice here to assume its legitimacy and take its measure.

As the usual sequence stands, we learn of a single drastic event – the 'risen-ness' of Jesus. All seems to happen with dramatic finality and immediate perceptions. We are shown an empty tomb. There are resurrection appearances, the most decisive concentrated into a single day. There is just a week for Thomas's absence to be made good. Then the sense of 'forty days' – plainly a richly symbolic figure.[12] Then a termination of appearances and the Ascension, followed then, and ten days later, by the historic 'sending' of the Holy Spirit. In immediate sequence the Acts of the Apostles launches the disciples on their preaching ministry and gives us vivid accounts of their first discourses. Leaving the issues here that scholarship must undertake, we sense the need to comprehend their comprehending less breathlessly. Could it be that the narratives have coalesced, as a dramatist might, the impact and the import of events? This will not render them untrue but as conveying truth that needs appropriate reception. It is clear that we neither can, nor should properly want to, reconcile the resurrection appearances, in respect to place, time and order. The Gospels are not 'the next day' sort of history – if any history is. Nor are the sermons in Acts remotely verbatim reports. All passes its light through prisms of comprehension, retrospect, and interpretation.

Will it not be right, then, to draw out the entire event, accepting the kind of literary convention by which brief hours of staged drama enclose days, months and years of the time needed to enact, say, Hamlet as in fact occurring? Suspension of disbelief does the rest. Timing encloses times. The disciples, we might say, were truly 'briefed' in the Holy Spirit about their remembered Jesus, the story being made 'brief' and 'instant' in the ultimate text. Thus, for example, may 'that same day' of Luke's final chapter, from dawn to commission on the mountain – for there is no break in one diurnal narration – be taken as the 'day' of their comprehending in many twenty-four hours the Christ of God?[13] Many later elements are there as well as immediate ones – consternation, despair, dispersal, a strange presence, puzzlement, 'opening of the Scriptures', and finally the 'knowing in the breaking of the bread'. The day reads like a whole decade or longer, through which the first Christians, in urgent dialogue with the Hebraic Scriptures, vindicated their witness by such appeal and in which they were learning their liturgy of broken bread and sacred wine.

Almost all the appearance narratives can be read in such fuller terms as more than immediacy can exhaust. Peter's role and leadership; the Galilean dimension within Easter faith; the reluctance to believe as not suppressed; 'the print of the nails' as crucial (meaning that the Messianic who and the Messianic where must be one identity); the queries about individual destinies – all these are fully intelligible only in the longer perspectives which, writing later the evangelists enjoyed. Yet, rightly, they set them by conscious authorship in the place where the long dawning began, 'very early of the first day of the week'. Let the wise reader understand the many first years of the new regime of 'Jesus as Lord'.

The third decade of them was hardly under way when we have the First Letter to the Christians of Thessalonica, probably the earliest piece of Christian documentation. It is addressed to a local community far away in the northern corner of the Aegean Sea; a community called a 'church', a term of which Palestine was always innocent.[14] From its opening greeting it writes confidently of 'God our Father and the Lord Jesus Christ'. Christian theology has arrived. Apostolic nurture of conduct and life is also under way, rooted in pastoral concern. There is warm evidence of expanding faith despite adversity. Moral quality derives directly from doctrinal conviction. There is a strong sense of peoplehood with no mention of ethnic lineage. Solicitude for other Christian communities is clear. A working faith, an enterprising love and a patient hope are the hallmarks of recipients as seen by the writers named.

It is, as those writers might have said, 'by these presents' that we have to understand what the Gospels – non-existent at the time – would later take back into origins. Those Gospels would recapitulate where everything epistolary had started but only because the reality that lived in the Epistles had actualised what that origin had meant. We read the New Testament wisely only if we have both angles of vision in focus, otherwise the way the Gospels end might mislead us into assuming a sort of graduation at Pentecost without the long, painful years of learning what graduation would ultimately be.

At no point is that lesson clearer than in respect of what 1 Thessalonians 1:3 calls 'the patience of hope'. Christian identification of things Messianic in suffering love breaking the entail of evil could not lack a future tense. No Messianism did, whatever its provenance. This first of Epistles has the Parousia in view, 'waiting for the Son from heaven' (1:10). Redemptive love, too, had its eschatology. When, years after 1 Thessalonians, that hope receded, or a longer future awaited it, the primitive Church was not chagrined or downcast. On the contrary, an interim futurity, longer or shorter as the centuries might require, was forever present in love's Messianic principle. For the principle was eminently repeatable in Messiah's body, the Church. Christ's role in the world would be perpetuated by the reproduction of redeeming non-entailing of evil by Messiah's people.

It is this which explains the otherwise remarkable survival of faith in Messiah-Jesus beyond the fading of Parousia hope. What became modern Judaic wisdom, namely that Messiah must be either hailed and proven premature by on-going evil, or never identified and so always expectable, was in no way the Christian option.[15] Thanks to the community to which he gave being, Messiah-crucified was both definitive and anticipatory. Epistles later than those to the Thessalonians would reflect this longer perspective, refining hope but in no way forfeiting it. It is this quality of maturing, in the Epistles, of which we need to be aware when the final chapters of the Gospels seem to leave us with a Church that already has in possession all it can ever need. Indeed it had – but only for the action which alone could draw out what it was that it possessed.

It was not only a longer patience of its own which it came to learn. It would arrive at comprehending 'the patience of God' (Romans 15:5). All that, in the Epistles, had to do with Christian character derived from the suffering-Messiah. The self-education of the Church pastorally is determined by the image of Christ doctrinally. 'The mind of Christ' perceived in the one is to be received into the other. 'Let this mind be in you . . .' says Philippians 2:5 which then moves into the founding theme of divine *kenosis*. They, too, are to be non-entailers of evil, 'reviled and not reviling again', translating their faith into conduct in the same terms, knowing of whom 'they have learned'.

In this way the Cross is the paradigm all the time. 'Receive ye one another as Christ has received us' (Romans 15:7); and how was that? – in the embrace of suffering love. Later 1 Peter repeatedly joins Christian readiness to suffer with the 'example of Christ'. 'Arm yourselves with the same mind' (4:1): 'If ye suffer . . . Christ also suffered' (3:14, 18): 'Hereunto were ye called because Christ suffered for us' (2:21). Throughout, the 'glory' of Christ is the concomitant of his 'suffering'. It was never so with other Messiahs, or – if there was suffering – it was that of warriors, not victims. When, in Acts 11:26, Luke explains how and why the term *christianoi* was derisively coined by pagan observers, it is clear that they saw it well suited to a folk deluded enough to confess as 'Lord' a crucified felon. 1 Peter 4:16 is happy to accept the implication and will in no way forego the honour. The governor, Agrippa, interrogating Paul, knows the word too and, as exemplified by his prisoner, intends its ignominious meaning.

There can be no doubt, then, what 'Christian-ity' meant in the world of these Epistles. What is there in the conjoining of 'the suffering and the glory' of Jesus as Christ and Lord was the sum and source of the Easter faith. But, some may ask, in tracing the comprehending that made Christianity in this way in the Epistles, are we not bypassing the empty tomb? No! On the contrary, we are understanding it. For it was not the emptiness of a tomb that warranted Christian believing: it was Christian believing (in the terms we have traced it) which revealed the tomb empty. The point is vital. Faith, as we know from Jesus' own temptations in the desert, is not evoked by arbitrary marvels: only superstition is. His rising from the dead must not be thought parallel to descending (had he done so) from the Temple's pinnacle to induce credulity in its courts below.

We have to realise what underwrites what. There *is* a genuine issue concerning the tomb which some exegetes and scholars have been too ready to ignore. It has to do with the fact that the first Christians were people whom authority – for reasons not far removed from those of the crucifixion itself – were eager to silence. To have produced the corpse of Jesus would have been the conclusive way of doing so. No corpse was ever produced – or so we must assume. The reason *could* be that none was identified, or none could be found. That situation, however, in no way *proves* resurrection. It is simply a circumstance not to be disregarded by historians. If no corpse was ever produced, or located, or identifiable, the fact would be highly relevant, given the pressures to have it otherwise. Such a negative, however, would never suffice to underwrite the risen Lord.

That the point persisted in the Church is clear from how Matthew, for example, meets it by asserting that the tomb was guarded because the disciples were alleged to be planning to steal the body, because they too realised how vital its dead evidence would be. Whatever we make of these allegations and counter-allegations, it is clear that the matter was *en courant*. The tomb could not have been misidentified for long. Nor could hypotheses about a missing corpse have been excluded from the post-Easter scene.

But 'He is not here . . .' not in these conjectures for detectives. 'He is risen', 'risen indeed', in the 'deed' of redemptive love. The empty tomb remains as enigma – and symbol. Detectives can never now resolve what history has to leave mysterious. But it is not the sort of mysteriousness faith either needs or invokes. On the contrary, it is simply there and believers who make it the main, or sole, ground of their conviction are failing the risen Christ. That empty tomb has no place in Paul's writings or theology. The Gospels present it as a private feature. If we keep central the Epistles/Gospels sequence for which we have argued, it is evident that Jesus 'alive after his passion' was where Christian preaching centred. It is the faith which contains an empty tomb as a circumstance, not an empty tomb which makes confident and legitimate the faith. Just as it is wise to ask, not Who crucified Jesus, but what? so it is well to wonder, not Who moved the stone? but Why the moving stone? No one saw it move. Anxiety about it belonged only with those with spices for the dead. Why, then, do the Gospels give it place?

If the point earlier made around the interest of the authorities in locating the corpse of Jesus is sound, it follows that we should wonder about the disciples' apparent disinterest in the same question. There is no doubt (the point will recur in Chapter 8) that the physical burial of the dead Jesus was central to the credal faith. It belonged with 1 Corinthians 15:3–7, where Paul states what is the very first credal formulation and gives it as 'the tradition he himself received'. It is a completely Messianic statement, confirmed by the phrase 'according to the Scriptures'.[16] It also illustrates the case for the priority of the Epistles. Paul's words, 'and that he was buried', had backward relevance to the fact of crucifixion. Though the context would have given him occasion, he made no reference to an empty tomb. Was he, or other founding Christians, uninterested in any corpse of Jesus and/or its location? Or could the matter of a tomb being empty, and proven so, seem irrelevant when Paul was writing to a far-away European folk?

The answer, surely, must lie in Hebraic concepts he shared about the Messianic exaltation. There were, to be sure, certain material matters – local topography would be in the range only of Jerusalemite Christians and there were important Christians in Galilee and beyond. After the chaos of the fall of Jerusalem in 70 CE, any tomb-location became virtually beyond any certain knowledge. But, more significantly, Jewish tradition had for some two centuries before Jesus come to hold a doctrine of general resurrection when the dead would arise physically from 'the dust of the earth', resting meanwhile in some proximate, hardly imaginable state, and status, of expectation. Messianic 'exaltation', however, Christianly affirmed of Jesus, was another thing. What, for the generality, was awaiting the Parousia was, for Jesus, already his at 'the right hand of God', exalted to be the final agent of general resurrection. In this light, any apostolic 'interest' in the search for a corpse, or in an identifiable grave, would be anticlimactic. The theme of a tomb and its emptiness would only begin to be germane to witness when pagan curiosity in the dispersion, like that of the Athenians on the Areopagus (Acts 17), began to be mildly fascinated by such earthy details, incredulous as they were about 'resurrection'.

Though dating is controversial, another factor was coming into Christian ken by the time the Gospels were finalised, namely Gnosticism, a bewildering influence with many ramifications. It found the corporeal at odds with the spiritual. If Jesus was 'divine' the 'flesh' about him, the physical, it said, must have been only a sort of façade, something unreal or illusory, maybe necessary to the crude and credulous, but discerned otherwise by the sophisticated.[17] It was urgent for any faith in Jesus' Incarnation and Messiahship to give the lie to this heresy so threatening to both, and to affirm unequivocally the reality of 'the Word made flesh', dwelling in authentic human presence that his glory, precisely his glory, might be known, and known there.

From this necessity of faith came, it would seem, both the larger accounts of resurrection appearances *and* the evidentiality of an empty tomb. When in 1 Corinthians 15:3f. Paul sets down the 'tradition', the latter is absent and the former are given in the simple 'he appeared to . . .' with listing of persons. In their later context, with pagan curiosity filtering in from the dispersion and Gnostic notions around, the Gospels give more incidental description of what 'appearances' might signify and how a tomb might also. That the grave had been shown detenanted and that it had been identifiably 'this same Jesus' with wounds in hands and feet, sharing bread and wine, were – in their context – vital witness *vis-à-vis*, in their different ways, both pagans and Gnostics.

As we must ponder in Chapter 8, the Gospels never succeeded in clarifying (for curious minds) what the spiritual-physicality of the risen Jesus actually was. How could he at once pass in and out of sight, elude locked doors, partake of bread and wine, lay a lake-side board, have his wounds open to Thomas, and yet in that actuality ascend into heaven? Beyond the anxiety of the empirical mind, the theme of the appearances simply held together 'the suffering and the glory', figuring the divine reality of all that had been human in Jesus, neither quality usurping the other but each as one accomplishing the Messiahship in the mind of God and in the anguish of Gethsemane. If that conclusion is right it bears out for us both the priority of the Epistles and the work of the evangelists. It gives us the New Testament by virtue of what the New Testament itself became as living text. The theme of the empty tomb follows at length from the task of the faith in the world, though the way we now meet it leaves us thinking that it originated the faith.

vi

That supreme association of 'the suffering and the glory', of 'the Lamb and the throne', was certainly in line with Messianic victory but in wholly different terms from those that Judaically obtained in Zealot, Davidic or other tradition. In comprehending what they believed Jesus had presented, the disciples had every reason for anticipating that 'their sorrow would be turned into joy' (John 16:20). The analogy of travail in birth was truly fitting, for it was only out of their travail around the travail of their Master that they could know what was coming to birth. It was they, we might say, who were born out of that double travail. In the self-awareness into which they grew by virtue of that birth there were two crucial dimensions. There was a new measure of the nature of God and there was a new realisation of human community. We only have their comprehending complete if we learn to the full these two realities they received in Christ.

The Resurrection stories turn eagerly on individuals: Peter, Mary

Magdalene, Thomas, James and 'that other disciple'. Paul insists that his Damascus story allows him to add his name also. Places matter – perhaps because they, like persons, were coming to matter also in the early Church – Galilee, Jerusalem, Emmaus, hillsides, lake-shores and upper rooms. Even so, all persons in all places were meant for comprehension, for understanding, that is, and for inclusion. It was this openness which marked the primitive Christian community. It is vital to understand it as the direct consequence of the Messiahship of Jesus.[18] Messiahs, by any count, were supposed to have retainers, a court, officers and an entourage. For, manifestly, they must have a future and, maybe, their 'Messiah-act' would come in stages, with things known and things yet to be revealed.

Such followings, communal and sequential, turned on who and how. Restrictive Messiahs could only mean restricted benefits and receivers of them: the nation, the godly, the pious, the elect, the fortunate with whom he coincided.[19] Only the crucified Messiah of divine redemption could inaugurate an inclusive peoplehood of all and sundry on a sole condition equally attainable by all, namely penitence and faith.

The Epistles and the Acts document how decisively, yet also painfully, the primitive Christian community came to comprehend this dimension of what Jesus had presented in and from the Cross. In their turn the Gospels have many hints that it would be so. Some scholars think that these were imported back there by hindsight and, as it were, accessory to the fact. How uneasily 'the mind of Christ' must relate to what the Church became we must face in Chapter 9. That, in some sense, 'church' was implicit in his ministry and passion cannot be in doubt. The 'great commission' in Matthew 28:19–20 was certainly being obeyed long before it had that credal formulation. The accessibility of Jesus to allcomers we noted earlier. His readiness for the renegade Jew within the covenant's people could argue his readiness for the 'Gentile', as equally, though differently, outside the legal pale. How the 'Gentile' evangelist, Luke, loved that phrase 'a certain man' in Jesus' parables, who need not be a Jew or any special breed at all. There was this latent universalism around the wisdom and the ministry of Jesus, saving the necessary economy of reach and location inseparable from his being Messiah at all.

But it was the Cross, most of all, with its beam pointing out as in embrace, which symbolised and transacted this readiness for a world. It was in those terms that the first Christians came to comprehend its range. A Messiah whose task had to do with sin and not merely (or at all) with Rome and whose intentions were human-wise, not Jewry-wise, could be read as warranting an ever-accessible peoplehood. 'Peoplehood' it would be, not some conglomerate, a mere throng of individuals. All the old pointers were that way, only that they now had to learn to dispense with birth, or race, or culture, or sex, as somehow exclusifying factors in their own right. Whosoever would might come. There could be a birth in the Spirit that could supervene on any and every parentage.

How the New Testament translated this into its life concerns us in the next chapter. We simply register here how decisive and how critical it was. The identity of Jewishness, as George Herbert might have said,[20] was 'double-moated'. Privilege was for the sake of vocation: vocation was the guardian of privilege. Together they had to be impregnable. Surrender privilege and you betray vocation: fulfil vocation and you require privilege. Election and covenant underwrote both and all four had to be inviolate. So, ultimately it was, despite the far-reaching Hellenisation of diaspora (and, indeed, some Galilean) Jewry in the time of Jesus and beyond.[21] The fall of Jerusalem, with the loss of the Temple ritual, could only intensify the self-securing of the Jewish mind. Yet in this very context, and by Jewish leading, the first Christians achieved a society for which the Jew-'Gentile' distinction need not obtain (Ephesians 2:11–22). 'Gentilising' of the rest of humankind by any Judaic necessity could cease in the conviction that 'in Christ' there were 'no more strangers'. The phrase, so loved by Paul, 'in Christ' was the sum of the new fellowship. It superseded being 'in Moses', or 'in Abraham', except in so far as that heritage could be trans-ethnically shared in respect of spiritual ancestry. 'In Christ' counterparted 'in Adam', which was the birthright of all. It generated that insistent sense of the world that characterised the new Christian fellowship, with its understanding of the Cross having to do with worldwide sinfulness and, therefore, with worldwide redemption.

The cost to traditional Jewry of this 'de-Gentilising' of humanity, this 'en-Judaising' of the non-Jew as fellow heirs of the covenant, is written large between the lines of the New Testament, notably in the Fourth Gospel. Those who rejected the vision in what they read as on-going loyalty felt threatened when the new Jew-Gentile entity cited their Scriptures, drew on their heritage and enlarged the community of their patriarchs. The tensions left their mark on the very text of Christian faith-confession. As we must see, Christianity could not duly scripturalise itself without wrestling with an ancestry that disowned its owning of it. The situation only served to test and try the perceptions that created it. The trust of the acknowledged Messiahship of Jesus could be said to have perpetuated what was implicit in the Cross itself, namely whether there were indeed in the passion of Jesus the true Christ-credentials and how, and by whom, they might be found authentic.

vii

Christ-credentials could not truly be such if not also the credentials of God. So much was explicit in the Messianic theme itself as having to do with history as the place for a divine answer adequate to the human predicament. 'The place of the Name' the old writers called it,[22] the inclusive event where God, in action, would be finally disclosed (as far as history might) for who and how He was, where humankind (or only Jewry?) might say: 'This is the Lord: we have waited for him. We will be glad and rejoice in His salvation' (Isa. 25:9).

In such joyful recognition of the inclusive thing the Church had come to birth. When the later Isaiah asked rhetorically, 'Who would have believed our report?' there was a double meaning in his very question. Like later Christian 'tradition', what had been so strangely rumoured to him could not help but be rumoured to others. Its very quality meant that.[23] So it was that the nearly incredible thing about God in Christ meant communication translating into the world the original comprehension of grace. Isaiah 53 had to do with 'the suffering servant', the puzzle of his identity and task. The primitive Christian community received what had come to them through Cross and Resurrection as authentic 'report' from God concerning God in being the authentically Messianic fact.

It remains, then, to 'let be told' what theology would for ever thereafter have to understand, embrace and tell of 'the arm of the Lord revealed' – God in His own recognizance. Faith would know itself Christian in the working-out of the Christ-event as 'the place of the Name'. In final summary to this chapter, this comprehending means that here is the only redeeming reality there is. In its reality faith finds the clue to how divine God is.

Overcoming evil with good has first to ensure that it is not overcome of evil. Analogies have their limits but let us draw one from twentieth-century history. During the Algerian revolution in the 1960s the West Indian activist Frantz Fanon, who gave himself to that cause, insisted that those who want to be free must necessarily hate. The French, he explained, had not only colonised the territory, they had colonised the mind. Imperialism only lived and succeeded by inferiorising 'natives', making them passive 'Uncle Toms' abjectly, or even religiously, subservient, as people denied all status, all pride, all dignity. These they must passionately recover by total repudiation, by savage self-assertion. The struggle itself, war, conflict, might well engender hate but, necessity apart, violence would itself 'redeem'. Satan would cast out Satan. Hate, denounce, defy, repudiate, and you will be free.

This was a philosophy that had no idea of incorporating its potential victims, its all-hated foes. It did not dream a strategy that might avail to free them from themselves or actually recruit them to liberating ends. When on 10 May 1994 some spoke of 'the greatest day in this twentieth century' they had in mind Nelson Mandela's accession, from prison to presidency. His was a faith that saw the need to help detach the agents of apartheid from their own crime and stain, to identify and foster whatever signs there might be of a will to its renunciation. Liberation, all round, demanded a will to forgive – all the more generous and eloquent because it related to 27 years of incarceration, deprivation and rank injustice. Mandela was able to turn his magnanimity into an argument for others – less massively sufferers – to emulate and share his vision of the need to co-operate with those who might be willing to undo their sin. There was, no doubt, much realism in the stance, but that in no way diminished the nobility. The old regime had somehow to be helped to relinquish the tyrannies made by its own pride and fear and enmity, its lust for power and security. Once there were any signs of heart-change they should be recruited to inclusive liberation, in ways that vindictiveness, talk of 'throwing the white past into the sea',[24] could never envisage or attain. Revolutions via hate have all too often achieved only their own new forms of tyranny and crime.

Perhaps the contrast between Fanon and Mandela – for all its incompleteness if translated into theology – at least suffices to indicate how *not* being overcome of evil is vital if ever there is to be an overcoming of evil with good. Reciprocal hatreds intensify. Cains breed their own curse and universalise the law, against themselves, of their own enmity. Only bearing bears away. 'Neither is there salvation in any other.' Could it then be otherwise, cosmically? Might the divine not be, by divine right, the willing sufferer in our redemption, even as the divine had ever been the willing ' sufferer' of our creation, our being, our freedom and our dominion?[25] Christian faith has it that the divine nature is the love that comes, redeems, forgives, and that the Cross of Jesus is where we know it so. If the Cross for ever stands as the focal drama of our human irresponsibility, our being Cains at heart, then it is also the focal point of a divine travail for us and because of us. We may then find there that to which all the logic points concerning ourselves and from which a logic flows, divine redeeming inaugurating its human emulation by the energising love of God, once we have been assured that God is such love and that such love is God. Then this 'Christ in us' becomes not only 'the hope of glory' but the hope of present peace and compassion here and now. From such divine *kenosis* comes both the measure and the means of salvation.

The perceptions of faith are always helped by imagery. Three converging images may illuminate this conclusion and also underline the pleas for an adjectival kind of theology for which to speak of the divine and the human is simpler than the usage 'God' and 'man'. Let us have in view the adjectives 'integral', 'supreme' and 'royal', each of which belongs obviously with divine sovereignty.

The seventeenth-century poet George Herbert, earlier quoted, was briefly Rector of Bemerton near Salisbury. Of gentle birth, he was a meticulous man, always prim, spruce, and well dressed, and he liked his music to be equally precise. In *Lives of the Poets*, Isaac Walton tells how Herbert came one day to his musical friends, all-bedraggled and dirty. He was reproached on arrival for appearing so oddly. However, there was a reason.

> In his walk to Salisbury he saw a poor man with a poorer horse that was fallen under his load. They were both in distress and needed present help which, Mr. Herbert perceiving, took off his canonical coat and helped the poor man to unload and, after, to load his horse again. The poor man blessed him for it and he blessed the poor man and was so like the good Samaritan that he gave him money to refresh both himself and his horse. . . .

At his coming to his musical friends at Salisbury they began to wonder that Mr. George Herbert, which used to be so trim and clean came into that company so soiled and discomposed. But he told them the occasion. When one of the company told him that he had disparaged himself by so dirty an employment his answer was: 'The thought of what he had done would prove music to him at midnight and that the omission of it would have upbraided and made discord in his conscience whensoever he should pass by that place. . . . I praise God for this occasion. And now let us tune our instruments.'[26]

It seems to follow that those who fail in compassion would compromise their music also. Could it possibly be also that way with the divine, with 'the music of the spheres'? The young Tolstoy once delivered himself of the opinion that 'You could no more have a bad God than a sun which is dark and cold.'[27] The comment is inept. For the sun burns and blinds and can never be ignored as God may be. All human things divine are relational and, therefore, never arbitrary as if wills were not involved. But, if we are to borrow Tolstoy's thought about God as 'never other than He is', the criterion must be unfailing love, and we shall need evidence of how and where it does not fail. Jesus and the Cross are where we have to look. We can tune the instruments of theological joy only where we have to ask about 'the print of the nails', which otherwise might seem to make God so strange.

So much for 'integral'; what of 'supreme'? On his own telling, about 23 or 24 March 1945, Supreme Commander Eisenhower was on the bank of the Rhine, talking with a common soldier who 'seemed silent and depressed'. 'How are you feeling?' he asked. 'General,' he said, 'I'm awful nervous. I was wounded two months ago. . . . I just got back from hospital yesterday.' Eisenhower replied: 'Maybe if we just walk along together to the river we'll be good for each other,' explaining as they went that he had made all the dispositions as carefully as a Supreme Commander should. Elsewhere in his *Crusade in Europe* Eisenhower writes:

At times I received advice from friends, urging me to give up or curtail visits to the troops. They correctly stated that so far as the mass of men were concerned I could never speak personally to more than a tiny percentage. They argued, therefore, that I was merely wearing myself out without accomplishing anything significant, as far as the whole army was concerned. With this I did not agree. In the first place, I felt that through constant talking with enlisted men I gained accurate impressions of their state of mind. I talked to them about anything and everything.[28]

All turned on how the 'supreme' understood the 'supremacy'. Is not theology, likewise, bound to be asking what it takes for God to be God and not excluding lowly things from the answer?

Analogies from war may have their limits – though Muslims will not object. There is another, more poetic than the last. It is Shakespeare's reading of what is 'royal' on the eve of Agincourt. Let us paraphrase the formula we must come to in Chapter 8 of the great Council in Chalcedon, defining the person of Christ for credal usage, adopting the phrase 'Very God of very God'. What then – if there is such a thing as 'basillology' – of saying, 'Very king of very king'? Shakespeare presents his Henry V as borrowing a cloak for disguise and visiting his soldiers in their tents at dead of night. He wears no crown. Around one camp-fire, he joins three common soldiers. They talk of 'the king' as an absent party and of the guilt of war and liability for it of 'the crown'. The exchanges are very spirited and their irony is deeply moving. But there is more than awed debate about the issues of power: there is evidence of its paradox as Henry enshrines it.

> The royal captain of this ruined band
> Walking from watch to watch, from tent to tent,
> . . . . .
> For forth he goes and visits all his host,
> Bids them good morrow with a modest smile,
> And calls them brothers, friends and countrymen.
> . . . . .
> That every wretch, pining and pale before,
> Beholding him, plucks comfort from his looks.
> A largesse universal, like the sun
> His liberal eye doth give to every one,
> Thawing cold fear. Then mean and gentle all,
> Behold, as may unworthiness define,
> A little touch of Harry in the night.[29]

Theology, too, has to ask, what may 'unworthiness' define. Is Henry – Harry in this setting – truly 'royal', less so, more so? Is 'royalty' here worthily defined? Is this conduct adjectival to the 'throne of England'? All will turn on the criteria of sovereignty. Shakespeare makes this clear by his deliberate contrast of the French royalty who lounge in their tents the same night vying with each other about the splendour of their horses.

We are left asking what defines royalty, what belongs with leadership – lofty superiority or lowly imagination, aloofness or generosity? If, as with Henry V, there is some apparent laying aside of pomp and glory, there will be, not forfeiture, but fulfilment of true kingship. This is what, in New Testament terms, is meant by *kenosis* in theology. There is no 'emptying' as of the contents of a bottle, so that what was there has gone, but a 'giving' in which 'divinity' is more truly present where, otherwise, it would seem to have been compromised.

The situation that required it so in these three analogies was real enough. There was nothing theatrical, or posturing, in the poet, the commander and the king. None of the recipients saw it that way, once they understood the identity they had encountered. The genuineness of our need is what we argued concerning the human situation. 'Very king of very king', if we see it so, becomes a way of understanding 'very God of very God'. 'God in Christ' was 'greater' (to use the Islamic *akbar*) not 'lesser', by this criterion. Indeed, the very criterion by which the divine could be known 'divine' had been transformed.

In the fact of 'God in Christ', of 'the Christ-reality in the being of God', there had been the presenting of the credentials of God. Comprehending them as being such had been the making of the Church. The reality of the two events would have to find its long and strenuous way into the form of Christian Scriptures.

7 Enscriptured

IT SEEMS evident that Jesus of Nazareth left no documents – unless it be the sort that walk around, disciples and hearers. We can readily imagine what his signature might have looked like in Aramaic, but there is no extant copy. He was certainly literate in that language – and probably also in Greek – as we know from the scroll-reading in the synagogue at Nazareth (Luke 4:16–21). The only occasion, however, in which the Gospels tell of his writing has to do with sand on the floor (John 8:6). Whatever the import was, it survived only until his hearers shuffled out in guilty confusion over their hypocrisy.[1] He was probably only pretending to write while his pointed words struck home, dealing patiently with the tense situation as both gentleness and severity required. The word 'pen' indeed occurs nowhere in the Gospels,[2] whereas there is 'voice' in abundance. The ministry of Jesus was never on the page. 'He who has ears let him hear.'

'Now herein is a marvellous thing' – if we may borrow the surprise of the blind man in John 9:30. The setting-down in script for other times and places of the Galilean words, the Jerusalem story, was wholly the task of the community that only found its being in the sequence and fulfilled itself in ensuring the record to the world. Having studied the 'comprehending' in the previous chapter, the need now is to enquire how those lived credentials came to be 'enscriptured' in the form we know as Gospels and apostolic Letters, with a linking narrative conjoining them. For by that process over several decades the New Testament writings took their place at the very core of Christian theology – not, in themselves, the primary source which was, and is, 'the Word made flesh', but crucial in their derivative status to any understanding of what is for ever primary. If we are to be adequate about perceiving the credentials of God we need the utmost rigour and imagination in possessing the New Testament.

Those two qualities have long been expended on the New Testament and in multiplied profusion this twentieth century. The task of the

ordinary reader in doing the scholars justice is formidable. The literature of New Testament study is enormous and a tribute to the will for
integrity in the faith within it. It multiplies into a wealth of issues –
historical, critical, literary, canonical, exegetical – so that the lay mind
can easily be bewildered or even dismayed. That temptation must be
resisted. The stimulus for doing so is in the very fact that the New
Testament happened, that Gospels and Letters are there. Memory made
it. Retrospect and gratitude explain its genesis and content. Memory
does not busy itself with what is not memorable. The whole text derives
from the possessing of Christ's meaning and the communalising of his
significance as an embrace of all and sundry without prior necessity of
right birth or noble culture or elect status. It is a missionary literature
in that its whole character has to do with a quality of telling, of
communicating and enlisting. The Gospels and the Letters come to be
because a history demands to be recalled and churches need to
be nurtured. Expansion of the people of faith means dispersion, in
place and time, and hence the means to return to the generating source.
Unless one is to betray the future one must ensure that the past
abides. If the one community is becoming many, the many must be
incorporated by an apostolic concern for their education into unity. So
the New Testament happened as a document out of the happening of
Christhood in Jesus, just as the central act of Christian liturgy lived ever
and again 'the night in which he was handed over' to his Cross.

That the Christian Scripture is there at all, and there as the sort of
Scripture it is, must be our courage in negotiating – as partially in this
chapter we must attempt to do – the manifold issues around it. There
is a place for poets and artists in a forest as well as timber merchants
and tree surgeons. First see a whole, and what a whole it is. How strange
on the part of the Holy Spirit to contrive a Scripture this way. When
John Bunyan was catechised about his refusal to use the Book of
Common Prayer, which he thought 'unspiritual' for not being spontaneous, he explained that it was 'a thing . . . patched together one
piece at a time and another at another: a mere human invention',[3] all
so different, he thought, from 'Holy Scripture'. Yet, had he known, he
could have made the same case there also. If not patched together, the
Gospels have to be matched together and they came to be what they
are by long, hazardous, intricate processes of rendition to reach their
familiar form. Epistles, too, came along one by one, as required by the
exigencies of a growing Church within societies full of threats to their
moral being and doctrinal understanding. It was only by so doing
that the Epistles provided precedents capable of being translated into
analogous issues by later generations. In this way the immediate setting which, as in Galatia, or Corinth or Colossae, occasioned the
expression of apostolic mind could educate other centuries into
the nature of freedom or the pitfalls of legalism. Possessing the New
Testament is thus no sinecure but a steady, imaginative vocation.
Examples abound, but first it will be well to see how Christians are one

with all religions in the fact of Scriptures and how distinctive in that universal category their own Scriptures are.

All systems of faith, even more recent ones like Baha'ism or Mormonism, have sacred texts, written oracles, the authoritative referent for all they claim and mean and offer.[4] The histories of how they came to be are as diverse as the concepts of the 'inspiration' believed to underlie them. The Qur'ān of Islam is understood as the direct speech of God mediated to, and repeated by, Muhammad to be recorded from his mouth by scribes as the very (Arabic) 'words of God'. Hindu Sruti Scriptures are received as from divine 'breathing', though they take their place among other writings with a less sublime origin. The Dharma-pada of the Buddha constitutes the ultimate 'wisdom', the 'master-teaching', by which the Sangha, or 'community of heeding', is uniquely guided and disciplined.

The biblical world has been variously perceived in respect of how 'revelation' and 'inspiration', the meaning and the means, should be related to each other. In the Qur'ān the distinction hardly exists.[5] Philosophers and poets in their realm were often at a loss to know whence form and import came and how either could arise within the other. Prophets were often a mystery to themselves, and, therefore, an enigma inducing in their hearers either conviction or incredulity. Everywhere the authority of Scriptures was involved in this mystique of origins and depended, however diversely, on how origins were construed.

The Christian Scripture, the New Testament, was not immune from many such considerations. Two factors, though, made it quite exceptional. They were its tie-back into recovered history and its engagement with on-going community. 'Epistles', of course, there were aplenty in the first centuries of the Church, but none attaining to be 'revelation' while also being (we might almost say) 'city guides'. On Islamic grounds 'epistles' cannot conceivably be 'divine word', for this can only be authentic as a 'verbal descent' from heaven. Human correspondence, albeit apostolic, can never be what God utters. In Christian reckoning Paul and Peter and John and others,[6] wrestling with the shaping of thought and conduct in nascent communities, are eminently qualified to participate in what will come to be received as Scripture, given that people in places are the focus of what faith stands to mean where life in it is lived. How their words came to be so received leads, later, into the study of the New Testament canon. For the moment we simply take the point of the criteria for being Scripture on which the New Testament is based.

ii

With those in place it may be useful to realise what the New Testament is not. Surprisingly, it is not a martyrology. It has far more kinship with Bunyan's Pilgrim's Progress than with Foxe's Book of Martyrs, or the like literature arising from bitter persecutions around the Reformation.

There are references aplenty in the Epistles to 'enduring hardness' and 'being of good courage'. Paul catalogues his tribulations in 2 Corinthians 6:4–5, but only to fortify his readers. The New Testament is silent on the final fate of Paul and Peter, and narrates the execution of James in Jerusalem (Acts 12:2) in astonishing brevity. The Stephen story in Acts 7 is crucial to Luke's authorial purpose and he allows himself a thrilling maritime narrative in Acts 27. Otherwise, the Christian Scripture makes no scenario of physical or other agonies attending on faith-confession. We find no hint of Nero or Caligula. The New Testament writers do not wear their scars upon their sleeves.

Nor, aside from Demas (2 Timothy 4:10) and Hymenaeus and Alexander (1 Timothy 1:20), do we hear of renegades, though the issue of apostasy after confession of Christ loomed large in sub-apostolic times. The Book of Revelation conceals the facts of persecution and oppression under its elaborate imagery of vials and horns and trumpets. Though there is no doubting the sufferings they portend and address, the burden of the text is not a yearning for pity but a celebration of divine 'Alleluias'.

The clue is evident enough in the Gospels. The writers and recipients of the Letters knew themselves standing in the tradition of the suffering Messiah and could read their trials in a context of redemptive continuity (2 Corinthians 1:5, 7). 'To suffer for the truth's sake' bound them into his Messianic role, given that they took what came to them by the paradigm of the Cross. Such Messianic reading of themselves left no place for martyrology, for explicit recital of what had been endured or its self-indulgent portrayal. This situation in the Epistles tallies closely with how the Gospels handle the crucifixion of Jesus. Emphatic as they are that its story and meaning are central to all else, they leave to discreet silence the physical aspects of its grim incidence. Unlike some later Christian art, they do not trade on anguish or give place to morbid curiosity. To go to the New Testament for the macabre or the sensational is to come away empty.

If the New Testament parades no catalogue of martyrs to attest its deep sufferings, it likewise exults in no tribes or nationalisms. The latter term may be out of time in this context, but the passions, the enmities and the prides it now denotes were real enough then, despite the overall community a *Pax Romana* might impose. The New Testament is no manifesto of some human exclusivism. We have traced the reason, in Chapter 6, to the Messianic decision of Jesus. Cities, like Corinth, were cosmopolitan enough to house a variety of origins, ethnic and cultural. It is mainly to cities that Letters go. 'Us whom He has called' (Romans 9:24) was how Paul noted this inclusion – Jews, *goyim*, Greeks, *ethnoi* of every tongue – even though the passage in Romans 9, etc., is one in which Paul is most ardently wrestling with what he should think about on-going Hebraism. The very heat of that problem (which we cannot think that he resolved either for himself or for us) witnesses to how real the new humano-Christian unity was. For otherwise, there would have been neither point nor purpose in struggling over being a Jew-in-Christ alongside *goyim* in the one company.

In Christ peoplehood had become a matter of faith, not of birth or circumcision. It emerged as something that could be neither exclusively Jewish nor exclusively Gentile, nor exclusively any other kin or kind. This did not mean some 'human unity' *per se*, lacking any sacred particularity. Like Jews, it was a holy peoplehood, but not thanks to ancestry and race. By the principle of 'new birth' its solidarity was grounded in the sole criterion of faith – a criterion freely and unconditionally accessible to all who willed to come.

Being such a peoplehood, its Scripture was not in any necessarily sacred language.[7] Its Greek was readily at home with the Aramaic of Jesus' local origins. Roman Palestine – at least for its crosses – was trilingual anyway and, down the centuries, the New Testament would happily be as cosmopolitan as readers might require.[8] It is true, as we must see in Chapter 8, that the three legal tongues of Roman Palestine played a critical part in the enlargement of Christian communities and the ordering of their mind. The legacies of that dominance would have to be transcended. The logic for that necessity was present from the start.

Among things the New Testament is not, we must thirdly note that it is not a credal formulation. It may be claimed that all the essential work of Christian theology is latent, if not achieved, within it. Yet we find only embryos of creeds as such and the presence of these reflects what transpired outside its time-range. Thus the baptismal formula in Matthew 28:19 is surely to be understood as synchronising, with what the passage relates, the formulae of lapsing years. It is certain, as we have seen in the previous chapter, that the disciples were into their mission long before their 'commission' reached the Matthean form. For it was implicit in the nature of Jesus' Messiahship. The formula postdated the obedience to it. It took time for a trinitarian shape of words to reach the kind of traditional usage evident in the conclusion of Matthew's Gospel.

The case is similar in Acts 8:37, where the formalised 'believing that Jesus is the Son of God' is said to belong at the Ethiopian's baptism. Some think it is a scribe's later insertion. Nothing is said between him and Philip about 'Son of God': the conversation revolves around 'the servant' in Isaiah 53.

Ephesians 2:18 is the only verse in the Epistles where we might read the rudiments of a doctrine of the Trinity, since 'Father', Jesus and 'one Spirit' come in the same sentence. This, however, is not credal. How creeds develop from New Testament sources must be our concern in the next chapter, with passages like Philippians 2:5–11 and 1 Timothy 3:16 in mind.[9] By the practice of lections in worship and through the canon in which its texts are enclosed, the New Testament exercises profound influence on Christian perceptions of faith. But the fact that it is not itself credal, nor a summary of 'articles of faith', is equally significant for the temper of Christianity.

iii

With the foregoing as a map-reading *en route* into the New Testament, the study of 'enscripturing' in Christianity has its central task in the formation of the Gospels. They followed from the comprehending of Jesus as the Christ which was the theme of Chapter 6. Without that conviction-experience they could not exist. Their business is to possess its origins and commend its sequel in the community of faith. The forming of the Gospels coincides, in large part, with the world of the Epistles. For the life in the Epistles sprang from the story in the evangelists. In that storytelling there was a steady marriage of faith-purposes with truth-concern.

It is this which gives the four Gospels their distinctive identity as literature. Unlike diarists who write alongside events occurring, the evangelists know the end already, as some novelists do who then enlist their prescience in the shaping of plot and the delineation of character. The contrast of the evangelists with such novelists is that they are handling actual history with a concern to be loyal to it. Yet, at the same time, they have a story to tell which they themselves are living – living with and living from.

It is important, therefore, to realise that they write as conscious authors, with a theology and a literary intention in deliberate control of what they narrate and portray. Belonging as they do to immediate centres of Christian dispersion, with local – but not crippling – perspectives and loyalties, their pens are not 'individual', but broadly moved by the perspectives of community. For it was on communal memory they had to draw as well as communal perceptions they were minded to express. The Gospels are, therefore, at once documents of history and of faith. It has to be appreciated that this makes for a subtle quality of 'fact' about them. In measure all history is this way. It cannot be told without a teller. Where the teller is responsive as such to community, 'fact' belongs with witness. If there is no song without a singer, there is no anthem without a choir. Without either there is no music.

What 'interprets' in history does not, however, 'falsify', unless there is a situation of 'bad faith' stemming from ignorance, enmity, distortion or deceit. In that event we are not encountering 'interpretation'. Given such attitudes, there is no singer and the song remains unsung. It is only by the help of such analogy that we can fully understand what sort of writing the Gospels are. The analogy is not to say that rightness always waits on writing, in any sphere of either. It *is* to say that there is never history without historians and that 'event' is always at risk in 'telling' precisely because, in 'telling', it is in care. It is Christian 'good faith', in this New Testament situation, to acknowledge it for what it is and to hold that the amalgam of happening and telling leaves the resulting 'happened-ness' trustworthy.

Since our concern is with the credentials of God as 'enscriptured' we must concentrate on how they stand there and not delve into the minutiae of scholarship, careful and honest as these are in their own place. Knowing the end from the outset, Mark begins magisterially: 'The beginning of the Gospel of Jesus Christ, the Son of God' (1:1). He continues, prosaically (1:9): 'It came to pass in those days that Jesus came from Nazareth of Galilee . . .', John the Baptist being already on the scene. The theological 'beginning' is down to earth at once – 'days', a man, a town, a lake, a ritual in which this man is baptised. The formula at the river may be read as a received symbol of servanthood and vocation. The narrative continues at once – for it has an urgent quality – into this 'servant's' rigorous scrutiny of the meanings and demands vocation faces.

Contrast the Fourth Gospel. 'Beginning' here too, but this time in eternity. Theological, like the other, but tied back to creation and setting that herald figure, John (1:6, 9), on a rich tapestry of faith and metaphors of 'light' and 'knowing' and 'birth', savouring the Greek mind but rooted in Hebraic tradition about 'divine Name' and 'flesh' and 'Moses' – the representatives of which come curiously interrogating the man who baptises about the nature of his mission.

The two Gospel openings are in the same theme, the angles quite contrasted. They symbolise the two levels, already argued, on which 'enscripturing' proceeds. As with Matthew and with Luke, the writers are in personal possession of their story, shaping it perceptively inside an intimate deliberation and a conscious literary will. We have to study, if only here in summary form, the sources on which they drew and the processes anterior to their steady work and those that attended on it.

iv

We have to realise a remembering community, expanding, scattered, circumstantially precarious, liable to aberration being so newly shaped and so rapidly spreading, bewildered in part by ecstatics and Gnostics, and with a lively instinct for sacred 'lections' customarily read in worship. All these factors can be traced in the Gospels. There was urgency – as for all time and place – by the sense of a lapsing past and a fear lest it be forfeited. Over all there was the difficult destiny to comprise Hebrew and Greek and Roman culture in the same community of faith.

On all these counts the cherishing of retrospect was paramount. We can assume that it was served by retentive memory. The sayings, parables and stories of and about Jesus, to have reached us as we know them in literary form, must have passed earlier from mouth to mouth and memory to memory. Clearly, we cannot be sure what verbal transit may have done to them before they reached written to-be-sources that Gospel formation could by and by enshrine. (We have already noted the divine risk-taking in the Gospel itself and will do so again.)

It needs no great subtlety in New Testament perusal to realise that, in the first three Gospels, whole sections of Jesus' teaching are given in wholly identical form, or almost so. Incidents around the teaching often tally closely. Thus, for example, the desire of James and John to have prime place at 'the Messianic banquet' (Matt. 20:20–28 and Mark 10:35–45)' occurs almost verbatim in the two evangelists, though in Matthew it is their mother who makes the request, while in Mark it comes from them. Similarly, there is difference about the number of servants sent to the husbandmen in the vineyard, but the story tallies closely in Matthew (21:33–40), Mark (12:1–12) and Luke (20:9–19).

The reasonable conclusion is that one or more drew on the other and probably all on prior material available to them. Many technical questions arise about 'priority' and here and there subtle differences of phrase, emphasis or imputation, from which scholars draw their academic, often conflicting, conclusions. But these do not affect the broad study of what is thus called 'source criticism', seeing that the whole situation is eloquent of a remembering community and a circulating tradition.

The main corpus of this common material is dubbed 'Q' – a topic which will recur in Chapter 10 below, since one of the main factors of Christian diversity with which the context there has to deal concerns isolation of a purely didactic teacher-Jesus from the Christ of faith. No Gospel writer makes any such isolation. Instead, they each preface their passion story with careful teaching content, and they culminate all their master's teaching in his suffering. It seems both wise and reverent to believe that the two are essentially inseparable. Christian concerns or memories interested in sayings and parables could never have been oblivious of how the story ended. Nor could the intense focus all the evangelists have on the climax of dying be disengaged from the itinerant ministry which had preceded it. However we allocate the several strands in the Gospels to varying sources, localities, or interests in their precarious arrival in the text – much of which must remain hidden anyway – it is a broad consensus that we find.

Luke has very precious material of his own including the parables of his chapters 15, 16 and 18. It must be a puzzle why his available sources yielded them to him only or otherwise why Matthew and Mark omitted them. (The Fourth Gospel, as we must see, is a special case.) The puzzle is no bar to a grateful enrichment and creates no sense of inconsistency. Whatever may be intriguing about their incidence in Gospel formation, the sources are in no way at odds with themselves in content. Variants of detail within the broad 'synopsis' (as it is called) of Matthew, Mark and Luke are attributable to vagaries of transit, to idiosyncrasies of the writers, to the setting in which they worked and to the factors obtaining in those local churches. For what is reported and treasured about Jesus' sayings could hardly fail to be seen in close relation to immediacies in the churches. We always have to watch for this double *sitz im leben* – that of Jesus in Galilee and Judea, that of readers in Anatolia or Achaia. The reaction of 'the elder brother', for example, in Luke 15:25f., after the return of 'the younger', signified not only about penitence and its acceptance but also about the tension over 'Gentile' inclusion in Christ which 'hard' Jews repudiated.

This synoptic consensus and the several variants of inner detail are the subject of scholarship around what are called 'form' and 'redaction'. Insights may be had, or are sought, into the processes behind the emergence of those three Gospels from close inspection aiming to discern in any *pericope* (literally what, in Greek, may be 'cut around' as 'core-unity') what was 'gist' and what, by comparison with parallels, or by conjecture, may be thought to be addition, or comment, or local colour. It is thought, or hoped, that clues may be had this way for how what is now on the page belongs with what was first in the oral origin. For example, is the puzzling story of the 'unjust steward' in Luke 16:1–12 rightly comprehended in the bewildering comment (added by Luke? or an earlier margin?) in verse 9, seeing that the parable can readily conclude at verse 8?[10] Or did Matthew somehow conflate two different stories in his grim addition to the 'wedding garment' parable (Matt. 22:1–14)? The story of the wedding feast is in Luke 14:16–24, where it has a congenial preface of its own (in the 'Messianic' comment of a guest already dining with Jesus), but Luke has no trace of Matthew's 'vengeance' on the surly refusers (does it echo the fall of Jerusalem?) nor of the 'wedding garment' prescript.

This meticulous study helps practitioners to see what analysis may suggest concerning the words that survive, the traces of their fortunes and the minds of their gospellers, as recipients and editors. It is those editing minds that are the quarry of 'redaction' criticism into details of whose present fortunes we need not here probe. It asks what can be deduced from a discernment stance, like Luke's fondness for the words, 'a certain man . . .', 'a certain woman . . .' – a hint perhaps of his non-Jewish quality, his sense of the universal, remembering however that Luke alone bathes his Bethlehem narratives in Hebraic hymnology. If we 'redact' Mark, we go for his characteristic *eutheos* ('straightway', or *tout suite*) some nineteen times, as his way of introducing his sequences. With Matthew it seems clear that he organised what he drew on with steady reference to associations he felt it to have with prophetic antici-pation. Some scholars even suspect that what he tells he tells in the form he does in order to have it fulfil prophecy. Thus his formula runs, 'that it might be fulfilled'. It is intriguing to compare Mark and Matthew in how they tally or vary, include or omit, when settings are given for the same episode or saying. It is possible to detect a heightening of Jesus' authority or impressions of it in Matthew who, incidentally, has 'two' where Mark has 'one', recipient of Jesus' healing.

In these ways the Synoptic Gospels yield ample scope for scholarly enterprise. This at least assures us that the 'enscripturing' of Jesus proceeded in careful terms which readily left place for lively authorship working with and from the lore of reverent retrospect. To be sure, we only have a mediated Jesus but with a confidence that the media, even with their manifest frailties in process, were congenial to his mind. Those who think otherwise are left arguing their scepticism from the very sources they distrust. The wide (some would say chronic) diversity of interpretation to which the Synoptic Gospels have been subject is witness to how far 'the testimony of Jesus is a trust of study'.[11]

V

Nowhere is that 'trust of study' more exacting than in respect of the Fourth Gospel. The lively reader senses a difference at once. It is, and it is not, the same Jesus. If one is imposing a square on a circle there is ample common territory but the shapes will never tally. Throughout the four Gospels there is teaching, healing, travelling, crowds, private people, public officials, a Galilee and a Gethsemane, an 'upper room' with 'bread and wine', a Judas who hands his master over to authorities of religion, a dying and a rising to new life. We have the same disciples, the same poles of history, the same climax but almost all else is different. The portrayer does not see from the triple perspective of the others when we come to the Fourth. The contrasts are many and perplexing. They have disconcerted generations of exegesis, even if sometimes, somehow, they have found little register in the devotions of the unwary.

We do not wonder, therefore, that the Fourth Gospel has evoked much consternation as to its compatibility with the others. Honesty can hardly have it both ways. If we take the Synoptic Jesus (apart from a few quite Johannine passages like Matthew 11:27), can we with any consistency accept the Johannine? They would seem to be two disparate figures had we not allowed our familiarity with John to affect our reading of the others. If we contrive to say that 'the Fourth is more theological' we only conceal the issue in what 'theological' might mean.

The point there could be our clue. We have to conclude that the Fourth Gospel is 're-presenting' the Synoptic Jesus with a radical initiative of interpretation. The author is 'reading' the same broad facts in his own idiom. He holds to history and, indeed, in some particulars is more reliable than the others and he is steeped in Palestiniana on the ground. Yet he 'renders' history with a freedom of insight that tells the entire significance of Jesus by clues that pass into credal Christology, of which he is the inspiration.

Yet, in this creative exercise, what, we ask, inspired him? Let us preface the answer by asking a naïve question: 'What did Jesus say?' It underlies Matthew's arrangement of 'the Sermon on the Mount' no less than the Johannine discourses. Either way, there was no stenography available. We have already studied in the Synoptics what we can gauge of oral transmission passing into Gospel formation. The Fourth Gospel belongs with that same process, in part, but – for the rest – in an entirely different way. Did Jesus ever say: 'I came to save the world' (John 12:47)? Or: 'He that eateth me shall live by me' (6:57)? If we answer with a literal Yes! are we not either in incomprehension or inviting ourselves into the incredible option that he, Jesus, was demented or ridiculous?[12] If we answer No! we miss the whole point for lack of a discerning patience.

But in what way is the answer Yes? Not *ipsissima verba* (as the Latin runs), 'the very words', if that is what we mean. We do not have them anyway in that sense, for Jesus did not speak English or dictate the *Good News* version. His Aramaic sounds and syllables are translated for us and have come, as we have already seen, through hazardous processes to reach the Greek Testament and ourselves beyond it. The Synoptics cite, we believe, as closely as possible. For that was their ambition and the intention of the processes on which they relied. We have confidence that, reading the Beatitudes, the Lord's Prayer, and so much else, we are hearing the authentic Jesus of Nazareth.

How differently are we hearing him, for example, in John 6 or 10? What 'Lord's Prayer' is it that we have in John 17? Will it ride with what Mark and the others report of Gethsemane? The Fourth evangelist, too, is 'translating', putting the whole 'text' that Jesus *was* into another way of speaking. Thucydides, in his classical Greek way, contrived to 'tell' significant story by having his heroes speak with their own lips the part they played.[13] The warrant he had for doing so was in what he believed the history meant and signified. So he gives us the actors as being themselves articulate with what they lived through. It takes a writing genius to do so. Only the incomprehending cavil about 'putting words into mouths'. That could only be an accusation from those who did not see what was in hand, who imagine 'words' as only ever 'saying' because they were once audible syllables.

The Fourth evangelist is such a genius too. He is capturing the significance of Jesus in the same immediacies as the Synpotics but from within what their significance had come to mean in the possession of resultant faith. The Thucydides analogy helps us only partially. For the Greek historian in-read his actors' minds enabling his reader to know them from within. The Fourth Gospel invites us to perceive, through discourse, the dimensions Jesus filled, transmuting into his consciousness their meaning in later Christian perception and making them articulate in encounters belonging with the story.

This in no way means that this Gospel 'coins' what is not so. If we want to speak of 'coinage' at all, it has to do with values present and authentic. These are given their currency by the evangelist so that we may occupy ourselves with their worth. Holding the Synoptics and John together – as we must, since there is deep reason in their juncture – we are in the way of what the Incarnation holds, namely the Jesus who 'speaks' where men listen on the hillsides and 'means' as the eternal referent of all he was, from 'the bosom of the Father'. We are not left (unless we are obtuse) with the literalists' Jesus as demented, ridiculous or divine. The divine could never conceivably belong with such an option. Nor need we find the Fourth Gospel incompatible with the others once we understand what contrasts them – and why.

So then, Jesus inviting to an 'eating of his flesh', having precedence on Abraham, being 'one with the Father', identifying himself with 'light', 'way', 'door', 'resurrection', 'truth', and coming forth from heaven and returning thither – this Jesus is the Jesus of the faith translated back into the history, the events, the milieu, in which that faith became the faith it was. In that fusion John's truth consists proleptically within the truth of the Synoptics. Hence all four comprise the Scripture.

Do we still have to enquire about the actual self-consciousness of

Jesus if we perceive the Fourth Gospel this way? Reticence will be right but integrity has demands. Let us face the issue at the most sacred point, the agony in Gethsemane. Clearly, 'the high priestly prayer', as it is called, of Jesus in John 17:1–26 reads altogether incongruously alongside what Matthew, Mark and Luke tell us of anguish, sweat, grief of heart and pleading prayer. In John 17 all is majestic, calm, assured, triumphant. It reads like the spiritual summary of an accomplished mission, as of one bequeathing his legacy of fulfilment into a future of anticipation. 'Now I come to Thee,' he says, with all those active verbs of realised redemption and of a discipleship charged and primed and ready. Where are those sleeping followers here, where the ones who fled? The passage even refers to Jesus in the third person: 'to know . . . Jesus Christ whom Thou hast sent'. Is it not the evangelist, from the perspective of the years, perceiving 'the finished work of Christ' and phrasing it on Christ's own lips, in that communion with the Father from whom all derived and to whom all returned?

He is the same Father to whom Jesus prayed: 'Let this cup pass . . . nevertheless not my will but Thine', and it is the one Jesus. Either prayer will only be fully known in the key of the other. If, in divine *kenosis*, we want to know 'what Jesus said' the Synoptics are the place, but the place Gethsemane truly was is told in John. How right he was to set the telling on the lips of Jesus. Where else could it be?

Do we not have to think this way about all the discourses of the Fourth Gospel? Then their disparity alongside the Synoptic parables will not perplex us. We are given the quintessence of meanings already there but only ours now through the medium of a pondering, absorbing mind. Yet the author in John does not wander into gnostic abstraction. He roots all in living history. In John 18:1 the magnificent strophes of Chapter 17 move swiftly across 'the brook Kedron' into the garden they illuminate and into the reality on its mortal plane. So it is throughout. Where this John is most sublime he is always close to earth, to time and place. He anchors all his discourses to events around persons – Nicodemus, a Samaritan woman, a cripple by a pool, a man blind from birth, even a prostitute. 'Signs' and discourses belong together. We are in a narrative, yet also a revelation.

We are aware as we give ourselves to the secret of him that this John is weaving his Jesus-history into a drama of deliberation in which an entire 'metaphor-in-life' is fitted into a sequence of 'signs' and imageries drawn from what happened – as Matthew, Mark and Luke had told – but with a sense of the import for which the eventfulness was divinely meant. We talk readily of 'eye-witness.' Is there not 'mind-witness' also? That is what we have concerning Jesus being the Christ in the genius of this Fourth Gospel. Is it not a clue to be happily read back into the Synoptics where, indeed, it is already partially in hand, though not in Johannine terms?

This sense of things in John can be evident for us also if, in those discourses, we ask where an initiating conversation ends and where the logic moves on beyond the one listener into themes of no one time or

place. Thus in John 3, where is Nicodemus after verse 12? John's exposition has him for an occasion of what addresses all. Similarly, the
discourse in John 5 beyond verse 18 develops into a long and profound
'theology' of Jesus' person ('the Father has life in Himself, so has He
given to the Son') which, though it moves from the incident of healing,
enshrines a whole Christology far transcending what occasioned it.

Again, in Chapter 6, it seems clear that later Christian dimensions of
the Eucharist enter into a discourse that *only* fits the immediate hillside
scene, after the feeding of the crowd, because it belongs with what the
evangelist, years and miles away, had perceived with his community as
the terms in which it could be read. The discourse was never 'recording'
Jesus: it was perceiving him. The discourses in Chapters 14, 15 and 16,
central to Christian experience, make, with Chapter 17, a strange hiatus
in the Passover time, between 13:38 and 18:1. John has his pivots of
chronology but his mind is free to subdue them to his faith-perceptions.
The climax of his narrative must accommodate the quintessence of his
witness.

Thus, for example, he can set the cleansing of the Temple at the
outset of his story whereas the others place it correctly as prelude to
the final week. John, however, sees vivid encounter between Jesus
and 'the world' as the salient theme: it can be truly symbolised at the
outset by the supreme challenge that cleansing signified. Similarly, in
his very first chapter he has two disciples summoned by John the
Baptist (who never used the term elsewhere) to 'behold the Lamb of
God'. Were they truly into the secret, raw as they were, at the very
outset? If so, how could it square with all the Synoptics tell us about
their failure to understand? What need for their long, patient, traumatic
education into that secret? Yet, if we discern him wisely, John is right.
The one they came to follow, by the Baptist's hand, was the one who
came to be what there in hidden-ness he was. As at a wedding, what will
ensue is already there, committed as the parties are.

vi

The Fourth Gospel is not unique in its linking of word with episode.
What we have earlier noted, however, around the Synoptics is sharply
intensified in John – sharply, because he has made 'encounter' as well
as 'sign' the motif of his narrative. It is almost as if Jesus stands accused,
is placed 'on trial' by the powers-that-be religiously. John's chapters
from 5 to 13 carry issues in this confrontation as they head into the
final arraignment in Chapters 18 and 19. The story of a gathering storm
in the Synoptics is here the more harsh and elemental. What is at stake
has to do with authority, tradition, liberty, truth and grace, law and life,
all of which centre in the crucial factor of Jesus' person and mission. As
we realised earlier with the prophets, 'reproaches fell on him' in
reproach of what he held concerning God so that, if the truth were with
him, they fell also on God (cf. Psalm 69:9).

Here we come again upon a point made earlier, namely the dual

reference that belongs with the Gospels. What John set forth of accu-
sation-in-trial of Jesus mirrored the stresses in the Johannine community in whose midst the Gospel came to be. They, for their part, faced
opposition and calumny from Jews resisting the Christian version of a
realised Messiah. Their confrontation echoed the earlier because in
essence the two were seen as linked. The claims about Jesus were as
controversial as those by him had earlier been.

Only if this situation is not in focus is it warranted to see the Fourth
Gospel as 'anti-Semitic'. 'Jews' are referred to there in gentle and
prosaic terms (cf. 1:19, 2:6, 3:1, 4:9, 5:1, 6:4, 7:2, 11:19, 31, 33, 36 and 45,
12:11 and 19:40). Where 'the Jews' occurs with the bitter animus of
confrontation it is in no way inclusive of a race: it denotes parties to an
issue. The issue was itself in its essentials inter-Jewish, inasmuch as a
Jewish sense of things Judaic had opened them to 'Gentiles', and opened
them so truly that this strange denominator, covering all *goyim/ethnoi*
while severally knowing none, no longer needed significant currency.
The perceptive reader knows equally that the bitter Johannine situation
had its counterpart everywhere when other Jews clung strenuously
to their exceptionality in God and felt obliged to oppose the new
inclusiveness. The elements of that crisis had been evident in Jesus'
own story and were the antecedents of his Cross.

Does not the Nicodemus story capture this situation and weave
together the brief years of Jesus and the lengthening years of Christ-
faith as John's artistry joins them? To be sure, Sanhedrin rabbis brought
their mingled curiosity and guarded admiration to Jesus, privately for
prudence' sake. While the conversation lasts, and when the discursive
'essay' begins, we are dwelling in two environments of place and time.
The pen is the pen of John (in Ephesus?), the theme is the theme of
Jesus (in Judea?). 'Birth' from Jewish womb was the vital factor which,
Jewishly, already ensured membership in divine peoplehood. Wombing,
of course, cannot be undone. What, then, is this teaching about being
'born again' — open to all and sundry who are already here by births
neither reversible nor Jewish? Nicodemus has it right. Birth can never
be re-evented. This 'new birth' will be like one's nativity in its newness
but only so as occurring within personhoods already there. These will
have it universally, available whatever their origins. Its necessity lies in
the fact of divine grace remaking the self from sin to love. The old
wilderness story of the serpent on the pole meant that if you would
receive the remedy you must first look honestly at the disease.

The writer uses a bold irony. 'Lifted up' (v. 14) was literal point
in Numbers 21:9, eventful reality in the Cross (cf. John 12:32), and
perceptible fact in Christian preaching. Faith, as trust in this redemptive
self-giving of the Lord, this divine *kenosis* into death, becomes the
crucial factor, always free and uncompulsive in any and every human
life. Only by a hint in verse 21 about 'coming to the light' does the
discourse keep Nicodemus in its sights. The evangelist has subtly
combined the central concern of the environment he knew and served
with the setting in which Jesus lived and taught. He has no less gently

wedded a Judean interview (which, entirely credible as it is, he may yet have purposefully contrived) with a faith-exposition which – in this form – relies on the vantage-vision of the years. But he has in no way 'falsified' Jesus. For this is what always was had come to mean. How characteristic, too, the gentle irony which brings Nicodemus finally (19:39) to share in the costly way that human love precedes the resurrection.

The foregoing does only scant justice to all we need to know – and all that necessarily eludes our knowing – concerning the Gospels. Hopefully, the primary perceptions are in focus. Before returning, as agreed, to the Epistles in their education of the churches, there remain certain general points about 'enscripturing'.

vii

A pen is a very singular instrument if we are thinking of a Thucydides, a Shakespeare, or a Goethe using it. When we pass from what is oral to what is scribal in the New Testament's formation it is well to think of plural pens. Idiosyncrasies in Matthew, Mark, Luke, John, Paul and Peter are evident enough and significant. Yet what we have from them we do not have of them as individuals. The processes that have to do with source and form and editing, with transcribing and amending, are all necessarily communal, and those who actually have quills on parchments dip into very local inks. We cannot be dogmatic about the identities of any of the evangelists. What now bears their names transpired in a society entirely familiar with attribution, setting texts under the authority of the famous and trustworthy, having 'reputable' wait upon 'repute'.

Thus the Gospels bear no authors' names but it was instinctive to have them carry names famously part of their own story. Matthew and John were personal followers of Jesus, Mark well known in Paul's story via Barnabas. The Lukan authorship of Luke-Acts could credibly be based on his close association with Paul and the personal pronoun usage that shows him to have been a fellow voyager. Ephesians among 'Pauline' letters carries, like Hebrews, no crediting. The Pastoral Epistles (those to Timothy and Titus), though 'as from Paul', require us by their tone and time to discern how 'as from Paul' should be understood.[14] Apostolicity, both for Gospels and Letters, is a quality of mind and authority and not always of individual identity. In that respect the term in respect of Scripture is one with the term in respect of Church.

Apostolic authorship in either sense belongs with community. Tradition associates Mark with Rome and Matthew with Antioch. That the Fourth Gospel emerges from a specific circle, its circumstance, its need and its mind, we have had ample cause to know. Was 'John' the son of Zebedee, 'the disciple whom Jesus loved', 'the elder', or one unknown? The question persists: what matters is 'his' Gospel. No New Testament writing is 'pontifical' because 'x' is writing. Even Paul in his most urgent mood appeals to 'the mind of Christ'. As for dating, we may reasonably hold that the New Testament literature begins with Epistles in the mid-fifties and concludes with Gospels in the mid-nineties of the first century. It is well to think in decades with Mark coming, as we now have it, between 65 and 70. Though its priority is not entirely agreed, Mark is broadly thought to have been followed by Matthew (though in some sense also in tandem) between 85 and 90, with Luke complete by 80–5 and John either side of 90 CE. Chronology is sometimes discernible by local reference or historical dating relating to several persecutions, the siege and fall of Jerusalem and expulsion from the synagogue.[15] Noting when quotations first appear in patristic writings helps to indicate likely dating but is uncertain evidence of actual timing of Gospel availability, given the vagaries of circulation and the doubtfulness of any and every argument from silence.[16]

Internal features are also studied for light they may cast on before when, or after when, the text could not have been what it is. Does John 21, for example – undoubtedly an appendix in the light of John 20:31 – reflect later controversy about the role of Peter in the Church? Is there already in Matthew's account of the post-resurrection scene the sort of heightening of drama that becomes more characteristic in the later apocryphal Gospels that play on credulity? The bifocal nature of the Gospels, as we have studied, properly means that careful exploration can conjecture relations between the 'when' of authorship at work and the 'when' in the story of Jesus.[17] How the role of John the Baptist is depicted, and how it may have turned on on-going discipleship to him in the dispersion, is one obvious example. But concluding from these clues remains elusive.

It is pre-eminently in the Book of Revelation that the author places himself firmly in the heart of the scene and the scene squarely in his personal travail. He belongs in the long tradition of apocalyptic visionaries who spelled out their meaning in coded symbols and allusions suited to the sufferings and perils of a persecuted and harried Church. His message is known *for* and *from* the actualities of tribulation and tells itself in the idiom of defiant hope.[18] Here imagery both interprets and informs experience.

vii

From Gospels emerging through the world of the Letters we turn to Letters inculcating in the life of the world the personal Christ-likeness the Gospels had portrayed. 'I in them and Thou in me,' as John had it (17:23). The evidences of God in Christ were to be enfleshed evidentially by grace and patience in persons in Christian community. An 'alembic' is a vessel which ministers its content through its very shape as containing and bestowing.[19] These Scriptures may be so compared: the Letters serve for the bestowing of what the Gospels are being currently shaped finally to contain. So much we have seen. Their very shape implies an audience and incorporates the terms in which that audience is already widening in the world. Thus, for example, the vivid conversation in

John 4 at the well of Sychar in Samaria has overtones beyond the immediacies of an apparently chance encounter. Dramatic imagination knows about 'five husbands' and five Books of the Pentateuch or the five deities imported there according to 2 Kings 17:30–31, by which the evangelist localises meaning. To localise is to personalise.

In their mainly 'Gentile' field of reference the Epistles do the same. What is presented of Jesus in his word and deed, in his death and resurrection, is made the text of life in his name. The precedent history yields precedents by which life is to be interpreted and lived. 'You were . . .', 'you are . . .', runs like a refrain in apostolic correspondence with the citizens concerned. 'Paganism' with all its licence, its profligacy or its sophisticated idolatry, is still their yesterday. They need to understand the will of Christ for sincerity, single-mindedness, and discipline. They have responsibilities to one another within the faith, to outsiders yet to be persuaded of their integrity. The context is mainly hostile and frequently bewildering. While Christians have no political pretensions, they are surrounded by usages in speech and demands in law that run painfully counter to their new-found loyalty in Christ.

While they rely (if they are Jewish) on old Scriptures, or (if they are pagans) the vocation to inherit them, they are still more parties to a new text, which is no less than the person of their Lord. Those who write to them are not consciously inditing Scriptures yet to be. Their pens have, as yet, no canonical status beyond the stature of their users. Recipients are thus part of the very process of 'enscripturing', and process has no prior guarantees. We have to think as if it were Jesus itinerating round the scattered churches, a Galilean preacher using the lips of other tellers writing their missives in his school. As Colossians 2:6 has it: 'The Christ you have received – live your life according to him.'

Two things are significant throughout. One is the central role of private persons, the *laos* or people of God, communal to be sure, but each there severally because of the uniqueness of the individual self. This feature underlies the whole sense of mission. While none are 'sufficient in themselves', none are superfluous in a hierarchy of the few or the élite. There is a compelling sense of the grace of God offered indiscriminately to all without the intrusion of birth or 'purity' of law.

The other is 'quietness' of vision for the world:

> Nowhere do we hear anything of the voices of oppressed peoples who gave vent to their rebellion against Rome's rapacity and destructive fury in the manner of the King of Britain in Tacitus (*Agricola* 30). Nowhere do we hear the voice of loathing with which the educated Greeks scorned the culture-less, snobbish and noisy activity of Rome, nor the voice of painful boredom with which Rome's own writers and poets . . . in the time of Civil War weighed and recommended to the prudent the surrender of the capital city and flight to the country.[20]

The New Testament handled slavery only by pleading a brotherhood of mercy between an owner and a runaway.[21]

This docility may have been due, in part, to often imminent expectation of the Parousia, or appearing of a returning Christ. Where the Scriptures in Christ portray this hope they do so in terms drawn from older traditions of 'the Messianic woes'. It is remarkable that when the Parousia hope faded and was seen, so to speak, as 'the horizon' of all history (for horizons by definition always recede) the essential quality of Christian living was unchanged, even though some 'sensationalists' persisted to trouble the waters.

Parousia either way left the rich potential of the Epistles to yield abiding precedents quite untouched. This potential came to be their very *raison d'être* as the decades passed. What Paul had explained to Corinthians about Christian freedom, in the context of idols and their 'meats', could be translated into guidance *mutatis mutandis* for any and every occasion of conflict between principle and practice in communities of love. Legitimate liberty in the strong has to give way to care for the foibles of the weak on more fronts than food taboos. For it is only in such forbearing that the bound are liberated.[22]

Similarly, what Paul intends in contention with legalists in Galatia serves to underwrite the menace in every area of false scrupulosity in religion. All too easily we 'build again the tyrannies from which we have been once delivered' (Galatians 2:18).[23] How to deal with sectional loyalties within the 'undivided-ness' of Christ is strongly shown in 1 Corinthians, with the danger of contriving 'parties' behind 'leaders'. Emulation of the 'Gentile offering' as a spontaneous sacrament of unity needs little conjuring from the two Corinthian Letters. In 1 Thessalonians 5 (the earliest of Christian Scriptures) the directives are explicit and detailed for Christian existence. Hebrews offers a rich theological example of how inherited religious culture, in any clime, may be read both for its relevance and its problematics *vis-à-vis* the new life in Christ. In the Pastoral Epistles clear directives about ministry and organisation are inclusive of more than their own time. Indeed, the epistolary ethics of the New Testament enter as deeply into Christian character as do echoes of older psalmody in Christian devotion. And there are passages like Philippians 2:5–11, Romans 11:33–36, and the great doxologies of Revelation which are a hymnology of their own.

It is in all these ways that we should understand the New Testament canon, for only so do we not have to apologise for it. The question is sometimes asked whether an on-going faith is well served by a confined Scripture, especially given – as we have seen – the cultural particularity circumscribing it. Indeed, the idea and fact of 'the canon' might be said to be a circumscribing (literally) of faith itself. If, today, we submit to the canon – we have no other option ecclesiastically – we need to do so with some register of inner protest. To do otherwise is to diminish what we mean by 'believing in the Holy Spirit'.

What, then, explains the finalising of the New Testament in the canon? There was, of course, the precedent, partly parallel and partly prior, of the Old Testament as a defined corpus, or *Tanakh*, of sacred writings. There was a keen sense of need for writings understood and agreed as normative, indeed as definitive. Issues around Christology and ecclesiology naturally attended on 'scriptures,' just as these had their status by association with apostles and first companions. Marcion, and later the Montanists, had views about Christ and about the Church which inevitably entailed controversy about the status of the writings to which they appealed or called in question. The urge to delimit divergent opinions and doctrines required authoritative standing for writings or their disqualification.

Thus the factors we have yet to study in Chapter 8 leading to the formation of creeds argued also the necessity for the canon of the New Testament. The basic list had taken shape by the middle of the second century of the Church, as we know from references, for example, in the second Letter of Clement and in Justin Martyr. It is fair to say that there was a canon in being by around 190 though, for two centuries after, a very few books (Hebrews, 2 Peter, 2 and 3 John and Jude) were some-times 'in' and sometimes 'out' of local lists. Athanasius of Alexandria, in 367, lists all the titles known now in the Muratorian or western canon. A papal declaration confirmed them in 405. The Nestorian Church contented itself with 22 Books, excluding 2 Peter, 2 and 3 John, Jude, and Revelation, but including Hebrews. The Syrian Church had Tatian's *Diatessaron*, or inter-weaving of the Four Gospels, known in Syriac trans-lation as the *Peshitta*.

The Church was heir to the Hebraic practice of 'lections', or *qeryana*, in public worship, and this undoubtedly contributed strongly to the concept of a Christian canon. It was natural for missives to be shared between churches and read, as some of them explicitly enjoined, to the congregations. The practice required – and effectuated – the recog-nition of writings worthy of this role. Indeed, efforts have been made to detect lectionary or calendar purposes as underlying the authorial shape of the Gospels.[24]

In this intrinsic interplay between the emerging fact and the official esteem of Scriptures as the Christian canon, it is important to see that 'canonising' does not confer authority on the text. It acknowledges authority already present – an authority, however, of a sort to come by this dignity only by cognisance of its worth and not by imposition or by criteria absolute in themselves.

In that quality the New Testament canon is symbol of the very nature of Christian faith, in debt to – and in trust with – what it did not originate but nevertheless accredits. In a different sense, however, the canon leaves us asking whether the Church should ever have finalised its written criteria so early and so confidently. The question is especially urgent in respect of what is read in worship. Should the treasures of subsequent Christian wisdom, devotion and spiritual enterprise have been so rigorously excluded from canonical status? Is not faith in part like some city, some Oxford, some London, some Damascus – on the same site, with the same aura, through the same centuries, yet transforming as it lives into new dimensions and presentations of itself? 'Development' in doctrine and liturgy, not to say in life, is conceded on all hands, though there are always those who want to finalise it at some attained point, halting further versions of the logic to which they have themselves appealed.

The canon has finalised Scriptural authority but has not resolved the larger questions of how that finalising consorts with its future tense. In worship and devotion, Hymnology – almost surreptitiously (for it is not 'approved' or legislated) – innovates, and changes thoughts and feelings, as the Wesleys and Methodism powerfully exemplified. But it is more doubtful how we do for doctrine and theology, outside the poets and singers, what thought and teaching need. The canon is now with us, in centuries of irreversible status entrenching for our security the fruitful penmanship of apostolic times. It is appropriate it should be so only by two provisos. The one is that we quarry it for precedents (as in previous paragraphs here) and find our bearings from them now by immersing them in what our own times show us of their relevance.

The other is the reality of the ever-present Holy Spirit leading us into all truth, according to Christ's promise. There can be no right reception – or theory – of scriptural canon that implies that the divine mind and presence are no longer brooding over all. The canon is historically closed. The Spirit behind it and before it makes of its closed-ness an open responsibility. In the following chapter we shall find that credalising has the same destiny.

8 Credalised

i

> Smothered in errors, feeble, shallow, weak,
> The folded meaning of your words' deceit.
> Against my soul's pure truth why labour you
> To make it wander in an unknown field?[1]

THE ancient Christian Creeds of Nicaea and the definitions at Chalcedon have often been greeted in such terms by those who demurred at the confidence of the credal clauses or were distrustful of any capacity to make them. The reasons will concern us in Chapter 11. 'A folded meaning' in the words' integrity a Christian honesty would readily concede, and there was much 'labour' in the credal story, not all of it commendable when ecclesiastical politics supervened. Yet 'the soul's pure truth' was always the intention, given the antecedents we have studied in Chapter 6 as these derived from the significance of what Chapter 5 presented.

'Meaning' and 'to mean' are versatile words and they usually entail a mingling of 'explanation' and 'intention', depending on whether reference is to a document or a purpose, a text or an aim. Politicians mix them well or a wily Shakespearean king: 'I mean that with my soul I love your daughter and mean to make her queen.'[2] To deal fairly with credalised Christianity we have to come to its explainings through its intention. Of the second there can be no doubt. The Fathers and the Councils intended three purposes – to affirm the reality of God, to understand the fact of Jesus as the Christ, and decisively to link the two, the reality and the fact. They saw Jesus as integral to what 'God', 'God is', 'God reigns', could 'mean' at all. Faith in God and faith in Jesus belonged together, for 'We cannot state the Christian thought of God except as we include Christ in our statement. The Name of God has the final meaning Jesus gave to it and part of that meaning is himself,'[3] and with it all other parts are consonant in the timeless 'before and after' of 'the Word made flesh'.

Intention and explanation proceeded together, each necessary to the other. Creeds were the form in which faith was made articulate in steady reflection for a world in life. Faith could hardly keep the inner meaning of 'trust' and lack the outer shape of words. Its truth would seek currency in the terms of receptivity that human perception might then receive.

This being so, it must follow that faith always transcends the forms of its expression. Those we have in historic Creeds dating from the third to the fifth centuries have the mind-set and the intellectual discoursing of their time and place. It belongs with our debt to them to be keenly aware of their limitations. There are for us now heavy liabilities incurred by our possession of them. Nevertheless, their story cannot be undone nor their legacy disowned. Generations of believers have said of them to a sceptical and incredulous world: 'How can these things in me seem scorn to you/Bearing the badge of faith to prove them true?'[4] The scorn has not diminished. It is rather heightened by the lapsing centuries and the flux of language. As historic, and conciliar in their consensus, the Creeds do 'bear the badge of [the] faith'. But 'prove' was never the right word. Faith wears no 'badge' except its own integrity – an integrity the Creeds both articulate and embarrass. The onus of that paradox is the crux of a confessional faith and of its faithful confession. We do not, as was said of John Henry Newman, 'believe in credulity'. It is well to take his 'Lead, kindly light' in some poetic, mystical sense, rather than as the unexamined *Ecclesia dixit* which was what, otherwise, he meant. For 'the encircling gloom' was alarmingly – for him – the gathering evidence of a liberalism which, in other terms than his, might well have been gratefully hailed.[5] 'Faith' and 'the faith' must always be in honest tension, with intention and explanation mutually alert.

ii

It will be a token of such alertness if we begin from the angle of those who deplore and dispute creeds and doctrine as ever religiously appropriate. Why not let God be God they ask, without subtle, elaborate, self-bewildering language so readily ridiculed as dealing in dipthongs?[6] And why not let Jesus be Jesus free of all accretions – as simplistically they seem – about 'incarnation', *Logos* and the rest? And why join God and Jesus so conceptually together as if they could not 'be' apart? Why incur at all the deep problematics of such association between God and this man, between the timeless and time, between transcendence and history? The naïvety of the queries is attractive – until we know them for the *simplicitas* they tell.

Letting God be God is obviously necessary. We have no other option. But how vacuous, if we have not stayed to search any content in the word. Suppose we turn the bidding into a formula and, free of all complexity of doctrine, simply say: 'God is God.' What can the saying mean? We have merely let the subject be the predicate. Neither has what might describe the other. Such tautology could only signify if we meant to imply a kind of incorrigible entity, as when we say: 'Well, politics is politics,' or 'East is East,' and think that realism forbids hope. Such defeatism, expecting nothing better, can hardly deter the task of theologians. Uncertainties require that they be more patiently perceptive – which brings us back to the necessity of doctrine.

Let us then venture further and announce that 'God is great' (Allahu akbar). An entire theology, we might claim, is now in hand – and with admirable brevity. Only so, however, if we go on to show how 'great' in both senses of the 'how' – the measure and the method of the 'greatness'. How, in particular, will it align with the human scene we faced in Chapter 3? How will 'greatness' prove itself sufficiently so in face of human history? Are we not 'case-hardened' to live at all, as the poet Wordsworth had it, encountering what 'seemed to offer proof that the world was poisoned at the heart'?[7] Tolstoy might ask: 'Can it be possible that in the midst of this entrancing Nature feelings of hatred, vengeance, or the desire to exterminate their fellows can endure in the souls of men?'[8] Only too possible. Must we then perceive a 'greatness' of malign and callous omnipotence – as such in no way great? Evidently we must have grounds, other than realist sight, for any 'great' predicate about God. The same situation will obtain whatever the predicate – wise, gracious, compassionate, merciful, or any of these turned into the cognate noun. It will equally obtain if we confine the predicate to 'God is . . .',[9] as some philosophy has been content to do – merely leaving a vacuity for other philosophies to respond that 'God is not.'

All theological formulae will be bogus unless they undertake what is owed to our own questionings. Each has to be sufficiently 'a theology of suspicion' set truly to understand what is to be understood, given the actualities of our own loves, our human ethics and our social experience. For the question of God, as we have argued earlier, is implicit in all other questioning. By its very nature it presupposes responsible freedom in us. For the reality of God is nowhere (except for mystics momentarily) overwhelmingly compelling. There is no external compulsion to belief (as rampant secularity demonstrates) by some unveiled manifestation of divine majesty calculated to exclude any liability of ours for personal decision. This being so an enquiring, probing, questing theology has to be steadily deployed. Merely to hold that 'God is God' will otherwise be treason and folly. We cannot take refuge in inscrutability.

Likewise with the reductionism that is content with 'Jesus the man', or 'Jesus the Jew', or 'Jesus the prophet', or 'Jesus the servant'. All these are true enough, as might also be, in some sense, 'Jesus the enigma' or 'Jesus the unknown'. It is for the honest sake of all these that we have to go beyond them. Certainly those nearest and most fitted to report him did so. With strong assurance, and in the immediate aftermath of his story and with remarkable speed, they were conjoining 'Christ our Lord' to his common name (for common it was in Jewry). The reasons we have seen in Chapters 6 and 7. The Christology by which they did so was and is a deeply Hebraic thing. Only later did the identity of Jesus find expression in Greek vocabulary. In that light we might read a strange poetic justice in the otherwise malintentioned question in John 7:35, 'Will he go into the diaspora among the Greeks and preach to Greeks?'[10] Indeed he did in the Christology of his followers and elsewhere into the human diaspora. There is nothing in early Christian Christology that does not derive from, and return to, profoundly Judaic understanding of divine ways in history. The 'Gentilising' of the faith about Jesus was neither a 'de-Judaising' in respect of the embrace of people nor in terms of vocabulary and concept. So much we have seen in the writing of the New Testament, so much we trace in the formation of creeds. It will, then, in no way suffice to observe naïvely or evasively that 'Jesus was Jesus'.

But what of the necessary – indeed, imperative – interrelation between God and Jesus? Why the steady Christian bond between theology and Christology, with neither viable without the other? Aspects of the answer can await Chapter 12 after we have reckoned with 'discounting'. The business of this chapter is to study how the two came to integral confession in the technical language of Nicaea and Chalcedon and other Councils around them. The controversies may seem arid and, in their political overtones, unseemly and deplorable. But what they had in trust as to 'God in Christ' and 'the Christ in God' required their utmost cherishing. What moves us now and here in reckoning with the history of doctrine is that the inter-association of God and Jesus (or credally of 'the Father and the Son') is at the full in the reality of the Cross,[11] understood as the heart of theology by its being also at the core of those things about the human world that have to be crucial for any credibility in the things of God. What being human is at its worst is dramatised in the crucifixion meted out to the master of the Beatitudes. What being divine is – at its most telling – must be at the same place. Love must be proved where the most outrage is done to it. It will be known where it is most vulnerable and what God is like known where the most god-like happens.

iii

The history of doctrine has often been traced and its intricacies explored. The aim here is not to retell a complex story but, rather, to clarify what credalising intended and how the past of it may serve us now. For the historic Creeds are part of a legacy. Yet there has to be a continuing possession and repossession of their intention and steady personal, as well as corporate, decision in accepting the inheritance.

The crucial thread in the story is the 'and' coupling God and Christ, Father and Son. We can reach the Trinity only that way. 'And' is always subtle in its apparent simplicity in every usage – 'male and female', 'time and timeless', 'ethical and holy' (as we shall see),[12] 'tragic and comic'. What do all these junctures mean? We have already noted how associated adjectives are more readily fused than coupled nouns.

'Christian and Muslim' (adjectives about, say, reverence) will more easily conjoin than 'a Christian and a Muslim'.

It will be our way here to think adjectival theology with the Creeds, before coming to the substantives – 'God', 'Man', 'nature', 'substance', 'person' and the like. Many of the issues that arose came from the 'what-ness' of nouns, the difficulty in their rendering from language to language and the sort of treatment their 'is-ness' demands. How can 'God' be 'man', we ask, still more a helpless babe, still more again a victim on a gibbet and a corpse in a tomb? How can the actual human, in these eventualities, be somehow, at the same time – indeed, eternally – 'reigning in heaven'? Or, conversely, who sustains the universe when 'God' succumbs to crucifixion?

The questions are unanswerable, but only because the posing of them has not understood that about which they are asked. But, if we can think that the power and majesty belonging with the divine are the same power and majesty we recognise in those human terms, we begin to learn in what sense 'God' is 'Man' and 'Man' is 'God'. May it not be that the purpose that hung the stars had – because of the humankind beneath them as part of that entire creation, indeed, its core part – an equal initiative to be the light of creaturehood? Would such a mystery of gentleness be less 'divine' than 'the silence of infinite spaces'? Is finitude excluded from infinity – given reasons infinitely authentic for such self-finiting? If, then, doctrine wants to speak of a 'pre-existent Christ' will it not simply be saying, and meaning, that such 'divine-ness' had ever been so 'world without end'? For, though the divine could never have started to acquire what earlier was lacked, the sense of something 'arriving' to be so was implicit in the nature of time – time into which the self-finiting came.

Similarly, in affirming credally 'ascension into heaven', where in some sense the human was eternally enthroned, was faith not saying that what the divine had ever been it would for ever remain, that the Incarnation was not undone? The pro-human character of the divine had been, and would for ever be, on both sides of the temporal enterprise in which that pro-humanity had been historical.

We can see at once what difficulties follow if we think in nounal, or 'substantial' terms. Can we truly concede – as many of the Fathers did and theologians like Pusey in the nineteenth century – that actual 'flesh' was somehow physically 'seated' in the heavens? Did the veracity of what the Incarnation affirmed about the divine necessitate a doctrinal insistence on the 'flesh' that historically served divine love being, as it were, 'eternalised', with all the potential absurdities such insistence would entail? Would thinking so not misconstrue Incarnation itself as, by its very purpose, 'episodic' – as all temporal things must be. The eternal abidingness of its meaning was ensured in the divine reality, not in incredible physicality on high.

One might suspect a crass mentality behind such misconstruing until one took due note of something else. The Church was beset on all hands by gnostic ideas, by docetic notions abroad, that 'flesh' was unworthy, illusory, compromising and impure and that, therefore, the 'real Christ' must have been altogether 'spiritual' with physicality only a charade, a strategy of make-belief, leaving us with only a kind of 'as-if' about Christ. Such thinking clearly made a travesty of faith, precluding altogether what the Incarnation meant and denying the very heart of divine self-finiting for love's sake. In gnostic terms the divine had ceased to be such.

Hence the perceived necessity to insist on the real, non-seeming, veritable and utterly relevant role of 'flesh', without which all else would be forfeit. But a right vigilance for what is meant can sometimes betray the very loyalty within it. That is what happened – whenever it was thought that the Incarnation required the Christian to assert that what came via Mary's womb was fleshly 'present' eternally with God and that what had lain in the sepulchre physically shared 'the majesty on high'.[13] Ignoring all the obvious incredulities, the Fathers were all too often tempted to give their faith corollaries it did not need or which would only confuse. The divine reality in Jesus was secure enough in the divine being for ever the divine, prior to, within, and beyond the historic drama of disclosure which, being necessarily human (and the pro-humanity being necessarily divine), had its incidence in a there and a then. The before and after were explicit in divine initiative and not – necessarily not – in the same idiom as the actualities of when and where. The Incarnation was from and of and in eternity, with time in human partnership. What had come through a womb and passed through a grave was the divine self-expression humanly self-expressed. Christian poets could rightly sing of 'the eternal Word unable to speak a word', of 'how glory's self should serve our griefs and fears and free eternity submit to years'.[14] Why should not transcendence wrap its clues in swaddling clothes?

iv

Through all the vicissitudes, mental and ecclesiastical, attending the progress of Christian experience into Christian doctrine and of doctrine into Creed, the adjective 'very' in its full sense could be said to have been the key to all that was 'meant', *qua* intention and *qua* explanation. 'Very God of very God', 'Very Man of . . . the Virgin Mary, his Mother'.[15] Echoing the 'verily' so familiar from Jesus in the Gospels,[16] 'very' is richly freighted. It is much diminished in popular usage but credally it means integrity of truth, legitimate assurance and intensity of trust. It contests agnosticism and denies doubt. It tells an authenticity. We saw its point in Chapter 6 via 'very king of very king', and saw too how the adjective captures what is inherently true and affirms it against all implication otherwise – the sort of implication it is there to dispel. A crucial word indeed.

But adjectives wait on nouns and it was these – God, man, nature, substance, person – that the credalising Fathers made their business. How much more appropriate to faith, and the faith's expression it had been if they had stayed with 'divine' and 'human' and let these adjectives be qualified by 'verily' like the parables of Jesus. Their explanation/intention, throughout, was to comprehend the divine dimension as truly there in the Christ-event, and that event as altogether human, with neither the divine nor the human attenuated, compromised or – can we say – embarrassed.

How, we might ask, could the divine *not* be incarnationally embarrassed, being identified with one who would be saying as a poet might: 'I pace the earth and drink the air and feel the sun.'? There would be other far more embarrassing situations in 'agony and bloody sweat'. Would these ever be compatible with the divine?[17] Answer must turn on what might be appropriately thought concerning God. Might these things even be credentials or could they only be unthinkable blasphemies to be insistently repudiated? It was because the Christian Creeds were minded the way they were by their first paragraph ('Creator', 'One', 'Father') that they could move without compromise to all that was 'verily' about the second paragraph with its necessarily longer detail of a credentialling story, the history that told the unembarrassed Lord, utterly uncompromised in advent-adventure 'for us men and for our salvation'.

If the divine could duly be this way in consistency with all that sovereignty in the universe and history must mean then 'very God of very God' would tell it so. The 'very' would simply underline that, contrary to all a dubious humanity might suppose, the *absence* historically of such divine advent/adventure would be the inconsistent thing. Hence the language about 'came down from heaven and was incarnate'. Arriving into history, entailing time and place, could be told by that analogy. Transcendence could not do other than stoop, being what transcendence is and yet having this enterprise in mind. Nor could the transcendent avoid to get born if the purpose entailed action-human. Such birth, in turn, would not be in the ordinary pattern, of contingency and 'the will of the flesh'. For it was divine will that lay within it. A fitting comprehension of divinely natal way into divinely conceived enterprise would have to be confessed, by those who believed it so, as different from what they did through one another in their lowly sexual way. The initiative, being God's, was not like theirs yet it had to do with what was birth like theirs, seeing it was 'coming where they were'.[18] For, birth apart, there is no personhood, no biography, no Incarnation.

> What greatly is done
> By prophet or poet, by scholar or king,
> Is a womb-cradled thing.

So 'and was born . . .' becomes part of a divine story.[19]

Since this is history, Mary is named in the Creeds and so is Pontius Pilate. Yet can this humiliation, this 'scandal' of brutal doing-to-death, be other than unthinkable embarrassment to any perceptions of the divine? 'Crucified, dead and buried' – the clauses have surely taken us incredibly beyond all credence as being feasibly said of the divine?

Again, the possibility we might be wrong should give us pause. Explanation will turn on divine intention and intention hinge on divine will. All depends on what we can predicate concerning God. Faith will ask what we *must* predicate if we are to recognise any sovereignty adequately relating to the wrongs of history. The point has been sufficiently made already in Chapters 3 and 5. In any Christian perception of God a realist love is the *sine qua non*. For such love there is no evasion of the Cross. Pontius Pilate has his place, like a fossil trace in a stone, because under his regime there happened the ultimate drama of the regime of God. The Creeds were wise to state it starkly as they did.

But what of their wisdom in that incredible comma? 'Born of the Virgin Mary, suffered under Pontius Pilate': 'and was made man, and was crucified for us . . .'? Why the life between elided, why the ministry left to total silence?

> No clue between, as though a day might dawn
> and promptly hour-less into night resign.
> Untimely comma! thus to dispossess
> The bearing womb of after-birth design
> And death's demise so tersely to confess
> Unpreluded.[20]

One can plead, no doubt, that Creeds are brief and do not mean to cover all. Yet all that Jesus said and was seems a wayward omission. Or one may think that 'suffered' intends to say all – as well it might – from Nazareth to Gethsemane. Or the Creeds, like the sacrament of 'bread and wine', concentrate where all the meaning culminates, in the knowledge that the Gospels are there already making good the silence of the Creeds. Or perhaps it was the reticence of loving familiarity.

For all our conjecturing mind about what might embarrass the divine we find ourselves tracing things believed to be entirely appropriate to transcendence. Their divine fittedness is seen as evoked by what is urgently responsive to the facts of humankind and eventuates from within what is apposite to the divine mind. In that confidence the Creed moves into celebration. 'On the third day he rose again . . . He ascended into heaven.' The verbs are twin words comprising one meaning. Divine redemption made actual in history has now the evident stamp of that authorship from whence it first derived. The initiative which moved by birth through suffering and death is known in resurrection by the origins it had in the divine. As things inaugural were thought of as 'descent', so things accomplished are understood as 'ascension'. 'Seated at the right hand' affirms an enterprise realised and joins it with the power by which the divine is for ever identifiable in the identity of grace and truth. The identifiability had necessitated human incidence where the divine found no embarrassment such as un-divine notions of aloofness, or indifference, or prestige, might have to visualise – but only so by misreading what sovereignty could mean. Intention has its explanation where the Creeds witness. 'Very God of very God' – self-giving and self-given.

V

If there is divine consistency in the human enterprise to which the Creeds are witness, we need to turn an adjectively expressed faith around and ask if all the foregoing is consistent with the human? For it will not, otherwise, be about Incarnation. Again, answer has to raise the question, what might 'human' conceivably be by the premise that there is the 'divine' recruiting it? If it 'means' at all, the Incarnation must be as much a human reality as a divine, not a truth about either without the other. If – given what it is inviting us to believe – it is in no way divinely inauthentic, must it be judged humanly unfeasible?

If it is by divine *kenosis*, or self-giving, that love is credible (and so cred-able) about God it must follow, by the same token, that it is not impossible in human terms. For all that might *seem* to make it impossible – divine aloofness, immunity, prestige, glory, omnipotence and the rest – is cared for in the divine *kenosis* which undertakes it. We cannot think of grief and find it incapable of tears. Nor can we posit majesty and forbid it condescension. What fulfilment necessitates initiative will achieve. The conditions the enterprise imposes the enterprise will undertake.

It took Christian theology much time and travail to allow that Incarnation had really happened. For the instinct to immunise the divine, to exonerate, to isolate, to elevate, came so strongly from the old tradition that shrank from even naming the divine Name. Yet in that same tradition was the sense the prophets had of divine pathos,[21] and of 'agency', whereby the divine as 'action' came forth from the divine as 'will'. We traced in Chapter 4 the inter-association of divine and human in servanthood and the Messianic. That believing in the ultimate sense about 'the Word made flesh' took so much misgiving to overcome may be welcome evidence of how finally and humanly acceptable the truth had to be.[22]

'And was made man . . .' then the Creed could say, comprehending all that might, otherwise, embarrass the divine or confound the human, and comprehend it as the single truth of the Giver in the given. 'Made' in context had no trace of duress but was a synonym for 'became', though both might be misconstrued. Hence the Gospel term 'begotten' (itself not unambiguous)[23] to link with what was earlier studied around the indispensability of birth but ensuring that the initiative was a divine intention behind a natal fact.

Outside the chain of human contingency, 'begotten' must be read so that the rich inter-analogy of 'the Father and the Son' may be understood. Translated, it must mean that what belongs inherently to the divine as power, love and truth 'authors' what expresses and fulfils the divine in the human realm. Musical genius 'begets' symphonies of genius and in them is fulfilled. Dramatists and drama are in the same 'begetting/begotten' unity.

It is sad that feminist concerns have confused this theme, seeing that analogy and metaphor must – and should – be understood in the sense in which they can be true. 'Sonship' and 'Fatherhood' here – if permitted to be analogical – have no sexualist connotation. There is no sound reason why 'and was made man' has to be read other than 'undertook humanity', since no exclusion of the female is there in the generic 'man'. If, however, there comes to be a concern that wants to think otherwise then the more patiently (reverting to the onset of this Chapter) must explanation underline intention, here, as everywhere, in credal doctrine. One might say, with masculine vulgarity, that no woman can 'beget', yet blessedly Mary did so by divine leave and mandate.

So we find the human side, in the same words of the Creed, of those events we earlier noted as divine. Then the problem was how they might be divine in such vulnerability to pain and grief and wounds. Now the point is how revealingly human they were, how explicit a sharing of the mortal scene and of the travail which the old prophets had shown to be the deepest splendour of the human heart. The touch on the leper, the laughter in the throng, the pause under a sycamore, the drink at the well, the feast in the house, the meal by the shore, the wine in the wound and the arms on the Cross – all these the Creed, satisfied with the Gospels, crowds into the one inclusiveness; 'and was made man'.

Yet, when we come to the climax, the Creeds content themselves with the tersest summary: 'crucified, dead and buried', one adding the rider: 'according to the Scriptures' in order to associate event with realised expectation. That incisive history is set back into the divine 'before all worlds' and forward into the divine sovereignty and 'the right hand of the Father', where an adjectival theology is complete.

vi

However, in the time and place of credal formation the adjectival theology we have read as the intention in the explaining would have seemed insufficient to the bishops and the Councils – insufficient because wanting in curiosity and a proper philosophic penetration. The contemporary mind then had a fixed concern about 'entities', about nouns that demanded definitions and required investigation into how their quiddities, or identities, could belong together. It was not only a cerebral instinct to see mystery as enigma and to turn wonder into quandary. It was, also, that there were familiars in the mind of both religion and philosophy that seemed to need substantial reckoning as things in themselves. Ought theology to be satisfied with 'ineffable' concerning God and 'incarnate' concerning 'God in Christ'? The Hebrew mind had come to cherish deeply ideas about divine 'wisdom', subsisting with God and of 'agency' whereby, in some personified way, divine action had being and identity, the same and yet somehow differen-

tiated. The Greek mind pondered an eternal principle of reason, or
Logos, underlying all order, meaning, and the very being of the world,
yet belonging with or emanating from the ever-beyond transcendent.
On all counts was it not imperative to pursue these clues in respect of
experience of Jesus' Christhood as the Gospel told it? Was not this
imperative already evident inside the New Testament, yet not there
completely credalised?

The credalising mind in the second, third, fourth, and fifth centuries
therefore felt obliged to busy itself with the kind of questions not
mooted had it been content with possession and interpretation of
experience as interrelating divine and human in a redemptive meaning
fully so enshrined. Aside, however, from intellectual ambitions, right
definitions were necessitated by conflict with 'heresies'[24] as these came
to be seen to be such. If doctrine was adequately to safeguard what it
meant, and had in trust, it had need explicitly to renounce what
obscured the meaning and violated the trust.[25] Inasmuch as local,
provincial, official sanctions were sought and found for all the issues,
defining became a thing, not only of 'Thus it is,' but also 'Thus it cannot
be.' What we earlier called in a sound sense 'a theology of suspicion'
had – it was thought – to be duly vigilant and, therefore, ready for
negation as vital to what was affirmed. Needless to add, the whole
process was thoroughly and untidily human.

We can best have the measure of all that was involved for a would-be
inclusively nounal theology if we go to the end of the story in 451 and
to the deliverances of the Council of Chalcedon. To be sure, there
was much post-Chalcedonian debate and demur and the Monophysite
formulae of much of eastern Christianity never accepted what Chalcedon promulgated. Nevertheless, for the western Church and for Byzantium in the east, Chalcedon became definitive. It was not lacking in the
complexities of its assumed competence, as may be gauged from its
finding:

> We all with one voice confess our Lord Jesus Christ one and the
> same Son, the same perfect in Godhead, the same perfect in man-
> hood, truly God and truly man, of a rational soul and body, co-
> essential with the Father according to the Godhead and co-essential
> with us according to the manhood . . . to be acknowledged in two
> natures, without confusion, without mutation, without division,
> without separation, the distinction of natures being by no means
> taken away by the union, but rather the property of each nature
> being preserved and concurring in one person and one hypostasis.[26]

'Our Lord Jesus Christ' had been the constant and loved watchword
in the New Testament Letters, fellowship turning on that embracing
pronoun 'our', and the three words defining each other in any order.
That 'Jesus is Lord' seems to have been the earliest form of Christian
Creed.[27] But here at Chalcedon – what defining refinements, refining
definings have supervened! Well might some overhearing Jew remark:

'This was one of our more obstreperous would-be rabbis, a preaching Nazarene!' Or some gravely schooled Muslim disdain such convoluted subtlety when 'God is great' could well suffice!

Yet the very carefulness of all these Chalcedonian clauses should give us pause before we consign them to futility. At least there is precision here – if it is not misplaced. There is evident sincerity, a desire to say with care what one means – always a necessity in meaning it. There is also travail here. For almost every word comprises a debate or undertakes an issue. The whole has ensued from long internal Christian faith-scrutiny in an anxiety to think rightly and to worship truly. Moreover, all relates to the second paragraph of the earlier Creeds. It is because it has to do with the first, with trust in a competent Creator in authentic sovereignty, that it must know – and say – what it thinks could verify such trust. There are deeply religious reasons for Chalcedon's theological temerity – if such we think it. Was it not the will to right thinking about God that taught – or at least encouraged – human mind to think, and trust, far-reaching thoughts?[28]

The counsellors at Chalcedon were aspiring to be definitive about a supreme paradox. Like many philosophies they ended by presenting the basic questions in answers that were in fact only the formulation of them.[29] The divine/human Jesus was 'one and the same' – excluding the view for which the Christ identity was, in effect, neither by not being both. This divine/human harmony impaired neither dimension ('perfect in Godhood, perfect in manhood') and rationally so in soul and body, 'co-essential' according to what God is and what man is.

The 'how' they were ambitious to explain persists in the 'thus' which states the answer. Why, we are right to ask, why not see all as within the *economy* of God, having to do with action and understand that 'economy' as expressing the divine nature? In terms of divine action for humanity we can readily understand (as we have argued throughout) how transcendence must be fulfilled in operative response to human wrong and need, that such response must seek out and stay with the human scene, that – so doing – it must take human shape and belong with human story. Then a human 'how' and 'where' will be entirely reciprocal to a divine 'why' and 'whence'. This is what faith has in the divine Christ and the human-caring Father. Recognising where such a divine economy is evident, we need neither doubt nor worry about the divine nature. For the credentials are ours.

Chalcedon, however, wanted to be sure of that final nexus of economy and nature and to define it lest the nexus be wrongly seen or incongruously said. So Chalcedon went beyond the single word 'person', applied to 'God the Son' and the term 'substance with the Father' with which the earlier Creeds had been content, and – with the term 'two natures' – sought to explore how 'personhood' divine and human should be understood. The impulse to this, in part, came from the concept of *Logos*, eternal, impersonal, sublimely rational, and how *Logos* could be inhering in fallible, particular, time-set human self and mind. Instead of letting that mystery lie implicit in the prerogative of a divine love to act in response to a wayward creation, the Council – against long antecedents of debate and perplexity – aimed to satisfy itself in philosophic formulae.

Christ was to be 'acknowledged in two natures', rather than being loved and trusted in a twin significance. Such 'acknowledgement' safeguarded itself with four exclusions of what would be false concerning these 'two natures' – 'confusion, mutation, division and separation'. Each of these words was directed against actual or potential 'heresy' and had its origin in long contention. They were designed to exclude what the several 'isms' along the way had put in jeopardy. The divine/human was to be known as authentic despite how either might be thought partialised, compromised, impaired or isolated, within the harmony. For better assurance, the final sentence affirmed that while the distinction was complete, 'the property of each nature' concurred in one *hypostasis*, or identity.[30]

It was all a splendid exercise in theological finesse but in statements that still leave the situation open to anyone who wants to go on asking, How? For that question remains present in what purports to have answered it. Does not that situation bring us back to the necessity of 'trust'? Yet not to a trust that has suppressed its own mysteries, but cares to set in writing what it wills to commend, not being a faith with scant concern for obligations in the mind. If, as Job's counsellor had it: 'We are of yesterday . . . because our days on earth are a shadow' (Job 8:9), the effort is noble that cares for a waiting future deserving of a text from the past.

Such Chalcedon achieved though 'of yesterday', a far 'yesterday', their terms archaic and their mind-set their own. The explaining will not suffice us now but the intention was authentic. They were anxious that what faith had in Christ *did* truly reach back into the being of God. For otherwise the pattern of love to which it summoned humanity would remain a precarious and tenuous idea with no sure purchase on reality. No Christ, no God. But, equally, no God, no Christ. Had Jesus as the Christ been essentially some charade, some gnostic 'insight', a private privilege of *gnosis*, a human fake, no genuine wombed, caring, serving, dying, tombed and risen 'man', then faith, in a miserable delusion, had no warrant and no hope. These were the cares of Chalcedon and our present debt.

vii

Debtors we present Christians are but not prisoners to Chalcedon. Our faith now needs to trust an active divine economy as sufficing for confidence in the divine nature. We return from Chalcedon to Gethsemane and to a Christology of action as sufficing for a Christology of nature. So doing, we return to the New Testament where 'God being in Christ' is known and shown in 'reconciling the world'. It is interesting to note that the Creeds and Chalcedonian Christology had no 'doctrine' about such 'reconciliation', no required theology of atonement. Content with the fact of the Cross they left the preaching of it to the Holy Spirit in the mind of the Church. It might have been well to have done the same with the Incarnation had not Gnosticism and other perils needed refutation for there to be any authentic redemption at all.

The Coptic, Ethiopian and some other eastern Christians continued to hold 'one nature' in Christ despite the careful circumspection surrounding how 'the two' were to be understood as inclusively compatible. The desire to think of Christ only 'divinely' could be seen as jeopardising a genuine humanity, though the Monophysites did not mean it that way.[31] The 'without etc.' clauses at Chalcedon ought to have sufficed them. The fact that they did not (apart from non-theological, political factors entailed) demonstrated how abstruse the whole exercise might be thought to have been. All agreed on a veritable Incarnation but the Monophysites wanted to believe it such in terms which the Diophysites – with justification – saw as putting in doubt the 'real' humanity of Jesus or else conceding it in terms that spelled some unreality.[32] For the Churches today the issue is either tacitly ignored or read with tolerance, for controversies can be outlived.

The Creeds and Chalcedon, with later fastidious refinements we need not here discuss, are with us still. We have saluted the good faith of their intention and acknowledged that the explaining folds back on itself. Hence the case for an adjectival theology which sees interaction, necessitated by any time-incidence to be human and by eternal reference to be divine. The infinite Self-finited is the theme of Christian credalising. If we read it as divine/human coinherence, coinciding as initiative/actualisation, have we called in question, perhaps unwittingly, that the Creeds tell of a once-for-all, a one-and-only Incarnation? It might seem that divine/human convergencies are occurring all the time, before and after 'God in Christ' – occurring in the prophets and saints of old, in ministries sacramental and compassionate everywhere. Can the work of the Holy Spirit be other than a continuous story of divine/human coinciding?

It surely is. Indeed, it would be possible to interpret Incarnation wholly in those terms.[33] So doing, however, we would not be superseding, still less suspecting, a single inclusive eventfulness in which the meaning had been for ever realised in what the New Testament called the *pleroma*, the 'fullness', of the divine in the human (Colossians 2:9). It would then be in the power and by the confidence of that event that 'the indwelling Spirit' – 'the Spirit of Christ' – would recruit and enthuse human partners, in poetry, music, teaching, praying, and every other realm of mutual ministry. We do not fully understand the incarnate Word if, knowing it the 'once and for all' that Word was, we miss what was and is everywhere 'the Word's' retinue of discipleship.

Here, in part, is the point of the Creeds' phrase 'the *only* begotten of the Father'. 'Only' equals 'one-ly' (from which it derives). The One-ness of the God-revealing is the One-ness of the God-revealed. The divine Word would not be 'Word' as partial, approximate or less than entire. It is not the 'only' of privation, but of entirety, not the 'only' of counting that got no further than 'one', but of identity with neither addition nor subtraction. It is the very unity of God which requires the singularity of the Incarnation. What is repeatable is the principle it exemplifies for that 'body of Christ' which is the people of faith, its members being 'one of another'.

The credalised truth of 'the one Christ' might point also to how, in fact, there is no other theism that holds, as Christianity does, a unison of power and love, of wisdom and grace, perceived operative in history in terms of crib and Cross, of sovereignty self-given into vicarious suffering. There is in all history only one 'crown of thorns' perceived as congruent with the mastery of the universe, no other confession of faith that moves from 'begotten . . . before all worlds' to 'crucified, dead and buried'. There have been avatars, deifications and apotheoses aplenty but none that were historical – to become credal – like 'the Christ of God'. 'Only' in the Creeds is the right word, alike for the historian as for the theologian.

viii

It is clear, therefore, why in their third paragraph the Creeds go on to affirm faith 'in the Holy Spirit, the Lord, the giver of life, proceeding from the Father and [or through] the Son'.[34] What is distinctive is thereby regenerative. The multiple 'and's which occur throughout the Creeds[35] link the several themes in one around the longer middle paragraph where redemption vindicates creation and is realised in the Church, its 'one baptism', its 'communion',[36] and its eternal hope. But a different term from 'begotten', namely 'proceeding', is used for the reality of the Holy Spirit. As the enterprise in Christ originates in the nature and love of God, so the regime of the Spirit proceeds, emanates, from the reality of the Christ. 'Brooding' over the creation and 'speaking' through the prophets, the Holy Spirit's 'day' climaxes in mediation of the meanings of Christ and in enablement of the people of God in the ministry and emulation of incarnate Word.

Credal confession of the 'proceeding' of the Holy Spirit means a kind of caveat about creeds themselves. For the living *traditio*, or 'handing on' of the faith which it is their function to enable, cannot be fulfilled if, so to speak, it is left perpetually to them. The terms they use, 'substance', 'quick', 'begotten', 'hell', may become misleading through the flux of vocabulary or be misconstrued in a different time. Beyond these verbal mischances there are the subtle disparities of the assumptions from which all reckonings start. 'Proceeding' is therefore the right word to control all 'concluding'. It will always be part of faith's fidelity to want, and to try, to 'say' its credal statements in another way, and do so without loss. For mere recital risks becoming an alibi for genuine thought. Risk will always be involved in thus 'translating' into a different mental 'vernacular' what we hold the Creeds as saying. But without such risk doctrine is only supposedly secure.

One clause where this alertness is mandatory deals with 'the resurrection of the body and the life everlasting.' We noted at an earlier point the credal concern about the term 'flesh' as meant in rebuttal of Gnostic and Docetic strains of 'unreality' which denied any veritable divine 'undertaking' of humanity. There was a consequent temptation to require that 'flesh' participate in 'ascension', if the truth of the sovereignty of the very love that suffered was to be ensured.

Likewise with 'the resurrection of the body'. The truth of sacred personhood, about us all, in which 'body' is mortally the vital locus of our precious individuation, is affirmed in this credal clause. So read, it means no resuscitation of the corpses that have decayed in the earth or been committed to the waves or burned in the fires. It has to do with the spiritual 'on-goingness' of what is most significant about us, in judgement and in grace, of which 'the body' is both crux and symbol. It is 'the body' where deeds are done and love is known and the soul fulfilled in the whole physical 'house of our pilgrimage'. Nowhere is the point more intimate than in the incidence of bereavement. When, in the Beatitudes, Jesus said, 'Blessed are they that mourn,' he did not merely suggest there would be some sort of consolation. He meant that only those who acknowledged the full measure of all mortal demise could learn the blessing of hope.

The discipline of present context must absolve this chapter of default in not being a full historical or analytical study. The aim was the role of the Creeds in their credalising of divine credentials. Beyond their explaining we return in conclusion to what they intended, which was to fulfil an intellectual obligation for the sake of the integrity and the sure perpetuation of 'things most surely believed'. The same sort of necessity lay behind them as the one we noted in respect of the canon of Scripture, namely the responsibility to safeguard a heritage of perceived truth and to define its perception. Their perception was one for which the divine and the human really 'mattered', and the unison was congruent with both. That conviction is the crucial and distinctive Christian understanding. God, seen as *both* transcendent and supremely relative (related), and in no way a sublime 'neutrality'.

The Creeds and Chalcedon enjoy a kind of privileged status, after and within the privileged status of the Scriptures. Yet it is a privileged status which admits of critical reckoning still. It might be thought a punctuation mark in Christian history at which we pause to understand what trust means as response to the trustworthiness of God. With all their anxiety to be right and comprehensive the Creeds repudiate the bland futility that versifies in

> We know Thee not nor guess Thee,
> O vague beyond our dreams.
> We praise Thee not nor bless Thee,
> Dim source of all that seems.
> Unconscious of our witness,
> The music of the heart,

O It beyond all itness –
If ought indeed Thou art.[37]

'A music of the heart' is where we rightly end in any response to credal themes, for that is where they began. Behind the New Testament passages we noted where creed is embryonic were the doxologies that shaped credence into choral music. The last book in the Bible is full of them with their prefatory 'Worthy is . . .' and their celebration of 'the throne of God and of the Lamb' – the summation of all Christian theology, the One both regnant and redemptive. For Creeds are about 'worth' and aim to set down the notation by which it may be sung. The 'and' of that phrase in Revelation is the 'and' that joins the paragraphs of the Creeds.

They are embryonic, too, in the apostolic prayers in the New Testament, notably the two in Ephesians 1:17–23 and 3:14–21. There the writer affirms as he prays. The terms of his pastoral ambition for his people are the strains of the music in his soul. So it must ever be. Even from the formalism and will to precision of the Chalcedonian Fathers we can believe that Jesus himself created the mood and the perceptions by which alone he might be truly understood. If 'the Cross was the coronation ceremony of sorrow',[38] the Creeds were the coronation anthem of the triumphant sorrow of God, of 'God in Christ reconciling the world'. It is in writing the score for an anthem that they have their place and warrant.

Always the Christian prescript around them is, 'Believe and trust,' not one without the other. We do not trust wildly or without things duly credible. But we do not credalise to attain a formula or to solve a mystery. The many conclaves and assemblies that underlie the credal texts had their full share of logic-chopping and sharp debate but they believed 'in the forgiveness of sins'. Community in faith is what they represented. It has to be ours still where 'Love takes the meaning in love's conference.'[39]

9 Hazarded in the Church

i

THERE are several Collects in the English Book of Common Prayer which strike a very apprehensive note about the Church and its faith. It would seem that both are beset by many hazards. Perhaps the language echoes an anxiety for the security of the Elizabethan Settlement and fears of a relapse into the pre-Tudor discords of the Wars of the Roses, or of Spanish Armadas plotting their way shorewards.

> Keep us, we beseech Thee, under the protection of Thy good providence . . . that by Thy mighty aid we may be defended and comforted in all dangers and adversities. . . . Put away from us all hurtful things . . . keep us by Thy help from all things hurtful . . . because it cannot continue in safety without Thy succour, preserve it evermore . . . that through Thy protection it may be free from all adversities.[1]

Being 'peaceably ordered' is the great aspiration: 'keep', 'defend', 'protect', the operative pleas.

'Hazard', then, seems the right word. Being ecclesiastical is being in a hard-hat area. Skulls and limbs alike are vulnerable. 'Hazard' is defined as a risk of loss or harm, a state of jeopardy, where chances are complicated by arbitrary rules, when things are staked and at risk, where bunkers, snares, bad goings abound, where the terrain is unfriendly to the traveller. All the aspects of the word plainly fit the history of the Church and the trust of its Gospel. Our study here has to undertake what the Christian truth has at stake in the Christian institution. We take it here after Scriptures and Creeds, though it was concurrent with, and instrumental to, both of these. There would have been neither text nor canon, neither formula nor fellowship, without the corporate awareness of the churches. In Christianity the primary fact is the fact of

Christ: the two derivative facts, which belong together, are the New Testament writing and the Church. These interdepend. The one is the documentary, the other the institutional, consequence of the reality of Christ.

The only tangible actuality at the end of the Gospel story is a group of men and women. 'They', notes Luke (24:52), 'returned to Jerusalem.' And 'they' were all there was – no structure, no gospels, no hierarchy and no power dimension, political, social or academic. They were neither rabbis nor priests – only fishermen, home-makers, artisans and erstwhile servants of imperial Rome, of largely insignificant Galilean origin, and only months, not decades, with Jesus in their story. Hazardous indeed for all that was to turn on their resources, their perceptions and their tenacity.

Paul, only a few years later (2 Cor. 4:7), caught their situation – and his own – in an intriguing metaphor about earthen pots. 'We have the treasure [of Christ and 'the Gospel of the face"],' he said, 'in earthen vessels, pots of clay, things that may quickly end as broken shards.' His idea has some kinship with provisions in the Pentateuch but his obvious allusion is to apostolic ministries and the minds and bodies of his readers. The sense of incongruity is both painful and exhilarating. As we have seen in Chapter 7, the passage from memory into document that Jesus and his meaning underwent at their hands was precarious indeed. The New Testament is a tribute of risk-taking to a capacity for love and fidelity. So it still remains.

The centuries have given ample evidence of this perception of a hazardous trust. Paul may well have had in mind the perils in which apostolic ventures were caught in his day. He lists them later in the same Epistle (11:23–28). The dangers were less brutal, more subtle, when the faith passed from crippling minority predicaments to imperial recognition and authorised 'establishment'. There is no place here for a bare catalogue of the vagaries, delinquences, crimes and compromises that have attended the long course of Church history, putting its faith in radical doubt and its fellowship into tragic anomaly. Assessment had better go at once to the inveterate temptation of institutionalism itself in every arena, that of religion most of all.[2]

An authentic sense of being 'in trust with' develops into a persuasion about being 'in charge of'. Indeed, the two words often interchange. Every exercise of power is likely to be exercised about its own perpetuation as a corollary of being there at all. Institutions have a chronic instinct of self-importance and can contrive a momentum even when they are most lethargic. Even 'the good philosopher-king' has little reason to doubt himself. It is somehow in the being of authority to keep on being. The phenomenon is most apparent in what has to do with God and faith. It might seem that it is 'the Almighty' who has most at stake in custodians and these, despite the paradox, are well skilled to think it so. Being on behalf of things vital to belief, and – if so – to salvation, is all too liable to develop into institutional prerogative. In the Judaic tradition Yahweh in some sense was believed to have staked His 'Name' in covenant with His people. A genuine Hebraic sense of that inter-society could be perceived as a sort of inter-necessity. This bequeathed to the Christian Church a precedent of 'God and . . .' which could easily degenerate into some structural assumption of monopoly of divine realities or of indispensability to God.

We have, then, the more need to explore the legitimate privilege of the vocation to be 'Church', for only so can we identify what is pretentious and why it must be known so. Sociologists have often distinguished sharply between 'sect' mentality and 'Church' quality. Sects instinctively demand tight allegiance, intense commitment and fastidious rigorism in tenets and identity, whereas the Church-mind may be assumed to 'comprehend' considerable diversity, embrace more varied culture and tolerate interior distances. The distinction is only partly valid. There are churches that behave in highly sectarian ways or, by their vagaries, give internal rise to sect-creation, just as sects can broaden into greater ease with themselves. Either way, these are still the vicissitudes of corporate identities for whom the truth-question is always and necessarily the 'us-question'.

The old biblical Chronicler (2:2.1) has the point exactly and is – we may suspect – oblivious of the irony: 'And Solomon determined to build an house for the name of the Lord, and an house for his kingdom.' There have been such Solomons ever since where temples for God have been also structures of prestige for their patrons. There is shared interest in the architecture, a shared presence in the precincts – precincts that are always more than physical, being a fabric of the sacramental, the doctrinal and the spiritual. Christianity has to be ever vigilant lest *ecclesia discens et docens* become for that very reason *ecclesia deformanda*. Things Christian, like all things human, cannot fail to need form, order, discipline and system – in a word, institution. Yet they can never safely admit that necessity without anxiety.

ii

Let us take the 'us-question' back to what we might discern of the mind of Jesus himself and how, in turn, the first apostles understood their corporate identity. To the question: Did Jesus intend the Church? the honest answer can only be, Yes and No. He certainly could never have intended much that the Church and the churches contrived to become. There can only be an enormous negation from the character, the mind and the personhood of Jesus, for the long and dark centuries of Christian story. The word 'church' (Greek: *ecclesia*) occurs in only one Gospel and there only twice (Matt. 16:18 and 18:17), though it is very frequent in the Epistles. The 16:18 passage in Matthew calls for the perceptive study that can negotiate gently and decisively the portentous controversy that has gathered around it.

Among the many questions there about the stature of Peter, the nature of the 'rock', the meaning of 'the keys' and 'the gates of Hell', we have the basic issue, studied in Chapter 7, concerning how far perspectives at the time of writing affected what was written about the past of origins in Jesus. Clearly the phrase, 'Let him tell it to the Church,' in Matthew 18:17, cannot refer to Christian community which did not then exist. It is surely a rabbinic provision about 'the congregation', the fellowship of the synagogue, adjudicating between members at odds with one another.

Therein lies our clue. Peoplehood deriving from the Christ-event was as essential as peoplehood deriving from Abraham, Sinai and Torah. The central principle of vital community, of inherent solidarity, passed from Moses' folk to Jesus' folk as crucially as it had been originally conceived and experienced – but with one essential difference. It was no longer ethnic, tribal, particularist or exclusive. It was rooted in inclusive grace, received freely by all on the one condition of penitence and faith – a condition inherently open to allcomers, without prior requisites of Hebraic birth and Torah-belonging.

Apart from being explicit in the logic of the Cross itself, there was one essential reason why peoplehood, in church form, was still mandatory and urgent as against some heterogeneous individualism or mere conglomerate. That necessity lay simply in the fact that community in Christ had to symbolise and achieve an evident oneness in which the Jew/'Gentile' distinction was transcended. It could hardly witness to that inclusiveness if it were not, demonstrably, incorporate. The key of peoplehood in the open form was central to the transformation of peoplehood in the private form. In retaining the people theme, the Church moved out of its old form only by retaining the urgent lesson of what that old form had been, as an instrument of divine ends. The Church paid the tribute of debt to its Judaic antecedent in the very act of radically revising it. The supreme task of incorporating 'in Christ' all who willed to come demanded a will to vocational solidarity no less intense than the old. The New Testament is vivid witness to the fervour and travail by which it was attained. The comprehending which faith brought to the Christ-event required the Church comprehensive.

Around the Messianic theme there had always been the idea of the Messianic community. 'Me' and 'us' were in some sense inseparable. His doing would be in his recruiting. His identity must mean identification of his followers, those who would implement what he pioneered, who would be, in Paul's language, 'the fulness of Him who fills' (Ephesians 1:25; 3:19).[3] The more inclusive his 'event' was perceived to be – as the Church certainly perceived it – the more crucial the communalising of its recognition so that 'Messiah and Messiah-ed people' could be truly mutual. If we understand Jesus in the terms studied in Chapters 5 and 6, there can be no doubt or question about whether he 'intended the Church'.

It is in this context that we must appreciate Matthew 16:13–23. There could surely be no individuated 'I' for Peter alone to override this necessarily corporate nature of Messiah's community. Interpretation has to reckon all the time (as noted in Chapter 7) with how far what the text says was sifted through the circumstances in which the writing, editing, construing church was placed by the lapse of time. The rocky contour of the location near Caesarea Philippi could readily have prompted Jesus' 'rock' analogy. It is clear from the sequel that Peter was very fallible, not to say confused, in his very confession. Neither he nor his notions were in any way rock-like! There might, indeed, be a strong irony in the whole exchange. If so, that would certainly be in line with the long fate of the passage.

Personal monopolies of truth or its custody, of grace and its benefits, are surely excluded in the economy of the Holy Spirit. If, by 'apostolic' we mean 'disciples contemporary to Jesus', that status is by definition not bequeathable. But, if the text and an intention of Jesus behind it cannot relate to Peter as a sole agent, it cannot well relate either to a bare formula, a statement in the abstract. Nothing Messianic could conceivably be that way, shorn of all zeal, commitment and the passion of love or, indeed, of still blundering search.

It must follow that the 'building of Christ's Church' is posited on a confessed Messiahship entailing by its very nature a responding and responsible community.[4] The meaning, then, is not in Simon 'pet-erised', nor in a *credo* without a *credens*, but in 'faith' in its double sense of the old *teneo et teneor*, 'I hold and I am held' – a perception that must be always singular in each and plural in the whole. As the dramatic response to Jesus' testing of his disciples' corporate mind ('whom say *ye* . . .', plural) it could be saluted in prophetic words, then quickly disabused of all that was fondly superficial about the quality of its perception.

iii

What has been derived, surely perversely, from Matthew 16 and 'the keys' is index enough to our common need to be alert always to the dangers of any institutionalised 'we' and 'us' in the things of faith. The need was urgent in Chapters 1 and 3 above as well as here. Accordingly, we may find point in reversing what, according to Luke 22:28, Jesus said to his disciples: 'You have companied with me in my temptations', and think him assuring us that he is with us in ours. The Greek *peirasmos*, 'time of trial', serves for things both testing and taxing. How, by the Holy Spirit, we might understand Christ being 'with us in the Church's testings and trials', outward and inward, will take us through this chapter and the two to follow.

We might well comprise these testing hazards under three heads: the proving of ministry, the care of the sacramental and the ethics of the holy. Ecclesiastical 'tribulation' is this threefold thing.[5] However, a few general considerations will be in order first. if, in all three, we are arguing that a requisite may become a perquisite,[6] it will be right to note that some aspects of the possessiveness in custodians are legitimate. If, as earlier emphasised, churches are embracing genuine cultural and ethnic diversity it must follow that variety truly belongs with them. Geography, language, history, will all sanction, indeed require, plurality of expression and criteria of loyalty. True unity is never monolithic, as true community is never wilfully centrifugal, however – thanks to culture – the 'centre' may be far to seek. It is when 'my-doxy' and 'thy-doxy'[7] transgress against 'unity of spirit in the bond of peace' that culture and tribal identity pervert faith in the interests of controversy. That cultural factors have abetted doctrinal issues cannot be denied. There has always to be a perceptive discipline about seeing Christ *and* ourselves in the bifocals of the mind – a discipline more often forfeited than fulfilled.

It must follow that all 'privacy of interpretation'[8] is suspect since 'a solitary Christian' is a contradiction in terms. The problem comes when, as it were, concentrations of 'privacy' become vast, perpetuated, prestigious, 'public' establishments, denominations and institutions with their respective canons of 'faith and order', devotion and authority. The will to ecumenism may have gone far this century to temper the conflicts around ministry, baptism, liberty, loyalty and validity, but – being on behalf of truth – ecumenical intent can never be an end in itself. For that very reason, it is well to have a mind like Richard Baxter's, to know that 'self is the greatest enemy to Catholicism', and to 'acquaint ourselves with healing truths':

> Every known truth befriendeth others and like fire tendeth to the spreading of our knowledge to all neighbour-truths. . . . Be sure that you see the true state of the controversy. . . . Bear with those that Christ will bear with: especially learn the master-duty of self-denial.[9]

In being ecumenically minded there is no proper escape from being truth-liable. Conversely, there is no responsibility to truth that can properly evade the onus of relationships. The very word 'catholic' denotes wholeness not only of doctrine but of fellowship. It is odd that it should be thought to need any qualifying adjective, whether 'Roman,' or 'Anglo' or other.

All praise of Christian ecumenism has, therefore, to be honest with history. It cannot mean that the past is undone or that pivotal events – 'protest', 'reformation', 'renewal' – have to be repudiated or deplored. Time is perpetual flux and only the current generation is currently served.[10] What had a past legitimacy will not argue a perpetuated necessity, the less so if it has done its work well. The bare concept of 'loyalty to loyalty' that earlier had to be radically confronted cannot well become the watchword of the challenge once made to it. If we want to think the Church *semper reformanda* it can only be as *semper informanda*.[11]

iv

To any such *informanda* the gift of ordained ministry has always been seen as crucial, though with conflicting estimates of how 'ordering' bears on the doctrines in trust. For reasons which will appear, the conviction here is that 'matters of order' cannot well be equated with 'matters of faith', only the inner integrity of ministry can. Indeed, the proving of ministry means two integrities in one – the integrity of the faith itself and the integrity of the faithfulness that serves it. The two are brought together in a significant exchange Paul had with his Corinthians (2 Cor. 1:15–24). Ill will on the part of some prompted them to call in question his entire good faith. It had initially to do with a minor matter, his failure to fulfil a promised visit at the time intended. Ignoring all the vagaries of travel in their world of chance ships and brigand-haunted roads, they magnified this circumstance into total distrust in his character.

Instead of giving them 'a piece of his mind' (as those are minded to do who have little mental to afford) he lifted the whole issue into the integrity of God. He grounded his own vindication and that of his companions, Silvanus and Timothy, in the fidelity of God manifest and pledged as such in the Gospel he preached. It was not possible, he argued, for them to be equivocators, 'Yes and No men', when they were servants of a Gospel about which there was no divine equivocation. Their word would be as dependable as the promises of God.

The whole passage is a classic example of how to turn idle or malicious polemic into authentic witness and so redeem controversy. But more – it locates the truth of faithful ministry within the trust of the faithful Word.

> Unfaith in aught
> Is want of faith in all.
> It is the little rift within the lute
> Which bye and bye will make the music mute
> And, ever widening, slowly silence all.

What ministers in Christian servanthood has to reciprocate what 'means' in Christian doctrine. This is not to say that unworthiness in ministries will alter the fidelities of the Gospel: it is to say that the Gospel itself will incriminate them. It is important for all religions to have built-in repudiation of inward treasons. It is the Cross of Jesus which has this role in Christianity. New Testament perceptions of ministry never lose sight of it.

Travel plans going awry in 2 Corinthians were one thing. The grounds on which contemporary assessors have to suspect what Christians are and say are deeper far. They dwarf the merely circumstantial things from which Paul's factious Corinthians began their questionings. Nor will they allow such ready alibis as Paul's journeys could provide. Corinth, however, being a major port, the ships frequent in Paul's odyssey may afford analogy for these larger hazards. Shylock, shrewdly calculating sea-going Antonio and his bond in The Merchant of Venice, puts the analogy well:

My meaning in saying he is a good man is to have you understand

that he is sufficient. . . . But ships are but boards, sailors but men.
There be land rats and water rats, water thieves and land thieves . . .
and then there is the peril of waters, winds and rocks. The man is,
notwithstanding, sufficient.[12]

'Sufficient' is an adjective much beloved by the apostles and by the
Church of England.[13] We have seen from the Collects how aware it is of
the 'perils'.

One peril – liable to put the trust at risk – is in reading, or misreading,
the origins of Christian ministry. 'I magnify my office,' says Paul in
Romans 11:13. The sentiment was, and is, legitimate. In context he is
alert to how some thought he lacked the prerequisite of 'office' in not
having physically companied with Jesus.[14] He is also insisting on his
vocation to 'the Gentiles'. There has, however, been much 'magnifying
of office' which has overplayed its hand in interpretation of the warrant
history gives it. It is not honestly possible to be categorical about the
authority for ministry, for its Orders and precedents, derivable from
the New Testament, beyond the propriety and necessity of ministry
itself. More decisive formulations have to invoke accumulating Tradition – which is then to raise the large question of the interrelation of
Scriptures and Tradition, the nature and legitimacy of 'development'.
Here issues of scholarship and theology merge together and take the
risks their cargoes undergo. For it is easy, under pressure of things
critical, to claim more for the warrant of office than the evidence allows.

The historic Orders of 'Bishops, Priests and Deacons' can properly
enjoy scriptural sanction. 'Priest', from the Greek *presbuteros* meaning
simply 'elder', is generational, like everything in time, and indicates a
degree of time-vested seniority and, thereby, responsibility for leadership. Within the New Testament it has nothing in it of the sacerdotal.[15]
The other two terms, deriving – with strange anglicising fortunes – from
episcopos and *diakonos* have to do with 'oversight' and 'service'. Both were
practical functions in the community. According to Acts 6:1–7, the
appointment of the first 'deacons, by the laying on of hands', was
explicitly to free the apostles for their prior duties in preaching. The
appointment of *episcopoi* became apostolic practice in the context of
widening mission and the multiplying of local churches. In New Testament context these 'overseers' are not distinguishable from *presbuteroi*.

There is more evidence of their necessity than of their distinctive
status in the Epistles. One ready case in point is the intriguing reference
in 3 John 6 – as incidental as the Letter is obscure – about 'speeding
Christians on their journey worthily of God'. Hospitality, expected and
forthcoming for 'believers', required letters of attestation in a setting of
danger and 'spies'. Such letters were obvious occasion for 'oversight',
indicative of much else in a growingly self-aware identity, rawly treated
by the outer world and often rawly fresh from pagan practices.

To realise the soberly practical origins of all three Christian 'offices'
is not to overlook 'the breaking of bread' and the patterns of baptism,
or aspects of emerging liturgy in the life of the congregations. Ready to

hand was the heritage of things Judaic, the lections of the synagogue and the love of the psalms. Some New Testament Letters, like those to Corinth, indicate spontaneous individual participation in these offices in the congregations. Others suggest a recognition of leading roles. It would be natural to think of these as aligning with the practical functions that gave prominence to persons of weight and esteem. No doubt the process happened in the other direction, as and when liturgical roles gave rise to administrative ones.

What is clear and beyond dispute – deferring to a later context the 'priesting' of the 'presbyters' in sacramental sense outside the New Testament – is that the 'priestly' there is wholly the pastoral ministry of preaching. In Romans 15:16 Paul sets 'ministering the Word' squarely in the realm of what his 'priesthood' constitutes. He describes his vocation as 'grace given to be a liturgist of Christ Jesus among the nations in the priestly task of the Gospel of God, so that the oblation of the nations should be acceptable, being consecrated by the Holy Spirit.' The whole passage has to do with preaching yet all the terms are sacramental, full of the aura of 'sacrifice', levitical propriety and 'making holy'. Thus he joins in one the two themes which Church usage, and Church architecture, have so long put asunder since his day. It is only in this amalgam of pastoral 'ministry of the Word' that the New Testament hints at the later sense of 'priesthood', but it does not confine it to *presbuteroi*, nor had that Greek word yet acquired the flavour that was to possess it from the different aura of the *hiereus*, a quite different Greek usage.

Brooding over all was the esteem of the apostles – a rank to which Paul laid vital claim on grounds unique to himself – thanks to the Damascus vision. Barnabas, it is true, and others outside the charmed circle of the twelve disciples, shared the title. If, however, we can argue from Luke's narrative of the deliberate filling, by choice of Matthias, of the place left vacant by Judas Iscariot, it must be assumed that the category of having been recruited *ab initio* by Jesus was a crucial distinction and dignity. 'The twelve' had precedent in 'the twelve tribes' of Israel. To them, as Matthew 5:1 signifies, Jesus entrusted his 'Sermon on the Mount'. As 'apostolic persons' their leadership, authority and precedence were obviously central but, by the same token, also irreplaceable. The sheer lapse of time, not to say also the widespreading of community, made apostolicity, as a one-generation reality, unique. The continuity of the term would have to belong with a continuity of doctrine and a perpetuation of fellowship (cf. Acts 2:42).

The terms in which such faith-fellowship perpetuation of apostolic mission and ministry could take institutional form via ordination, and what such 'laying on of hands' might in fact confer, have long been at issue in Church history. Our concern here with 'the proving of ministry' is surely obliged to set apostolic credentials primarily in the loyalties of faith, in other words, in a discernible apostolicity of mind and spirit. To be sure, credentials in those terms may be subject to question, even to ambivalence and uncertainty, as and when claimants to them differ and dispute. But we have ceased to believe in the reality of the Holy Spirit if we yearn to foreclose that situation or obviate that fear of disparity by some invocation of institutionalised guarantee. For any such yearning will violate the freedom of the Spirit. Furthermore, the authenticity of that which supposedly ensures the apostolicity will itself be always subject to contention.

This is not to disparage, nor in any way to disavow, the place that concern for means and symbols of apostolic quality must have. (They will better come below in passing from 'Word' to 'sacrament'.) It is, however, to insist that such means and symbols can only rightly avail to true ends when they underwrite, and undergird, the apostolic truth of 'God in Christ' and an entire personal consecration of heart and mind in an apostolic emulation of the quality from which all things began.

The credentials in faith-terms of the truth of 'God in Christ' have been studied in Chapters 5, 6 and 7, with the creed-problematics noted in Chapter 8. Those credentials in serving terms demand the kind of 'priesthood' of the self, of mind and spirit in unambiguous discipleship, which might hope to experience what moved the first apostles when they graduated from their Galilean discipleship into the vocation of a world faith. A writer early this twentieth century has the theme in fervent apostolic clarity:

> The *verbal* identity of 'priest' with 'presbyter' has its own significant suggestiveness. . . . True priesthood requires the dedication of the inward life to Godward. . . . The more complex and responsible the work the more inclusive it is of the whole life and character and the less can it be defined by its outward operations. . . . True priesthood is pastorate and true pastorate based in priestliness.[16]

Only so will the thing said and the life lived corroborate each other in 'the proving of ministry'. If 'the Word' is 'to dwell in us richly' (Col. 3:16), it must speak as a unity of doctrine and communal life captured, as Paul says in the same passage, in the arts of Christian praise and mutual society. It is all these that ministerial Orders have to serve and quicken and sustain. All that is comprised in the ancient ritual of 'laying on of hands' – whether of continuity, authority, apostolicity or enablement – is only fully perceived if 'the hands' are known as those of the wounded Christ. Ministry of the Word only has its Easter confidence out of its Gethsemane experience. It is enough for disciples that they be as their Lord.

V

In moving, as earlier proposed, from 'the proving of the ministry' to 'the care of the sacramental', it becomes clear that in one sense we do not move at all. The two are one. They should never be sundered. The ministry of the Word is a sacrament of language and personality. It is a pastoral exercise of mind to mind bearing on will from will. In every way it is deeply priestly in its intention towards the conviction of truth, the retrieval of error, the deliverance from wrong, the hallowing of society through transformed personhood. In all these terms it is the heart of Christian oblation, the offering of a ready mind, a consecrated self and an intention of love. One cannot care for meaning and its bearing on the past and present of both persons and community and not be engaged in transactions that represent God to humanity and present humanity to God. There has to be an altar in the heart of every preacher, in every pastoral care. 'The shepherd' and 'the table', according to Psalm 23, are one theme.

This all-pervading priesthood has found its most assured symbol and fulfilment in the Christian Eucharist. It is precisely here that those 'perils of waters, winds and rocks' have been sadly evident in the aberrations of pretension or perquisite which have befallen the sanctuary of 'holy mysteries' known in 'bread and wine'. The authenticity of sacramental meanings and devotion is not in question, only their capacity to be perverted or misconstrued. Here the very criteria are at issue. The yearning for that which somehow 'evidentialises' divine things (if the word is permissible) is for many almost overwhelming. So much is clear from the long centuries of Church history. The tactile, the tangible, the palpable, around 'this is my body', 'this is my blood', have, for many minds and pieties, been indispensable to conscious faith, and their appeal irresistible. Yet, measured by the simplicities of Jesus' original institution in 'the upper room' where all began, that yearning and appeal have been fraught with the tragic menace of superstition and the danger of 'canalising' grace as some prerogative of ecclesiastical power. The Christian task has always been to bring and hold into one discipline the devotion that properly attends on outward senses and the perceptions that alone are spiritual. The sacramental dimension in Christianity is where, at one and the same place, we are most wonderfully authentic and the most desperately at risk.

Few can doubt that 'High Mass' must seem very far removed from what Jesus intended and enacted 'the same night in which he was betrayed', assuming we can be finally certain about the significance there and then. It is, in fact, only Paul in 1 Corinthians 11:25 and 26 who records the command to repeat the rite. Luke's account (22:19) has the clause 'in remembrance of me' but without Paul's addition of 'as oft as you drink . . .'. Mark (14:22f.) and Matthew (26:26f) omit both and even suggest that the next occasion will only be 'in the Father's kingdom'. By the time of the Fourth Gospel, it is clear from its Chapter 6 that the ordinance has assumed greater subtlety as a liturgy both of participation and of incorporation in Christian society.

There has to be around Holy Communion the same questing as to Jesus' intention as we noted earlier in respect of the will in him for the Church. There are perhaps two salient clues. The one is the context of the Passover meal, however we discern the detail of that incidence. The second is the significance of the initial concept of 'remembrance'. The two can illuminate each other.

'Breaking bread' and 'pouring wine', his words were: 'Do this.' So familiar has the Liturgy become that we are rarely minded to question the choice. Earlier it was asked: If Jesus were pre-eminently, and essentially, 'teacher', should we not have anticipated some ceremonial lection from the Sermon on the Mount, or recital of some characteristic parable? It would have been surely suitable to have 'done *that* in remembrance of him'. Such recalling would have suited Socrates or Demosthenes or Confucius. Qur'ānic recital was the very core of Muhammad's mission and is still known as *dhikr*, or 'reminding'. Jesus ordained otherwise. In the aura of the liberation of the Exodus, he centred remembrance on his imminent suffering.

Yet, in terms either of memorable teaching or of travail in death (without isolating either from the other), was he ever forgettable? It was right earlier to put to ourselves the urgent question whether *anything* was necessary by way of 'remembrance'. In retrospect or in sequel, could he ever be out of mind, the disciples (for whom any 'rite' was first meant) having companied him through all until their final abandonment? To *habitués* of frequent, perhaps daily, Eucharist, the questions may seem almost irreverent. Yet there is much relevance every way in pressing them.

For if, with his unforget-able-ness in mind – and the meaning of his resurrection – what he ordained in the upper room can have nothing to do with some concern about oblivion. It was not about that sort of 'remembrance', struggling to keep alive what, otherwise, had no claim on memory. 'The bread and wine' were never about *whether* he would be 'remembered'. They had to do with *how*. They meant, and mean, not the mere fact but the manner of recall. They focused on his passion and they required participation. 'Take this and make it your own.' The ear-reception of wise words can lead to admiration, even warm applause. But Jesus did not come to be admired. 'Never man spake like this man' can be said by the uncommitted. The heart-reception of 'bread and wine' must lead – on the food analogy of faith – to total discipleship. It is in the nature of the sacrament that it must internalise its meaning in the mind and will.

That is why it may never properly be reduced to a spectacle, an object of veneration as some external icon of the eye. The rite in the upper room was incorporating the disciples into the meaning which would await them on the farther side of the Cross. How else could they have been retrieved from their abject failure on the eve of it? He would 'be known to them in the breaking of the bread' – as Luke's story has it at Emmaus – with a vividness that surpassed even his 'opening of the Scriptures' by the immediacy of a shared communion. Given the inclusive truth of 'the Word made flesh' in incarnation, 'the Word' is made experience in 'bread and wine' partaken at his hands. The divine hospitality to humankind which creation enshrines, bearing 'the marks of the nails' from human history, comes intimately to each and all in the sacred emblems of our creaturehood, our guilt and our redemption.

vi

These dimensions must never be lost to sight nor should they ever fail to discipline the situation when – as happened by the late second Christian century – the administration of 'these holy mysteries of bread and wine' passed exclusively to the hands of *presbuteroi* and *episcopoi*, now coming to be seen in hieratic and separate responsibility with the sacramental means and meanings. There are evidences already in the late first century of the leadership and administrative roles undertaking also a presidential role in 'divine liturgy'.[17] In many ways it was a natural and entirely legitimate development. Does not the very term 'liturgy', as we have seen, like the later English usage 'service', properly cover sermon, street, soul and sanctuary alike – and equally? The history need not detain us here, nor the salient part in it of such figures as Cyprian.[18] It is rather the theology with which we have to deal as, urgently, a 'hazard' of our very life in Christ. When *presbuteros* has become in effect *hiereus* in the sense of being indispensable to the rite of 'holy communion', seeing that the consecration of the sacred elements is now uniquely his, vigilance is imperative. For lack of it, and of the due perceptions which attend it, we may so readily fall back into something like the old hieratic scene deriving from Leviticus and the Temple – the scene for ever made obsolete by 'the finished work of Christ'.

The Letter to the Hebrews is occupied with a careful and sustained exposition of the Christian contrast from the incessantly – and necessarily – repetitious 'sacrifices' of the old order. They were artificial, contrived, schematic, ritualistic and credulous – the last in the sense that they could only 'hold' as long as priests and people alike 'credited' their being there with divine sanction and ceremonial order. They had about them nothing of the inherent relation to human wrong which – as studied in Chapter 5 – belonged to the actuality of Jesus' Cross, to his bearing of human evil concentrated there and the forgivingness in which he did so. These were no idle form or formula. They involved no bloody animal immolation but transacted veritable historical issues central to realities both divine and human. For 'the blood of his sacrifice was his own' (Hebrews 9:12).

It therefore becomes a tragic aberration if Christian Eucharist is ritualised into anything resembling the old order in which somehow divine anger is arbitrarily placated, with the emblems of the redeeming Christ reconstituting what that old order incongruously thought to find in daily animal holocaust where altars dripped with blood and the floor was strewn with ashes. In those terms Eucharist would find no warrant from the ever heroic, ever love-luminous Cross, nor yet from the risenness of Christ present with his people in the fellowship of 'bread and wine'. Nor could any 'presidency' around those sacramental gifts rightly be thought, or known, or used, as a purveyance.[19]

The historical and spiritual reality of the Cross should serve us – and indeed suffice us – to identify and resist two tendencies of the religious mind that are evident in the story of the Church. The one is deep in the psyche, the other is at the heart of theology. Let us take them in turn.

In earlier chapters we have noted the demand for guaranteed certitude in the things of faith – the kind of absolute surety that is not sanely to be had, or spiritually appropriate, ultimate wonder and mystery being as they are. Yet the urge for it persists, even grows at any suggestion of the lack of it. The lust for the immaculate, the infallible, the indubitable, the precise, is all too often unready to give way to the right spiritual and intellectual quality of trust and good faith. As with love, so with truth: pledges are reciprocal to honest belief and meaning to responsible perception. The whole art of Christian faith is to 'know *whom* one has believed' and such believing neither seeks nor gets any 'guarantee' that is extraneous to what either confides to the other. We have seen this situation in the previous chapter around the nature and significance of Creeds.

It belongs no less with the relevance of sacraments. For here also there is the instinct to think, and want, grace canalised, to be able to demand what the Latin phrase *ex opere operato* captures, namely a rite which, by an automatic process, does what it symbolises. This instinct in the religious mind may conspire with the perception of the officiant. Indeed, the two may belong together. The concern for what is sought in the bestowal is mutual with the role fulfilled in the bestowing. Grace then has its rite as a vehicle and both have their priestly auspices. What we have earlier called the food analogy of faith then has an almost literal connotation, especially when greeted with the words, from a very different context in the Gospel: 'I am not worthy that thou shouldst come under my roof' (Matt. 8:8). As with metaphor, so with sacrament – the nature is distorted if taken with crude literalism. True sacraments are never magical or automatic.

Where clear and unequivocal differentiation from the magical is not made, and made steadily, all the dangers of the institutional temper come all too gladly into play. The 'president-priest' at Eucharist is then in danger of becoming a perquisite-holder, administering that which is vital in the receiving yet operative only in and by the 'office'. The sanctuary is then liable to be likened to a kind of divine dispensary where 'vehicles' of grace – rather than the humbler 'means of grace' – are transmitted from the right auspices to the dependent recipients.

We have to be patient and vigilant in how we see the sacramental situation. It is not that there is no 'real presence' of the Lord or that 'bread and wine' have no more than a token significance or that no ordered auspices could be consonant with the mind of Christ. The reality is all these within a total significance where perquisites and purveyancing cannot belong. It is clear from the very attractiveness to some of the wrong perceptions, that order and symbol, rite and ritual, ceremonial and 'offices' around it, not only hold great fascination but play a legitimate role in the imagination. It is not the fact, but the temptations, of the institutional that are at issue. The original meaning in the upper room, in immediate anticipation of Gethsemane and beyond, can truly obtain in the Christian sanctuary that now possesses an ordered ministry, an alert liturgy and a perceptive faithful. 'The mind of Christ' in his 'taking bread and wine' is perpetuated in a discipleship which recapitulates his own ordinance, in the larger context supervening on those origins, via the trust of faith, the experience of community and the patterns of his apostles. In all these visible tokens, ordered ministry and sacramental expressiveness have their vital place, but only in being consonant with how truth and grace were by him once and for all achieved and defined.

Their being so consonant takes us to the second of our two themes, the one that goes to the heart of theology. The difference between the actuality of the Cross and the contrived sacrificial ritual of the Temple already stressed is pattern to another radical contrast between the two realms. This contrast has to do with the very nature of God. Ritual Hebraic sacrifice meant a placating of Yahweh and expiation for wrongs and sins by which He had been offended. It may well be that early forms of Semitic sacrifice expressed a will to fellowship, a sort of sacred meal in which God might be in some sense a guest, or 'smell a sweet savour' and relent, or be lenient or forego offence. But, in broad terms, the full Temple ritual had to do with 'sin-offering', with symbolic guilt-shedding on to animals slain in expiation or driven into the wilderness. 'Atonement' signified a very necessary, if ritual, 'making things good again' with God.

The Cross was none of these. It was not 'a ritual offering' in any sense. It was history, life, event, and realism. Nor may Christian theology see it as in any way 'external' to the divine heart or placatory of the divine mind. On the contrary, faith sees it as reality within the divine being in that 'God was *in* Christ reconciling the world.' The meaning has been fully told in Chapter 5. Part of the very nature of Jesus' 'sonship' is that when we hear him praying, 'Father, forgive . . .', we should understand it as like a soliloquy in the self of God. Its being said, in the there-and-then, is because it is – and it has to be – 'history', if we were ever to know things so. Therefore, the dying of Jesus is not some device, some subterfuge, some formal requisite, extraneously to bring about some divine pardon not already explicit in the divine intention, and not already implicit in the very way that Jesus suffered. The Cross is what happens in a world like ours to a love like God's.

As with the father in the story Jesus told of a returning penitent from his 'far country', forgivingness is present *ab initio* in the father's heart but only through the pain and shame the wanderer's enmity inflicts. Only the repentance is necessary: the price of redeeming is being paid in and by the father's unchanging will to be the father despite all that it costs him being so. Such is the way it is with God, and the Cross of Jesus is where we see and know it so. Gethsemane is integral to the divine nature having created and willed us humans into being. To think the Cross of Jesus external to God is to deny it the meaning by which only we know and understand it.

A right theology of the Eucharist cannot then derive from a wrong reading of the Cross. If God is not 'being placated' by the Cross He is not being placated at the Eucharist. The Cross throughout the New Testament is seen as Jesus' 'obedience'. Reciprocal to all obedience is the will that has it, one with the will that brings it. Thus it follows that what is, by divine *kenosis*, abidingly within the being of God needs no 'presentation' before Him in any 'foreign' sense. Some Eucharistic practice has often seemed to imply the contrary. The meaning of the Ascension is that the divine reality in the Cross is eternally 'second nature' (indeed primary nature) in God. The throne is 'the throne of God and of the Lamb'. Jesus' enthronement is 'the throne of grace' already, not a throne of dubious persuadability into compassion. The language of pleading is inappropriate, given the exalted Lord Christ.

There is, to be sure, a 'presentation' but of that which is already 'present'. Ours it is in Holy Communion to 'present' all that we have in Christ as the ground and shape of our own surrender. We do not re-enact that which happened 'once for all', but nor do we merely recollect a pure past. Christian *anamnesis*, or 'remembrance', is living again that 'same night in which he was betrayed', so that we take again to ourselves its achieved redemption and 'represent' to the world its nature and its cost. 'Bread and wine' are then no mere memorial emblems but the intimations of a drama through which we live again, and the elements of a communion in which, by incorporation, we belong in Christ with one another. Intimation and invitation together demand the consecration of the selves we bring.

To find and know it so is to know, for the perversities they are, the institutional temptations. Beware of a Church that thinks itself in charge of grace. Ministry can only think itself in trust. There is an old distinction between the *esse* and the *bene esse* of the Church. Oddly, the distinction almost invariably is held to refer to Orders and ministry, rather than to doctrines about God and Christ. On the one view, criteria of office and ministry have to be validly defined and implemented for there to be any 'Church' at all. On the other view, the agreed criteria spell the well-being of the Church, that is, they constitute the desirable, but not the exclusive, condition of its churchness. Concerned, as we are here, with hazards, we need not take up all the ecumenical issues that turn on the *bene esse*, leaving the *esse* view to be adamant about its own variant of what is essential. An ironist might wonder how 'the fellowship of the love of God' could want, or make, the distinction anyway and apply it in terms that have to do with structure, power and prestige. *Cum privilegio* used to be printed, for good reason, in English bibles to indicate that publishers had legal warrant. There is indeed a *Cum privilegio* in the very being of the Church and of its ministry in Word and sacrament. Hazard comes in knowing of what sort it is.

Reflecting on that conclusion suggests one briefer note. So much of what is at stake in the foregoing about apostolicity, ministerial orders, the authority of sacraments and the mutual relations of liturgy and life, hinges on the loci of authority in Scripture and developed tradition. There can be no complete excluding of the latter. For the viability of biblical Scripture, and its exegesis, depend upon it. The New Testament itself was formulated within an on-going tradition without which, as we saw in Chapter 7, it could not exist. Should we, then, absolutise it in canonical form so that no development of faith or structure shall accrue beyond it? Post-canonical 'development' is with us and that crucially.[20] But, conceding legitimate 'development', can we give it absolute warrant, so that whatever 'Mother Church' comes to pronounce *de fide* is indeed such?[21] So to conclude, apart from leading us far from the moorings of real history, would be manifestly invalid, enshrining as it would a sort of fideism, for which 'believing made it so'.

If we can neither absolutise *sola scriptura*, nor admit any absolute licence to develop, the Church is thrown back on trust in the Holy Spirit, in the context of scriptural primacy and with a reverent liability to think and live in a trust of faith and structure that is dynamic and creatively responsible. Hazards there will always be, but in that temper the Collects with which we began – most urgent in this very field – will have their answer.

vii

The third duty of this chapter, after the proving of ministry and the care of the sacramental, has to do with 'the ethics of the holy'. This is the final dimension of the other two. In all three Semitic faiths there has ever been, and there still remains, a tension between the ethical and the holy. The holy, of course, should be the setting and the spur of the ethical. Rituals should make for righteousness. 'Do justly, love mercy and walk humbly with your God,' said Micah (6:8) in that order. But how were these virtues of the prophets evident in Joshua's 'holy' mandate to conquer the land and slay its population? Then there was neither justice nor mercy nor humility. There are features of contemporary Zionism which see possessing of land and disposessing of people mandatory in 'the name of the holy'. Yet the land also is meant for due hallowing and its possession presupposes a 'holy people'.

'The holy', to be sure, is much more than the 'emotion' that, as was said, might 'tinge morality'. It has to do with awe, wonder, mystery and love, such as no mere ethicism can command. Yet all too often the holy (recalling the point in Chapter 3), far from kindling ethical right and motivating truth, obscures and impedes them, competes for itself at their expense. If we paraphrase Matthew 5:23f. we 'bring our gift to the altar' and, lost in the mystique, ignore what our 'brother has against us', and 'go our way' fortified in our negligence and hardened in our self-esteem.

Muslims have condoned the belligerence and violence of political forms of *Jihad* by arguing 'the greater *Jihad*' of personal ethics and social morality. But the distinction, as necessary to make, confirms a 'holy *Jihad*', albeit 'lesser', that makes 'unbelievers' due prey. 'The holy' is not then tributary to the ethical. Christian history has many dark examples of immoral invoking of 'the name of God' in the pursuit of crimes unspeakable. What did the Fourth Crusade do to Constantinople or the conquistadores to the Amerindians? There was from the outset, something discernibly and deliberately unworthy about the election 'ethics' of Richard Nixon, so that what finally culminated was no aberration but the cumulative evidence of what was always there. Yet his presidency enjoyed the sustained attentions of America's most renowned Christian evangelist. Why was 'the holy' so available for the unethical? Do we not hear the saintly John Keble, in the Assize Sermon of 1833 (often taken as inaugurating the Tractarian Movement), sounding strange strains about violation of 'the holy' in the 'secularising' of the iniquitously oppressive Irish bishoprics by a newly reformed House of Commons? He seems not to have seen the ethical legitimacy in Ireland in caring so dearly for the 'rights of God' in the status of the Church of England. Newman, some years later, was to coin the term 'illative', to denote a theological capacity to draw inference from premises. All intellectualism does so. If the premise is 'the holy', let the inference be ethical. Only when the premise is ethical can the inference well be holy.

The tension between them has ever been the hazard of being Christian and of a Church. The reasons are not far to seek. The people of Hebraic covenant knew them well enough and they of 'new covenant' no less. Being designedly 'on behalf of God' – by divine design – may be thought to legitimate whatever such status is perceived to mean and to leave the criteria wholly to inward reckoning. Then comes the illusion that God is committed to them in terms that make them somehow the regents of His will. The truth must be that all proprietors of 'the holy' can truly be only servants of that which for ever transcends them. Some aspects of 'ethical holiness' and 'holy ethics' in living terms will concern the arguments in Chapter 11 about the many 'counts' on which Christian faith is discounted.

viii

There remains one final significance to all that is hazarded in the Church. It lies simply in the fact that things Christian should be this way at all. Muslims think that Allah has cared for revelation, law and society far more tidily and securely in the patterns of the Qur'ān and Islam. Judaism seems capable of a sublime assurance in peoplehood to God about which – anti-Semitism apart – there need be no misgivings as to its authenticity as a datum beyond doubt.

In the Christian situation there seems to be a sort of divine readiness for greater risk, for a Scripture that waits on a perceptive integrity, for a structure of ministry so liable to be misconstrued by its very custodians, and for a vision of God itself so divinely vulnerable not merely to doubt but also to unworthy trust – the unworthiness known such from the very magnanimity it handles.

So indeed it is. There is, parallel to the deep *kenosis* of the Incarnation and the Cross, of 'God in Christ', a *kenosis* of the Holy Spirit, bearing patiently with the vagaries, the ill usings, of unfaithful faithful, of disloyal loyalists. 'Grieve not the Holy Spirit of God' (Eph. 4:30) is no idle warning. There are those whom the Holy Spirit 'makes friends of God and prophets' who delight in the heavenly wisdom. But there are many more whose responses are dull and their wills sluggish and, as we have seen, there are in 'holy office' perils in many waters, the 'loss-makers' of the kingdom. The metaphors of wind and fire that belong with the Holy Spirit presuppose open human sails and glowing human coals. When these are wanting, there is a kind of Gethsemane of the Spirit waiting on our willing. 'For that which we believe of the Father, the same also we believe of the Son and of the Holy Spirit' – the God who wills His way through the way of our wills. The hazards He takes are the hazards He risks. The Church is where the vulnerability that makes the Gospel sets the Gospel at risk – but only by its being thereby in ever sacred trust.

10 Suspected and Neglected

i

'SUSPECTED and neglected' – the words might almost fit into Handel's deliberative music for 'despised and rejected'. Indifference, however, can be hardly less disconcerting to faith than outright hostility. Having surveyed Scriptures, Creeds and Church in their trust with divine credentials, we have to carry forward into the contemporary situation the present fortunes of all three, concentrating here on suspicion and neglect and leaving to Chapter 11 the more sceptical, intellectual issues. Both chapters are intended as preface to the positive task of a concluding Chapter 12.

Faith cannot well 'advertise' or see itself in market terms with believing as a kind of purchasing. Yet the nonchalance with which its earnestness is often treated could well be likened to wandering vaguely through the stalls of a market and eye-browsing through shop windows. Faiths, even Christian faith, have so many purveyors, a range of stallholders and vendors of grace to make the analogy appropriate. Secularity has a ready mind for sales resistance, confused by where to look or whom to trust. Allegedly divine credentials are made dubious by the wide variety of their proponents or, in Paul's analogy, 'the trumpets give uncertain sound'.[1] If we put a plural gloss on the familiar New Testament phrase we noted in Chapter 8 as the possible genesis of creeds, we would have 'faith-saying' 'worthy of all acceptations' and be at odds about which to choose and why (1 Timothy 1:15).

Faced with potential confusion, minds are often too lazy or preoccupied to bring any attention to bear. Or they are liable to 'cut out' as engines do, or they turn away as from something vaguely familiar yet not of immediate concern. Scriptures, Creeds and Church, for all their age-long status, dwell all too often in some limbo of neglect where they are left to languish . Too often the popular criteria of relevance itself conspires against the content and the claim of truth. If 'faith' comes by 'hearing' (Romans 10:17) it has little chance with the deaf, their deafness hardened (as we say hearing is) by the competition of a bewildered society incessantly subjected to factors for ever diminishing its attentiveness. Even divine credentials become casualties of human indifference. In such a strident world what has to do with wonder, mystery and awe is hard-pressed to gain the ear at all, much more to reach the mind. Indeed, reachable minds are fewer in respect of the realms of the sacred and the spiritual. There are lobbies everywhere for this and that, some blatant, others insidious, but all of them partisan in their different demands on appetite or gullibility. How does any 'good news' of God compete in such a market, such a climate? Can 'competition' ever be its word? Yet competition is its fate unless it is to abnegate. Some evangelism has been ready to turn itself into crude lobbying for God but at what cost to 'the precious blood of Christ' which is often its overfamiliarised text. Indeed, has not 'precious' come to signify, not merely a thing invaluable, but also its precariousness in an over-robust world?

When Paul was taking the 'foolish Galatians' urgently to task, he told them that 'Christ had been placarded among them', (Gal. 3:1). His Greek verb *proegraphe* means exactly what we now do on hoardings. He had in mind the fearful 'publicity' of crucifixion itself when it happened to Jesus. But that was Roman doing. The preaching of the meanings of the Cross has to show the same reticence the four Gospels had for its physical reality. The Gospel can only properly be told on its own terms – the terms of patience, long-suffering and awe. These qualities do not compete well in a time full of the raucous, the vulgar and the cheap.

Preaching with humility has always been something of a paradox – a paradox of grace. For one of the frequent reasons why people stall when summoned to faith is their assumption that preaching is axe-grinding. The clergy are paid 'professionals' and, therefore, have a vested interest in the truth of what they affirm. This, it is thought, makes them less than open to doubt and so unready for genuine interrogation, even if hearers were minded to bring it. Theology has become, in some quarters, a synonym for abstruse unreality. In any event, what 'preaches' is suspect. It means taking sides for private motives. 'Thus says the Lord' is only a cover for 'We are in the know,' and it is better to have opinions rather than texts. Convictions, in such a climate, especially if proffered for commitment, are liable to be dismissed as no more than the capacity of their purveyors to be the victims of their own propaganda. Indeed, sincerity itself in a go-getting world is, for some sociologists, no more than the readiness to be self-deceived.

For divine credentials, in trust (as they inevitably are) to human care, the going is hard in the contemporary world. For some Christians the answer is seen to lie in absolute versions of authority, an advocacy of counter-culture, the will to have the Gospel a sort of 'public truth' possessing a claim to belief like the patterns of mathematics or chemistry. But if, in faith realms, authority absolutises itself, it may do violence to what authority can only be, namely the 'commendation' of that which 'finds' us and is found only in freedom. An evangelism that purports to offer guarantee makes faith the less necessary. Integrity in believing presupposes integrity in the inviting to belief, and we have seen in Chapters 7 to 9 the call to honesty implicit in the very shape of Scriptures, the intention of Creeds and the retrospect of the Church. Only honesty will best vindicate the splendid Christian reality that true faith embraces and wise ministries commend.

It is true that exasperation about being understood or, more likely, about being wilfully misunderstood can generate a dogmatic impatience that falls back on sheer assertion. There are many situations for Christian language analogous to a comic exchange in Oscar Wilde's *The Importance of Being Ernest*, where Cicely remarks, 'When I see a spade I call it a spade,' to which Gwendolen responds, 'I am glad to say that I have never seen a spade. It is obvious that our social spheres have been entirely different.'[2] Such perverse respondents are everywhere when faith is the conversation.

It is true also that those who claim to be freeing the mind of crusty dogma demonstrate a remarkable capacity for their own more 'liberal' dogma. Thus, for example, Don Cupitt, in a recent work. Religious institutions he opines, are finished. We are now beyond the great romance of the transcendent God in search of His human creation. There is nothing left of the Christian story. Our will is for ecstatic immanence in a void of cosmic indifference where we are all the better, not to say the wiser, for the bleakness of this true vision. It is not only the issue that is at stake here: it is also the pontifical manner in which the claims are made. Cupitt's final advice is oddly unaware of its own metaphorical limits:

> We should live as the sun does. The process by which it lives and the process by which it dies are one and the same. It hasn't a care. It simply expends itself gloriously and, so doing, gives life to us all.[3]

Without the earth's atmosphere the sun would not forebear to burn us mercilessly in totally destructive fire. There are clouds too in the economy of God. Yahweh in the Psalms had much to do with them. How can a mindless star, which Genesis 1 refrains from naming lest the name denote an idol, be a simile for conscious selfhood in the Christian art of true *kenosis*? Those commonly dubbed 'fundamentalists' are not the only people capable of absolutising their acknowledged authorities. There are liberals who do no less with their own.[4]

It is right and wise to shun the assertive in this stalling world unless we are to be caught in a futility of sorry impasse. 'Come now, let us reason together,' was the prophet's plea in Isaiah 1:18. The context shows that he was in no way unrealistic about what the issues were and how perverse his hearers proved themselves to be. Even so, he invited them to a meeting of their minds with his meanings and evidently believed it possible. 'Commend' is the favoured word in the Epistles for Christian faith-presentation in reproducing what it believes to be the pattern of God Himself (Romans 5:8). The Greek word *sunistesin* identifies a certain community of relevance between the parties, which exists and can be recruited for the transmitting of what is at first opaque or dubious. The wise witness makes the other man his ally as well as his quarry and his meanings potential of recognition even in their strangeness, if only the strangeness is willing to 'unstrange' itself. The Gospel has always been a very patient thing.

In settings dominated by market-led products and television and journalism 'giving people what they want', this patient task of satisfying need only by first having people rethink it, is a stretching one for both parties. 'Television', remarks one practitioner who knows the media, 'imposes, or at any rate reinforces, cultural values most powerfully when they are least explicitly stated.'[5] But how is Christian faith 'least explicitly' told? Or its wealth compressed into a feasible 'sound bite'? Media experts may no doubt contrive some contributory technical answers but the deeper problem remains of the very means to meaning where the time and the temper are so coarsely tuned to markets and the sit-com. Apart from 'greetings' there, the only context in which the Gospels speak of 'markets' is of children playing funerals and weddings – the analogy Jesus used for a 'generation' that could neither mourn deep nor celebrate hilariously, people incapable of authentic tragedy and genuine comedy (Matthew 11:16–17). As then, so now. The 'kingdom' that measures both has the perennial task of bringing them to light in the option of faith.

ii

The inattention the Church must deplore is no matter for dismay, still less for reproach, unless the reproach be inward. For much of it, as noted in the previous chapter, derives from the churches themselves. Their presenting of divine credentials is made dubious for many by how multi-versioned they seem to be. Is there really one core expression, one definitive Christianity where they may be said to be conclusive? Their content and character as studied in Chapters 5 and 6 cannot claim unanimous assent. We have honestly seen in Chapter 7 how given the Christian Scriptures are into responsible, and therefore non-simplistic, trust, and in Chapter 8 how dependent on wise discernment are the historic Creeds. A faith that intended to be entirely categorical would surely have contrived more absolute testimonials than these. So much had been duly recognised.

It follows that Christian diversity has to be frankly undertaken. This is the ecumenical task in the familiar meaning of the adjective.[6] It is true that the diversity of world religions adds dimensions larger still to the truth-question for reverent and enquiring minds. To think of final things as optional or as incidental to birth and nurture may well unsettle their authority. We defer that larger issue of religious pluralism to Chapter 11 and confine ourselves here to what is plural inside Christianity in the broadest reach of the word. The analyses in Chapter 9 will not need repetition, being presupposed.

William Blake, who had fertile imagination to produce 'visions' enough of his own, has the multiplicities of Christian faith well in his lines:

> The vision of Christ that thou dost see
> Is my vision's greatest enemy.
>
> . . . . .
>
> Thine is the friend of all mankind,
> Mine speaks in parables to the blind.
> Thine loves the same world that mine hates,
> Thy heaven's doors are my hell-gates.
>
> . . . . .
>
> Caiaphas was in his own mind
> A benefactor of mankind.
> Both read the Bible day and night
> But thou read'st black where I read white.[7]

Anyone attempting to assemble a bibliography of 'Lives of Jesus' and of ventures in 'harmonising' the four Gospels has reason to doubt there is hyperbole when the addendum to the Fourth Gospel concludes with the guess that 'If the many other things that Jesus did should be written every one . . . the world itself could not contain the books that should be written' (21:25). The concluding 'Amen' has a ring of truth. Warren S. Kissinger, a scholar in New Testament studies and a bibliographer in the Library of Congress in Washington, lists almost three thousand titles there, and surveys the course of the several 'quests' of Jesus in his 'history' and in the devotion of the centuries.[8]

Recalling the tradition that Jesus was a 'carpenter',[9] the poet W. B. Yeats surmises that

> The true faith discovered was
> When painted panel, statuary,
> Glass mosaic, window-glass
> Amended what was told awry
> By some peasant gospeller,
> Swept the sawdust from the floor
> Of that working carpenter.[10]

His irony is sharp but works both ways. If there is pious licence in haloed brows and jewelled crosses there is false reductionism in the sawdust. Had the sawdust been all, the carpenter too would have been swept into oblivion and the workshop with him. Nazareth is known to history, not from a sermon in its synagogue but from script in Hebrew, Greek and Latin over a cross.

The varieties of Christian belief stem from this diversity of reckonings with Jesus. Some stray very far from the Messianic dimension and its criterion at the Cross which has to be central if the name 'Christian' is in control. This centrality has been clear enough in Chapters 5 and 6.

Having seen in Chapter 9 the ecclesiastical sources of diversity that come with institutionalised faith, our task here with disparate Christianities as making them all suspect turns on two related issues. The one is between an ethical Jesus and a redeeming Christ. The other concerns the tie between history and faith.

iii

'Jesus came teaching', said the Gospels. 'The Son of Man must suffer,' said the teacher. Especially in the eighteenth and nineteenth centuries New Testament study sought to take the former, to treasure the ethical and dismiss the christological, to salute the Beatitudes and the parables and read Gethsemane as their unhappy sequel. It was congenial to such minds to imagine they could jettison what they saw as tedious or abstract about credal doctrines of the person of Jesus and seek to recover that 'person' as essentially a master of ethical wisdom. We noted earlier the impact of J. R. Seeley's *Ecce Homo* in this connection, despite a title joining it squarely to the Passion.[11] Perhaps there was more point in the title than his reproachful critics realised. For it would seem finally impossible to isolate the teaching ministry of Jesus from the fact that he suffered. We were careful in Chapter 5 to trace the 'contradiction' Jesus underwent by teaching as he did and how this antagonism culminated in his crucifixion.

We must here note (deferred from Chapter 7) a long tradition in New Testament scholarship of a discernible source, usually labelled 'Q' to which appeal is made as a corpus of Jesus' teaching, existing in its own right in the early Church and utilised by Matthew and Luke as the place where they drew the material they share which they did not have from Mark. The case assumes the priority of Mark among the three Synoptic Gospels, a priority which not all experts concede. The detailed issues need not occupy us here. Whether Matthew is prior and Mark abridged him, or Mark is prior and Matthew elaborated him, we still need to ask about non-Markan material so nearly shared by Matthew and Luke.[12]

The 'Q' thesis is that it consists of a collection of the sayings, or 'Wisdom', of Jesus preserved by a 'Q' community which, it is argued, was a distinctive element in the Church separate from the sources, oral, literary and communal, from which came the emphasis on the Passion narratives that all the canonical Gospels present. This 'Q' community may have acknowledged Jesus in some sense as 'Son of Man', and have retained strong Jewish sympathies, choosing to remember Jesus for his 'words' rather than as 'the Word' suffering to redeem.

Careful as the documentation is, there is much that is cautionary here. The 'Q' idea serves as a salutary reminder that there may well have been other patterns of recollection from which we do not hear at all. We do well to have a sense of the 'silences' around New Testament tradition.[13] What is known as 'Q' we do have and it is eloquent witness to how the teaching Jesus sounded. Was 'Q' ever significantly isolated to characterise a distinctive community? At least the finished Gospels integrated it firmly into a common tradition about the Passion.

It would seem inconceivable that any 'Q' community did not know of the Passion. Reluctant though they may have been about the inclusion of 'Gentiles' in the expanding Church, they could not have ignored the logic from the Cross that required it. That Jesus' teaching could be treasured in wholly (reformist) Jewish terms remains significant, and even if the 'Q' hypothesis is discounted we still need some source – like it – to explain the non-Markan material Matthew and Luke employed in ways that suggest a common debt. This will still be true even if we think either or both of them actually prior to Mark.[14]

However, sources and debts apart, there is one final argument against the effort, at any time and from whatever motive, to confine Jesus to the teaching role. It is simply that the very survival of the teaching turned critically on the reality of the Passion. 'Q' is only conjectured because the Gospels exist. They are the one and only source for all that Jesus said and taught. The only agency that ensured his being accessible to us at all is the one that believed him crucified and risen. This is not to say that the New Testament is indubitable portraiture: it is to say that anyone venturing to correct it can do so only by conjecturing precariously from it. Even so, there are still those who suspect a faith they think has a divided mind about its Lord.

There is another formidable consideration against claiming to be wiser than the Gospels. It is the fact that the teaching of Jesus proved eminently unsuccessful. His ministry was not a gathering crescendo of acceptance and acclaim. One can well evaluate his teaching without reference to his death: one cannot, ignoring that climax, relate it to this world. Aspects of what his words meant might have been betrayed from within had he refrained from the encounters that entailed the Cross. Was not the most sublime tuition there in the suffering, there most of all? The sweet, inclusive invitation and promise in Matthew 11:28–30 may indeed be read, as 'Q' advocates suggest, as from Jesus as 'Wisdom', a figure who throughout the Wisdom literature is properly self-advertising.[15] How much richer still if we think the promised rest and the 'learning of him' as being 'in that he suffered'.

Those who feel with the full etymology of the name 'Christian', to which these chapters have been loyal, have, nevertheless, to allow that a bewildering diversity exists around what claims the name. If our fear is that this forestalls what divine credentials mean, wise custodians will not despair. Given realism, the ethical way in can be carried forward to the redemptive fullness. 'He who has ears . . . let him hear,' was Jesus' own way with his parables and wisdom. The diversity of 'hearings' can still avail if there is any will to realism about the whole. Fire may still glow under many embers and precious metal yield its worth in different currencies.

'Have I been so long time with you and yet have you not known me?' was a question addressed by Jesus, according to John 14:9, to intimate disciples. It reverberates through the long centuries among remoter folk. He has been read by quaint sentiment, revolutionary fervour, liberal rationality, juvenile wistfulness, psychotherapy theorists and scores of other interests – all reading their own image in his own. Scholars impatiently reacting have proposed a due 'historical quest' and differed sharply about where the 'quest' should end. The one who, as we saw, never wrote has occasioned more writing than anyone else in history. And all came almost totally from four Christian Gospels which are not themselves biographies, or 'lives', in any sense.

Indeed, the genre 'Gospel' speaking, as it does, 'from faith to faith,' and coming to be through the vicissitudes studied in Chapter 7, poses in very direct terms the underlying question of the relation that obtains between the 'who?' concerning Jesus the historian must ask and the 'Who?' the believer finds. The only honest way to deal with Christian plurality, past, present or to come, is to undertake that issue. It need not be as inconclusive as many have feared in respect of its bearing on a Christian unity of mind concerning the heart of faith. The strains on such unity which have been studied in Chapter 9 deriving from things institutional and sacramental may well be more incorrigible.

iv

That the four Gospels are event and faith, woven in one fabric, is evident in their very form. It is also frankly stated in the conclusion to the Fourth, the one which has most at stake over the issue. 'These things are written that you might believe' (20:31). The Gospels intend to persuade. If they are imparting information they are also seeking belief. It would be foolish to want them to be 'neutral'. In some measure *all* history-writing is this way, for it is interpreting significance in the act of recording happenings. To be sure, the historian must renounce deliberate distortion but, so doing, the writing will select, assess, imply, explain and shape so that what the reader receives has been sifted and conditioned by the ordering mind. Bias, of course, may be excessive and then, as with Gibbon's *Decline and Fall of the Roman Empire*, it betrays itself and readers can adjust accordingly. There is always the option to think the story might have been otherwise told. It is precisely that option we are leaving open in respect of the Gospels. But histories totally free of such options do not exist. There are always perspectives, angles of vision, a positive 'bias', or 'interest', that wanted the event(s) to be remembered and explored.

A critical reading awareness of this situation is vital. No one can say that the Gospels lacked it. Volumes of scholarship attest the contrary. The question, therefore, is resolved into asking whether the point of view has 'falsified' or 'possessed', has 'depreciated' or 'appreciated', what it handled. If we keep the significance of the Epistles firmly in view, the case is strong for the view that the Gospels represent an event-faith, a faith-event, a literature that deserves to be trusted if perceptively received as such. We have always to ask what kind of 'event' must Jesus and his 'Christhood' have been to have had this reporting, to have issued into this shape of recognition. To discount the documents as self-generated, self-deluded, or self-opinionated would be the ultimate credulity.

This makes for trustworthiness – a surer quality than infallibility. The 'happening' of the teaching, the ministry, the Passion of Jesus matters. We are not falling back on some sheer fideism for which it suffices that certain things are 'believed' in a way that remains indifferent, or even averse, to any event-quality. Faith is not faith in faith, whereby mere believing suffices or is itself the only 'event' there could be. History is not self-generating: it is event-generated. Equally, the event would not be one, if it had not been noted, greeted, memoried, digested, treasured and interpreted in a recognition that became itself an event. The Gospels offer themselves precisely as such an event from event, at once inviting the utmost scrutiny acceding to their character as its first wisdom. They do not allow us a Jesus without Christology.

This being so there will remain room for some disciplined diversity in inter-Christian scholarship that need not be fatal to a unifying consensus, provided it understands a suffering Christhood as vital to being Christian and such Christology as crucial to an adequately Christian theology. 'Worthy of all acceptance' (1 Timothy 1:15) will be the terms of the self-confidence it draws from its Christ-confidence. In conceding that Christian diversity is a fact of our situation, we can still be set to serve the criteria on which consensus deserves to be found, while accommodating differences in emphasis compatible with it. That consensus is identified here in the Christ-event, in the Christhood of Jesus incorporating his entire ministry and Passion, and read as the eternal index to the divine nature at the heart of theology.

The crucial interplay of history and faith and such Christian consensus of what is definitively Christian may be illuminated by discerning attention to first-century, and subsequent, Judaism. If we are confined to a teaching Jesus then, as Jewish scholarship this century has shown, near parallels – for example, to the Beatitudes – are evident from Judaic sources.[16] In respect of ethics alone the teaching of Jesus can be seen to be less 'unique' than it was traditional to think.[17] There is a remaining sense in which 'never man spake like this man' (John 7:46) if the whole impact of Jesus' personality is recognised.[18] Nevertheless, a liberal Judaism can readily, even possessively, own the Jesus of the 'Q' passages and, indeed, find joy in isolating them.

The parting of company occurs in the interpretation of the Passion and in the opening out of the faith to all so that the instinct to characterise all non-Jewry as 'Gentiles' could be radically challenged and repudiated. What remains distinctive about the emergent Christian faith is precisely this 'world awareness', this consciousness because of the Cross of a single human community. Doubtless, there was in Jewish dispersion a Hellenising of many things Judaic. Philo was no stranger to Greek wisdom. But always there was the ruling necessity of the special category of the circumcised.

'O Saviour of the world, who by thy Cross and Precious blood has redeemed us, save us and help us we humbly beseech thee, O Lord' became the early heart of Christian Liturgy, giving a currency to the plural pronoun 'us' and linking it with the Passion. The Cross and the world, in their mutuality as where sin had its drama and Messiahship its achievement – these were what gave Christianity birth and remained its insignia. Yet the teaching Jesus whom Jewry, no less than Christians, could salute was always present and articulate in that worldwide redemption. Those who want to isolate that Jesus from the Cross-eventuation in the world are necessarily debating the destiny of their own Judaism.

v

This vital relation of faith to history does not belong only with their fusion in the Gospels. It arises also from the faith's current encounter with contemporary time. The western world has drifted significantly away from familiarity with the biblical world so that the allusions and associations of that world no longer register as they did formerly. This is especially so in respect of vocabulary and the mysterious 'feel' of words. The way faith speaks differs pointedly from the language of modern advertisement. The meanings of words are inevitably and ultimately at the mercy of those who use them. They cannot be immune from the caprice of actual usage nor be made absolutely exempt from the vicissitudes that beset every living thing. Dictionaries can 'define' only by citing examples of use, and their historical register can readily be seen to be tending always to diversity and change.

It is venerable institutions, like the law, the Church and doctrine that are most susceptible to finding their forms of speaking made archaic because speech around them, being less richly cargoed, has shifted ground. In every language situation it is the participants who matter and who, by their familiars and their prejudices, will determine what is transacted between them. Poets can, perhaps, be free of any necessary readers, for they are simply coding their thoughts and impressions. Preachers, publicists, can never be free of their context – advertisers least of all. There is a sense in which beliefs are not only that we think *on*, or *about*: they are also what we think *with*. Thus language always turns on a capacity to register as well as a capacity to tell. Between these words will always be the crux.

Christian faith is, therefore, caught in every generation in this quandary of an ever articulate trust and an ever shift-making reception. Ambiguity can, no doubt, sometimes be an asset and give a useful elasticity to meaning, but more often it will breed perplexity and hinder comprehension. There is one notorious example at the heart of Catholic devotion, where so much disconcertingly turns on so little. K*haire kecharitomene* is the Greek in Luke 1:28, the salutation to Mary, where there is a play on words. 'Good day to you, God being so good to you,' is the immediate meaning. In Jerome's Vulgate we have: A*ve, Maria, plena gratia*, 'Hail, Mary, full of grace.' What should we understand? The play on words seems to require that 'grace given gives Mary reason to be glad', that is, news of a vocation such as to explain Mary's evident perplexity. The Latin has come to carry an implication of pre-existent status, even endowing Mary with immaculate quality from before her own conception. Then a whole theology of Marian 'grace' can follow.[19]

'Grace' is evidently a very Christian word but what does it, how will it, signify? What is at issue about it within the churches may not satisfactorily convey to those outside them. That meanings may turn a somersault on themselves is what time and usage can do anyway,[20] without further connivance from ecclesiastical confusions. That this happens, and has happened, has beset divine credentials ever since they were Christianly confessed. The problem is not only in the translation from Hebrew or Aramaic into Greek, from all three into Latin, and from all four into the sundry tongues of multi-cultures. It belongs also with the elusive hope of stable equivalence in any and every language where words lapse as well as times.

Consider how many vital Christian words are either archaic, in that they do not register in current speech, or are confined to their own sphere. Either way, their import requires an effort of will, or enquiry which many are quite unwilling to make. 'Beseech', 'miserable', 'prevent', 'fear', 'pardon', 'pity', 'merit', 'bosom', 'evermore', 'confession', 'Ghost', 'comfort', 'lay hands', 'begotten', 'behold', 'verily', 'help' and 'mortify' are a few drawn at random from Scripture and Liturgy that obviously qualify as only peculiarly registering what they hold. Further, many pivotal terms of Christian faith and worship have no currency – or almost none – outside those realms. 'Atonement', 'resurrection', 'redemption', 'soteriology', 'substance', 'only begotten', 'proceeding', 'absolution', 'repentance', 'ascension', 'Catholic', 'Godhead', are an obvious few. Others from the Te Deum Laudamus alone are: 'worship', 'everlasting', 'cherubim', 'seraphim', 'Sabbath', 'Comforter', 'right hand of God', 'world without end', 'vouchsafe' and 'confounded'. If we think of 'the quick and the dead' it could well be the hazards of the street-crossings, or if 'we mention the name' it will be some chance or casual remark, not the having ever in mind which the psalmist meant by the words. Examples are legion of how Christian speech 'betrays', not because it is still 'the Galilean accent' warming itself at the world's fire, but because its vocabulary is stranded on the sands of language.

Emotions as well as meanings are deeply involved here as controversies have demonstrated around 'alternative' Liturgies and 'revised' versions of the Scriptures. A case can be made for necessary archaism. Even the unintelligible Latin Mass could long survive. It may well be right that some religious language should stay 'venerable', 'traditional', suited to sanctuary mind, lest unduly conversational idiom should enter into worship and jeopardise both reverence and mystery. It is surely well that Scripture should not forfeit the resonance that the long generations cherished and that wrought the very genius of the English language. It is well to be suspicious of innovation.

Nevertheless, an outward-looking faith in debt to all the world, through all the times, can never be complacent when museumisation threatens its vocabulary. Its existence being for the sake of its non-membership, it must care about the remoteness from them of its traditional language. Technicalities of doctrine are no doubt inevitable and we have earlier negotiated some of them. The concern here is with the trust of meaning at every level of popular and intelligent expression. We do not meet the issues if, with some charismatic 'hymns and songs', we fall back on endless repetition. Reiterating may enthuse the faithful: it will not reach the indifferent or enlighten the perplexed. Properly understood, all that prompts the insider to cherish a loved vocabulary has to be the spur to realistic ventures in leaving it behind for the sake of its ultimate possession more widely.

There is help in this task if ministry of the Word will always conjoin exploring with persuading. If one is bent on enlisting another's 'seeing' of meaning, it is well to be steadily discerning one's own. Convictions are best offered when they are vitally possessed. For Christian truth is never merely for private or intellectual savour. It intends to 'find' all, and ministry with it has to be part of that intention. It follows that all obstacles, all that suspects and neglects, must be means to interpretation. The Gospel itself, as we have seen in Chapters 5 and 6, was truth *sub contrario*, shaped under opposition. It remains in dynamic relation to all human capacities, both for belief and for unbelief. We shall be wrong if we think the Church has a declaratory *magisterium* than can ignore the demands of doubt and despair. Indifference or perplexity around it are the waters it must navigate. 'Give me a clue,' as in the first occasion in Acts 8:34, will always be a plea to heed – and, indeed, to excite.

vi

The art of bringing Christian meaning out of the limbo of indifference requires a lively appeal to imagination. Meanings for many are stalled in suspicion or neglect because people have ceased to think with the heart. A dearth of vivid emotions is on many hands a feature of the time. It must be the Gospel's task to rekindle them. This will not mean some improper suppression of the mind, some call to self-persuasion. Intellectual responsibilities remain rigorous but they are only fully discharged in what has to do with faith by a lively partnership with soul. Any summons to belief has to be accompanied by a call to the suspension of disbelief, a will to let imagination in where cold reason may for ever veto what it has to learn.

Consider what happens in the theatre. No meaning is registered except within acceptance of the nature of the medium. 'Can this cock-pit hold/The vasty fields of France?' asks the Chorus at the opening of *Henry* V. The stage of the Globe Theatre invites the 'in-clue-ing' of the audience.

> Piece out our imperfections with your thoughts:
>
> . . . . .
>
> For 'tis your thoughts that now must deck our kings,
>
> . . . . .
>
> Turning th'accomplishment of many years
> Into an hour-glass.[21]

Drama must wilt and perish for lack of will to think within the requisites of presentation. So it is with Gospel-faith. There is no reckoning with the content without comprehension of its form. It merits a will to believe that perceives both form and content for what, to each other, they must be.

Writing to the Corinthians (1 Cor. 4:9), Paul saw the apostolic story as 'a theatre for the world'. How much more, then, the apostolic Gospel? The poet Robert Herrick seized on the idea and said of Jesus crucified:

> The Cross shall be thy stage   ·
> And thou shalt there the spacious field have
> For thy theatre.[22]

That sense of things must always inform the ministry of the Word. Enquiring Greeks knew their own clue when they said, 'We would see Jesus' (John 12:21). There is a perennial vividness in the sacred history in the New Testament. It is for ministry to present it, as 'producers' do, not only in the skill of argument but in the grace of poetry – the poetry of recognition. There have indeed been inveterate sceptics who realised this 'drama' of the Word yet thought themselves inhibited from response. Thus A. E. Housman:

> I never over Horeb heard
> The blast of advent blow,
> No fire-faced prophet brought me word
> Which way behoved to go.
>
> Ascended is the cloudy flame,
> The mount of thunder dumb:
> The tokens that to Israel came
> To me they have not come.
>
> I see a country far away
> Where I shall never stand.
> The heart goes where no footsteps may
> Into the promised land.[23]

To be sure, even imagination can contrive its own vetoes. Unbelief may insist on its non-suspension, but 'footsteps going with the heart' will still be the way to Christ.[24]

Poetry, we might say, is where the heart goes without leaving mind behind. Even that down-to-earth writer, James, in his Epistle (1:22) calls on his readers to be 'poets of the Word' (*poietai logou*). He is in line with Ephesians 2:10 which has the intriguing idea of the Church as 'God's poem' (*poema*). Examples abound in the New Testament of how (as in all true poetry) we come by content only in savouring form. Metaphors and allusions are only liberated for their purposes by minds taken out of apathy or negligence by those who will care for the clues and make them understood.

Often, in this ministry, it helps to start with puzzlement. What does a reader first make of Matthew 5:48: 'Be you perfect, as your father in heaven is perfect.' It sounds nonsensical. There is clearly an echo of Deuteronomy 18:13: 'Thou shalt be perfect with the Lord thy God.' *Tamim* (Hebrew) and *teleios* (Greek) have the idea of 'wholehearted', 'entire', 'above reproach'. The Deuteronomist is writing in context about witchcraft, necromancy and other superstitious ways that are plainly incompatible with any due sense of Yahweh. Jesus in his sermon has just observed how the Lord 'sends rain on the unjust and the just alike'. Divine hospitality in nature does not turn on our merits. Our being 'perfect', then, must mean a will to the same inclusiveness which does not stint or condition its generosity. Clearly we are being led towards the thought that there has to be a mutuality between how God is and how we should be. The divine nature is reproducible in the human. Ethics, in other words, is theological. Was there not an old and foolish idea that linked the moon with madness (hence 'lunacy')? Shakespeare puts it:

> It is the very error of the moon:
> She comes more near the earth than she was wont
> And makes men mad.[25]

Something reciprocal, an exploded notion, illuminates a Christian truth. There is that which we can be because of how God is: the transcendent may be counterparted in the human.

There is nothing in faith which will not yield its riches more by dint of honest imagination. The 'face' has always made poetry in every tradition. In one of his finest insights, Paul tells the Corinthians that they 'have the light of the knowledge of the glory of God' as in a face. He means in Christ Jesus as 'the divine countenance'. There is no more perceptive image of the Incarnation (2 Cor. 4:6). Even 'Gentiles' among his readers must have known of the old Aaronic blessing (Numbers 6:24–27). Paul finds it fulfilled for the world in the Christ-event. The face is a mysterious sacrament of things spiritual housed in things physical. Joy, pain, surprise, questioning, fear, hope, a swift sequence of emotions, pass across the face. There biography inscribes itself in wrinkle, line and gaze. Yet all is nerve, sinew, muscle, skin, blood and flesh. Comparably, divine glory sheds its light upon us in the recognisability a face enshrines, which 'face' is Jesus being Christ and Lord.

The comprehensibility of things Christian is today obscured by the degree to which New Testament writers, in their day, used *argumenta ad homines*, presentations suited to the hearers' world. These very rarely register in ours. A rich example is the first chapter of the Letter to the Hebrews which for centuries has been read at Christmas, doubtless leaving many quite clueless about its logic, for all its sonorous prose. It has several citations from Coronation Psalms in making its point about how much 'greater than the angels' is the divine 'Son', 'begotten that day'. How might the writer's case be clarified – angels being so far outside our willing 'suspension of disbelief'?

We need to think of divine sovereignty, of God in will towards the human world. Will means action: action means agency. Both are human related. For humanity was/is the crux of divine purposes humanly entrusted with the 'dominion' of the earth. In this dignity, according to an old Semitic tradition, the 'angels' were bidden to 'worship' human creaturehood (Hebrews 1:6).[26] It follows that they symbolise the divine concern with human freedom and decision, to which divine purposes are entrusted – the concern to guide, inspire, inform and educate the crucial creaturehood. But supervening on such 'ministries' (1:14), the legislating and sustaining relationship of God with us, there is the ultimate redemptive relation that is the role of 'the Son'. The writer is expressing the central Christian conviction, via his own idiom, that the God who ordains our human being achieves His crowning concern with us in the enterprise of Christ, deriving from His very nature. 'Sonship begotten' is the very self of God given in the deed of grace, as drama is 'begotten' by the dramatist. To hand in the writer's day, among Hebraic-minded readers, were psalms that celebrated the accession to power of new kings whose 'royal name', in their adopted role, was more excellent than lesser ministries. Old hymns about them could yield the themes of celebration and majesty which the Letter was ascribing to the Christ of God.

We are a far cry from the thought-world and the exultant psalmody of the first readers of Hebrews, but a patience that sees beyond initial mystification readily unlocks the abiding relevance. Patience it must be, with interpreting perceptions to reward it.

Situations of indifference were evident enough in the Gospel scene itself. The parable in Luke 14:16–24 puts the point with gentle irony. A listener, when Jesus is himself at table, enthuses about 'the Messianic banquet' – popular idiom for 'the kingdom of God'. Jesus' response is the parable of 'the great supper', when invitees had ready excuses – all of them rather hollow, having to do with commerce, goods and a recent marriage, and only produced when the final 'call' (according to Jewish custom) had reached them. Odd to have bought land and oxen without having inspected them! Honeymooning was maybe a rather better alibi. Were they hinting they might perhaps come later? When, at length, the supper was finally 'furnished with guests' it was by other folk whose urgency ruled out prevarication. There are hidden issues here about 'the Gentiles', but one thing is clear – the summoners to the supper were not made idle by the excuses.

Sometimes aspects of faith's call can penetrate by surprise. The parable of the labourers idle in the market-place is a ready example (Matthew 20:1–16). When the proprietor decides to pay a whole day's wage to those he recruited only in the late afternoon the compassion which moves him cuts across the law of the cash nexus. He wills to resist the injustice and inequality which stem from 'the state of the market' when this applies to human life and labour – the only commodity basic man has to 'sell'. This flouts the market rates per hour. The disgruntled first-comers demand that such compassion be disallowed unless it maintains the differentia at stake in economic laws. Their claim would mean that compassion is forever excluded and humans can be only market fodder. The proprietor asserts his right to liberate his employing power from sheer economic control. A fair wage for employment does not exempt recipients from the harsh incidence on others of the system by which they prosper. Human meaning is more than economic justice – the more so when even justice is market-distorted. The full-day workers are invited to a suspension of their disbelief about the late ones.

Such clarity of import is harder to detect when, many times, rich metaphor or obscure allusion are entailed. When some translations have Paul telling his Corinthians (2:14) that we are 'always made to triumph in Christ', it sounds too extravagant. Paul is too often suspected of hyperbole. In fact he is calling up a piece of imagery familiar enough in the Roman world of victorious Caesars leading their captives through Rome as tokens of imperial power. Or the imagery may have more than a hint of Palm Sunday and how Jesus, differently, gave Jerusalem evidence of his healing retinue of liberation. 'Thanks be to God who continually leads us captives in Christ's triumphal procession.'

That picture in the mind is quickly followed by another which likens the faithful to 'incense' 'offered by Christ to God'. What an odd reversal of ancient sacrificial lore where Yahweh was thought, in very crude analogy, to 'smell the savour' of the food of sacrifice and so doing assured the offerers of their acceptance, ritual meals being an ancient exchange between gods and men. Life itself in moral quality and personal discipleship is that which makes the praise of God significant. Elsewhere (Romans 12:1), Paul makes the self-oblation of Christian people the very 'logic' of life. One might detect the same imagery when Isaiah 40:26 pictures the starry hosts of heaven as 'responding like soldiers at muster on the parade-ground', crying, 'we are all here' as each name is called. The sense of God present to us and we present to God pervades the biblical scene. In the New Testament it is 'in Christ' that the reciprocal meanings of grace us-ward and obedience God-ward are known to be realised.

'In Adam' – a usage of Paul in 1 Corinthians 15:22 – both belongs with, and contrasts to, being 'in Christ'. It has been much miscomprehended. It captures the truth of human solidarity, of common birth ushering us all into an entail of our nature and our history, from which there is no exemption. It does not connote some inherent judgement against us before we have begun to be active or a taint that inheres by genealogical connection arbitrarily contrived. It witnesses to a non-exemption from the realities of self-centredness that are implicit in the very possibility of selfhood and of self-unselfishness in a world where society is corporate and time has momentum.

How puzzling to 'a master in Israel', if not indeed offensive, was Jesus' point about being 'born again', which Peter echoes in his Letter (John 3:3, 7; 1 Peter 1:23). Nicodemus did well to ask how it could be. Truly no one re-enters mother's womb to be born a second time. In spiritual terms also, no Jew needs to. For a Jewish mother has ensured membership of the very people of God as no other mothers do. Hence Nicodemus' puzzlement. As with all metaphor, it is vital to read the sense in which its tenor can be meant. Being 'in Adam' means that we share the matrix (kindred word), with its social liabilities and human gravitation. No life begins in contextual neutrality. The work of grace is not to cancel out personhood but to enable it in negation of the evil and embrace of the good. 'A death to sin and new life in righteousness' are frequent New Testament accents in this remaking of the self. It is like birth in the 'newness' of the experience, not like it as the genesis of the physical being without which, of course, no regeneration could happen for lack of any locale. Indeed, remaining 'in Adam', in solidarity with the human situation in all its hope and despair, is the only context of 'newness of life'.

vii

Doubtless the opaqueness, to many, of the things of Christ in an age of jaded secularity goes far beyond the reach of these examples. Yet a will to suspension of disbelief, of impatient literalism and the crass obduracy we would never bring to dramas on the stage, could readily kindle comprehension. Christian meanings must be taken for what they mean to say, as all necessary formulae, metaphor, sacrament and imagery can render them. It is crucial to witness that these its media should be known for what they are. It is on witness itself that the onus lies to have it so, but it must also somehow enlist a kindling imagination from the other side.

Any such kindling is not only, or finally, to verbal forms, to thought as doctrine, to credentials in active commendation. It is to experience, to inward participation in the grace these bring. The hearer becomes in turn a part of their evidence. 'O taste and see that the Lord is good' was an old bidding of the psalmist (34:8). There has always been this food analogy of faith. 'A table spread' has ever been the rendezvous of grace. 'Come eat my bread and drink of my wine' leaves hospitality, *qua* invitation, a matter for inspection. After response it becomes experience where truth is inwardly transacted and, in the most ultimate shape of knowledge, 'We know whom we have believed.' George Herbert quaintly ended his debate with his own unworthiness and the divine magnanimity in the words: 'So I did sit and eat.'[27]

11 On Many Counts Discounted

i

'WHY doth thine heart carry thee away and what do thy eyes wink at?'[1] Job's questioner might well be voicing the secular dismissal of religious belief in general and of Christian faith in particular. The heart is suspected of responsibility for carrying away believers where honest mind cannot go – into desirable solace and comfort, into some tidy, reassuring dependence that will ease life's puzzles and make its mysteries tolerable. The price, however, is always a readiness to 'wink at' awkward evidence of vacuity and enigma that genuine thought would not evade. Divine credentials, properly seen, are human credulities, no more. Religion is a search for trust that cannot itself be trusted or, if trusted, then only at the price of 'winking at' the disconcerting facts. So, at least, the argument runs.

To attempt any inclusive contemporary reckoning with Christian faith is a large proposal. The literature is vast. To compress that attempt into as many pages as the decades of some two centuries as the range of our retrospect suggests the impossible. Even so, the intention in this chapter is to take the business of scepticism further and deeper than the broad indifference that concerned Chapter 10. The task now is more squarely intellectual. It presupposes the climate earlier reviewed which it knows for the dissuasive it is either way, whether for the serious critic or the open-hearted respondent. The latter must have place in Chapter 12. We stay here with the arraignment of 'winking' believing.

The sundry 'counts' in the 'discounting' of Christianity resist any neat tabulation. We may well discover a partial clue in the degree of 'connecting' the mind is prepared to make. For there are 'disconnectings' and reductionism in many aspects of unbelief which may be seen as reciprocal to what are regarded as the pretensions of confident faith. We shall be wise to let that issue hum like a refrain below the surface of more precise matters. For it may well be the clue we need to carry forward into Chapter 12.

More precisely here, the plan is to review credulity minus credentials under four heads. Those offered have to be discounted as being too ambitious, narrow, naïve and self-assured.

ii

The ambitiousness of Christian doctrine is evident enough to any remotely familiar with the *Summa Theologica* of Thomas Aquinas or the soaring confidence of Augustine's 'O God, Thou hast made us for Thyself and our hearts are restless till they rest in Thee.' There was something admirable, if also vaguely suspect, as we saw, about the will of the Chalcedonian Fathers to 'come verbally clean' about their dogma. 'To love the Lord with all the mind' is no mean ambition and the mental assurance of theological enterprise gave abiding stimulus to the confidence of the very sciences that now purport to have displaced it. When seventeenth-century doubt instigated a search for what might be indubitable it was theology in divines like John Donne, with his 'Tis all in pieces, all coherence gone', which prompted it to do so.[2] Even scepticism must exert its wits, and it was belief that stimulated it to do so by the very boldness with which faith strove for understanding.

It was this theological will to inclusify all meaning, via the concept of God, that provoked, where it did not generate, the contrasted option of non-inclusive pursuit of particular knowledge. There might be poly-maths like the great Ibn Sina (980–1037) aspiring to master all learning, but with the growth of awareness of the physical world, its endless data and the means – like lenses, machines, computers – for ascertaining them, sciences, perforce, became ever more specialist and sharply focused. The scientific mind became ever more and more involved with less and less by virtue of its own principle of precise exploration and intimate immediacy of concern. To be sure, every part presupposed the larger wholes in which alone they had their being and their laws. Yet these had to be exempted from the purview of the concentrated pursuit of ever ramifying, proliferating parts. Where the laboratory was all engrossing, God and the universe could not intrude. One might peep and botanise, obliviously, on one's mother's grave.

Doubtless, wholes, mysteries, perplexities, anxieties, might break through as truly inseparable from these exacting, imperative special-isms. But for many the enterprise they exacted and rewarded all too readily forfeited the wide dimensions to which the same interrogating reason had need to relate. For there was nothing which curiosity addressed or scientific efficiency contrived that did not reach back into more total issues about whence and whither, why and wherefore. Much, however, in the scientific instinct dismissed these as either diversionary or abstract. God Himself might be overlooked in a test-tube. Artificial light could forget the stars.

This concentration of mind and reason on purposes of curiosity, invention and control, via the evidences of the senses was formidably reinforced by the patterns of seventeenth- and eighteenth-century empiricism in philosophy urging the necessary confinement of reason to sense-experience as alone furnishing data to mind. Metaphysics came to seem a pretentious pursuit. Rather, let doubt reach for the indubitable. Finding it in himself as 'thinking his own doubting', Descartes bequeathed a potent legacy. For, having centred the indubitable on the *thinking* self, he raised the vital question of the competence of that self-as-mind. His 'I think and so I am' might so differently have been 'I am and so I think,' or 'I suffer and so I am,' or 'I love and so I am' − any of which would have been more 'theological'. If, however, his 'I think and so I am' was to escape solipsism, it had to legitimate sense-experience − where all thinking starts.[3]

That academic venture into universal doubt, yielding self-as-mind for its basic 'certainty', required Locke to formulate the cautionary principle that 'there is nothing in the mind that is not first in the senses' (the dictum, 'I am and so I think' would not have dictated such limits). With mental 'knowledge-structuring and structures' thus limited to sense data, it followed that the mind was confined to empirical realms and forbidden to range beyond sense data − a necessity which ruled out medieval scholasticism and its long love-affair with theology. For such pretentions (as they must now be seen to be) presumed to operate outside what sense-experience afforded. If the empiricists retained any theology it would have to be by other means such as moral criteria or direct 'revelation'.

Here in the empirical tradition lay the clear modern disqualification of the 'ambition' of natural theology proposing to attain what 'there is nothing in the mind not first in the senses' disallowed. When, in the next century, Immanuel Kant qualified that principle by his rider, 'There is nothing in the mind which is not first in the senses except the mind itself,' the curbing of theological 'ambition' was still more stringent. For Kant argued that the human mind, being the presiding organ to which the senses ministered their perpetual impressions, imposed its own order and categorisation on them. Honesty, therefore, required him to insist that, so doing, the mind yielded knowledge only of 'phenomena', that is to say, things as the mind thought them to be. Inasmuch as the mind did the 'phenomenalising', what things were − the mind's activity apart − could never be known, seeing that the instrument that 'knew' them was always in the way. But it was necessary to leave room for what things might be in other 'knowing' than ours, which Kant called the noumena.[4] Though always *ex hypothesi* unknowable, these had yet to be acknowledged as arguably 'other'. Since all knowledge via sense-experience was thus mentally contrived, and since there were no data about God open to sense-experience as mind had it in 'phenomena', it followed that what Kant called 'pure reason'[5] could never legitimately 'theologise'.

It is necessary to follow this sequence in philosophy, familiar and elementary as it is, to appreciate the broad philosophic indictment of the ambitiousness of Christian faith. The case might be more subtly and variously made but, in context, if suffices to review it this way. Natural theology, such as the Bible seems to commend ('The heavens declare the glory of God') and such as Aquinas magisterially system-atised, must be *verboten*. Let reason renounce all pretension about what can be divinely 'proved' and learn the humility of its necessary confinement to the physical sciences and what might be crudely dubbed 'common sense'. To 'love the Lord with all the mind' is to fantasise about what one cannot reach with what one has not got.

There is much else that might be said which, indeed, Kant and others would aid us in saying, but the present point can stay with the case against false ambition. Disallowing 'natural theology' must throw the whole weight on 'revelation', or 'historical, special, theology', where reason, it might properly be thought, could claim to have a mandate. But the effect of empiricism, broadly, was to forbid this also, seeing that – though 'data' of such historical revelation may claim to be 'factual' – their being (as the curious term goes) 'supernatural'[6] must disqualify them on empirical grounds.

More recent thinking, though still in this empirical tradition, has shifted somewhat away from 'what you can properly think' to 'what you carry truly prove'. The term 'verification' comes into play to clip the wings of any ambition to know and love God. The traditional so-called 'proofs' of the existence of God must be disqualified, not only because in Kantian terms they trespass beyond what the senses-mind situation can admit, but because they are unverifiable. 'Prove that God is love' demands the sceptic, sure that all 'proving' is out of reach. The demand begs the whole question about the nature of verification. Having, however, limited that issue to the realm of visual, tangible, practical evidences, the sceptic has ensured a sceptical answer. Intentions can be satisfied when they have carefully confined the criteria.

The case for discounting Christian – or indeed any theism – as a viable faith by demanding verification on one's own terms of what 'verifiers' should be is often reinforced by turning the matter round. Let us forget, for the moment, about feasible verification, the argument runs. Let us ask instead: How much *counter*-evidence can you stomach before having to concede that your faith is illusory? Here the mysteries of evil, natural and personal, come into full play. The clear strategy is to leave faith exposed to its own futility. Believing, if it persists, will be seen to be an obdurate persistence. Go on believing in a wise, good, loving omnipotence in the light of cancer, tidal wave, famine, tyranny, holocaust, Alzheimer's disease, muscular dystrophy, 'the thousand natural shocks that flesh is heir to', and you stand wilfully, pitifully, demonstrably self-deluded. Faith is proved an obstinate recalcitrance, unwilling or unable to confess its own vacuity. Lunacy is so named because, as noted earlier, it was once thought that the moon made people mad. Reality cannot have it so but the parable fits. A fiction above the sky has made people credulous. Science can absolve the moon from responsibility for continuing lunacy. It still struggles to rid devotion of comparable delusions, though its own mind remains perplexed about its own certainties.

iii

Lurking around the questions: What may we think? and What can we prove? is the further question: What can we *mean*? 'You know what I mean' is familiar enough verbiage when people converse and seem to be asking for help around what, somehow (they hope) is already rightly guessed. The phrase captures the deep philosophic problem of language itself which, in this century in the shape of logical positivism, has come to preoccupy the issues in all religious meaning.

We can come into what is at stake here by way of tautology. 'A spade is a spade.' 'Very God of very God.' The statements are self-enclosed. In some measure all definitions are. Dictionaries purport to tell you the meaning of 'cynosure', 'benefit', 'quorum', 'wheelbarrow' and the like. They do so by suggesting other words. The famous *Larousse* can be 'illustrated' and pictures will convey. Simple empiricism would allow that all this is satisfactory. We name what we know and we know what we name. But language is more than simply descriptive. It is societal and transactional. Undeterred by the empiricists' cautions we have studied to stay with senses, language moves out into metaphor, rhetoric and imagery. Words acquire a currency, if not a meaning, by contexts to which, empirically limited, they do not belong. We hear tell of 'the meat of the matter' or 'the trickle-down' theory of wealth creation. We are warned against 'pie in the sky' or exhorted to 'get off the ground'.

What is happening here? Associations are being made which can only be taken perceptively. Language is itself creating its own discoursing. Is 'get off the ground' a bidding to trespassers or to enterprises who, like aircraft, are still on a runway? Language is not, now, saying unequivocally what it means, nor is it unambiguously meaning what it says. The context, it might be pleaded, takes care of 'meaning', but only if we stay with it. The secular accusation is that religious language deceives itself and gives false currency to 'non-meaning' via the extension of a word's legitimacy. Thus faith may speak about 'surviving death'. But will that be like 'surviving an accident'? Obviously not – but what is the intended meaning? Has it been conjured into mind by a distortion about what can be meant by 'survive'? When we are told by Matthew that 'the Lord warned Joseph in a dream' can it mean other than that Joseph dreamed that the Lord had warned him? Either a form of words has embroidered a 'fact', or assertion has taken over language for its own purposes. When Scriptures talk of 'the arm of the Lord' positivists must suspect that they are concealing the meaningless under apparent sense, by sleight of words.

It is alleged, therefore, that language can only be trusted in the spheres of logic, mathematics and empirical 'fact'. Analogy, metaphor, poetry, must all be sceptically scrutinised as emotive betrayers of factuality, in effect if not always in intention. Rhetoric exists to evoke the answers it wants. Questions can only properly be asked where answers exist – a precept which limits intelligible language to sense data. Even doubt, not to say conviction, must be held to relate only to what is factual. Emotive or uncritical use of language beguiles its users away from this salutary principle and emboldens them to 'give to airy nothing a local habitation and a name'. Words, constantly repeated, bestow solidity on the vacuous and, unlike coins that wear thin, wax convincing by sheer circulation, acquiring a pseudo-realism which must be disowned.

Philosophies of language in this twentieth century have been significant in remonstrating with all religious faith over what they see as wilful mystification, a reliance on language which eludes both verification and falsification, and therefore offers, in so doing, only a deceptive assurance. It utilises – as of necessity it must – terms of human provenance like 'make a covenant', 'send a son', 'smell a savour', 'hear a cry' and 'taught with a pen' and supposes them legitimately said, and meant, concerning what surely transcends all such devisings. By such instinct language is allegedly betrayed, made to carry what it cannot say and may not signify.

Such strictures from the linguistic positivists may recognise that there are 'insider vocabularies' in all specific areas of human activity and converse, whether the factory floor, the golf club, the garage, the farm, the village, the mosque or the cathedral. It is not the gregariousness of particular vocabularies which is in question but the pseudo-reality for which there can be no honest 'insiders'. Is there not also a sense in which certain things can only be said in certain languages? Do not all translators realise this? The reason may partly be with culture, inasmuch as what 'goes' in one does not 'hold' for another. Language, however, interweaves and connives with this. Is there not, then, a clear case for holding that language shapes, if it does not sometimes create, the meanings it purports to make objectively actual? Then perhaps we have to acknowledge that the language I am using is the language that is deluding me.

Then there is the constant matter of reiteration and association. Religious people have simply told themselves so often that 'the Lord is my shepherd', and that 'Muhammad is the apostle of God', or that 'Yahweh covenanted with Israel' that it has come to be so, but to be so only for those who use the language with the conviction the language itself has generated. Must it not, therefore, be proper to suspect all religious language as an actual or potential schemer of confidence tricks and to restrict words, verbs and nouns, and the sentences that arrange them, to realms that remain accessible to experience and logic alone? Linguistic positivism is minded to reinforce, from its own angle, the reservations of philosophical empiricism. In short, the entire idea of God with credentials or of credentials about God must be renounced. 'Vaulting ambition has o'er-leaped itself'[7] and had better learn the humility which Christianity has always commended. Theology should consent to keep its feet on the ground and cease theologising. Pleading poetry or mystery will not save it.

iv

If those who would credential God must curb that improbable ambition they must also forego their interest in monopoly. Even if credentials could be conceivable they may not be exclusively taken into trust. Religions are manifestly and incorrigibly plural and custodians are hopelessly narrow if they think to defy that situation and present themselves as the sole proprietors of truth. The pride of ambition must not allow itself the arrogance of spiritual privatisation.

There is nothing new about religious multiplicity. What is new late in the twentieth century is the pressing awareness of it inside the several main sanctuaries of belief. The former isolations of cultures and peoples behind mountain ranges and wide oceans are ended. The earth is one uneasy neighbourhood in which mobility, information media and world agencies concerning trade, health, population, commerce and finance, transact a single humanness while they also accentuate economic disequilibrium and political strife. Religions have often contributed malignly to tension and disorder, enemies to mutual peace and human community. In an age when technology both unifies and chronically accentuates what divides, it is surely imperative for religious faiths to forego their interior self-sufficiencies and respond worthily to the claims and perplexities of co-existence. If we are to have divine credentials at all let them be mutually concerted and concerned.

Faiths have, of course, long reacted to each other historically and, in measure, owed themselves to interaction. The interplay of things Judaic and things Christian is implicit in both.[8] There is a fascinating possibility that Christian influences contributed to the development of the Mahayana from within the Hinayana tradition of Buddhism.[9] Islam would not be the faith it is apart from debt to and reaction against the Christian story. Hinduism is perhaps the most interacting and spiritually promiscuous (we might say) of all religions though stoutly tenacious of its own proper identity.[10] It is further true that in many areas the issues between religions are also issues interior to each of them. It is out of things common that they diverge and in their divergences they quarrel about adjacence.

It follows, so the current case runs, that uniquely custodianised divine credentials must be condemned as impossible. Truth, it is urged, will not allow proprietors in those terms. At worst, religions by their sheer multiplicity must all be wrong: at best they must co-exist, whether in parallel or possibly convergent lines. If, among those credentials, there is any provision for 'providence', any philosophy of history, it must be axiomatic that the absolute has eggs in many baskets and that no market-vendor has ever, can ever, will ever, offer lonely wares in a solitary market. Nor has any one religion, in spite of Jihad, crusade or 'empire', ever acquired the governance of the world. Dar al-Islam, by

definition, has to concede there is Dar al-Harb or Dar al-Sulh.[11] Something mentally counterpart to all those flags at the United Nations must
emerge somehow to align all dogmas with 'universal human rights' and
freedom of worship, of belief and of transit into or out of it.

How any faith responds to this contemporary destiny lies with its
concept of itself and its capacity for self-doubt and self-search. Insiders
must retain paramount responsibility but there may be ways in which
outsiders can also participate. What tethers each to its own heritage
will be at once the determinant and the problem. There are many ways,
in current dialogue, of negotiating this situation. There is a bland and
facile inclusivism which purports to think that, in the end, all faiths are
virtually the same, or would be, were it not for excessive rigorism or
possessive loyalty in their story. This alleged transcendental unity of all
religions needs to be allowed to emerge within the diversity that has
always, if unwittingly, housed it. All tracks lead up the same mountain.
The summit is one but the mists are many, the clouds low and the
climbers confused.

There is a wiser sort of inclusivism which turns on a logistic of
prepositions – truth for, truth in, truth through and truth of. The last,
this view holds, can only be had in terms of truth for, since there are no
agreed criteria by which we can affirm the truth of a faith. That it is truth
for its faithful is all there can be – the only form of truth of. One must
beware here of seeming to say that 'believing makes it so', since, in
many areas, there are perhaps feasible, and agreeable, grounds of
verification and falsification. Not, however, in the depths of religious
conviction. There, believing does, and must, make it so. Let 'faith', as
'hope' may, function as a verb and let us speak of 'faithing'. This is what
all believers do in giving form, rite, code and creed, to the perception of
the transcendent their 'faithing' acknowledges. There will be neither
place nor need for any one of these 'shapes' of 'faithing' to require
its exclusiveness or impose its criteria on the others. The several
authenticities will be in 'faith' as a set of soul, not in 'faiths' (beliefs) as
doctrines.[12]

This formula for constructive pluralism will not disown Christian
credentials of God provided they are allowed to Christians alone. It will
disallow their necessary relevance to all and sundry.[13] It may be seen as
implying that 'God' is at once Christian, Jewish, Hindu, Muslim, tolerat-
ing the adjectives all these apply to Him by owning them themselves.
There happens a kind of inter-identity between people and deity,
between this culture and this transcendent. Jews and Judaism always
held that sort of nexus as definitive both of Yahweh and themselves.
We must leave to Chapter 12 the question whether there can ever be
meaning in saying that 'God is Christian', and if so, in what sense. Any
faith that divine credentials have, indeed, been divinely presented,
comprehended, entrusted and custodian-risked, will be well alerted
by the question. That the credentials admit of it will be reassuring.
Meanwhile, discounted for narrowness will remain firmly on the charge-
sheet.

V

Perhaps most disconcerting of all for Christian faith in any 'Christian' God is the Buddhist interrogation of the Christian self. Christian-Buddhist dialogue is the more exacting in that it travels, for the most part, beyond all territory of Semitic (or even Hindu) theism. Selfhood, in you and me and all humanity, is its most crucial issue. Christian belief in personal significance incorporates both creation, Incarnation and redemption. It presumes to hold: 'I am created and so I am', 'I am eternally loved and so I am', 'I am redeemed by Christ and the Cross and so I am'. Personhood is thus rooted in the reality of the Christian (alleged) dimensions of God whose credentials incorporate and authenticate our personhood. Beliefs about the divine and the human are necessarily reciprocal.

Buddhism, at least in its original and bleaker form, would disavow all this. Such convictions about a significant self are a sorry illusion of which we must be disabused. The Eightfold Path will enable us to be so with its disciplines of right thinking and right willing, and the rest. It is necessary to undertake the steady abnegation of this illusory selfhood and that, not merely in the very Christian sense of renouncing what makes the self morally self-centred, but of conceding the fact that we never could be rightly self-centred existentially. For there is no real 'me', ontologically valid and authentic. On the contrary, appetite deceives us into the will to be satisfied, whereas all existence is fleeting and can never yield abiding satisfaction. We go on thinking it can, and must, because we fail to appreciate our essential nothingness, or rather, 'nothing-ness', and are thus caught in *dukkha*, or the pain of the suffering of transience, in the *anicca* that spells *anatta*. This doctrine of the 'no-self' (*anatta*), though modified somewhat in the less austere Mahayana strain of Buddhism, must be totally rejectionist of the Christian reading of a legitimate selfhood as the creation of God and the theme of 'the Word made flesh'. These must go with the illusion of the self they supposedly underwrite.

Given the basic philosophy, one can discern an enormous sense of pathos in the Buddhist interpretation of the human condition, and also in its wistful aim to retrieve the human from the burden of its illusion. Postponing a positive reckoning, there is from Buddhism an onus on Christians to cease believing wishfully in the comfort of assumed significance. They need to forego the kind of confining exuberance that had Walt Whitman cry: 'I sing of Myself,' greeting the wide Pacific as all rolling in for him, and stooping down to caress the grass as 'the handkerchief of the Lord'. Such extravagancies might seem to turn the accusation round and accuse the Buddhist of a churlish rejection of the senses, of time and of history, of earth and universe as fit for human quest and converse. But, seen through 'enlightened' eyes, the narrowness is precisely that the panorama is imprisonment until we have stripped it of the deceptions it suggests. Liberation is not into it but out of it. The true wisdom is to distrust what only captivates.

What prompts desire must prompt distrust. Oceans are for the oceanic feeling.[14]

The 'narrow' in reading the world is that which ignores decay, mortality, flux and satiety, for these, time being time, will ever more constrain and confine. Desire, ignoring them, will obviate the attainment of 'non-being' which is the goal beyond illusion. This is not (as some erroneously suppose) final 'extinction' seeing that, truly, there is 'nothing' in you and me to 'extinguish' (though Buddhist *dharma* uses the analogy of fires not fuelled and left to go out). The language of the 'oceanic feeling' tells of a bliss in which 'drop-ness' (a simile for individuation) is forever lost yet somehow for ever, unidentifiably, there.

We may find ourselves later faced with an inclusive decision about whether or not all that we experience is, or is not, intentionally trustworthy, is or is not designedly inimical. For the moment we leave a most radical disallowing of credentials, in the terms the Christian knows them, as being ever rightly ours either to desire, to search out or to attain.

vi

What is overly ambitious and religiously narrow must also be discounted as sadly naïve. If philosophy must sober the Christian to healthier reservations of mind and plurality of faiths challenge his narrow confidence, there are other critics who expose any reliance on the objectivity of doctrine. It will be simplistic to imagine that any faith-system can warrant its truth seeing that all knowledge is culture-bound and finality-free. Is there not, necessarily, a sociology of everything – of law, of art, of ethics, of education, of religion most of all? The science of sociology sees all things as 'phenomenology', not in the Kantian sense that the mind registers all experience according to its own knowing equipment by which 'things in themselves' become 'things as cognised', but in terms of 'value-free' assessment of social function, pattern, behaviour and relation as these present themselves to sociological study. Observation can, and should, conclude that religions, their scruples, practices, fads, patterns, devices, are discerned as social phenomena without reference to any spiritual credibility or ultimate sanction. These latter can be seen as extraneous to observational study with, in many quarters, the likely assumption that they do not exist.

This approach, legitimate as it may be in sociology, can be quite lethal to any faith in divine 'given-ness' about doctrine or the worship that responds. If the referent in religion is always and only social, a function appertaining in society, it becomes naïve in the extreme to suppose any absolute reference of a transcendent order. A habit anyway supervenes for which belief-structures have meaning only in respect of how they work. Judgements made about them are 'value-free' in that they relate only to a role in society, not to a vision of truth.

It is intriguing to note that much of the early stimulus to sociological study came from fascination with religion, though anthropology was more likely to be the term used if the studies related to 'primitive peoples'.[15] Was religion, in some sense, 'society worshipping itself'? At least it seemed clear that religion provided, regulated and enforced by its sanctions a structure of relationships based on perception of the external world. Rites and rituals, codes and conduct, though conceived as religious, were in fact contrived by social forces for societal needs. Life and its continuity depended on attitudes to nature, to sexuality, to physical being, and so in turn required regulators and symbols whereby fertility, resources, needs, could be ensured. Hence the taboos and traditions by which these could be socially secure. Once such reading of the situation was attained in the intelligible human sciences, it became naïve to relate these phenomena to any transcendent order.

The same 'grown-up' wisdom enabled so-minded sociologists to perceive all religious reference as a social conditioning. Social structures are conventions by which behaviour and conviction are determined. The truth about us is that we are, in fact, puppets on strings. Though we can appreciate the fact that we are pulled and jerked beyond ourselves that realisation – by necessity of the analogy – cannot save us from it. The knowledge may be disillusioning, but it is honest and realist. It is something to know our predicament even if we cannot gain exemption from it. It is the naïve who imagine themselves free. To think oneself sincere is to be deceived by our own propaganda. All is conditioned by the context that makes things carry the norms they do, the assumptions they impose.

Unwilling to be dubbed naïve, we might think to protest that there *are* minorities who have in fact, in due time, changed the conditioning ethos, that there *are* eccentrics who demonstrate a personal escape from alleged confinement to 'what goes'. Sociological theory is not impressed. All is grist to the mill. Creative minorities, indeed. But how did their transformations succeed? Only by being ultimately adopted by society, otherwise they could never survive. The collective always emerges in control. As for eccentrics, they prove the point – as exceptions. For how would they be identified as such, without the norms that make them so?

Sociological determinism seems proof against naïve dissuasives. Society is the form of our imprisonment in history, even though it builds its own world. There is no real paradox here, if consciousness itself is entirely a social product, being formed by that social thing – education, with its array of prejudices,[16] whims, interests, blind spots and anxieties. Scientific and objective it may aim and claim to be, yet never exempt from economic, ethnic and political factors which will both engage and disconcert any sociology of knowledge. Certain Marxist ideas as to 'ideology' arise in this same context. For Marx did not allow to ideas any derivation from 'pure reason' or independent mind. For Kant's 'things in themselves' and 'things in the knowing', he had 'things in their utility and utilisation'. Ideas were sublimates of economic reality in its several social forms determined by systems of production. Philosophy is no more than the form in which economic-social situations are expressed and – when duly activated – the means to change it. Only the naïve in their obstinacy, or gullibility, could suppose otherwise or allow to religious faith any genuine mystery, wonder or awed perplexity.

vii

If sociology purported to expose the naïvety of trustful theology by study of society, the psychologists proposed to do the same by study of the self. They went back to where Buddhism saw the nub of the human puzzle but they did so, not in the *angst* of the Buddhist soul around the paradox of 'desire', but in the confidence of empirical science and techniques of observation, analysis and theory, drawn from the physical sciences and recruited to the very different world of human emotion and behaviour. What if religion was no more than the psyche, in its disorder, its dreams, its responses and its fantasies?

The approach was again phenomenological. Observe obsessions, ceremonials, mechanisms of consciousness, neuroses, and read all that religious behaviour reveals as no more than psychic phenomena relating, not to genuine transcendence but to sex, soul, society and death, to the id, the ego, and the super-ego. Pursue these beyond consciousness in realms of the unconscious, whether individual or collective, and find the key there to the drives, the instincts and the 'religious' shame, guilt, zeal, habit, routine and ecstasy, formerly and mistakenly attributed to divine reality.

Contemporary psychology ramifies into a diversity of theory and practice, often sharpened into 'schools' and 'heresies'. Its relevance in therapeutic terms deserves the careful, perceptive respect of theologians. What is at issue, however, is its essential reductionism of Christian theology, as relating to transcendent sovereignty, grace and redemption. There is no quarrel with the open-minded theologian when it explores the underlying, collective factors present in culture-boundness, and brings into the theological equation factors of symbol, myth and imagery that were earlier unidentified or unknown. In those terms there had long been a believing naïvety that needed to be accused. It will be right and honest to reckon with what, in religion, is owed to factors wholly in the psyche. There is more, however, in the self than its psychic workings. Religions, Asian and Semitic, differ sharply on the degree to which what we find in the psyche warrants what we affirm about man in the universe. We may not exclude the genuine influx of the transcendent. Nor is psychic development in persons or societies a closed system. We remain in total, lifelong responsibility for selfhood within a common humanity, seeing that ego-consciousness, however atrophied or distorted, is never mortally withdrawn. Religious are, or can be, means whereby the immediate self is alerted to, and perhaps enabled for, what that responsibility implies and imposes. Christian doctrine insistently refers us to knowable, divine, gentle, sovereign compassion, where all our vagaries are known and our secrets unhidden. What may seem, in the theologian, to be naïve to the psychologist may well identify a reverse naïvety.

viii

The ambitious, the narrow and the naïve in the discounting agenda we have in hand lead on to the indictment of the plausible. All four merge together. Self-assurance might be said to characterise all religions. Self-doubt, especially among their appointed custodians, has seemed inappropriate to their authority even if sometimes present in their soul. Though Christianity might well claim a greater capacity for self-doubt than any, it has not seemed so to other belief systems. These, by their own lights, have found much to reproach in Christian credentialling of God. The several grounds they find devolve, inevitably, from their own characteristic cast of mind. The general charge of presumptuous exceptionality which we have already noted is distinctively underlined by the Hindu mind. Christian assurance about *the* Incarnation and 'the saviour of the world' offends against the inherent multiplicity of the Hindu pantheon. The self-assurance of the New Testament cannot ride with the Hindu need to find the transcendent essentially untidy, multiplex, inconsistent and immune from the law of necessary contradiction. We must concede, in worship and in concept, a plethora of powers, deities and beings, never unified into a single dominion, unless it be that of the inconceivable *Brahma* that contains them all. Shiva must have place, and Krishna with his whims and moods and forms. Theism has to make sensible room for polytheism. Myths and the beings that inhabit them can never be credibly reduced to singular divinity. The sort of theism Christians affirm is guilty, not only of crass self-assurance, but of wilful betrayal of sheer mystery, in purporting to proclaim 'One Lord, one faith, one baptism, one God and Father of us all' (Ephesians 4:5). The 'One' Christians make their 'only' is forever among 'many'.

Perhaps in the very reproach there is no less a self-assurance. Maybe religions cannot escape this. The Hindu stance would seem to imply that reproach cannot be laid unless it is reciprocal. Just as tolerance cannot be practised on the intolerable, so transcendent plurality cannot avoid being 'one' interpretation. If, then, we are confronting the insoluble, at least we can learn humility.

The Judaic reaction to Christian credentials of God as proving only Christian self-assurance can readily be guessed from the conclusions in Chapter 4. The case is that Messianic identification in Jesus crucified is pure romanticism. If, as in writers like Gershom Scholem, Martin Buber and Leo Baeck, it is necessary to see all Messianism as the shape of ever-unrealised 'hope', then any historic actuality of truly Messianic order is ruled out. This will be so even without the incredible 'foolishness' of a victim made victor in the Christian frame of cross and resurrection. Easter faith is self-indulgent credulity in sharp contrast to on-going Judaic fidelity to the divine covenant, 'capable (in John Keats's words in another context) of being in uncertainties' and not lusting after proven rescue from them. Traditional Christianity, on this view, is merely self-assured (and self-deceived) when it locates a world's redemption in a single and an actual Christ and proposes to share him with all humanity and that, in a world so evidently, so desperately, unredeemed.

Islam, in its own different self-assurance, sees Christianity as indulging in self-delusion from another angle. Unlike Hinduism, it has no quarrel with doctrines of unity but only with the Christian engagement of them with Christology. 'God in Christ' is seen as a travesty of 'Allah in Himself'. In creation, law, revelation and prophethood, the divine indeed engages with the human world, but these are where engagement stays. Christian confidence about divine initiatives of grace and redemption go unwarrantably beyond what is attributable to Allah. Indeed, they contravene what is conceptually tolerable to genuine theology. Divine relations with humanity are didactic, hortatory, legal and judgemental.

Creation is a blessedly common conviction between Muslim and Christian, as is the divine beneficence it tells. In respect, however, of what creation undergoes, in history, at human hands, Islam has no place for those measures of divine gentleness and vicarious love which Christian belief in the Incarnation and the Cross enshrines. Divine sovereignty relates to human story with sterner power. From its context in Meccan society, Muhammad's mission – and so the whole Qur'ān – perceive a world so prone to idolatory, so given to *zulm* and *shirk*, dark wrong and false worship, as to necessitate the structure of belief and discipline Islam alone afforded. Its very finality sounded a verdict on less adequate theisms which had preceded it. To persist in these, when the Qur'ān was given, could only be a wilful persistence.

It followed that Christian measures of divine compassion could only be improperly meant about God and unfitted to the human scene. Islam saw itself as rebuking the original – and continuing – assurance about itself that Christianity enjoyed. It had always been plausible to believe in divine compassion and *kenosis* but, as Islam saw it, something not to be forfeited, had gone. Of Allah it must be insistently affirmed: 'Exalted be He above all that they associate.' That dictum must exclude the Christian doctrines. For do they not 'associate' Allah unwarrantably with Jesus as 'His Christ'.[17] Moreover, those central points of Christian faith entail paradox which is mostly seen in Islam as either a laziness of mental perception or a mystification of truth. Such Christian self-assurance merits anathema.

ix

This issue of what is, or is not, theologically conceivable about divine liability to humanity in history and its suspicion of mere plausibility have a very different echo in an intellectual handling of theology in the nineteenth century. Having origins further back, it is associated with the name of Ludwig Feuerbach (1804–72). For many in his day it occasioned the kind of erosion of faith, experienced, for example, by the novelist, George Eliot, who translated his *The Essence of Christianity* from the German. For Feuerbach, Christianity gave a pseudo-objectivity to the elements of religion which, rightly identified, were human subjectivity projected as divine reality. It was human feeling that gave an assured, but illusory, substance to its content. Human consciousness had a capacity for the infinite in its very nature, which was thought for the sake of thought and loved for the sake of love. All was subjectivity objectified. The absolute was human sensitivity. Feeling had its 'God' in itself, not by crude wishful 'creation', but as the correlative of the human capacity *qua* worship, dependence and intuitive sense.[18]

It followed for Feuerbach that faith was human self-love reassuring itself by the hypothesis of God, God being an abstraction of our innermost desires. What humans urgently desired to see on earth they contrived in the heavens. Faith was, therefore, both true and false. It was right in its aspirations, its intended values, but wrong in its location of them. It devised for its peace a man-oriented supreme. From Martin Luther, Feuerbach derived, as he thought, the clue to guilt, sin and justification, in human yearning for pardon and peace. If, in this way, 'God' existed for man's sake, it was easy to account for doctrines, like the Incarnation and the Cross, as the desired response to human need.[19] This also explained the prominent role of miracles in religion. Faith needed them to vindicate its feel for an objectivity reciprocal to its hopes.

Basic to estimates of Feuerbach and his thesis of a pseudo-objectivity is the real concreteness of nature itself. While he wrote of religious gratitude – with nature's benison in mind – as a genuine element in subjectivity, the puzzle persists as to how to relate that natural order to the Feuerbachian 'God'. Karl Marx, who owed much to Feuerbach, saw the point and used the concreteness of things economic to require 'values' more realist than those of human projection on to some divine only constituted by such projection.[20]

Basic also was any referability of all to reason and rationality. Underlying all else was the question (to which we must return in Chapter 12) whether all that is is human-friendly in its actuality, or whether we see it only as the ambiguous setting of our wistfulness, ignoring the challenge it presents to our toil and brain, our ways and means and ends, our arts and science. Might values projected be values neglected? Marx, at least, thought so.

Nevertheless, many were the literati and the literate in the nineteenth century who reckoned, via Feuerbach, with what might be called 'the fiction of faith'. His thesis certainly nibbled away at the sort of dogmatic assurance the Creeds had enshrined and purported to uphold. It had always been implicit in Christian faith about 'God in Christ' and 'the Word made flesh' that what was believed about God and what was believed about humanity were one whole, but not in these subjective terms. If there were no divinely 'real' reciprocal to nature and to history, and if the divine was none other than a human securing of human values, the shift to human grounding might induce other conclusions. If there was really only us, projecting, why not simply 'Only us'? Burdened or exhilarated by Darwin and much else, many took that path. Classic, doctrinal Christianity began to seem at risk precisely in being too definitive, too credal, too assured, too anciently derived. If Christ, as Feuerbach wrote, was 'an existence identical with the nature of feeling . . . on him are heaped all the joys of the imagination and all the sufferings of the heart'[21] history was no longer crucial as the faith claimed and everything was relative to option if not open to scepticism. By projection, doctrine might begin to look absurd.

X

A keen observer might detect in the issues, of which Feuerbach stands for symbol, a further dimension with which we might conclude this chapter's counts against orthodox Christian faith. The notion of 'projection' suggests the question whether faith is not somehow 'telling its own story'. The novel, since Fielding, Sterne and Richardson, and in its rich fulfilment in Dickens, George Eliot, Thomas Hardy and Conrad, has come to seem not only the genius of modern English literature but a sort of index to the shape of meaning.

The status and sustained appeal and popularity of the novel form since its creation may be taken for proof that it corresponds existentially to the core of human experience. It is, therefore, no accident that theology *qua* story is drawn into the implications. In the novel, the author is in control of plots and sequences. The characters relate, develop and contrive as the pen wills. The novelist probably knows the end from the beginning. Though, reputedly, Dickens, for example, devised schemes and personalities as he went along, by instalments in magazines, the logics that he set in train were his own. He, like Thomas Hardy, could engineer sub-plots to underline his schemata, with sudden eventualities, odd mischances, convenient demises, to reach his ends. There is about such novelising a mastery that via story depicts a vision, shapes a world and recruits time to tell meaning.

It occurs to many a sceptic that faith about divine credentials is doing exactly this, out of its own 'genius' for forming response to the known, the felt, the pondered and the suffered. It is, like the novelist, making fiction as a way of questioning what is and depicting an answer. Doubtless the novel, as its best, relates to the real, to life, to meaning. Otherwise it could not intrigue, persuade, fascinate and portray. But it does all these things, for 'reality', only in the form of story of which it is itself the *fons et origo*. Hence the necessity for creed to be story, for doctrine to be drama, for – in a word – belief to be fiction. On this understanding, we can rightly speak of 'the truth of fiction', but only if we realise 'the fiction of truth'. The will that writes, the will that controls, is 'making its own points'. Story is the place.

The next chapter must take up the sharp challenge this poses about objectivity itself. It may be protested at once that believers are inheritors, not novelists, that they accept their 'story' and in no way, 'write' it. Indeed, but (the analogy argues) novels of course have readers and readership goes along with what has been 'storified' precisely with the expectation that it would. Readership thus becomes a ready metaphor for faith-reception, or what ancient usage called the cat-echumentate. Might religious fanaticism then be seen as some kind of fan loyalty, and more gentle believing a literature appreciation? The second suggestion gives a hint that there might be in faith a counterpart to literary criticism. There was surely a place for it when George Bernard Shaw pronounced himself a better dramatist than Shakespeare. Let us defer the hint. Faith may well be living into, and with, a story without thereby misreading the reality that gives the story being. For the moment, however, the charge is that the assurance Christians find is no more than the gift of a good story. If, as was reputedly said, 'a good book is the precious lifeblood of a master-spirit', faith, thinks the sceptic, may be a satisfying read provided we appreciate that its reality is fiction.

xi

That there may be a role, if not a place, for agnosticism intelligent faith has always acknowledged. No summary in the compass here available, both of space and range, could hope to do justice to how dismissible are the Christian credentials of God. We have not noted how far and how often the presentation of them in Church history has veered and altered tack and quite transformed its emphases by inward pressure or external charge. Anselm, Calvin, Donne, Jonathan Edwards, the Wesleys, Simeon, Newman, Gore and Temple preached the same Cross but not the same atonement. The Logos of John meant one thing to the Cambridge Platonists, much else to Origen, Hegel and the Oxford Tractarians. Heirs and heritage have shifted with the centuries. Theology has often seemed in tactical retreat, withdrawing from one bastion, no longer 'impregnable' like Gladstone's 'rock of Scripture', to stand (as it seemed) further in with a beleaguered sanctuary set to be shown 'impregnable' in other terms, if these could still be found.

As much, however, could be said of the columns of dictionaries, those havens, as we often think, of the definitive, yet steadily the victims of obsolescence and flux. As the author of one of them noted, 'What is so much in the power of men as language will very often be capriciously conducted.' Caprice can be malice as well as confusion. We have need of patience. It is – and must be – in context and exchange that language had currency. It is likewise with things of faith. We began with a sense of possible, or real, reductionism in the postures of static unbelief. Simple notions of language and fact betray the subtlety inherent in both. To be confined to what is often called 'literal fact' is to fail to see that meaning is never 'embalmed' in statements or caught like amber. Language is transaction with meaning, ways of ascertaining and exchanging it, which incorporate much more than logic, in respect of contexts, gestures, nuances, implications and the very shape that sentences must take. 'Fact', likewise, can never be intelligently limited to propositions. It belongs with fields of reference. More things than logic turn on whether words are 'true', and if so how?

It is necessary to carry forward to Chapter 12 this suspicion of reductionism at the core of unbelief. It must be seen as reciprocal to the charge of extravagance at the heart of faith. Ludwig Wittgenstein has the dictum, 'To believe in God means to see that life has a meaning.'[22] But what meaning? Is faith's meaning only and forever interior to faith itself, constituting the world for itself as rules constitute games? What, then, does it 'mean', to mean? How, in language, does 'saying' relate to the 'said'?

In tracing the suspicions that divine credentials in their Christian referents are overly ambitious, oddly narrow, intellectually naïve and only self-assured, we have set a large agenda for finding them otherwise. 'Finding' will be the just word. That will never be faith that has not meant a search. Perhaps it has been sufficiently honest about the maze it sets itself. 'Maze', however, yields 'amazement'. Amazement may be only entanglement and frustrated perplexity, or it may spell wonder, astonishment and delight. To these the Christian is no stranger.

12 Finding Credentials Divine

PAINTINGS which could find no market a century ago are now well-nigh priceless. How potentially rich, unknowingly the artist Vincent van Gogh was making a friend on whom he called in Dordrecht, Holland, saying with his customary, gentle courtesy, 'This is really your room and now I would very much like your permission to paste some little biblical pictures on the wallpaper.' Who would resist his enthusiasm?

> Of course I immediately acceded to his request and he went to work with feverish haste. Within half an hour the whole room was decorated with biblical scenes and Ecce Homos and Van Gogh had written under each head of Christ: 'Ever sorrowful but always rejoicing.'[1]

The story opens this final chapter well. When it knows itself truly the Christian faith intends a similar respect to the personhood of each and all. It has to do with one who knocks and waits. 'This is really your room', is its instinctive greeting. For about each and every 'I' there is something inviolate. Everyone's soul is their own. A body is the individuation of us all and ensures the same privacy to the consciousness and the conscience it separately houses. In the appeal of faith, as in awareness of being, there is no escape from the personal pronoun. Each, as we saw at the outset, has to be asking what they make of the world. The answers they live will be their own.

For that same reason there is a capacity to accommodate a guest – a guest with a theme, a wealth, a waiting handiwork for which he covets vacant places it may fill. An enthusiasm brings him. For it is his own artistry he carries. It is an artistry that tells itself in scenes from Scriptures, in pictures that are biblical. From that source it has what dominates and determines the meaning of the whole. It possesses the

Bible only in the final terms of *Ecce Homo*: 'Behold the Man', 'ever sorrowful but always rejoicing'.[2] That paradox of the Cross the artist underlines. For it is the utmost he means to say about God. Painting is the way he finds to say it.

The previous chapter promised attention to some strenuous problems of theology and faith. Has this one lost its way already in fine sentiment? What, it might be asked, would Feuerbach have made of Van Gogh, had they been contemporary? He might well have recruited him for evidence of unusual subjectivity. Was not everything about the painter simply the vividness of his imagination? Van Gogh never made good his early ambition to be a Christian preacher, and preachers have to believe in objectivity.

Be these conjectures as they may, there is a single counter-question which will bring us to the heart of the matter and, so doing, qualify to comprise all the issues remitted from Chapter 11. It is to ask: To what did such intense personhood relate? We cannot well be content simply to say: To the landscape, to the natural scene. His passion to depict, his ardour with the brush, his insistent struggle to participate signify more deeply. There is something transcendent breaking in.

Vincent van Gogh was a soul immersed in the thereness of the world, its beauty, wonder, terror and demand. Let us use this vexed word 'subject' to learn the real objectivity it must connote. For, in being a 'subject' he is truly having one. The entire situation is reciprocal. All artists have their 'subjects' – faces, scenes, clouds, hills and valleys, seas and furrows, wheat and scarecrows. Having them, they, the artists, are 'subject'(s) to all these – 'subjects' who sense, wonder, aspire and belong, who recruit their colours for the glowing panorama with colours of its own. Their 'subjects' to which 'subject' are the queries in a peasant's face, the dark frown of the clouds, the rippling corn in the wind over the field. They and these are alike 'objective' and mutually so to each other, the painters and the painteds. The brush 'objectifies' the 'subjects' only because the 'subjects' are objects already in their own right – objects to which the 'objectifiers' are kindredly 'subject'. In the strange double sense of the word the human spirit 'realises' by dint of art and canvas what has availed to be realised by being real. Art, as we must say, 'takes' only as, and because, it receives. It does not 'project': it registers. The same happens between God and faith – in terms we must be careful, and honest, to explore.

This analogy, it will be urged in protest, has to do with art and may not be transposed to things of faith. It suffices, for the moment, to require us to see a situation in which 'projection' is inconceivable. On the contrary, here there is reception, interpretation, in congenial response. There is mutuality. Meaning is being transacted only because meaning is there. That real situation is ignored if we presume to talk of pure subjectivity projecting itself upon what, or where (such subjectivity apart) would be a void. The only subjectivity is one that lives by virtue of the 'other', the 'given', the really real. That 'other', in its turn, is subject to the skill, the love, the mind, that 'finds' it.

Keeping for the present, to the adjectival theology for which we have pleaded from the start, and speaking of 'divine' and 'human', the case being made is that Christian faith responds to the divinely real and that the credentials we have studied are where it happens. It happens there by virtue of an import, not unlike that of theme to art, akin to a capacity, a disclosure that responds to a discovery. The experience of the 'something mutual' is not self-assured: it is Christ-assured. Christian faith would not be the thing it is were it not about what was genuinely reciprocal. The Christian believer relates no less than the artist. Faith interprets, registers, and comprehends what truly reciprocates those respondings. What results, as in art, is a verdict, a verdict reached and held and so commended. In affirming, it will still explore: if ill serving it will refine. It will always be a self speaking, but not in self-persuasion. As a human awareness it is taking in what is truly mutual in divine transcendence, because, as Baudelaire hinted, transcendence is divine transdescendence.[3]

This is why 'finding' here is such an apt word, for its double meaning illustrates the point. We 'find', as archaeologists do, for example, relics, remains, coins, strata, from which we 'find' conclusions, as juries do in courts, for or against the parties to the litigation. 'Finding' binds evidence in being to evidence as meaning. 'Credentials', in any sphere, have this same quality, confirming the belief in presenting the believable. Credentials are fit to be found such by the finding they enable. This is no passive thing in either part. It is had by a 'subject' but only by virtue of the object.

Experience of hunger may clarify. Hunger is a yearning of any subject to it, a yearning for food on the part of food-needing entities. Outside that category it could not exist. It is a kind of seeking which belongs only with the reality of what must be found. It does not happen, presumably, to grass or stones. It is a privation and, as such, is no illusion. It argues the meaning of food, the meant-for-food-ness of the hungry. It is, therefore, fit parallel to Augustine's famous words about our restlessness for rest and his conviction that both the yearning and the satisfaction have to do humanly with God.

ii

However, bringing all the cautions, caveats and doubtings reviewed in the previous chapter into one summary, may we not conclude that all our 'finding' and hungering restlessness are no proof that this divine/human encountering is more than a 'say-so' of ours? Is it only that thinking finds it so, the inducements to such thinking being so urgent, so traditional, so obviously motivated? We want solace, we need assurance, we face death, we lose friends, we forfeit hopes, we miss opportunities, we sense boredom, we break trust, so we invent comfort. Do we not detect in all these what more than suffices to explain our prayers, our churches, our mosques and temples, our proneness to belief? Is not confirming evidence that it is so writ large in our pieties?

Does it not breathe in our hymns and betake us to our Masses? 'Is their trouble anywhere?' runs the wistful question. 'Take it to the Lord in prayer' certainly rhymes but can it avail, except by make-belief? If Christians want to take analogy from hunger, or from restlessness, or from search, and proceed to argue food and rest and finding for the soul, let them take their analogy the other way and concede that there is death in hunger, a fiction in rest and futility in search.

We state the issue harshly as the issue deserves. For here, we are at the heart of it. Nor has faith in credentials ever been immune from the threat of 'only a say-so'. In his stressful youth, John Bunyan knew it well. 'How,' he asked, 'if all our faith, and Christ, and Scriptures, should be but a think-so too?' He was one with all of us in this quandary in reaching for some straw to clutch. Paul, the great apostle, came to his mind, 'of whom and his words we made so great a matter'. Paul could not be deceiving us. We could reasonably chase away doubt on the strength of Pauline faith.[4] That bulwark, however, if we are minded to undermine it, will offer no security. Plainly there are no guarantees. If there were, there would be no occasion for faith. Meaning has never been a literalist, a sky-writer. Truth has always to be taken in trust.

It seems clear that we are faced with an option. Theology *will* be 'faith saying-so', co-existing with others saying 'not-so'. The psalmist must have sensed this when he sang, 'Let the redeemed of the Lord say so' (Psalm 107:2). Such faith always pointed to event and claimed to tell event's significance. Christianity has always done so about the event of Jesus Christ. Witness is about perceived fact: fact carries truth: and truth requires witness. The circle is complete. 'Let the redeemed, say so.'

But wait, says the other option. They are *only* 'saying-so'. The circle, witness, fact, faith, witness, is obviously circular. It arrives where it was intended. The 'saying' about 'redeeming' is from the lips of 'the redeemed'. It is open to the sceptic to retort: 'They only thought so.' The event they interpret cannot bear their interpretation. We wonder: Did it happen? Even if it did, it was, maybe, fortuitous. The history was a toss-up. The exodus was a fluke. The claim was a verdict and the verdict was prejudice. Wish, illusion, conjecture, rumour, were all involved. All we dependably have is credence with credulity.

An option of interpretation, then, let it be. But, if we stay here, are we not just back, more devastatingly, in the discountings of Chapter 11, to which this one was supposedly responding? Indeed we are, but on purpose. For now we have all those discountings in a single focus and faith at its most radical stretch. For, in all the foregoing chapter, we were not concerned merely with points in a discussion but with a plea for faith-sincerity. It is a poor apologetic that only aims to entrench a dogma. We have to be ready for the depths and heights into which theology has to take the honesty of faith.

'Say so'? Or truly so? Does it matter which? Some would say not. Yet, if faith is only what *we* affirm, can it 'do' what it does, namely interpret all there is? Why not? Is there not a sense in which it is doing so all the time, even if the faith-people do not realise that it only works for them because of them? If and when we, in believing, realise this is, or may be, the case, will we not have to think again? Perhaps we shall acquiesce that we are believing for believing's sake and so have, in effect, engineered all conviction without any real or necessary relation to what is there. We may pronounce ourselves content to do so even though what we held, prior to this discovery otherwise, we held from authority, inheritance, or heavenly *imprimatur* in good faith. We should then, in effect, be sustaining, of and by ourselves, what hitherto we thought was sustaining us, opting to decide what previously was supposed to be deciding us. We are, then, so to say, making our own faith.

That, the cynic or sceptic may say, is the way it is, the only way it could be. This is the only option you have. For reasons given, no criteria exist to escape it. We are, inescapably, believing to believe. Or, in other terms, we are consenting to be deceived, whether nervously, complacently, or doggedly. Have we not said already that 'Truth is reciprocal to trust'? Then, so be it. Let the truth/trust situation talk no more about 'credentials'. Faith is a self-made world.

This, however, is not the kind of dubiety that faith can allow. Indeed, this stance evacuates even the business of doubting honestly. A living faith cannot be content with the suspicion that it has engineered itself, nor with a conspiracy to renounce interrogation. The will for credentials, a sense of their necessity, a hope of their possibility, will be inseparable from any authentic faith, any faith worthy of the name.

Proceeding with this liability, there is one immediate point. It is that the case against ascertainable credentials of God is no easier undertaking than the contrary positive case. When Iris Murdoch opines that 'there is only us', with no theological referent, she adds that it 'is a view as difficult to argue as its opposite, and I shall simply assert it. I can see no evidence that human life is not something self-contained.'[5] It is important to recognise that this is so. In 'the grand perhaps', as Robert Browning called it, doubt and denial are as much at issue as faith and confidence. Atheism does not escape the suspicion of being a crude 'say-so'. It can derive from motives of sloth, guess, posturing, no less than faith can. Reality deals to all the same cards even within circumstances that may be tragically contrasted. We can find mental genius and the simple-minded in both camps. We must beware of believing, or disbelieving, by proxy, trusting in the credentials, either way, of other minds, except in so far as these can belong with divine credentials in our steady personal exploring.

iii

If what is thus at stake could be seen as 'the con of a pro' and 'the pro of a con', it will be right to continue with any truth/trust situation by asking whether trust, in another sense, is what must decide about truth: not now in the earlier terms of trust 'making true', but rather of truth 'making for trust'. In short, let us ask whether all that is is meant, means well, and is meant for humankind. If neither No nor Yes can be 'proved', and both have their grounds, why not opt for the glad option? Ample, massive evidence will sustain us. Other evidence could urgently dissuade us, but the choice remains and choice is ours. If we take the glad one we have convincing reason for tipping the balance that way. Perhaps things will turn on our 'sort of mind', but then we shall want to have others share it. The misanthrope may well be nourishing a sombre psyche. The glad choice will not be threatened by immensity or over-awed by infinite distances of space and time. We shall not be implying that the universe is exhausted in the phenomenon of man. Its vastness does not obviate, still less annihilate, our here-ness. In noting the starlight we are contemporary with the millions of lifespans through which it reached us. The sun warms us from 93 million miles away which we acknowledge a benign distance, since its surface temperature is 6000 degrees Celsius. We need not stay here over tokens of a happy, mysterious tolerance of life, of mind and spirit, and of option – and wit – to register its meaning. We might even conclude that there is an odd churlishness about the soul that throws all away in sceptical vulgarity or nonchalance or cynicism. Yet, nevertheless, all are free to make that case and take their option. It could be honestly adopted.

Let us not carry the evidences further than we have already done in Chapters 2, 3 and 10, but comprehend all that has been listed in Chapter 11 within this single angle of decision and say at once: If we opt for human meaning meant and known and meant well, we must incur the full onus of our gladness. We will need to face what must give us pause.

To argue only from nature will not suffice. For perceptions remain ambiguous – surely an overall beneficence, yet 'cons' persistently present. Appeal to moral law will not suffice. For while there is a beneficence in the very fact that law belongs in life, that we are not unmoved to good or unrebuked by wrong, manuals of right and wrong and codes of ethics do not fit our perpetual liability for what they should contain and how they may be lived. A transcendence that is only legal and hortatory, that has only Decalogues and prohibitions, will not meet our human case.

The option of gladness in celebration of meant-ness must measure the contradiction of sin and evil to that choice. Since it has ruled out transcendent malignity, it must undertake the mystery of how wrong concerns the ultimate beneficence it sees. If not in doubt about 'whether' it sees an ultimate love, it must be urgently knowing When? and Where? Unless we are to be back with faith as 'self-made', we must ascertain how and where it might be 'God-made'.

Such ascertaining brings us again to the insistence made throughout on the divine/human theme in theology and, within it, the centrality of things vicarious. There is something about wrong which, in both senses of the phrase, does not, will not, 'leave us alone'. It frequents us, to be sure, but it also entails us with each other, beyond what retribution, law, restitution and the like, can either regulate or undo. What is beyond these has simply to be borne, and how it is borne will be the vital clue to its defeat.

There is little need to recapitulate. The intermeshing evils of human society are self-evident. The suffering of their entail, from the guilty on to the innocent, is everywhere. History may do little to prosper good causes: it certainly witnesses to evil ones, and to their consequences in blight and tragedy for the wronged as well as guilt and shame to the doers. As one of her clerics in George Eliot's novel tells its hero, Adam Bede:

> There is no sort of wrong deed of which a man can bear the punish-
> ment alone: you can't isolate yourself and say that the evil which is
> in you shall not spread. Men's lives are as thoroughly blended with
> each other as the air they breathe: evil spreads as necessarily as
> disease.[6]

There is not only contagion. People do more than 'catch' evil from each other. They undergo it. Nor is the 'punishment' ever solitary. It comes arbitrarily where it has no due place, on those who underwent the wrong. What George Eliot has in the conclusion of her longest novel, *Middlemarch*, only partly suffices for this truth. It may have been the mind of Feuerbach inhibiting her. Yet she finely writes:

> Her [the heroine's] full nature . . . spent itself in channels which had
> no great name on the earth. But the effect of her being on those
> around here was incalculably diffusive. For the growing good of the
> world is partly dependent on un-historic acts: and that things are
> not so ill with you and me as they might have been, is half owing to
> the number who lived faithfully a hidden life and rest in unvisited
> tombs.[7]

The redemptiveness is deep here but very modest. 'Hidden', 'growing', 'partly', 'half-owing', are all cautious and all 'diffusive'. By 'unhistoric' she meant 'not notable'. All, so far, is well. 'Good', here, is 'not being overcome of evil'. But are there not (historic or otherwise) occasions where good is positively overcoming evil, where something more delib-erately vicarious undertakes wrong done in order to restore what wrong had violated in the only terms available, the terms of love?

If there is such human vicariousness in the incidence of wrong, and its repair in forgiving-ness, can we think it due to any counterparting original in the divine mind and competence? If so, where? For, if there is, it will have a human story. It will radically engage the divine in the human situation.

We noted earlier in these pages the interaction of the divine/human in the suffering of the greatest prophets, the Isaiahs and Jeremiahs of the Hebraic tradition. There was a divine/human partnering in their sending and their readiness to be sent. That mutuality surely persisted when they underwent contradiction, even death, in their experience of mission. For these reactions were meant for the God they represented, or at least for what the divine claimed. Is it, then, a thing not to be thought that the divine was somehow there also when the human suffered? There could hardly have been desertion.

Chapters 4 and 5 have argued how this dimension of the divine in the human, of the human for the divine, might lead us to vicariousness as where theology arrives. It knows itself doing so in reckoning with the Cross of Jesus, the crowning place of this same sequence via love's passion to love's victory. Ever since, Christians have been saying: 'Herein is love . . . God commends his love towards us in that while [seeing that] we were sinners, Christ died for us.'

Immediately, however, the question arises whether this, too, is only our 'say-so'. Has faith simply inserted the Cross into that same circularity that earlier gave us pause. Is it simply 'the redeemed' still 'saying so' with Jesus crucified as now their plea? Take the glad option about the world, if you will, but why, or how, can you underwrite it – as they say 'objectively' – by invocation of Good Friday? You have no better rescue from a trust/truth equation than you had before. What will you say to Feuerbach's repeated charge?

> the very luxury of egoism. . . . Thus, in and through God, man has in view himself alone. . . . God as Christ is the sum of all human misery . . . Christ is the self-confession of human sensibility . . . God is the love that satisfies our wishes, our emotional wants, he is himself the realised wishes of the heart. God is the optative of the human heart. . . . Omnipotence does nothing more than accomplish the will of the feelings.[8]

We can reply that his option, likewise, is his own. Yet note how entirely lacking from his pages is the vicarious theme, either in its splendid human incidence or in its divine, discernible, inherent possibility. Instead, he sees the Cross 'so little superhuman that it even sanctions human weakness', and upbraids Jesus in Gethsemane for lack of the sort of proud courage with which Socrates drank his hemlock. He fails to see that it was never a 'superhuman' Christ the Christian faith perceived. Quite the contrary. There was no reproach in tears for Lazarus. Feuerbach has ironically understood how the Cross captures the heart but fails totally to see the reasons why, misstating as he does the Incarnation. 'God', he thinks, 'empties himself of his Godhead, for the sake of man, lays aside his Godhead. . . . If God loves man, is not man then the very substance of God?' Kenosis had to do with 'very God of very God' in other terms than these, as told in Chapter 6.[9] Faith has always been at risk from misconstruings.

The issue, of course, is wider than its juncture with The Essence of Christianity, influential as Feuerbach's thinking was. That 'God was in Christ reconciling the world' remains a truth of witness, not of geometry or its QEDs. But it may think itself deeply fitting to God, as God needs to be, if we are to 'make sense of the earth', still more if we sustain a conviction about the seriousness of creation and the ultimate 'good-ness' of the world. In the light of history, a wise omnipotence is not likely to be unscarred. The crown of thorns may well be truly divine insignia.

Conversely, if what can be divinely meant needs, for those divine reasons, to have the measure of the human crisis lest its meaning be in forfeit, must there not be something like what made Jesus the Christ-figure? If to be vicarious in respect of wrong is the nature and vocation of love, and if there is, world-size, a wrong in human history, may the wrong and the love not meet? Will their meeting not be an event carrying the dimensions as they are, thereby telling them beyond all illusion so that it might be truly said: 'Behold the sin of the world'? 'Behold the Lamb of God who bears . . .'?

It is not conjecture but realism that has us reading in what transpired on Good Friday the epitome, in quality, of 'the evil that men do'. What conspired to make it the human thing it was contains and incriminates us all. So much is history. That Jesus ever said, 'Father, forgive them . . .' we have only from the good faith of Luke who tells us so. The sceptic who doubts it, wills to doubt it. It will not override him. For the Cross is not the overriding sort of truth. The utmost scepticism will be free to think it false. We shall be justified in pinning our glad acceptance of the world on the symbol that most comprehends the reasons why it might not be so and gently cancels them from reckoning, the 'All-great being the All-loving too'.

iv

It may now seem a long way to come back to those philosophical empiricists with whom we began in Chapter 11, but they have their place. It is, however, a place in this whole context. Kant's very honest duty to distinguish between 'things as they seem' when humanly cog-nised and 'things as they are' (*noumena*) such cognising apart, will not affect Christology. For that, as we have seen, derives, not from empirical study of sense experience, but from inclusive dimensions of human existence. The overambition of the old 'arguments' for the existence of God, known as cosmological and teleological, we can readily, indeed thankfully, allow to be repudiated. It is agreed that, starting from sense experience, we cannot postulate a designing Creator with that sort of 'designing'. An 'uncaused cause' in those old terms indeed involves a rational contradiction. Moreover, the tracing of causality within what senses can observe and mind organise into law and theory can be better understood as nature-bound with Darwin and his successors coming into their own.[10]

Our point of departure is not from sense-experience in the context set by Cartesian concern for the self as rational and with doubt also as the mind's business. It has been with the person as more than a *Cogito* and with the ultimate alternatives either of radical despair or wagered conviction. Creation, thus, is not a bare matter of some 'start', involving

Kantian antinomy. It belongs, not with 'when' or 'how', but with 'why'. 'Why' is a question, not springing from sensa data and so subject to empiricist veto, but from the 'given' of being with its moral liability and its spiritual demand. It does not fall into, and fail as, a category of pure reason but of radical need and decision. The charge of overambition can be readily allowed, on its stated terms. It cannot require that we be under-alert. The pretension of which theology stands accused by the empiricists has no relevance to the wonder of rationality itself and the onus time and life place upon our human personhood to 'connect' with all its dimensions. *Noumena* mean nothing to a would-be suicide.

There may well be a sense in which, so saying, we return to a teleology. For we are allowing the questions that contain the whole and assuming intention in the world, its story and its meaning. This is not the old, discredited 'argument from design' but one that thinks beyond empirical confines, not to violate them by purporting to enquire about sundry parts, but to enquire about a whole – the whole which such 'confinement' itself admits to be its larger context.[11] One can hardly forbid a territory and deny that it exists. The human soul has a wider reach than, admittedly, human senses can read for data.

The most rigorously specific sciences cannot for ever escape the wider connections and bearings of what, for study's sake, they properly isolate. We noted in the previous chapter how Charles Darwin found a presiding genius for his theory in 'Mother Nature', working through means to ends. It would only have been a further step to relate such 'personal' purposiveness to the still larger issues of *human* history, society and hope. This, precisely, is what Christology does, in reaching the conviction of a 'mother grace' and identifying it in love incarnate.

The question, surely, about all intelligent relation to life and time and personhood, is not *whether* a teleology but how far and how full it might be. A teleology, a sense of ends in means, that stays (as Darwin did) only in the natural order might be held to have foreshortened teleology itself.

The old cosmological argument that the world was not self-explanatory and must, therefore, have had a 'cause' – not itself 'caused' and to be called 'God' – must properly concede itself ruled out in the light of Kantian critical 'realism' about the limits of reason. Yet it remains legitimate, indeed imperative, to enquire about 'being' inclusively, as well as about particulars severally. Sense-fed reason may have to confine itself scientifically to the latter: mind at large (and there is no full mind otherwise) cannot be itself in such a prison. It must occupy itself with the whence and whither that envelope the this and that of means to ends, the minutiae of empirical knowledge. To be so occupied is not undue ambition but due integrity.

It becomes clear, further, that a right theology refines the old philosophical form of the ontological argument which was the most exposed of all to Kantian accusation of pretension. It used to run somewhat as follows: 'A perfect being can be imagined; lacking existence it would not be perfect; therefore the perfect being necessarily exists.' The movement was from the idea to the reality. The critique of pure reason was bound to veto this on the ground that thought was wandering where it could not go. One could imagine a hundred dollars in one's pocket but the thought would not put them there. There was no necessary link between the idea in the mind and the idea's 'thing' in the real.

A sequence from notion to fact, in these terms, could not well hold, still less sustain a right theology (though the analogy about the dollars is not apt since the argument always claimed that the sort of case it made could *only* be made about God). Nevertheless, theology, as a proper discipline of human life, can in no way dismiss what, crudely, the old argument was feeling for. We have been living here with a feel of it all the time. 'God' and our 'thinking' are in no way mutually alien. Mind duly reaches for totality. Being, here, particular, seeks being, also here, universal. Or, better, the human and the divine partake in one transcendence – the human in the sense of it, the divine in the possession of it. For this the old form of ontology was groping, in detecting some inter-necessity in 'thought' and 'reality' interrelating here. Hence, again, the emphasis on adjectival theology, the divine presence to the human, the human register of the divine.

It is this, as noted earlier, that makes unfortunate the customary confusion about 'supernature', with talk about some 'placement' of God 'up there', or (in reaction) 'down there'. The term 'supernature' is sadly tied to 'nature', the latter a question-begging term. If we mean by it the physical order, from grass to galaxies, rocks and rhythms, winds and waters, then we set the divine over against anatomies, biologies, geologies, chemistries, pathologies, structures of investigative knowledge of every kind searching into materiality. 'Supernature' will then be some externality, liable, even likely, to be thought of in similarly material terms. We may then visualise some entity thought of in the same terms, yet unhappily eluding them and so called 'supernatural'.

If, however, we let the human have its whole dimension, including these many 'ologies' that properly have their place, we find ourselves connecting with a much larger discourse in which all else belonging to our humanness will be engaged, tested, pained, awed and celebrated, in memory, society, history, poetry, love, mystery and death, in which the divine will no longer be 'super' in remoteness, scientifically excluded, but 'intra' as the ineffable counterpart of all these elements of our dignity and of our perplexity. This will be ontology – faith in 'being', not as an abstract logic but as experience.

V

It might be claimed that the techniques of sociology and psychology had indeed brought the 'supernatural' down into the web and woof of daily living. So doing, some of their practitioners are thought to have elided the 'super' altogether. Analysing religious behaviour they conclude that social factors and psychic needs or patterns sufficiently explain the ways of worship, the sense of guilt and pardon, the credibility of creeds and the content of religious codes and cults. The cultural and personal manifestations of 'the divine' could all be understood as phenomena, things as instinctual drive or collective models made them.

In so far as 'supernature' thus became 'human nature' the old 'objectivity' of God was dissolved into the mores of society, the structures of the self, and the mind-sets of culture. The techniques of observation and analysis which achieved, or sponsored, this, however, modelled themselves on the patterns of the physical sciences. The psyche could be studied like ocean currents, the soul like starfish, worship like bird migration. It was assumed, in crude terms, that society was amenable to the investigative assurance of the botanist or the archaeologist, the psyche to the skills of the engineer. The instinct was a part-truth that could demonstrate achievement validly only when it conceded its necessary limits. It is there that overambition or, better, unhappy pretension, had to be the proper charge in reverse and that reservations had to be those a lively theology required. As with the empiricists of the nature sciences, so with those of the human sciences, the flaw was an unhappy disconnecting from the fullness of the human meaning. In so far as this was true, these practitioners were the victims of their own functionally necessary, but undetected, partiality.

Faith and theology may be held naïve in unawareness of Durkheim and Malinowski, Freud and Jung, and in ignorance of the collective unconscious and the super-ego. They stood to gain by a perceptive attention to these tutors into human origins and human factors in what was held divine. The subtlety of myth in the meaning and pursuit of devotion and in the sacramentalising of society needed recognition. These dimensions, however, needed to be received as factors in a context larger than their reach. The criteria of naïvety may be themselves naïve. The inter-meaning, or inter-definition, of the divine and the human transcends what mechanisms and analyses detect only as phenomena.

vi

What of narrowness as the indictment of the religious mind, of privatisation of truth on the part of faith-custodians? The way the charge was phrased in the previous chapter was intended to show how right it was. There can be no doubt of the crime of religions down the centuries in cornering their meanings as absolute in themselves and adversarial in their communities. The truth and 'us' has been a tragic instinct of the religious mind which it is now more urgent than ever in history to deny and renounce.

A clear way to do so is to explore and mutually identify the elements in common. For these are significant both for hope and truth's sake. It should be the business of every faith to identify where its meanings inter-belong with other belief-systems, to search out what it sees it has that warrants its continuing separate persistence and to hold that crucial thing open, hospitable and peaceable for all.

A stateable objective, the realist will say, but an impossible agenda. (Don't escape from the 'narrow' by returning to the 'naïve'!) To be sure, religions do not possess such resilience, being vast heritages of culture, prejudice, bigotry, torpor, zeal, inertia and confusion. Only a negligible élite within them are capable of such a programme and, as such, liable to be ignored. Admittedly, the deterrents are many, the obstacles massive. Many contemporary indices are not encouraging. Counsels of mutual converse are daunted by what is visual at Varanasi on the Ganges, at Mecca in pilgrimage, or festivals of the Queen of Heaven in the southern Amerindies. And there are those hard, sometimes savage, introversions of religion in reaction to the rumour or the threat of secular hostility and the pervasive mores of alien culture. Where these entrench suspicion and mental agoraphobia the habits of faith are more introverted still.

Our business here is not with prognosis of what may be, or how, in the religious scene, nor with the possibilities between this faith and that, in respect of concord and discord. We must, however, examine the claimed distinctiveness of Christianity and try to show cause why it may not 'dilute' but can yet converse and mediate in the trust of it. That there are large areas of common territory the Christian has with the creation, law, and prophethood themes of the other Semites, with the devotional theism found among Hindus, and with the self-disciplines of the Buddhist Path, is clear enough.[12] Our duty is to confess and possess them together if only partially to overcome the 'them and us' instinct that, in privatising meaning, erects frontiers and sanctions rejections. That situation might be captured in Shakespeare's lines at Agincourt:

> fixed sentinels almost receive
> The secret whispers of the other's watch:
> . . . . .
> Each battle sees the other's umbered face:
> . . . . .
> Proud of their numbers and secure in soul.[13]

That is the temper of confrontation and 'umbered' is the word for any 'face' that can be seen, in the twilight of battle.

To all such possible converse the Christian credentials of God bring a distinctiveness that has to be in careful trust. The 'only' mentality has often been deplored in dialogue and, wherever possible, it has to be renounced. For this reason it is well to forego the word 'unique' so often on the lips of so-called 'exclusivists'. 'Distinctive' is the legitimate word, reserving what has no parallel, but not confusing or denying, as 'unique' does, the common elements which are implicit even in the contrasts. 'Unique' overlooks what joins in insisting on what divides. For that reason it is a usage lacking in discernment.

There needs to be a *nota bene* here, for it is true that 'only' has important place in Christian creed and that 'unique' tallies with the Latin *unigenitus* in the Gospel and the Creeds in reference to Jesus's Sonship. He is 'the only begotten of the Father'. We must not let the term have for us the sense of the usage, 'only child'. That is limitation, privation, in the human idiom. 'Only', or 'One-ly', in the Gospel has to do with the divine unity, real both in the revealing and the revealed. Divine unity is not singularity in the numerical sense of 'one day' as twenty-four hours, or 'one' and not 'two' days. God is never limit or series in that way. Neither is divine Sonship, which does not 'pluralise' the divine or admit of being 'duplicate'. 'Only' here denies plurality in the sense in which it needs to do, namely to exclude both in God revealed and God revealing all duality.

To use 'unique' for the whole complex of Christian doctrine, because it was the term for incarnational meaning, would be to obscure that meaning itself. It would also exclude precious themes about creation, mercy, divine 'sending', and divine 'peoplehood', all of which are biblical as well as Christian. It would also isolate Christians from shared dimensions of Islam. 'Distinctive', therefore, is the happier, sounder word. It will be part of our answer to the charge of narrowness that we prefer to use it.

In what does the distinctive consist – in Christology as crucial to theology and in Christology as cruciform? Christians find finality, not in the enigmatic serenity of the Buddha countenance but in a crown of thorns. The God of Islamic 'great and manifest victory',[14] is the God with wounds. Leonardo da Vinci had it graphically, if only locally, when his *Note Book* on Good Friday had the entry: 'In all parts of Europe . . . lamentation by great nations for the death of one man who died in the East.' He felt it right to add on the same page: 'Many who hold the faith of the Son only build temples in the name of the Mother.'[15] 'Lamentation' was a right but partial word, staying with the grave clothes. The Easter faith is celebration, Eucharist, 'the knowledge and the love of God', but only because of how Jesus suffered, 'the just for the unjust to bring us to God'.

It is this faith in the divinely vicarious as the clue to a world's redemption which is *sui generis*, entirely distinctive, *sans pareil*, in the Christian heart and Gospel. That is a careful, legitimate and honest verdict, not a theme of private relevance but the due possession of all by means of an open custody which does not fail its meaning or obscure its originality as God-given and human-meant. It is the focal point of what is, and must be, mutual in those two adjectives.

There are other theisms, to be sure, but they see the Christian one as foolish or offensive. There is, happily, a sense of things vicarious in ethics elsewhere but nowhere attributable to the divine, or enacted in history. For Christian conviction a mythology of immolation, rituals of expiation, cults in martyrology, do not belong and could not obtain. Nor is the Messianic in Jesus futurist or conceptual or its alleged incidence in time a fantasy, an esoteric secret only for those who qualify for knowledge. It remains an open secret, only 'passing knowledge' in the glory it enshrines. Its openness does not confine its relevance to accidents of birth or culture. In the idiom of extending arms, this Cross wills an embrace of all who will. Preceding chapters have tried to discern and tell what is Christian-distinctive. This final one is simply concerned with finding it for what it is and with the finding as a trust of mind and heart.

This means a perceptive use of biblical texts. In one sense, it is necessary to say that the Bible cannot greatly help us in contemporary inter-faith thinking, inasmuch as no apostle (within Holy Writ) had dealings with India, nor with Buddhism. Explicitly, Islam did not exist. The New Testament is wholly Mediterranean in its outreach. The biblical mention of China is only incidental (Isa. 49:12).[16] These cultural limitations of the Bible throw us back more squarely on the promise of the Holy Spirit and make the Spirit's task with us the more exacting than simple text-citation.

Three passages are specially relevant. That in Acts 17 concerning Paul on the Areopagus in Athens gave us a conclusion to Chapter 3. The others are John 14:6 and Acts 4:12. 'No man comes to the Father except by me,' and 'Neither is there salvation in any other. For there is no other name, given to mankind by which we may be saved.' Both verses have usually been cited as requiring a total Christian disinterest in any other faith, seeing these as excluded from any relevance to the sole auspices of 'the Son' and 'the Name'.

It is those two very themes, however, that we need to weigh carefully. We cannot doubt that Abraham came to God as a pioneer of obedient faith, or that Job came to God in anguished quest, or that Jeremiah came to God in all the burden of prophethood. But we must notice the predicate. They did *not* come 'to the Father'. That predicate, at least in its fulness, awaited the disclosure of the 'Sonship' reciprocal to it.[17] We have 'the Fatherhood' only in 'the Sonship' where its significance is fully shown. It is very clear in the Johannine theology that 'Father' and 'Son' are interdependent terms. 'He who has the Son has the Father also.' For it was Fatherhood in God that was expressed in 'the Son's sending'. There were many authentic predicates by which God was known, and continues to be known. Only in the fact of the Son, in the event of the Christ, in 'the Word made flesh', is 'the God who is Father' fully known for Who He is by that name.

The context in John 14 – and indeed in Matthew 11:25–27 – makes this reading plain. Philip has asked to be 'shown the Father'; Jesus replies, 'He who sees me sees the Father,' meaning that the divine compassion is credentialled in the whole significance of Jesus, personality and story, prayer-life and obedience. The concurrence of wills that lay behind all that eventuated made the earthly 'obedience' index to the divine nature. To know Jesus as 'the true and living way' does not mean disparagement of faiths that acknowledge and revere God in creation, law, mercy and sovereignty. It is precisely these that call for initiation into what 'the Son' alone authenticates.

This understanding of John 14·6 must illuminate what Peter's sermon summarised, as Acts reports it. The audience are Jews, of Jerusalem and the diaspora. Acts has not yet arrived to 'Gentiles'. The crucial Jewish topic was 'Messiah', the anointed, expected one. No one in the audience lacks that word, though they differ in who, or what, it connotes. We can hear Peter saying:

> The Messiah we all await, the central pivot of all Judaic hope, the fulfiller of Davidic promise, the one and only saving Name – well, men of Israel, know now for sure that it is Messiah-Jesus. His is the Name who fulfils all, this crucified. Imagine! the very stone our builders threw away as useless proves to be the very corner-stone.

The thrust of the passage is to underscore the Messianic reality in crucified terms. It is insistent and emphatic because this is such astounding news. In the light of all we have studied in Chapters 5, 6 and 7, we might rightly paraphrase: 'Only in the love that suffers are we loosed from evil.' 'The Name than which there is no other is legible in the meaning of Gethsemane.'

'The Name', biblically, was never a bare formula, a mere cypher, a code by which to spring a lock. It always had 'a place' – the 'place of the Name', an identity within a story. Salvation is not by multiple 'formulae', nor is what is exclusive here an arbitrary verdict, like some 'trespassers prosecuted'. It is inherent in the very nature of saving, sin being the stubborn thing it is.

Furthermore, religions mean many disparate things by the term 'salvation'. It is confusing to ask about 'whether X is saved', or to comprehend all issues in that one question, until we have sorted out what the question might mean. To quote Acts 4:12 woodenly will prevent vital disparaties from being brought to light and the full significance of the verse brought to bear on them. 'The Name' is not a password we have to use like magic. It is a surpassing mystery we have to interpret and commend. 'Commending' always means listening, the listening that alone learns how to tell. Peter's words anyway were in a sermon: a conversation might serve a different need.

The foregoing may meet the case about narrowness mounted in the last chapter. If concern is for the intense concentration Christian faith perceives in the Christ-event, it is of the order that belongs with all dramatisation – the moment that can make the momentous. Does not the word 'symbol (Greek *sumbolon*) mean a 'throwing together'? The Cross of Jesus being the Christ has cosmic inclusiveness in that it joins at one and the same point 'the sin of the world' and the love of God in symbol as event and event as symbol. It is where the meaning of the divine in relation to the human has its fullest measure, and its most inclusive credential.

vii

That there are pitfalls for faith in the use of language we have been made well aware. It is right to be attentive, lest we conjure into being with words what has no reality or conjure 'truths' out of mere ideas. If believers deplore the disconnectings that go with secularity, they may need to make some of their own, if links that do not honestly exist beguile them. Belief has to be alert to make-belief. Yet, happily, a vigilance with language can bring positive rewards. For what happens *to* words, as well as *by* them, can itself be a window into meaning.

There is much for theology, for example, in the Greek word *karakter*. It began life as shape inserted into clay, then denoted the 'mark' made and thus a 'character', or 'letter', and thus, again, a sign of something meant when associated with other letters. Then it grew into a person-age, a 'character' in a drama, who might be tragic or comic, a Hamlet or a Don Quixote. Thus, finally, it became ethical and told the inner personal quality, not now an actor in a part but a *persona* in authentic life. The fate of words this way, both up and down, for richer or poorer, turns, of course, on the connectings, designed or fortuitous, that usage actually makes. Such usage will always be index to experience. The liabilities of vocabulary will give us to realise that 'saying' is never merely propositional but transactional.

The sequences of *karakter* might well serve to clarify the reading we have made throughout from a point in history to the 'character' of God. For it is 'character' with which credentials have to do. 'A bit of history' is all that might be said of the Cross of Jesus. That is how Tacitus, for example, saw it.[18] Much recent Jewish thinking has asked why Christians make so much of what, in that brutal Roman world, seemed so trivial. Secular minds also wonder why Good Friday signifies and matters so. Leonardo, as we quoted him, would seem now ridiculous. It was only a little mark in history's clay. Even so, it registered. It identified dramatic action – thanks to 'Father, forgive . . .'. What could be perceived as a 'sign' became an identity. A figure in a role, grimly visited on him by time and place (for which read all human sin), became the person known by it. In that reality, historical, real, recordable, 'character' in the final sense could be understood. For, reading the sequence backwards, how could the quality it had be known? In that 'Father, forgive . . .' we could believe we had arrived at 'the character of God', but only in its being humanly prayed – and prayed in all the evident implications of the whole event.

Theological language, then, is of this order – not merely propositional but confessional. If we are asked about 'verification', we must be clear about the 'verifiers'. They will be of the range, and of the sort, that we have the wit to require and the depth to want. The stance of 'phenomenology', whether it be of the natural order or the psyche or society, has its due place in legitimate enquiry about how things work, physical, psychic and societal, and how, after enquiry, they may be organised, manipulated, managed, regulated, technologised and controlled. There is appropriate fascination and potentially beneficient efficiency in all such skills. But can phenomena be ultimate? Can they be all? Phenomena – manifestations – of what? will always be the rearward question. What makes for efficiency is relating to what is beyond efficiency alone, and has to connect with it. We cannot attain what might 'verify' belief if we have foreshortened what needs the verifying. Only when we have appropriately enlarged it will we know what verification would need to be. Agnosticism has a noble history as an honesty capable, like John Keats, of 'being in uncertainties'.[19] But there is a kind of agnosticism which is content to be unknowing because it does not *want* to know, being sufficiently engaged with phenomena. A full 'acceptance to be' is, thereby, with and also beyond phenomena in awareness of decision, verdict, faith, as alone responsive to our human stature.

As we saw at the outset, life offers us many 'parts', many ways in which we impress ourselves into the clay and so express some final character. 'A partner's part' is the one which heeds the invitation of grace – the grace of natural being and the grace of divine/human society in love and truth, the grace of the society Christian faith finds in the shadow of the Cross, the shadow thrown from the light of God.

We took note earlier that perhaps 'What can we mean?' was the more vital question than 'What can we believe?' Unwilling to ignore it, we further noted that 'meaning' concerns both explanation and intention. It suffices us in conclusion. After all 'explaining' about divine credentials, their 'meaning' will turn on our 'intending'. Not that intention will be cavalier about explanation: quite the contrary. Rather, that all witness, all credalising, all theology, have to 'intend'. 'Intend' is a transitive verb, waiting for what must follow. 'Follow' was the very word Jesus had in his call to his disciples. Who wills to know let him do. The meaning of faith is known in actively meaning it. In meaning it the meaning deepens into personal truth. The language of explanation translates into the language of possession.

Was it a right case we made from that word *karakter*? We read its story forwards from a fragment of cuneiform to full 'character'. As only a vagary of speech that might seem an inapt way to think these present thoughts. Let us read it backwards and seize on its parable. All things begin in the character, the ineffable mystery, the transcendent reality, of God, so desperately enigmatic to the soul of Job. Then there is a figure in a setting, a history-character that transcendence identifies. That drama is imprinted in 'the Word' – 'the Word' that earlier stands intimated by impressions in the Hebraic soul, impressions which draw themselves from the earliest shapes of human wistfulness set in the clay of time.

Have we not now the whole story? Then this 'character' of God holds for our finding all we need to know about the destiny and the quality of ours. 'Be characterised by the character of God.' No less the meaning intends; no less the meaning demands; no less the meaning awaits.

When John Milton wrote his poem on 'The Passion', in his youth, he added a note which ran: 'This subject the author finds to be above the years he had when he wrote it and, nothing satisfied with what was begun, left it unfinished.'[20] That might well be so about any theologian, young or old. To mean by explanation remains always something 'left unfinished'. To mean by intention to follow is to have begun the satisfying of love.

Notes

Chapter 1

1 J. A. Froude: *Thomas Carlyle: A History of His Life in London*, London, 1884, Vol. 2, p. 18.
2 William Wordsworth: *Poetical Works*, Oxford, 1905, *The Prelude*, Book VI, lines 339–42, p. 680.
3 Edwin Muir: *Selected Letters*, ed. P. H. Butter, London, 1974, p. 137 (21 March 1944).
4 Elie Wiesel: *Gates of the Forest*, New York, 1968, p. 94. One might compare Wordsworth's lines: 'The deeper malady is better hid:/The world is poisoned at the heart.'
5 So the sculptor tells the playwright in Hochhoth's play *Soldiers, An Obituary for Geneva: A Tragedy*, trans. R. D. MacDonald, New York, 1968, p. 75.
6 Even in grammar indicatives yield imperatives. What transcends cannot be also 'inferior'. Its doing so is, therefore, a necessity that is ethical as well as ontological.
7 Job is challenged in Chapters 38 and 39 to 'enter into the treasures of the snow', to 'know when the wild goats bring forth their young', and to 'walk in search of the depth'. Technology has done all these things and presented the findings in glorious technicolour on a million TV screens. No doubt the intention of Yahweh's challenge abides but not its details.
8 This is not, of course, to exclude the dark, almost Buddhist, awareness of 'the vanity of human wishes' in Ecclesiastes from the contents of Holy Writ. It may well be salutary there. The point – made urgent by public reading – is to ask in what sense is it 'the word of the Lord'?
9 A very definitive event in the career of Muhammad in that his adversaries, the Quraish in Mecca, were signally defeated in the first martial encounter and the new Islamic movement received great impetus and prestige. The Qur'ān refers to the day of Badr as *Yawm al-furqan*, 'the day of the criterion' (Sura 8: 41). *Al-Furqan* is a title of the Qur'ān itself.
10 In John Hick (ed.): *The Myth of God Incarnate*, London, 1977, p. 4.
11 Using 'emmanuel' here with a small 'e' understanding divine transcendence as 'with us', and not only 'over' or 'beyond' us, reading 'us' as inclusively human.

12   William Wordsworth: *The Prelude* (1805 text), Book 12, lines 85–7.

13   Jomo Kenyatta: *Facing Mount Kenya*, n.d., New York, p. 225.

14   Ibid., p. 121. B. Malinowski, the eminent anthropologist, was Kenyatta's teacher in that discipline. *Facing Mount Kenya* thus comprised both the first-hand 'native' experience and the techniques of professional exposition.

15   R. S. Sugirtharajah, (ed.): *Voices from the Margin: Interpreting the Bible in the Third World*, London, 1991, p. 289.

16   One historian of religion who sensed deeply the way in which being 'institutional' can distort or corrupt religion was Arnold Toynbee. He returns to the theme often in his several studies. See also my *Troubled by Truth*, Durham, 1992, pp. 222–41.

17   As, for example, a writer as perceptive as C. S. Lewis nevertheless posing the alternative, 'Either megalomaniac or divine' in respect of the Johannine Christ. See R. Selby Wright (ed.): *Asking them Questions*, Oxford, 1953, where, pp. 95–104, Lewis thinks that if Jesus were not divine his saying, 'I and my Father are one' makes him a 'megalomaniac in comparison with whom Hitler was the most sane and humble of men'. He asks, further, 'what would Muhammad have done if asked: "Are you Allah?" ' This, sadly, is to misconstrue all that the writer is meaning in the Fourth Gospel, failing to realise how it is not verbatim but interpretative. Lewis is writing as if a stenographer were present in those supremely theological discourses and no John.

18   Robert Browning: *Poetical Works*, Oxford, 'A Death in the Desert', p. 489. He adds:

> 'A proof we comprehend his love, a proof
> We had such love already in ourselves,
> Knew first what else we should not recognise.'

19   Echoing King Lear's language in Act 3, sc. 4, lines 32, 33, 100, 101.

20   Sages in the Talmud were ready so to acknowledge, including Egyptians in their sense of pity around the Exodus, thus qualifying the triumphalism of 'Then sang Moses . . .' in Exodus 15:1f.

21   L. Trilling: *The Opposing Self*, London, 1955, p. 75.

22   The analogy is Edward Dowden's in *Life of Robert Browning*, London, n.d., pp. 103–4.

23   William Shakespeare: *The Tempest*, Epilogue, lines 15–16.

Chapter 2

1   Robert Browning: *Poetical Works*, Oxford, 'La Saisiaz', p. 554.

2   'The curious stars' is a phrase of R. S. Thomas in his poem musing on a Welsh peasant, farming the high hills: *Selected Poems, 1946–68*, London, 1983, p. 3.

3   In the one as an orderly in hospital during the horrors of the American Civil War, the other in New England sorrows of family tension, insanity and suicide.

4   Miss Egerton-Smith.

5   It was 18 Ocrober 1892, when Hardy was fifty-two. See F. E. Hardy: *Life of Thomas Hardy, 1840–1928*, London, 1962, p. 251.

6   Andrew Marvell: *Poems and Letters*, eds H. M. Margoliouth and E. Legouis, 3rd edn, Vol. 1, Oxford, 1971, pp. 21–2.

7   Alice Meynell: *Complete Poems*, London, 1940, p. 123.

8   This, in context, seems to be the meaning rather than any implication

about 'eternal life', if we take the Hebraic parallelism from the first part of the verse about 'all the days of my life', with 'goodness and mercy' characterising the hills, streams and sheepfolds as 'the Lord's house'.

9   'Hypostasis' has to do with thinking or writing of abstracts as 'personal', as when Proverbs 8 and passages in the Wisdom literature give 'wisdom' a personal pronoun: 'I was daily His delight', etc. We then think of that which is 'divine' (the wisdom of God) as in some way 'other than God', yet not so. A sort of equal subsidiarity enters into our thinking when divine agencies are personalised and become, thereby, at one and the same time truly, but differently, 'God'. How evidently this bears on Christian credal formulation of 'God' as 'God in Christ' will come below in Chapter 8.

10   Echoing the words of 'the old man of the sea' to the young boy in Ernest Hemingway's epic story of that title.

11   George Herbert: The Works of, ed. F. E. Hutchinson, Oxford, 1941, 'Man', pp. 90–1.

12   Gregory of Nyssa: quoted from Sources Chretiénnes, 6, Paris, 1943, p. 126.

13   See, for example, Bernard Lovell: In the Centre of Immensities, London, 1979, p. 122f. 'If the proto-proton interaction had been a few per cent stronger then no galaxies, no stars, no life would have emerged because the protons which were the available energy from the building of heavier atoms would have formed into helium in the first few million years of the universe and would have stayed there. A 1 per cent change in the balance between negative and positive electricity would blow, not just your mind, but your head straight out of the solar system. If at that moment (when the universe was one second from the beginning of its expansion) the rate of expansion had been reduced by only one part in a thousand billion, then the universe would have collapsed after a few million years, near the end of the epoch we now recognise as the radiation era, or the primordial fireball, before the matter and radiation had become decoupled.'

14   Paradise Lost, Book vii, lines 621–2, and 225–31 and 242.

15   Antonio Machado: Juan de Mairena: Maxims, Epigrams, Memorabilia and Memoirs, ed. Ben Belitt, California, 1963, p. 118.

16   Thomas Traherne: Centuries, Poems and Thanksgivings, ed. H. M. Margoliouth, 2 vols, Oxford, 1958, 'The Preparative,' Vol. 2, p. 22, Centuries 1, 72 and 29.

17   William Wordsworth: The Excursion, Book 1, lines 211–16, Chapter 1, note 2.

18   Vincent van Gogh: A Self-Portrait, Letters revealing his Life as a Painter, selected by W. H. Auden, London, 1961, p. 55.

19   Collected Poems of Thomas Hardy, London, 1932, pp. 59, 521.

20   Richard Jefferies: The Story of My Heart, London, 1923 pp. 3–4.

21   Note 19, 'Before Life and After', p. 260.

22   The argument ran that since 'existence' was crucial to 'perfection' 'the perfect being' must necessarily 'exist'. Otherwise, too, a capacity to conceive it would be inexplicable. Kant insisted that human rationality could only operate within what sense data afforded to it.

23   In The Hallowed Valley, Eng. trans. Cairo, 1977, the Egyptian writer Muhammad Kamil Husain described 'atheism [as] a failure to understand what human nature is', pp. 1, 32f.

24   There are numerous versions of Jalal al-Din's famous Mathnawi and of the Islamic love-romance of Yusuf and Zulaika. cf. Mashavi-i-Ma'navi, ed. E. H. Whinfield, Book II, Story 10, 2nd edn. London, 1898, (translated and abridged).

25 Such sentiments have been attributed to Origen but are hard to reconcile with the depth – if the aberrations – of his celebrated intellectual stature.

26 C. G. Jung: *The Undiscovered Self*, trans. R. F. C. Hull, New York, n.d., p. 110.

27 Ezra Pound: *Cantos*, London, 1964, Canto 94, and *Selected Poems*, ed. T. S. Eliot, London, 1928, p. 69.

28 William Shakespeare: *King Henry IV, Part 2*, Act 3, sc. 2, lines 235–7.

29 John Milton: *Paradise Lost*, Book 10, line 1045.

30 William Shakespeare: Sonnets 12 and 64.

31 John Betjeman: *Collected Poems*, London, 1962, 'What to Say', p. 374.

32 John Donne: LXX *Sermons*, 1640, quoted from *The Sermons of John Donne*, eds E. M. Simpson and G. R. Potter, Berkeley, 1963, Vol 1, pp. 90–1.

33 G. M. Trevelyan: *The Life of John Bright*, London, 1914, p. 43.

34 Charles Wesley: A stanza from the poem-hymn, 'Wrestling Jacob'.

Chapter 3

1 The aphorism summarises Lawrence's view of religion, cf. *Reflections on the Death of a Porcupine*, ed. M. Herbert, Cambridge, 1949: 'On Being Religious', pp. 185–93 and: 'On Taking the Next Step', pp. 387–90. Also: *The Symbolic Meaning*, Cambridge, 1949, p. 137.

2 D. H. Lawrence: *Women in Love*, London, 1921, p. 102.

3 Baron Von Hugel: *Eternal Life*, London, 1912, p. xiv.

4 D. H. Lawrence: *The Rainbow*, London, 1915, the opening of Chapter 1.

5 Robert Browning: *Poetical Works*, New York, 1897, Vol 1, p. 117, lines 188–97. The 'man in sympathy' line is in 'Prince Hohenstiel Schwangau', Vol 2, p. 304, line 948.

6 Using the non-theological title of Iris Murdoch's study, London, 1970.

7 Author (1057–1111 CE) of *Ihya' 'Ulum al-Din*, 'Bringing to life the Ways of Religious Knowing', a study in ten books of theology and the human self.

8 cf. T. S. Eliot's play, *Murder in the Cathedral*, London, 1935, pp. 37–43, where Thomas's 'Fourth Tempter' offers him a martyr's posthumous victory ministering to 'sinful pride'. Thomas asks: 'Is there no way in my soul's sickness/ Does not lead to damnation in pride?' 'doing the right thing for the wrong reason'.

9 John Milton: *Paradise Lost*, Book 1, lines 264 and 49.

10 The term is *Zann* meaning evil surmise, antipathy to truth. 'Surmise has no place where truth is concerned' (Sura 53:28).

11 R. M. Brown: 'Ignazio Silone and the Pseudonyms of God', in G. B. Tennyson and E. E. Erickson (eds), *Religion and Modern Literature*, p. 353. Grand Rapids, 1975.

12 Albert Camus: *The Fall*, trans. from the French by Justin O'Brien, London, 1957, p. 96.

13 *Ibid*. p. 80.

14 Albert Camus: *The Stranger*, trans. from the French by Stuart Gilbert, 1946, where the central character, Mersault, seems impervious to all but the physical immediacy of the moment and incapable of genuine emotions, whether of love, hope, grief or sorrow.

15 Albert Camus: *The Rebel*, trans. from the French by Anthony Bower, 1956.

16 A favourite note in Camus's lyrical writing – may be aligned in differing idiom with how Jeremiah, making a play on words, salutes the almond tree as the first of the spring blossomers, using it as a token of the divine vigilance (Jer. 1:11–12).

17 Note 15 above, p. 256, citing without reference.

18 Vincent van Gogh in youth strove to be a Christian 'pastor' and preached his first sermon in Richmond, England. His text, perhaps prophetic of his own distraught story, was from Psalm 119–19: 'I am a stranger in the earth: hide not Thy commandments from me.'

19 David Hume: *Dialogues Concerning Natural Religion*, Part xi, cited from Edwin A. Burtt: *The English Philosophers from Bacon to Mill*, New York, 1939, p. 751.

20 Robert Browning: *Poetical Works*, Oxford, 1940, 'Easter Day', p. 411.

21 *Kenosis* is the term used in Philippians 2:5–11, to denote the divine 'self-emptying' the meaning of which will be central to Chapter 5. 'Emptying' is not to be understood as of some container whose contents when 'emptied' are no longer there. It concerns an expression of 'rank' or 'quality' or 'status' in ways that lay aside what is normally assumed of it and, by so doing, transform ideas of what such 'status' truly is.

22 This is a steady theme in the New Testament Epistles: 'Beloved, if God so loved us we ought also to love one another' (1 John 4:11).

23 The indefinite article 'a' presupposes the possibility of the plural in the thing denoted, and indicates single membership in a genus or category: 'A shilling is a coin.' The Arabic word *Allah* is generally seen as having incorporated the definite article *Al* into *ilah* (the common term for 'god'), making a name incapable of plural or indefiniteness.

24 Can one truly think of 'inter-relevance' and yet suppose it one-sided (ours) as R. S. Thomas seems to do in his lines 'A presence, that compels me to address it, without hope of a reply?' R. S. Thomas: *Frequencies*, London, 1978, 'Absence', p. 48.

25 'Our children' here is restrictive, meaning Jewry not humanity. That issue has to engage us in Chapter 4.

26 Wallace Stevens: *Collected Poems*, London, 1955, p. 320.

27 Alfred, Lord Tennyson: *Poems and Plays*, Oxford, 1965, 'Lucretius', p. 151.

Chapter 4

1 The opening sentences of Joseph Conrad's novel *Victory*, London, 1915.

2 H. Graf Reventlou: *Problems of Old Testament Theology in the Twentieth Century*, Eng. trans. John Bowden, London, 1985, p. 80. History has been 'mythicised', for example, in American history in the 'story' of Abraham Lincoln, or the Boston Tea Party, where a paean about liberty clothes the matter of a tax which was quite reasonable in the light of the cost of defending the colonists. The shot that 'rang out at Lexington' was more than musketry.

3 See, for example, R. E. Clements: *God and Temple*, Oxford, 1965. 'Baal' and 'El' were Canaanite deities and 'cherubim' mythic figures in the local milieu which Israelite religion adopted. Zadok may have been a Jebusite priest confirmed in office by David. That monarch who, in early years, was something of a bandit, had many 'Gentiles' in his entourage as bodyguards, or *gibborim*, e.g. Ittai the Gidite. 'Cult sites' and 'cult figures', like Jerusalem and David, had counterparts among the Canaanites. Later prophetic sense of the nations owes much to the experience of Jews in, e.g. Egypt, at the time of Zephaniah. Years later does not Ezekiel say, of Jerusalem: 'Thy birth and thy nativity is of the land of Canaan: thy father was an Amorite and thy mother a Hittite' (16:3)? The tone may be satirical but only in recalling a fact. Was this why Elijah avoided Jerusalem when

going to seek the Lord at Horeb? There are fascinating allusions in Psalm 48 which must give pause to excessive isolation of 'chosen people'.

4   In Roman times, not least in Galilee, tenant farmers owed shares in the harvest to non-resident landlords. These could be rapacious and it is strange that Jesus could involve them in analogy with 'the heavenly Lord'. The point, however, was that tenants might contrive to take over the vineyard either by acting as if the absentee were dead or ensuring that he would be. They could ill treat messengers to test reaction and conspire with neighbours to defraud. Hence the sending of 'the son'. For only the heir, not servants, could assert ownership in response to such provocation. Hence, in turn, the urge to murder him to ensure the future. It is clear that, otherwise, the sending of the son is lunacy in the light of what had been done to the servants. The core point is that the stakes are being deepened all the time. Every new violence takes the issue beyond mere 'fruits of the season' to 'what is your relation to the Lord?' Sin, in Jesus' experience of rejection, is on a mounting spiral and so, matching it, is the love that comes and claims. The commentary on his own consciousness is unmistakable. (See Matt. 21:33–46, Mark 12:1–12 and Luke 20:9–19; important enough to appear to all three Synoptics.)

5   A Latin hymn written around 1250 by Thomas of Celano, inspired by Zephaniah's imagery about the 'last judgement of the nations' (1:2–6 and 8–13; 1:14–2:3. It had great appeal throughout the later Middle Ages. Goethe borrowed from it at a dramatic moment in his *Faust*.

6   The Psalm is an idyllic celebration of royal Messiah in full tide of universal peace, submissive nations 'bringing gifts', of justice to the poor, compassion for the needy, 'blessings invoked on him all the day', and enduring till the moon is no more in empire 'from sea to sea'. All a far cry from the actualities of the original Solomon.

7   'Crucified' here of course metaphorically but by no means improperly. Jeremiah never sought ministry, shrank instinctively from publicity and the pain of solitariness in its demands. Yet he found no respite and no reprieve, unavailing as it all proved. He felt that God had 'taken crude advantage, like a seducer, of his simplicity' (20:7). His travail was unremitting. It was that his 'Confessions', his pleas and anguish became the surest index to the Messianic implications of a preacher's tragedy. It is in Jeremiah that 'the lamb' language has its deepest significance (11:19).

8   Unless we want to say that these precedents from psalm prophet affected the actual narrating of the Passion, seeing that apostolic faith had found its clue there to the Cross. We need not think the details wrong since they linked event and meaning, foreshadowing and fulfilling, entirely.

9   The 'anointed' here seems to refer to the whole 'seed' of the patriarchs. The idea here of their being in divinely guarded immunity from harm would, of course, totally exclude what the Gospels, and prophets themselves, tell us about 'with his stripes' being 'healed'. The psalmist's sentiment is also a very Islamic one. Messengers finally oppressed or open to their enemies are thereby discredited.

10   For the Maccabean connection with the Magnificat, see; *Bulletin of the John Rylands Library*, Vol. 37, No. 1, Sept. 1956, article by Paul Winter: 'Magnificat and Benedictus: Maccabean Psalms?' pp. 328–47.

11   The question, as we must note later, is very close to Christian Christology. If we are to think of God 'reigning' 'in the midst' here on earth, it can only

be by some 'mediation' into time of that which, so acting, has in no way abandoned eternity.

12 For inter-testamental writing, see J. H. Charlesworth (ed.): *Old Testament Pseud Epigrapha*, 2 Vols, New York, 1985.

13 Quoted from E. G. Urbach: *Types of Redemption*, Leiden, 1968, p. 194.

14 *Ibid.*, pp. 220f. Even Ruth's 'vinegar' (2:14) could be equated with Messianic suffering, not to mention Joseph's affliction.

15 See Gershom Scholem: *Sabbatai Svi, The Mystical Messiah, 1626–1676*, Princeton, 1973.

16 This issue is enormous and the literature likewise. See, e.g. Arthur Hertzberg (ed.): *The Zionist Idea: A Historical Analysis and Reader*, New York, 1973. For my part, some effort was made in *This Year in Jerusalem*, London, 1982. Simon Dubnow (1860–1941) stood for diaspora 'nationalism' via minority rights, constituting Jews as 'one of the peoples of Europe'. No emigration was necessary or proper.

17 Note 15 above, p. 94.

18 Echoing Theodor Herzl's famous phrase in *Der Judenstaat*: 'If we will it it is not a dream.'

19 Gershom Scholem: *The Messianic Idea in Israel and Other Essays*, New York, 1971, pp. 34f. He writes of Jewish life as 'Lived in deferment in which nothing can be done definitively, nothing can be accomplished irrevocably'. Living in hope is 'grand' but 'profoundly unreal'. Many Jewish writers have reproached Scholem for this verdict and hotly disputed it. Yet the idea of the necessarily 'unrealisable' persists.

20 Having 'a failed eschatology' – as Jewish thinking often alleges of Christianity – would be, for minds like Scholem's, simply the other alternative to 'futurism'. But are these the only two alternatives? Chapter 5 must live the question.

Chapter 5

1 Two interacting and characteristic words of the New Testament. (cf. Romans 5:8, and 2 Corinthians 5:11, Romans 8:38, 14:14 and Galatians 5:8) The Gospel does not 'impose' or 'dictate': it reasons and almost 'consults' with a present intelligence, cf. the Greek term *sunistesin*. 'Persuading' is close to the idea of a rhetoric (in the original sense) which aims to lead to free conviction, all the firmer for being personally attained.

2 William Shakespeare: *Hamlet*, Act 2, sc. 1, lines 64–5. 'Bias' is a fair word here and not derogatory. We have seen how Hebrew thought had its own interior prerequisites. If, as earlier argued, 'indirections' they proved, 'directions' were, nevertheless, only reached by 'assays', 'testings' of their experience.

3 John Ashton: *Understanding the Fourth Gospel*, Oxford, 1991, p. 245. Paul was far from disinterested in Jesus from Galilee onwards as his several echoes from the teachings indicate. Nothing could be more 'Messianic' than the theme of the 'subsidiarity' in 1 Corinthians 15:24–28. In Romans 1:2–4 he stresses the Davidic link. What, perhaps, misleads the unwary is the notion that in 2 Corinthians 5:16 Paul is somehow dismissing knowledge of – or care about – the Jesus of the story. That notion is obtuse. Paul, as the whole logic of the passage shows, is insisting that former worldly ideas of 'the Christ' have gone. He no longer thinks in those old politico-national, zealot, or other terms that are 'after the flesh'. Jesus the Christ has revol-

utionised the entire perception of Messiahship. *Ho* may have been elided in Paul's grammar but, as with him in Romans 9:5, it is present in his thought. No other reading makes sense of 2 Corinthians 5:16 – apart from the inherent oddity of thinking Paul disinterested in the one whom, with such ardour, he called 'My Lord'.

4   See the perceptive discussion in W. H. Vanstone: *The Stature of Waiting*, London, 1982, pp. 1–33.

5   J. R. Seeley: *Ecce Homo: A Survey of the Life and Work of Jesus Christ*, London, 1865. This eloquent work was, by some, suspected of 'liberal' intentions read by them as wilfully hiding behind a 'Passion' title. This was grossly unfair to Seeley.

6   The Greek bears both senses. One may compare the Qur'ānic verdict about *zulm*, or defiant 'wrong' against God: 'It was their own selves they wronged' (Suras 2:57, 3:117, 7:160, 9:70, 16:33 and 118,29:40 and 30:9).

7   See Chapter 4, note 4.

8   D. H. Lawrence: *Reflections on the Death of a Porcupine and Other Essays*, ed. M. Herbert, Cambridge, 1988, p. 233. There is, it is said, a Jewish proverb which runs: 'If God came to live on earth, people would smash his windows.' Or, break his heart?

9   The point can be recognised from the word 'Christology' itself. Of Greek provenance, it has come to stand for what being 'the Christ' means, just as 'biology' deals with 'life', and 'geology' with 'earth'. However, it came to be almost exclusively concerned with the 'being' – not the 'doing' – of the Christ, with terms, like 'nature', 'substance', 'person', which concern us in Chapter 8. However, before such 'ontology', or concepts of 'being' could 'mean' at all there had been the action, the event, of Messiah. It is high time to recover a Christology of action and let it control all else.

10 See, for example, Matthew Black: *An Aramaic Approach to the Gospels and Acts*, Oxford, 1967. What is called the Aramaic 'passive' occurs some one hundred times in Jesus' sayings. 'There is one who will . . .' as in the sequence after: 'Blessed are those who mourn for. . . .'. See also C. F. Burney: *The Poetry of our Lord*, Oxford, 1925.

11 Hebrews 5:8. Greeks were fond of that play on words. It occurs in Herodotus 1:207, *Mathemata ta Pathemata*. Through the experience of suffering one learns what it is that has to be obeyed, cf. Isaiah 50:4 where 'shame and spitting' undergone warrant the right to have 'the tongue of the learned'. Thus, with Jesus, the 'Sonship' which is immanent in the divine nature is only made real in the action. This confirms note 9 above. See also Chapter 7 below, where we find this the central theme of the whole New Testament. Messiah is learner, then teacher.

12 Its most familiar formulation was that of W. Wrede: *Das Messiasgeheimnis in Den Evangelien*, 1901, whose thesis was that Mark's Gospel presents a Jesus whose Messianic identity is 'concealed'. It only came to be believed of him in and by the Church after Easter. However, to be authentic it must have been so all the time, whereas Mark depicts the disciples as never comprehending it. Accordingly, Wrede argued that it was hidden deliberately. By this hypothesis, the Church could validate a Messiahship which, in fact, Jesus had never himself understood to be such. He was only, so to speak, *post facto* Messiah in the faith of the Church. Mark devised the secrecy idea to allow that/faith to be reconciled with the other fact of uncomprehending disciples. The thesis ignores the whole issue of Messianic ambiguity *in situ*. We have to conclude that Jesus was indeed

confessed as Messiah in the faith of the Church but only because of, and in the terms of, his existential experience of Messianic meaning in the story. Not 'secrecy', but Messianic decision and then Messianic recognition. Some scholars prove too inventive.

13 The emphasis that Geza Vermes made central in *Jesus the Jew: A Historian's Reading of the Gospels*, London, 1973. Vermes sees Jesus as a wandering charismatic preacher, a not unfamiliar phenomenon there and then. Is it not too attenuated view for a 'historian' to take?

14 The demonstration on Palm Sunday may be thought disproving the point. Though, indeed, a deliberated event, its purpose – and its outcome – can be seen in full accord with the pattern here argued.

15 Such a 'sharing of mind' and then of 'will' is explicit also in how the Gospels later present the baptism of Jesus. That 'This is My Son, my beloved,' is not some admiring satisfaction. It means 'one whose will is one with Mine'. The same is the point with 'men of goodwill' in the Christmas song, not some general goodwill, but a 'willing of what God wills' as the condition of 'peace on earth and glory in the highest'.

16 Robert Browning: *Poetical Works*, Oxford, 'Two in the Campagna', p. 238.

17 Albert Schweitzer developed the thesis in his *The Quest of the Historical Jesus* (Eng. trans. 1905) of a Jesus who died anticipating an immediate divine intervention. His disciples never understood him: he was desperately wrong in his expectation but unwittingly profoundly right in the paradox of his mistaken trust.

18 Though doing so is to be left with no credible explanation of how the disciples could have come to see it so on their own without warrant from Jesus and, indeed, in spite of him. For the case against the 'suffering servant' precedents having been operative with Jesus, see: Morna Hooker: *Jesus and the Servant*, London, 1959. The positive case is in C. R. North: *The Suffering Servant in Deutero-Isaiah: A Historical and Critical Study*, Oxford, 1948.

19 See, for example, Philip Carrington: *The Primitive Christian Calendar*, Cambridge, 1952, and *The Primitive Christian Catechism*, Cambridge, 1940. See also E. Trocmé: *Jesus and His Contemporaries*, Eng. trans. R. A. Wilson, London, 1973.

20 Certainly, *post facto*, that was how the Church saw it. We are assuming throughout, though we have yet to examine, the interplay of event and record, the mind of Jesus and the mind of the Church.

21 For, in that event, his memorialising would have been some ritual reading, e.g. of the Sermon on the Mount.

22 Eng. trans. of *Qaryah Zalimah*, Amsterdam, 1958, Paperback, New York, 1965. Reprinted, Oxford, 1994. It was remarkable that Kamil Husain furnished the advocates of force among the disciples with arguments drawn from his own Qur'ān. On his authorship, see: *The Pen and the Faith*, London, 1985, pp. 126–44.

23 *Contra Celsum, loc. cit.* note 25. Chapter 2, Book 2, p. 68.

24 See note 4 above, p. 99. 'Created' is not the right word here if it suggests anything artificial or contrived. Vanstone speaks later of God 'surrendering His impassibility', i.e. foregoing immunity in a pursuit of love to humankind. What we have in the Passion of Jesus measures all that is human-bent in the being of God. So unanimously thinks the New Testament.

Chapter 6

1   Edwin Muir: *Selected Letters*, ed. P. H. Butter, London, 1974, p. 92.

2   The principle is there in Genesis 9:6. The words quoted are from the Talmud alluding to Cain's deed. Pirke Aboth Rabbi Nathan xxxi. Sura 5:27–32 of the Qur'ān repeats the words, though it exempts 'murder and corruption in the land' from the writ of non-retaliation. If this were to benefit Cain we would have to see his crime as 'manslaughter' and not 'murder'. It is not clear what crimes are meant in 'corruption in the land'. The Qur'ānic passage tells vividly how Cain, seeing a raven scratching the ground, realised how futile it would be for him to try to 'conceal' his brother's death by scratching earth over his corpse.

   It also has another telling detail, having Abel say to Cain before the fatal deed: 'My wish would be to have all my sins be on you as well as your own.' Commentators have found this enigmatic. Did Abel mean that all his actual sins would somehow devolve on his brother if he (Abel) was killed? Does being murdered outweigh all that, otherwise, might be culpable? Or is the meaning very close to 'I will not justify your enmity by returning it'? Abel's sufferance of Cain means that the wrong of the situation is wholly Cain's.

3   It is important to see that 'vicarious' is *not* in respect of guilt but of consequences undergone. The Qur'ān, for example, is repeatedly insistent that 'no burden-bearer bears any burden but his/her own', and that 'God calls no soul to account' except for that soul's sins. The dicta are sound and right. It is, however, sad that they have often been cited to exclude the possibility of anything vicarious in life. It is not others' *guilt* that burden-bearers 'take': it is what that guilt does in its effect. The point is highly relevant to Christian interpretation of 'atonement'.

4   The word has the resonance of the Authorised Version in Isaiah 53:5, 'he was bruised for our iniquities'.

5   Jesus brings out this crucial point by the studied contrast between the father and 'the elder brother', who significantly avoids the word 'brother' which the father uses in appealing to him ('This thy brother is come'). 'This thy son' he prefers to say, meaning: 'Call him your son if you will: he's no brother of mine.'

6   It has proved impossible to trace the source of these lines.

7   W. B. Yeats: *Variorum Edition of the Poems*, ed. Peter Allt, London, 1957, p. 506.

8   The verb 'entail' in the usual sense 'to involve necessarily', as a consequence, derives from the legal 'fee entail,' which ensures property without alienation to a series of persons in succession. It thus usefully describes the onward connections inherent in human wrong.

9   So, in the Prayer Book version. The psalmist's meaning seems to turn on the individual soul being always unable to make good the wrong in his/her own life story. Record, that cannot be reversed or undone, must be eschatologically awaited.

10   This being the double sense of the Greek *airon* in John 1:29.

11   The paraphrase at the beginning of Chapter 1 of Thomas Carlyle's comment on the French Revolution ('knowing what to make of the world') will be taken up finally in Chapter 12, bringing 'Cross' and 'credential' into unison.

12   Reminiscent, surely, of the 40 days of the wilderness temptations and, in turn, the 40 years of post-Exodus wanderings. Moses' 40 years with Jethro, Elijah's 40–day journey to Horeb, not to mention Goliath's 40–day defiance

of the Israeli army, may be associated. Forty was also the biblical overlap of a generation.

13   If we read 'day' here, as with many biblical precedents we may, its wearing away, time-wise, to 'evening' would still be apposite for an emerging awareness. See Barnabas Lindars: *New Testament Apologetic*, London, 1961, Chapter 2, where he traces how 'Messianic value' was discerned in Jesus's life and passion and fitted, for proofs' sake, into Hebrew prophecies, to show that Jesus had been *Christus designatus* before, via the Cross, he became *Christus revelatus*. The disciples' earlier non-comprehension stemmed from their confusion about the role.

14   The word occurs only in Matthew 16:18 and 18:17 and belongs to the developing tradition of an *ecclesia*, as 18:17 clearly indicates. It is fair to wonder what word Jesus used in Aramaic in 16:18, and how far the passage hinges on what could only be understood of him *post facto*. See Chapter 9.

15   Much Jewish thinking this century emphasises fidelity in hope in 'the God of Israel' without striving to identify where it is 'fulfilled'. For it will always be future, seeing that any alleged 'fulfilment' will inevitably be falsified by on-going history. This perception also chimes with an acute sense of how far and how often Jews have been misled about 'Messianic actualisation' and have paid dearly for their aberrations from hope without sight. All eschatologies must fail except the last one. See, for example, Gershom Scholem: *The Messianic Idea in Israel and Other Essays*, New York, 1971, and Martin Buber: *Two Types of Faith: A Study of the Inter-Penetration of Judaism and Christianity*, trans. N. P. Goldhawk, New York, 1961.

16   The passage is crucial, as the earliest 'shape' of Christian creed concerning Jesus, in this context less than three decades from the events and explicitly cited as handed on from a still nearer time. The formulation is Messianic precedent-in-fulfilment. See also note 13.

17   Gnosticism presents a labyrinth of issues for the historian as to its origins, its dispersion, its bearing on Christian awareness and on Judaism through two or more centuries.

18   The point is more thoroughly explored in my *What Decided Christianity*, London, 1989.

19   'Fortunate' is a subtle word here, if one keeps in mind the 'Messianic woes'. If Messiah was to deal conclusively with evil it was assumed, in much Jewish tradition, that evil must reach its maximum prior to his 'act', for – otherwise – evil would persist after him and so disqualify his defeat of it. This was the logic of the concept of 'Messianic woes', the zenith of darkness and chaos in which it would not be good to be alive. Hence the saying: 'May Messiah indeed come! but may I not live to see the day!'

20   'Blessed by God, whose love it was/To double-moat thee with His grace, and none but thee.' Presumably Herbert had in mind the English Channel and the Elizabethan settlement. See: 'The British Church,' in *The English Poems of George Herbert*, ed. C. A. Patrides, London, 1974, p. 123.

21   The most signal evidence was the Septuagint, the Greek translation of the Hebrew Scriptures, done over several centuries before and after the Christian calendar.

22   'The place' and 'the Name' figure largely in Hebraic story through all the sequences of sanctuary location and the geographical bearings of theology. See Psalm 132:4, Isaiah 18:7, and 1 Kings 8:29–35.

23   'Report' is both passive and then active. What has been 'heard', received,

is in turn told in order to be heard again. The same double meaning belongs with the Christian 'tradition'.

24   This was the stance, for example, of the Pan-African Congress whose graffiti ran: 'One settler – one bullet', to 'encourage' whites to emigrate. Ibbo Mandaza, a black editor, wrote of 'the white factor in southern Africa being transient', 'on the way out'. On that basis, one might say, apartheid was justified. It supposed necessary exclusion as mutual, making hatred reciprocal. We have to be careful what we wish for. To suppose there can only be enmity is to entrench it and prevents wrongdoers from knowing their own guilt.

25   There is 'suffer' in the old sense of 'allow' (as in 'Suffer the children to come to me'), then the more usual meaning of bearing wrong. We have certainly been 'let be' in creation: 'redemption' belongs there, since God is One.

26   Herbert's Poems with A Life, by Isaac Walton, London, 1826, p. 34.

27   Leo Tolstoy: Complete Works, Moscow, 1928–64, Vol. 1, p. 290.

28   Dwight D. Eisenhower: Crusade in Europe, London, 1945, pp. 425, 343.

29   William Shakespeare: Henry V, Act 4, Chorus.

Chapter 7

1   The passage in John 8:2–11 does not appear in many Greek texts, and several of the early Fathers make no use of it. On internal grounds also it would seem to belong more readily to the Synoptic tradition than to the Johannine. The main point in context, however, is not affected. The incident serves graphically to underline how Jesus left no documentation from or of himself.

2   Or indeed in the whole New Testament, with the solitary exception of 3 John 13 where the writer refers to 'ink and pen'.

3   John Bunyan: Appendix to Grace Abounding. The magistrate before whom he appeared, one John Keelin, told him: 'We know that the Common Prayer Book hath been ever since the Apostles' time.'

4   A comprehensive study can be found in Wilfred Cantwell Smith: What is Scripture?, London, 1993.

5   The Qur'ānic term wahy means both revealing and inscribing since these, as Islam sees it, are necessarily one. The Qur'ān, unlike the Gospels, is not about something more ultimate than itself. It is, qua text, 'the Word of God as Book'. It follows that no human correspondence, however well meant, could be divine. If Paul chooses to write to Philippi, so be it. He, or his 'letter', cannot conceivably be God speaking.

6   The familiar names are used which identify the four Gospels, though all of them are anonymous. See later in this Chapter. The authorship of some 'Pauline' epistles is in question. Throughout, it is wise to keep in mind the instinctive practice, before and after the New Testament period, to link writings with revered names by which actual authors meant to invoke higher repute and claim affinity of mind. Almost all apocryphal writing is pseudo-named. No subterfuge was involved, the pattern being well known. See further, note 14.

7   The contrast with Islam's Qur'ān is complete, whose Arabic is inseparable from its identity as 'Scripture'. Translation into other languages has only been reluctantly conceded and is held to forfeit the essence of Qur'ānicity. The New Testament by its very nature assumes translateability.

8   Lamin Sanneh in his intriguing study Translating the Message, The Missionary

Impact on Culture, New York, 1989, examines how the enterprise of biblical translation has given receiving languages and cultures a spiritual articulacy they did not previously possess, giving new range and consciousness to vernaculars.

9   And see also Chapter 9, note 20.

10   The very meaning of verse 9 is elusive and, even if identified, is hard to make tally with the clear – and humorous – import of the story which has to do with the 'hidden usury' of adjusted buying and selling by contract which concealed loan and interest. The steward curried favour by simply rewriting bills in cash value terms.

11   If it is allowed to echo the words of Revelation 19:10, reading 'a trust of study' for 'the spirit of prophecy'. The way that Jesus was in life, word and death is the theme to which the 'prophets' in the churches must be loyal, letting it possess them.

12   It is sad that thinkers as eminent as C. S. Lewis have sought to argue in these terms, as a way of explaining belief in the Incarnation, i.e. these alternatives being unthinkable, he can only be divine.

13   No conscious parallel, of course, is suggested here. The point is simply that in his Melian dialogue and the 'speeches' in his *History* Thucydides (460–400 BCE) aimed to convey the situation, from inside, by having his action told on the lips of the main participants. He was not 'reporting' what was ever 'heard', nor was he citing informants. Dismissing what he called mere 'story-telling', he gave the crucial figures words that dramatised and 'told' the motives and meanings the events inwardly possessed as interpretation might. The Fourth Gospel gives us faith's perception of Jesus being Christ in dialogues and signs that, while rooted in the day-to-day scene, convey the 'over-meaning' of the history. *Kenosis* may be likened to a tapestry with its one design viewed beneath and above. There has been no *kenosis* unless both are there in one fabric and one texture. What is visually that way about a tapestry is done in writing by John, ascribing to Jesus in words what Christology saw him to have been. To appreciate John's achievement we need to understand his intention.

On Thucydides as analogy, see further, M. I. Finley: *The Use and Abuse of History*, London, 1986, who writes: 'It was necessary to compose speeches which would lay bare . . . both sides of an issue. . . . He accepted the need to narrate events in sequence but . . . he wished to extract from the events the essence . . . and consequences of power,' pp. 31–2. For 'power' read in the Fourth Gospel, 'grace and truth', 'Jesus in his Christology'.

14   'Pseudepigrapha' is a current but dubious term for the several writings in the New Testament that bear names other than their actual authors. In modern usage 'pseudo' suggests 'false'. Modern practice supposes that names are of authors and that authors 'assert their right' to be acknowledged for whom they are and whose the writings. Such tradition did not obtain in Biblical times. Given the safeguard of communal mind, it was feasible to write under the name of a 'celebrity' – Enoch, Isaiah, Barnabas, Ezra – who had no conceivable authorial part in the text. The pattern was well understood, namely that the actual writer intended the 'higher' association to give weight and 'association' to his message. In the New Testament the Letters to Timothy and Titus arguably reflect a more developed stage of ministerial order than belonged to Paul's own career but which could be duly associated with his influence and assumed approval. The circumstantial references about his prison conditions and

companions register what was certainly true to life as belonging to his ministry thus linked with the text. See further, T. D. Lea: 'Pseudonymity and the New Testament', in D. A. Black and D. S. Dockery (eds), *New Testament Criticism and Interpretation*, Grand Rapids, 1991. Also: J. D. G. Dunn: *Unity and Diversity in the New Testament*, London, 1977, and, for a strongly opposite view, arguing 'fraud', see E. E. Ellis; 'Pseudonymity and Canonicity of the New Testament Documents' in M. J. Wilkins and T. Paige (eds), *Worship, Theology and Ministry in the Early Church*, Sheffield, 1992.

15　Expulsion from the Synagogue – a traumatic thing in Roman context – is referred to in John 9:22 and 16:2. There are numerous other references, e.g. who is the true Israelite (1:47); being Moses' disciples under challenge (9:28). In the late 80s the synagogue authorities introduced a reworded Birkat ha-Minim, or imprecation on deviators, into liturgical services in order to be able to expel them. To confess Jesus as Messiah qualified for this. (There were Jewish Christians who held to the synagogue while keeping their beliefs quiet. Some may have reported on 'full' Christians.) Preachers from the Johannine community were arrested and put on trial, with capital sentence, for 'misleading' Jews, a situation reflected in 5:18, 10:33 and 16:2. Numerous other fields for 'detective work' are present in all the Gospels to help in ascertaining when they were complete.

16　The dates of actually surviving documents of New Testament texts are even less usable means of dating the texts, given the loss of manuscripts. It is intriguing that the earliest surviving papyrus of John (in the John Rylands Library, Manchester) is from John 18, parts of the passage in which Jesus is interrogated in private by Pilate.

17　For example, 'Blessed are ye . . .' in Matthew 5:11, where the Beatitudes move from 'they' to 'ye', could apply equally to disciples listening on 'the mount' in Galilee *and* Matthew's readers in circumstances like those of John's in footnote 15.

18　See, notably, George B. Caird: *The Revelation of St John the Divine*, 2nd edn, London, 1984.

19　The metaphor is drawn from distilling. Did not Moses say: 'My doctrine shall distil as the dew' (Deut 32:1)? One might compare how Wordsworth's poetry, via Dorothy, his sister's eyes, drew out of 'hiding places ten year's deep'. Events are given 'through the alembic of John's own mind'.

20　G. Bornkamm: *Early Christian Experience* trans. P. L. Hammer, London, 1974, p. 21.

21　*The Epistle to Philemon*.

22　The issue had to do with idol names invoked over meat. For the weak brethren who had not yet realised the utter non-entity of idols, such invocation would make the meat significantly different, to eat which would imply acknowledging the idol. A robust Christian like Paul would find the implication baseless since idols are non-entities. Yet, free to eat as he is, he would forego such freedom lest he mislead his brethren, but only until they had been liberated from their illusion of the idols' 'reality'.

23　The Galatians hankered after the old 'wrapped-up-ness' of legal precepts which they found less demanding, more passive, than their exacting liberty in Christ to proceed in faith alone.

24　Alleen Guilding: *The Fourth Gospel and Jewish Worship*, Oxford, 1960, and see note 19 in Chapter 5 above.

Chapter 8

1   William Shakespeare: *The Comedy of Errors*, Act 3, sc. 2, lines 35–8.

2   William Shakespeare: *Richard III*, Act 4, sc. 4, lines 249–50, substituting the second 'mean' for 'intend'.

3   H. R. Mackintosh: *The Person of Christ*, Edinburgh, 1912, pp. 286, 290, 292.

4   William Shakespeare: *A Midsummer Night's Dream*, Act 3, sc. 2, lines 126–7.

5   The hymn was written by Newman in a mood of deep soul-anxiety in his quest for a truth that needed no questioning and his disquiet, like Keble's, about signs of 'secular' erosion of the authority of the Church.

6   Thomas Carlyle's well-known gibe at *Homoousios* and *Homoiousios*, 'of one substance' and 'of like substance' with the Father.

7   William Wordsworth: *The Borderers*, Book 2, Sect. iii, line 344.

8   Leo Tolstoy: *Complete Works*, Moscow, 1928–64, Vol. 3, p. 86.

9   As some have thought Exodus 3:14 does in 'I am that I am,' where the meaning, however, is not philosophic but existential about a 'God of Exodus' whom only exodus will prove so.

10 Another of those 'bifocal' questions noted in the previous chapter in which what is at issue belongs *both* to the Jerusalem (or Galilean) scene *and* to what obtains when, and where, the Gospel is written. Consorting with 'the Greeks' in certain Jewish circles in either locale was an occasion for scorn and sharp satire.

11 'At the full' needs to be rightly read. It is not implied that the divine and the human in Christ was any varying reality, only that its significance throughout was most intensely known in the Cross – known both in the time-consciousness of Jesus and in the awareness of a right theology. See below. In theology it is necessary, in saying what one means, to avoid saying what one does not mean. Sometimes, as here, one is cast on perceptive good faith in the reader.

12 In Chapter 9, section vi.

13 The adverbs are important here. Without them (i.e. 'fleshly' and 'physically') the sentence would be entirely true. It is precisely the Incarnation which makes its meaning eternally divine *and* its eventuation historical in actual human terms. Those human terms of 'flesh and blood' partake in the divine/eternal precisely as the necessary arena, while what is and happens there partakes of the nature of the divine in the divine/human duality of ends and means.

14 Richard Crashaw: *Poetical Works and Quarles' Emblems*, Edinburgh, 1857, p. 38.

15 Clauses in the (so-called) Nicence Creed and in the Christmas Preface in Holy Communion (Book of Common Prayer).

16 'Verily' in the Authorised Version anglicises a Semitic *al-haqq al-haqq* 'in truth in truth', 'the really real'.

17 In some Muslim-Christian medieval controversy one finds alleged embarrassment in crudely corporeal questions about excrement and other bodily functions, pressing polemic about incarnation which could have no reference to its point.

18 Echoing 'he came where he was' in the good Samaritan story. The divine is not 'other-sided' on the human road.

19 See my *Poetry of the Word*, London, 1987, p. 65. Inasmuch as 'birth-incidence' is inseparable from being human there has to be an understanding of divine Incarnation via birth as necessarily distinguishable from the birth-thing we undergo in general. That essential 'otherness' about divine,

incarnational birth has been traditionally symbolised in Mary's virginity –
as it may well be. However, it needs to be insisted that the passage in
Isaiah 7:14 which gave occasion to the concept of virginal conception has
nothing to do with it. Isaiah 7:14 appeals to the familiar theme of pregnancy (in any 'maiden' or 'girl') followed by birth and weaning. 'Virgin' is
not what the Hebrew *almah* conveys. Nor is the point of the passage any
'miracle' but simply how a troubled king, beset by political coalitions, may
be comforted by assurances that his fears will be disproved in the brief
time it takes to wean a youngster who is significantly named 'Emmanuel'.

20   *Ibid.*, p. 38.

21   It was always clear that prophethood entailed suffering from a hostile
world – suffering incurred by being on behalf of God. It could not be, then,
that the God whose service spelled His servants' travail should be aloof,
or immune, from it. Hosea, for example, saw a direct correlation between
his own anguish and 'yearning' in Yahweh. See also Abraham Heschel: *The
Prophets*, New York, 1962.

22   Some of the factors concern us shortly. 'Humanly' is used here in the
sense, not of having to pass muster because humans might demur out of
enmity or pride, but as being unworthy of such divine grace.

23   Seeing that 'beget' and 'begotten' are normally used, and often biblically,
of ordinary human family lineage (so used in Matthean genealogy of Jesus'
'line' through Joseph). There is no single word that suffices as the verb we
need in this regard. Begotten is used in the sense discussed in context. On
the force of '*only* begotten', see below. The Qur'ān of Islam in Sura 112
reads 'begotten' in the normal sense and, so doing, rightly denies it in any
divine reference.

24   The word derives from the Greek *hairesis*, 'an opinion of one's own'. According to Acts 24:14 it was a term applied to the emerging Gospel itself. It was
often used in the first centuries about deviant (as later seen to be) ideas
of, for example, Arius, Apollinarius, Nestorius and Eutyches who gave
their names to the 'isms' which the Creeds and Chalcedon sought to
exclude. While 'heresy-hunting' is an unhappy impulse, 'heresy-probing'
(before the word is applied) has its due place in truth-concern.

25   It was this need, of course, which required the 'Ecumenical Councils' to
make explicit what needed to be so made. Inevitably, again, the stresses
of the doctrinal issues spilled over into the standing of the Councils which
purported to resolve them.

26   Quoted from note 3 above.

27   Such is clearly implied in 1 Corinthians 12:3. We note in the Pastoral
Epistles the emergence of the phrase: 'This is a faithful saying . . .' (1
Timothy 1:15 and 4:9; 2 Timothy 2:11; Titus 3:8) clearly enjoining what is to
be taught and accepted.

28   As A. N. Whitehead remarked: 'The habit of definite exact thought was
implanted in the European mind by the long dominance . . . of scholastic
divinity.' *Science and the Modern World*, 1925, p. 13.

29   Muslim theologians, for example, did the same when they 'reconciled' free
will and determinism by saying that 'God willed the deed in the will of the
doer', virtually turning the question into the answer. Must one not go on
to ask: 'Could the doer help willing it when God willed it in his will?' An
unfree will is then part of God's 'doing'.

30   The term, from the Greek, is used to denote divine attributes or activities
from divine essence, 'doing' from 'being', seeing that these can be, or need

to be, thought of as distinct from the divine reality which is through and beyond them. No theologies – Jewish, Christian, Muslim or other – could escape what they meant in speaking of divine 'Name', 'Face', 'presence' or *shekinah*, 'Wisdom', 'Speech' or 'loving kindness'.

31   The 'one nature' theology in the Monophysite view more suitably upheld the divine-ness as entrusted with the humanness on its own terms. In resisting 'the two natures' theology, it risked, without conceding, a less than full humanity.

32   By allowing, for example, a dichotomy in perceptions of Jesus so that 'weariness' at the well or 'sleeping' in the boat were obviously 'human' things while 'stilling the storm' or foreseeing resurrection were divine power and knowledge. Such a dichotomy was ruled out by the 'two natures' doctrine as being 'without separation or division'. Even so, many in Chalcedonian orthodoxy for centuries made such division in understanding their faith about Jesus. Witness, for example, the resistance the Lux Mundi essayists found after 1890 (from H. P. Liddon and others) in repudiating notions that denied authentic humanness in a real *kenosis*.

33   Geoffrey Lampe, in *God as Spirit*, sought to bring the Incarnation entirely within the work of the Spirit, and so coming to a binitarian theology. He thought that the classic understanding of the Incarnation was untenable except in terms of 'spirit'. His plea has not been heeded. The divine/human in 'the Word made flesh' – as argued here – consummates and controls all 'proceedings of the Holy Spirit'. *God as Spirit*, Oxford, 1977.

34   The alternatives of the well-known *Filioque* clause dividing east and west and turning on the interpretation of John 15:26, which spoke only of 'from the Father', though the same Gospel joins the Son with the Father and has the Son promising the sending of the Spirit. The issue is more one of subtlety than substance.

35   Some twenty times in the Nicene Creed, four in the Apostles'.

36   The clause 'the communion of saints' may well be 'the communion of holy things', i.e. 'bread and wine'. Otherwise the omission of all reference to that sacrament is puzzling. *Communio sanctorum* may be either 'saints' or 'things'.

37   A composition of the New Testament scholar T. R. Glover. See H. G. Wood: *Life of* T. R. *Glover*, Cambridge, 1953, p. 137.

38   A phrase of Oscar Wilde's in his 'De Profundis' in *The Works of Oscar Wilde*, ed. G. F. Maine, London, 1945, p. 869.

39   William Shakespeare: A *Midsummer Night's Dream*, Act 2, sc. 2, line 52.

Chapter 9

1   Collects for the 2nd, 3rd, 8th, 15th, 16th and 22nd Sundays after Trinity. Being 'peaceably ordered . . . in all godly quietness' (5th Sunday after Trinity) is the dearest ambition. If, however, we are rightly minded to deplore this lack of adventure we must recall the stresses, early and late, that taught this language.

2   William Temple once remarked: 'Institutions must be run on their own lines.' See Adrian Hastings: 'William Temple' in Geoffrey Rowell (ed.), *The English Religious Tradition and the Genius of Anglicanism*, Wantage, 1992, p. 216. It is the obvious realism of the remark which gives us pause. Institutions' 'lines' readily become their 'ends'. The theme of the bane of institutions was central to the thought of Arnold Toynbee in his *The Study of History*. The

point is developed, with references, in my *Troubled by Truth*, Durham, 1992, pp. 222–41.

3   If Ephesians is not Paul's, it is very Pauline. The term *pleroma* is very rich, being here an absolute accusative, 'that which fills' as a content, or that which 'fulfils' as a purpose. It can mean at once the crew and the cargo of a ship. It signifies what is there when all 'potential' is achieved. It means 'plenty', 'stature', 'completion', and 'perfection'.

4   The 'binding' and 'loosing' in this passage belongs with rabbinic usage and does not refer to any power to adjudicate on the incidence of divine forgiveness. The words relate to 'enjoining' and 'prohibiting', i.e. affirming the will of heaven *vis-à-vis* human behaviour. The John 20:23 passage concerns us later.

5   'Tribulation' derives from the Latin *tribula*, a heavy threshing device made up of three logs strung together and studded underneath with iron spikes.

6   'Perquisite' is defined as 'an article which subordinates claim a customary right to take for their own use', in the abeyance of its original use.

7   'My-doxy' is, of course, orthodoxy and 'thy-doxy' is heterodoxy. The terms are used by Thomas Carlyle in *The French Revolution*, London, 1837, Vol. 1, p. 462. He attributes the terms to Bishop Joseph Butler.

8   The meaning in 2 Peter 1:20 is that no Scripture can be well understood except within a corporate mind. Exegesis is not a matter for insistent individualism. Nor should a particular passage be forced against a sense of the whole. The directive is linked by the writer to the conviction that the source of Scripture was never a purely individual impulse but always the Spirit's initiative.

9   Richard Baxter: *Self-Review*, London, 1910, p. xvi.

10 cf. Acts 13:36. Even the great David was not exempt.

11 The Latin *informo* is not 'to give news' but 'to give shape', 'to delineate truly'.

12 William Shakespeare: *The Merchant of Venice*, Act 1, sc. 3, lines 15–17, 21–5.

13 e.g. 'Our sufficiency is of God' (2 Corinthians 3:5), cf. same Epistle 2:16, 9:8 and 12:9. The word *autarkeia* means 'adequacy'. Article 6 of the Book of Common Prayer, in affirming 'the sufficiency of the Scriptures', dissociates them from the notion of 'infallibility'.

14 It is clear from Galatians 1 and 1 Corinthians 15:8f. that this was a vital matter for Paul – a 'lack' he believed made good by the Damascus vision. Its importance to him argues its being central in the thought of his fellows in Christ.

15 The Greek word *hiereus* ('priest' in some ritual sense) is nowhere used in the New Testament in respect of the Christian ministry. It occurs, narrative-wise, in respect of the Temple hierarchy and it comes in the argument of the Epistle to the Hebrews concerning the priesthood of Christ. See below. In Revelation 1:6, 5:10 and 20:6, and in 1 Peter 2:5 and 2:9 it echoes the Hebraic theme of 'a holy nation and a kingly priesthood', i.e. the biblical concept of the human *imperium* hallowing the natural order by a right political, national order of power, science and government.

16 R. C. Moberly: *Ministerial Priesthood*, London, 1907 edn, pp. 293, 295, 299.

17 It is important, however, in studying early Christian leadership, both func-tional and sacramental, not to overlook the central significance, in the first century, of 'prophets', men and women of 'the Word', whose capacity for ecstatic utterance had greater immediacy and impact, even though (by the same token) it made the more crucial the will to 'order' and due discipline,

the more so by the time that 'lapsed Christians' in persecution became so large an issue.

18 Cyprian (c. 200–58) was Bishop of Carthage through the final twelve years of his life, being made bishop almost immediately after his Christian conversion. By training a lawyer, he was a major figure in the development of a doctrine and practice of episcopacy as necessarily constitutive of the Church. The setting of his time goes far to explain the exigencies behind his thinking. In fierce, if intermittent persecution, what of the lapsed? Could they be received again, after penitence, by appeal to the merits of the saints or of loyal 'confessors'? Should there be re-baptism? By whom were sacraments valid? The 'trueness' of the Church, not to say its unity, demanded, in Cyprian's view, a clear, decisive, unambiguous role for episcopacy.

19 'Purveyance' is defined as 'procuring, providing, supplying and controlling anything necessary for others'.

20 The point was brought home to me when in Beirut we employed a Maltese verger at All Saints' Church. As a Roman Catholic he wanted to be 'received' as an Anglican in order fully to 'belong' in the context of his duties. Knowing little English and no Arabic, and I no Maltese, we agreed on a Maltese New Testament as a gift. When I handed it to him he asked: 'Where can I find the Creed in this book?'

21 Such right, and ability, of on-going 'faithful' to read into, or out of, their scriptural heritage what they wish, or think, it to have come to mean is a phenomenon also in other faiths. Some Jews believe that all that Moses received on Sinai enlarges into all that the oral law and its exegesis chooses to hold. Some Muslims, likewise, hold the Qur'ān to be prescient of meanings its first hearers never realised nor the actual text suggests. The Roman Church has successively invoked and exercised an alleged right to 'develop' doctrines and devotions that have no arguable apostolic or traditional warrant. Lack of such warrant is freely acknowledged. Papal authority, including its own 'infallibility', makes the lack good.

Chapter 10

1 Paul's words in 1 Corinthians 14:8 have often been cited in calls for doctrinal purity. His own context, however, has to do with the moral compromises which distort the sound.

2 Oscar Wilde: The Works of, 1856–1900, ed. G. F. Maine, London, 1948, p. 353: The Importance of Being Ernest.

3 Don Cupitt: After All: Religion without Alienation, London, 1993, p. 105–9.

4 Shabbir Akhtar, with some justice, made the same point about the 'liberal establishment' in his critique of its reaction in the contention over The Satanic Verses. See his: Be Careful with Muhammad, London, 1989.

5 Clive James: The Dreaming Swimmer, London, 1992, p. 103.

6 'Ecumenical' means 'belonging to the whole inhabited world'. However, until lately, its current usage confined it to inter-Christian relations. Now it tends to be used in wider bearings on the inter-religious.

7 William Blake: The Prophetical Writings, ed. D. J. Sloss and J. P. R. Wallis, 'The Everlasting Gospel', Oxford, 1926, Vol. 1, p. 25.

8 Warren S. Kissinger: The Lives of Jesus: A History and Bibliography, New York, 1985.

9 Matthew 13:55 and Mark 6:3. The term may include 'mason' or 'builder' in

more than wood alone. One might recall Thomas Carlyle, aged 14, asking his mother: 'Did God almighty come down and make wheelbarrows in a shop?' D. A. Wilson: *Thomas Carlyle till Marriage*, London, 1923, p. 78.

10   W. B. Yeats: *Collected Poems*, London, 1923, p. 246: 'Wisdom'.

11   See Chapter 5, note 5.

12   Among recent discussions see David R. Catchpole: *The Quest for* 'Q', Edinburgh, 1993.

13   We cannot argue from those about whom we do not hear but it is important to realise that there may well have been minority verdicts, so dramatic were the issues. As Samuel Beckett remarks in another connection: 'It is all very well to keep silence but one has also to consider the kind of silence one keeps' – or undergoes.

14   For insistence on the priority of Matthew, see, for example, W. R. Farmer: *Jesus and the Gospel*, Philadelphia, 1982.

15   See, for example, Proverbs 8:1–6, 9:5, etc.

16   The text of the Qumran Beatitudes, echoing phrases from the first Psalm, exalts 'the meek' over whom the Lord's 'spirit will hover', and extols the 'pure in heart'.

17   'Unique', in any event, is not the surest of words to use in a theological or ethical context. 'Distinctive' is a more perceptive word in acknowledging characteristics that are not shared while allowing those that truly are. That which is totally non-participatory with others must be incompatible with the whole meaning of Incarnation.

18   One useful study of Jesus' distinctiveness (which may also help the point of note 17) is John Riches: *Jesus and the Transformation of Judaism*, London, 1980.

19   It is noteworthy that the same greeting to Mary at the Annunciation is echoed as one to all Christians in Ephesians 1:6, where they are said to be 'graced in the Beloved', i.e. truly 'favoured' (*echaritosen*).

20   Examples are everywhere. 'Proselytism', these days is an ugly word, meaning the making of converts by means foul or fair. Etymologically, the 'proselyte' is simply one who seeks, who comes to enquire in order to understand. The word 'prestige' which now has to do with pride of place, honour and worthy reputation originally came from *praestigium*, in which observers were eluded by imposture, by conjuring tricks intended to deceive.

21   William Shakespeare: *Henry V*, Prologue to Act 1.

22   Robert Herrick: *Poetical Works*, ed. L. C. Martin, Oxford, 1956, p. 398: 'Good Friday: Rex Tragicus.' The poem continues: 'Thou art He who all the flux of nations come to see.'

23   A. E. Housman: *Collected Poems and Selected Prose*, ed. C. Ricks, London, 1988, p. 148: 'Out of Egypt'.

24   Housman's early biography reveals that a crippling academic disappointment remained with him as almost a grudge against life and goes far to explain the deep distrust of hope and truth that characterised his exquisite poetic gift.

25   William Shakespeare: *Othello*, Act 5, sc. 2, lines 109–11.

26   The theme is a very central one in the Qur'ān, cf. Sura 2:30f. The angelic 'worship' of the creaturehood symbolises the dignity of the human as the arena of divine experiment with the 'trust' of the earth.

27   *The English Poems of George Herbert*, ed. C. A. Patrides, London, 1974, p. 192. 'You must sit down, sayes love, and taste my meat.'

Chapter 11

1   Job 15:12 (Authorised Version). Perhaps the seventeenth-century trans-
    lators did not quite get the Hebrew, which often in Job is hard to get
    anyway. It may be 'flashing' rather than 'winking' eyes that the writer
    meant. The Vulgate has: *Quasi magna cogitans attonitos habes oculos* which
    might serve us here almost as well.

2   John Donne: *The Poems*, ed. H. J. C. Grierson, Oxford, 1933, pp. 213–14. 'The
    new philosophy calls all in doubt/ . . . /'Tis all in peeces, all cohaerence
    gone: All just supply, and all Relation.' He adds: 'This is the world's
    condition now/ . . . /Thou knowest how lame a cripple this world is.' 'The
    First Anniversary', p. 214.

3   Solipsism means the reductionism that allows itself only assurance about
    the individual self and that self's experience. It is, of course, true that 'only
    I is I', and that all awareness is self-located. But no self is self-explanatory
    or self-sufficing. Selfhood is a social reality. There was very much else that
    could not reasonably be doubted if the self was to be dubbed indubitable.
    Conversely, as some absurdists have felt, the self could readily be included
    in all-embracing deception.

4   One might crudely illustrate by imagining oneself wearing green-tinted
    spectacles which one could never remove but which one knew were
    imparting greenness on to all in one's vision. Thus it would be both
    possible and necessary to acknowledge what the seeing was contributing
    to the seen and postulate the unattainable, ungreened noumena.

5   'Pure' he distinguished from 'practical' reason. The latter determined
    moral judgements and formulated the principle of the law of contradic-
    tion. If the principle of one's action would be self-defeating if universal-
    ised, that principle was manifestly wrong. Thus, fraud and dishonesty
    destroy the basic trust on which society proceeds. If all were frauds no
    fraud could succeed. Practical reason also yielded the 'categorical impera-
    tive', the command without any qualifying 'if'. By these in turn Kant was
    able to affirm the reality of God as the third postulate of that imperative –
    the other two being freedom and immortality.

6   See, further, Chapter 12. 'Supernatural' is a question-begging word. In
    what sense 'super', or what is 'nature'? Charles Darwin was the greatest
    'supernaturalist' of them all, in the sense that beyond the immediacies of,
    e.g., botany, or biology, he discerned an all-embracing teleology, a 'Mother
    Nature', working (divinely?) towards ends and purposes. Darwin has been
    called 'the Paul of evolution'. On his own showing he personified the word
    'nature'. See, for example, Stanley E. Hyman: *The Tangled Bank*, New York,
    1959, pp. 38f.

7   Echoing William Shakespeare in another context: *Macbeth*, Act 1, sc. 7,
    line 27.

8   In both, inasmuch as, while Christianity owes itself to the Messianic hope,
    much in Judaism after the fall of Jerusalem owes itself to insistent reaction
    against the Christian perception of a crucified, Gentile-incorporating Mes-
    siah. The point is important. For it sometimes assumed that Judaism
    wishes merely to be left alone, since it has no 'liability' towards Christ-
    ianity such as Christianity has towards Jewry.

9   A conjecture that deserves much exploration. See, for example, R. L. Slater
    in R. L. Slater and H. D. Lewis (eds): *World Religions: Meeting Points and Major
    Issues*, 1966, pp. 65f. He notes the coincidence of dates, the Mahayana

tradition developing in the first Christian centuries, reproducing, Buddhist-style, the ideas of 'Gospel', 'Saviour', and 'grace'.

10 'Promiscuous' – 'confusedly mingled' – was not initially a sexual descriptive.

11 The Islamic theory of the three distinctions made Islam, from the Hijrah, a politico-religious 'realm' destined by Jihad to comprise all the world. Until it did so, the areas outside its rule were, by contrast, 'the realm of war' (Harb). The third was a pragmatic compromise wherever power or delay required, as 'the realm of armistice-peace' (Sulh).

12 Wilfred Cantwell Smith who uses 'faithing' in this way insists on a radical distinction between 'faith' and 'beliefs'. 'Faith' ought never to be plural, cf. The Faith of Other Men, New York, 1962. Also Towards a World Theology, New York, 1981.

13 'Necessary' is needed here. In Smith's view, while there is no vital need to require, or seek, or elicit, conversion, freedom of movement of belief must ensure that the opportunity is always available. It is in those terms that mission can still have point, as the holding in place, for access, of a form of 'faithing' not yet followed.

14 The 'ocean' was a familiar analogy for the Nirvana of ultimate emancipation from the 'suffering' of individuation into the bliss of immersion into the undifferentiated totality where identity would be no more. Walt Whitman's Leaves of Grass, with his 'I sing to myself', uniquely expressed American vitality and the vibrant sense of personal meaning. He could salute the oceans as his wondrous friends and find himself participating, via his being the Walt he was, in all human experience.

15 Some anthropologists thought that by 'going back to origins' they could more readily understand the fusion of religion and society than by reference to more sophisticated culture. Thus James Frazer's The Golden Bough, at the turn of the nineteenth century, gathered material from many sources to furnish the sociological study of religion. It was inspired by E. B. Tylor's Primitive Culture (1871). Both thought that in assembling this material of 'religion and magic' they were reaching 'the embryology of human institutions'. Durkheim had the same broad idea in his Elementary Forms of the Religious Life, Eng. trans, 1965.

16 Not 'prejudices' here in the derived sense of attitudes deliberately hostile or perverse but in the original sense of mental 'set-of-mind' innate and not consciously adopted – the myth-bound, socio-religious ethos that cannot (or does not) think itself other than it is.

17 cf. 1 Corinthians 3:23. The sort of 'association' of God with 'will', 'Word', 'speech', law, mercy (all of them understood as 'His') that is inseparable from any doctrine of creation and sovereignty Islam entirely accepts. However, fortified by its necessary anti-idolatry, it required itself to resist the Christian understanding of 'God's Christ' as 'pluralist' when, in fact, it fitted exactly into those other 'associations' with God that Islam and the Qur'ān directly or indirectly affirmed and needed in order to be Islam.

18 It is important not to misread Feuerbach's view to mean there was nothing to theology but 'wishfulness'. Worship, faith, prayer could all be 'genuine', as being humanity's own meaningfulness symbolically transacted and transacting.

19 The need, e.g. for significance, for guilt-awareness, for a rendezvous with penitence, for pardon and assurance, for being loved as the corollary of loving. There is something mischievous in the very truth of readings,

like Feuerbach's, that 'justify' what faith denotes and 'possesses' while detaching it disconcertingly from what other minds would consider the nature of fact. Perhaps, in the end, it is precisely what constitutes 'fact' that is the issue at stake. See Chapter 12 below.

20   Marx's debt to Feuerbach can readily be seen when, so to speak, he turned the theory on its head. Religious belief indeed a subjectivity of the human soul? Then appreciate that it connives with injustice, fortifies acquiescence in wrongs and palliates situations which should be challenged and changed. Feuerbach's wine became Marx's 'opium' (of the people). 'The cry of the oppressed' pointed to the socio-economic and demanded the denunciation of the socio-religious.

21   Ludwig Feuerbach: *The Essence of Christianity*, trans. George Eliot (Mary Ann Evans), London, 1854, pp. 144f.

22   Ludwig Wittgenstein: *Note-Books*, 1914–16, trans. G. E. M. Anscombe, eds Anscombe and Wright, Oxford, 1961, p. 16.

Chapter 12

1   Vincent van Gogh: *A Self-Portrait*, ed. W. H. Auden, London, 1961, p. 38.

2   Quoting Paul in 2 Corinthians 6:10, he perhaps echoing Jesus' words about those invited to the comedy and tragedy of life who had no measure of either. That clue runs through the whole reach of Christian meaning (Matthew 11:16).

3   An intriguing coining of word. The French writer and libertine wrote in *Lettres inédites à sa mère*, 1833–6, trans. A. Symons, London, 1928. 'I desire with all my heart to believe that an external, invisible being is interested in my fate, but what does one do to believe it?' (p. 224.) He thought that even human vices contained proof of a thirst for the infinite.

4   John Bunyan: *Grace Abounding*, Paragraph 98.

5   Iris Murdoch: *The Sovereignty of Good*, London, 1970, p. 79.

6   George Eliot: *Adam Bede*, Chapter 41. The prophet Haggai knew as much, cf. Chapter 2:10–14, an 'oracle' on contagion.

7   George Eliot: *Middlemarch*, Finale (last page).

8   *Loc, cit.*, note 21, Chapter 11, pp. 27, 30, 59, 121, 125.

9   *Ibid.*, pp. 60, 57.

10   See note 6, Chapter 11. It is clear that Darwin was hesitant, even appalled, by what he foresaw would be the consequences, to traditional faith, of his theories, and by the travail into which they would bring him. Yet traditions of purpose and ends that his upbringing had instilled found their way – as it were, 'evolutionised' – in his 'Mother Nature' faith. It remains a significant feature of his 'unbelief'.

11   One might recall G. K. Chesterton's comment about 'those for whom everything matters except everything'.

12   Some effort to explore what these 'areas' might be was made in *The Christ and the Faiths*: London and Louisville, 1986.

13   William Shakespeare: *Henry V*, Act 4, Prologue, lines 6, 7, 9, 17. The last line is only about the French.

14   Echoing the repeated Qur'ānic phrase, celebrating the triumph of the faith. *Al-fawz al 'azim, al-fawz al-mubin*.

15   Leonardo da Vinci: *The Notebooks*, ed. I. A. Richter, Oxford, 1952, pp. 248–9.

16   Assuming that China is meant. The Septuagint has *Ges Person*, which may mean Elam, eastward. The Vulgate has *Terra australi*, 'southern land'. Some

translators read Syene for Sinim, and identify it with Aswan in Upper Egypt, where there was a colony of Jews at the time of this writer (see Ezekiel 29:10 and 30:6 where Syene is mentioned). If Sinim were derived from Tsin named for a Chinese dynasty, it would be too late for the time of this writing or preaching.

17 The term 'Father' is indeed found, as in Psalm 103:13 and Malachi 1:6 and 2:10, by way of analogy or in relation to mercy within creation. It is, however, in Jesus' Sonship that the divine Fatherhood is fully comprehensible.

18 Tacitus: *Annals*, 14:44. This Roman historian (55–117) wrote contemptuously of Christians as a 'subversive cult', which he derived from one, Christus, whom, he noted, was crucified in the regime of Pilate in Judea.

19 John Keats: *Letters*, 1814–1821, ed. H. E. Rollins, Cambridge, Mass., 1958, Vol. 1, No. 45, of 28 December 1817, to George and Tom Keats.

20 John Milton: *The Poems*, ed. J. Carey and A. Fowler, London, 1968. The note following the poem is p. 122.

Post Scripta

'The Word Made Flesh'

'O mind has womb' where quickened thought conceives
A wistful shape that weighs its willing way
Toward life till ripening words convey
Imagination to embodiment.

So ever was the muse of prose and verse
Interpreting intelligent intent
Through verbal pregnancy a thing that breathes.
By very birth is very meaning meant.

Mind's child becomes a character impressed
Into the clay of 'there' and 'then' and 'thus',
With literacy in sequence to rehearse
The many-storied thing. No longer pent
In slumbering expectation of release,
The bearing text with language in consent
Finds destiny in being understood
And signifies a comprehendedness.

God's drama *verbum caro factum est.*
'To us child is born, a son is given,'
Beyond whose natal prelude lie in wait
Dimensions written into scene and plot
Where it suffices that the day will end
And then the end is known – the end the known,
Divinely authored proven masterpiece
Enacting into time the theme of grace –
In *profundis et excelsis gloria.*

Begin to read at Bethlehem but more
'Behold the man' – the sacrament in life
Of Jesus as the Christ, the hills and haunts
Of Galilee his proving ground. Weigh well
The breathless 'straightways' of the Markan tale
That brood and breathe in retrospect of John.
Regard the retinue of multitudes
In claim on heart compassion, the touch
On leprous scar, the weary hungry fed,
Disciples by the rock of Banias
In blundering imperception given pledge
Of rock-like strength against the gates of hell.
From sanguine palms and Temple's disarray
Come share where bread and wine will educate
The broken twelve. In far Gethsemane
The burden learn of love's full final word,
The whole of truth for which first birth was meant.
Stabat Mater juxta crucem where wounds
And dying state what love has writ – has writ
For signature in every human script
Across the face of Pilate's titulus.

The pre-existent Christ the doctrines say,
The-yet-to-be that in reality
For ever was. By intercourse of heaven
And earth, through history from crib to cross,
Nativity fulfils eternity.
Transcendence, giving comprehension leave,
Has wrapped in swaddling clothes the clue to God.

Index

Aaronic blessing 177
Abel 88, 228
Abigail 89
Abraham 54, 57, 102, 118, 148, 214
'Absence', divine 48, 134, 165
absolutes 34, 40, 41, 45, 48, 188, 196, 211
absolution 44, 174
absurditiy 2, 27
Achaia 115
Acts of the Apostles 13, 95, 101, 122
  cited:

  4.10   91
  4.12   214, 215
  6.1–7   152
  8.37   112
  8   56, 175
  11.16   92
  12.2   117
  17.16–31   50, 214
  27   111
'Acts of God' 54
Adam 32, 36, 102, 179, 180
Adam Bede 206
adjectival theology 20, 21, 46, 48, 104, 132f,
  201f, 210
Aegean Sea 96
aestheticism 25
agency, divine 137f
agnosticism 35, 50, 198, 217
Agnosto Theo 50
Agricola 124
Agrippa 98
ainigmata 33
Alexander 111
Alexandria 126
Algeria 103
Allah 6, 162, 195, 223
Allahu akbar 2, 11, 107, 130, 139
almsgiving 78
Amerindians 10, 11, 162
Amos 8, 59, 61, 62
  cited:

  5.24   15
  9.11–12   64
anamnesis 160
Anatolia 115
anatta 190
'Ancient of days' 65
Anselm 27, 198
anthropology 10, 240
antilogia 74
antinomy 21, 209
Antioch 122
Antiochus Epiphanes 65
anti-Semitism 74, 162
apartheid 103
apocalypticism 66f, 82, 123
apostasy 111
apostolicity 122, 152f, 160
Aquinas, Thomas 183, 185
Arabic 110, 230
Aramaic 65, 77, 108, 112, 117, 174, 226, 229
Areopagus, the 50, 99, 214
Arimathea, Joseph of 93
Aristotle 16
'arm of the Lord' 103
Ascension, the 95, 132, 135, 160
Assyrians 56
Athanasius 126
atheism 28, 49
Athens 50, 99, 214
atonement theology 140, 141, 174, 228
Augustine 28, 183, 202
authority 5, 7, 19, 47, 59, 71, 76, 110, 126, 127,
  153, 160, 165
autonomy, human 4, 43

Babylon 63
Babylonians 56
Badr, Battle of 8, 219
Baeck, Leo 194
Baha'ism 110
baptism 44, 227
baptismal formula 112, 114

Bar Kochba 67
Barnabas 122, 153
Bathsheba 59
Baudelaire 202
Baxter, Richard 150, 236
Beatitudes the 75, 79, 83, 118, 143, 169, 172, 232
 – in Qumran 228
Beckett, Samuel 49, 238
Beethoven 45
Bemerton 104
Benedicite Omnia Opera 22
Bethlehem 116
Betjeman, John 32, 222
Bho Tree 86
birth narratives 13
Blake, William 168, 237
'body', the 143, 144
Book of Common Prayer 109, 145, 228, 230, 233, 235, 236
Brahma 194
Bright, John 33, 222
Browning, Robert 13, 18, 39, 46, 204, 220, 222, 223, 227
Buber, Martin 70, 194, 229
Buddha, the 110, 213
Buddhism 12, 19, 188, 190, 214, 219
 – Eightfold Path in 190, 212
Bunyan, John 109, 110, 203, 230, 241
Byzantium 138

Caesar 45, 74, 79
Caesarea Philippi 81, 83, 149
Caiaphas 168
Cain 83, 88, 89, 104, 228
 – law of 88, 92
Caligula 111
Calvary 85, 86
Camus, Albert 25, 27, 44, 45, 49, 222
 – The Fall 44
 – The Rebel 44, 45
 – The Stranger 44
Canaan 9, 10, 11, 15, 58
Canon, the 7, 110, 124, 125f, 143
Canterbury 27
Carlyle, Thomas 1, 2, 19, 228, 233, 236, 238
Catholicism 150
Celsus 85, 227
Chalcedon, Council of 11, 13, 160, 128f, 183, 234, 235
Chemosh 56
China 214, 241, 242
'Chosen people' 52f, 62
 – privacy of 69f
'Christhood', of Jesus 72f
Christianity 7, 8, 72f, 88f, 97f, 128f, 151f, 169, 194f
 – The Essence of 196, 207
Christianoi 97
Christology 72f, 117, 120, 125, 130f, 172, 195, 208, 209, 213, 224, 226, 231
 – of action 140
'Christos, Ho' 72
'City of David' 83
City of Wrong 84
Clement of Alexandria 126

Cobden, Richard 33
coinherence 141
collectives, human 37, 38, 39
Colossae 109
Colossians, Letter to
 – cited:
   2.6   124
   2.9   141
   3.16   154
Comte, Auguste 68
concreteness 69, 70, 196
Confucius 156
conscience 40, 41, 58, 59, 77
Constantinople 163
Corinth 109, 111, 125, 153
Corinthians, First Letter to
 – cited:
   4.9   176
   11.25   155
   15.3–7   99, 100
Corinthians, Second letter to
 – cited:
   1.15–24   151
   4.7   146, 177
   5.16–22   85, 87
   6.4–5   111
   11.23–25   146
cosmology 21, 208, 209
covenant 54, 56, 58, 61, 77, 101, 102, 147, 162, 187
 – in blood 83
 – paradox in 60
Crashaw, Richard 233
creation 12, 14, 20, 21, 22, 23, 37, 52, 56, 69, 132, 195, 208
Creeds 20, 91, 94, 96, 99, 101, 106, 112, 126, 128f, 145, 164, 166, 167, 196, 212, 213, 233, 235
Crusade, Fourth 162
Crusade in Europe 105, 230
Cupitt, Don 166, 237
Cyrus 63

Damascus 101, 126, 153, 236
Daniel, Book of 65
Dar al-Harb 189, 240
Dar al-Islam 188
Dar al-Sulh 189, 240
Darwin, Charles 197, 208, 209, 239, 241
David 54, 57, 58, 59, 64, 66, 89, 236
 – dynasty of 64
 – 'Son of . . .' 67
'Day of the Lord' 61
death 31, 32, 33, 53, 85, 86, 88, 121, 191, 206
Decalogue, the 205
Demas 111
democracy 40
Demosthenes 83, 156
'denial of denials 35, 39
Descartes, René 184, 208
design, argument from 27, 209
desire 190, 191, 193
determinism 234
 – in sociology 192
Deuteronomy, Book of 48, 56, 58, 177
 – cited:

2.21–22   55
4.32–39   55
18.13   177
29.29   48
development, doctrinal 127
Dharmapada, the 110, 191
dhikr, in Islam 156
Diabolos 36
diakonos 152
diaspora 65, 67, 68, 102, 131, 215
Diatessaron, the 126
Dickens, Charles 197
Dies Irae 61
disbelief, suspension of 96, 178
diversity, human 38, 39
Doceticism 133, 143
Donne, John 183, 198, 222, 239
Don Quixote 216
Dubnow, Simon 68
dukkha 190
Durkheim, Emile 211, 240

earth's exceptionality 22
Easter 94, 96, 98, 154, 194, 213
Ecce Homo 74, 169, 200, 201
ecclesia 147
Ecclesiastes, Book of 219
economy, the divine 139, 140
ecumenism 150
Edwards, Jonathan 198
Egypt 10, 15, 28, 54, 55, 62, 223
Eisenhower, Dwight 105, 230
Elijah 6, 223, 228
Eliot, George 196, 197, 206, 241
Eliot, T. S. 222
Elizabethan Settlement 145, 229
'Emmanuel' 80, 219
Emmaus 101, 156
empiricism 45, 185, 186, 208f
England, Church of 145, 162, 229
Enlightenment, the 68
Enoch, Similitudes of 67
episcops 152, 157
Epistles in New Testament 72, 74, 85, 95, 96, 97, 101, 108f, 233
Ephesians, Letter to
  – cited:
    1.17   144
    1.25   148
    2.10   177
    2.15–22   102, 112
    3.14–21   144, 148
    4.5   194
    4.30   163
Ephesus 121, 122
Esau 34, 55
eschatology 65, 66, 67, 97
  – and Schweitzer 227
esse and bene esse 160
Ethiopia 56, 112
Eucharist 120, 155f, 213
evangelism 164, 165
exclusivism 111, 112, 212
exile 8, 56, 57, 63
Exodus, the 8, 11, 15, 37, 54, 156, 220, 228, 233
  – Book of, cited 9

Ezekiel, Book of, cited 64
Ezra, Book of 63, 64, 65

'face' imagery of the 146, 177, 235
factuality 54, 199
fanaticism 198
Fanon, Frantz 103, 104
'Father', the 76, 77, 82, 87, 93, 112, 120, 131, 142, 235, 242
  – 'coming to' 214, 215
  – 'from the bosom of' 118
Fathers, the 128, 132, 183, 230
feminism 137
Feuerbach, Ludwig 195, 196, 201, 207, 241
Filioque 142, 235
finality 95
'finished work of Christ' 119
forgiveness 62, 77, 82, 90, 93, 206, 236
  – and the Cross 86f, 159
form criticism 116
Foxe's Book of Martyrs 110
French Revolution, the 1, 228, 236
Freud, Sigmund 211
Frost, Robert 18
fundamentalism 6, 11, 166
futurism 63, 70, 71, 213
  – in Judaism 97

Galatians 92, 109, 165, 232
  – legalists among 125
  – Letter to, cited:
    2.18   125
    3.1   92
Galileans 28
Galilee 13, 75, 79, 82, 83, 96, 99, 101, 108, 114, 115, 146, 174, 224, 232
'gates of Hell' 147
Genesis, Book of, cited:
    1.2   23, 166
    4.1–15   88
    9.6   228
    32.22–32   34
Gentiles 11, 52, 67, 101, 112, 121, 124, 148, 152, 170, 172, 179, 239
Gethsemane 13, 73, 82, 83, 84, 93, 100, 117, 118, 119, 135, 140, 158, 163, 169, 207, 215
Al-Ghazali 42, 222
Gibbon, Edward 171
'gift to the altar' 78
Gnosticism 99, 100, 114, 133, 140, 229
'God in Christ' 102, 103, 107, 128f, 140, 154, 159, 162, 195, 196
'God of mercy' 47
Goethe 122, 224
Good Friday 207, 208, 213, 216
Gospel, the 50, 74, 75, 77, 83, 138, 163, 167, 175, 213
Gospels the 13, 31, 50, 60, 81, 84, 91, 94, 95, 96, 97, 100, 108, 113f, 165, 168, 170, 171
  – anti-semitism in 121f
  – Apocryphal Gospels 123
  – the Fourth 13, 72, 74, 80, 84, 102, 114, 115, 117f, 155, 168, 171, 225, 231
  – Synoptic Gospels 114f
grace 47, 85, 87, 124, 174, 193, 195, 209, 217
  – and birth 121

– and sacrament 155f
Grasmere 26
Greek/Greeks 112, 116, 131, 174, 226, 233
Greek Testament 118
Gregory of Nyssa 21

Habakkuk 92
Haggai 64
Halakhah 67
Hamlet 96, 216, 225
Hardy, Thomas 19, 24, 25, 26, 37, 197, 220, 221
Hasmoneans, the 66
Hebraic tradition 36, 69, 147, 178, 206
Hebrews, Letter to the 74, 91, 92, 122, 125, 126, 178, 236
– cited:
    1.6–14   178
    9.12   157
    12.3   74
Hebron 57
Hellenisation 102, 172
Henry V 106, 175
Herbert, George 21, 102, 104, 105, 180, 229, 230, 238
heresy 138, 234
Hermon, Mount 9
Herod 66, 67
Herrick, Robert 176, 238
Heschel, Abraham 234
Hexateuch, the 54
Hezekiah 68
hiereus 153, 157, 236
Hinduism 188, 194, 195
Hobbes, Thomas 40
'holiness' 59
– and ethics 59f, 161f
Holy Spirit, the 44, 95, 96, 109, 125, 127, 141, 142, 154, 161, 163, 214
– kenosis of 162
Hosea 62
– cited:
    4.1   75
    12.2   75
Housman, A. E. 176, 238
humanism 29
Hume, David 45, 46, 47, 223
Husain, Kamil 84, 221, 227
Hymenaeus 111
hymnology 127
hypostasis 20, 22, 140

Ibn Sina 183
ideology 41
idolatry 36, 58, 124, 232
Iesus Kurios 72, 130, 138
imperialism 15, 45, 103
Incarnation, the 8, 20, 21, 80, 100, 118, 129, 132, 133, 136, 141, 142, 156, 162, 190, 194, 195, 196, 207, 235
inclusivism 189
India 214
infallible, the 158, 172, 236
inspiration 110
intention 78, 128, 209, 214, 218
– in creation 21, 36, 37, 42
– and explanation 128f, 143, 217, 218

inviolability 58, 59, 60, 67
Ireland 91, 162
irony 73, 147, 168
Isaiah, Book of, cited:
    1.13–18   15, 59, 166
    5.1–7   60
    7.14   234
    25.9   102
    30.11   59
    40.26   179
    42   63, 82
    50   63, 82
    52   63, 82
    53   63, 82, 103, 112
    63.10   44
islām 2, 29
Islam 2, 9, 11, 14, 38, 42, 110, 162, 188, 195, 213, 214, 234, 240
Israel 58, 61, 68, 176, 187
– 'God of' 10, 62, 229
– 'Holy One of' 59, 67
– land of 60
– tribes of 53, 56
Italy 68

Jacob 34
James the Apostle 76, 101, 111, 114
– Letter of 177
Jefferies, Richard 24, 25, 221
– 'Story of My Heart' 24
Jeremiah, 8, 45, 61, 66, 92, 206, 214, 224
– cited:
    7.4   60
    11.19   82
    22.24   64
    23.5–6   64
    25.31   75
    33.14–18   57, 64
Jerusalem 54, 59, 64, 65, 77, 79, 81, 83, 86, 101, 108, 111, 223
– fall of 67, 99, 102, 146, 215, 230
Jewish War, the 67
Jewry 42f, 58, 60, 62, 69, 102
– and Goyim 111, 112
Jihad 161, 188, 240
Job 4, 5, 29, 182, 217, 219, 239
– Book of 4, 5, 48, 140
Johannine community, the 120f, 232
John the Apostle 76, 110, 114, 123
– Gospel of, cited:
    1.6–9   114
    1.29   92
    3.9   92, 180
    4.4   79, 124
    6.57   117
    7.35   131
    7.46   172
    8.6   108
    9.30   108
    9.39   80
    11.32   124
    12.6   73
    12.21   176
    12.27   84
    12.47   117
    14.6–9   170, 214, 215

16.20   100
17.1–24   119, 123
18.33f   84
19.30   85
21   123
John, Letters of 126, 152
John the Baptist 78, 114, 120
Jordan, the 9, 15
Joseph 28, 68, 186, 215
Joshua 10, 15, 57, 68, 161
Josiah 55
Judah 64
Judaism 7, 14, 65, 68, 78, 121, 162, 172, 173,
    188, 239
    – Messiah in 53f, 65f
Judas Iscariot 72, 73, 90, 153
    – suicide of 73
Jude 126
Judea 56, 64, 115, 122
Judges, Book of 54, 56
Jung, Carl 211, 222
justification 92, 93
Justin Martyr 126

Kant, Immanuel 21, 28, 184, 208, 221
Karakter 216f
Keats, John 23, 194, 217, 242
Keble, John 162, 233
Kedron 119
kenosis 46, 97, 104, 106, 119, 121, 136, 160, 162,
    166, 195, 207, 223, 231
Kenya, Mount 10, 220
Kenyatta, Jomo 10, 220
Kere-Nyaga 10
keys, the power of the 147, 148, 149
'kingdom of heaven' 75, 78, 79, 178
'king of the Jews' 84
kiss, betrayed with a 31, 72, 73
Kissinger, Warren 168, 237

'the Lamb' imagery 120, 145, 208
laos of God 124
Lawrence, D. H. 36, 39, 75, 222, 226
Lazarus 207
lebensraum 39
Leonardo da Vinci 213, 216, 241
Leviathan 40
Lewis, C. S. 220, 231
liberalism 11
    – as dogma 166
liberation 12, 13, 14, 15, 156
Liturgy, early Christian 83, 109, 112, 114, 125,
    126, 156, 173, 227, 232
    – vocabulary in 174f
Logos 129, 136, 138, 139, 198
'Lord of hosts' 10
'Lord of this house' (Mecca) 9
Lord's 'anointed', The 61, 64
Lord's Prayer, the 118
Lucretius 49
Luke the Evangelist 66, 91, 97, 101, 114, 115,
    119, 122, 123, 156, 169, 170, 208
    – Gospel, cited:
        1.28   173, 174
        4.16–21   108
        14.16–24   116, 178

15.1   76
15.11f   90f
16.1–12   116
19.18–22   80
20.9–19   115
22.19   149
22.28   149
22.48   31
24.52   146
Luther Martin 196

Maccabees, the 66, 224
Machado, Antonio 22, 221
Machiavelli, Niccolò 40
Magi, the 75
Malinowski 211, 220
Mandela, Nelson 103, 104
'And was made man' 136, 137
Marcion 126
Mark the Evangelist 72, 80, 114, 115, 116, 119,
    122, 123, 169, 170, 226
    – Gospel, cited:
        1.1–9   114
        8.27–33   81
        9.12   82
        10.35–45   115
        12.1–12   115
        14.41   74
        14.44   31
Marvell, Andrew 153, 220
Marx, Karl 32, 192, 196, 241
Mary 31, 133f, 173, 174, 238
Mary Magdalene 101
Masada 67
Mathnawi 28, 29, 221
Matthew the Evangelist 72, 75, 98, 114, 115,
    116, 119, 122, 123, 169, 170, 186
    – Gospel, cited:
        5.48   177
        9.36   77
        11.16–17   147, 148
        11.28–30   75, 76, 214
        16.13–23   81, 147, 148
        18.17   147, 148
        20.1–16   179
        20.20–28   115
        22.1–14   116
        26.48   31, 72
        28.19–20   101
Matthias 153
Mazzini 68
'means of grace' 47
Mecca 9, 86, 195, 212, 219
Melville, Herman 2
meschalim 77
'Messiah' the 4, 14, 53f, 61f, 88f, 100, 215
    – Messianic dimension in God 43
    – 'hidden' 66f, 81
Methodism 127
Micah, cited 6.2   75, 161
Michelangelo 45
Middlemarch 206
Milton, John 22, 32, 43, 217, 222, 242
'mind of Christ' the 101, 122
miraculous, the 12, 13, 95
Moab 84

Monophysites 138, 235
Montanists 127
Mormonism 110
mortality 32, 33
Moses 6, 9, 15, 54, 57, 68, 75, 77, 78, 86, 102, 114, 148, 228, 232
'Mother Nature' 209, 239
Mount of Olives 95
Muhammad 6, 8, 38, 86, 110, 187, 195, 219, 220
Muir, Edwin 1, 88, 219, 228
Muratorian Canon 126
Murdoch, Iris 204, 222, 241
Muslims 28, 29, 161, 162
mythicisation of history 54f

Nabal 89
Napoleon 1, 45
Nathan 59
natures, two 140f
Nazarenes 78, 139
Nazareth 80, 108, 114, 118, 135, 168
Negro folklore 15
Nehemiah 64, 65
Nestorians 126
Newman, John H. 129, 162, 198, 233
New Testament 60, 61, 65, 72, 74, 76, 85, 89, 91, 92, 93, 94, 95, 100, 102, 106, 108f, 122, 125, 131, 138, 148, 161, 164, 168, 170, 194, 214
 – slavery in 125
Nicaea 128, 131
Nicodemus 92, 119, 120, 121, 122, 180
Nietzsche, F. 47
nihilism 45
Numbers, Book of, cited:
  6.24–27   177
  16.38   74
  21.9   121

oaths 60
objectivity 201f
omnipotence 46, 47, 136, 186, 207, 208
'only begotten' 75, 136, 137, 141, 142, 178, 213, 234
ontology 27, 209, 210
ordination 151f
 – in New Testament 152
Origen 85, 198
Orontes, River 58
Osage Indians 11, 15
Oxford 126
Oz, land of 4

paganism 50, 51, 58, 100, 124
Palestine 57, 58, 96, 112
Palestinians 72
parables, of Jesus 74, 75, 115, 169, 178
paradidomai 73
Paradise Lost 32, 43
paradox 7, 10, 38, 42, 61, 65, 69, 139, 165, 192, 201
 – of law 42
 – of power 44
Parousia 97, 99, 125
particularity 53, 54, 56, 86

Passion, the 74f, 83, 85, 94, 99, 169, 170, 172, 224, 227
Passover, the 82, 83, 120, 155
Pastoral Epistles 122, 125, 234
patience, God of 11, 22, 46
Paul the Apostle 33, 42, 43, 50, 51, 92, 98, 100, 101, 102, 110, 111, 122, 146, 148, 165, 176, 179, 203, 214
 – and 'Messiah' 72f
Pax Romana 111
peace, the king's 40
peirasmos 149
penitence 44, 77, 93, 101, 159
Pentateuch, the 141, 146
Pentecost 97
perplexity 13, 33, 35, 140, 183, 210
Persia 63
Persians 56
person of Christ 139, 140 passim
personhood 19, 20, 24, 25, 30, 31, 32, 38, 190, 201f
Peshitta 126
Peter the Apostle 76, 81, 91, 94, 96, 100, 110, 111, 122, 123, 215
 – and 'Rock' saying 147
 – First Letter of, cited:
  2.21   97
  3.14   97
  4.1   97
  4.16   98
Philip the disciple 112, 214
Philippians, Letter to
 – cited:
  2.5–11   85, 97, 112, 125
Philistines 58
Pilate, Pontius 13, 74, 84, 86, 87, 91, 134, 135
Pilgrim's Progress, the 110
'place of the Name' 8, 17, 36, 103, 104, 215, 229
pleroma 141, 236
pluralism, religious 37, 188f, 211f
Pompey 65
Pound, Ezra 31, 222
prayer, in Gethsemane 118, 119
 – in Richard Jefferies 25
'precious blood of Christ' 165, 172
pre-existent Christ, the 132
presbuteros 152, 157
'print of the nails' 96
Proceeding, of the Holy Spirit' 142
Prometheus 45
'proofs' of God 27
prophets, the Hebrew 15, 58f, 62, 82, 120, 161, 163, 195, 206, 214, 234
Proverbs, Book of 221
 – cited:
  8.36   74
  13.12   66
  29.18   30
Psalms, the 22, 65, 125, 152, 166, 180, 224
 – cited:
  2   56f
  8   22
  22   83
  23.6   20, 155
  32.1   180
  40.1   69

42.7	29
49.8	15, 92
69	83, 120
72	61
72.9	56, 64
74.3	5
74.22	4, 5
89.3–4	64
89.20–37	64
105.15	64
107.2	203

pseudepigrapha 230, 231, 232
Pusey, E. B. 132

'Q' (source) 115, 169f, 238
QED's 207
qeryana 126
Qoheleth 6
quietism 68
Qur'ān, the 3, 6, 7, 35, 43, 88, 110, 156, 162, 195, 219, 226, 227, 228, 230, 234, 237, 238, 241
 –cited:

2.2	6
2.30	35, 36
2.186	6
3.7	6
4.165	3

ransom 82
rationality 41
realism 12, 42, 47, 79, 130, 208
 – Messianic 80f
'real presence' 158f
redaction criticism 116
Red Sea 15
Reformation, the 110
Resurrection, the 85, 88, 91, 94, 95, 97, 98, 100, 103, 122, 124, 135, 156, 194
 – of the body 143
retaliation 90
revelation, concept of 6, 7, 16, 53, 185
Revelation of St John 111, 123, 125, 145, 232
reverence 24
rewriting of Messiah 72f
Rhine, the 105
'righteousness' 15, 29, 41, 43, 62, 78, 83, 94
 – and 'the holy' 59, 60
'right hand of God' 99, 135, 137, 174
risk divine 22, 43, 44
Romans, Letter to 42, 43, 92
 – cited:

5.8	207
7.21–23	42, 43
9.24	111
10.17	165
11.13	152
11.33–36	125
12.1	179
15.7	97
15.16	153

Rome 67, 79, 86, 122, 124, 146, 179
Rumi, Jalal al-Din 28, 29

Sabbatai Svi 68
Sabbath 66, 77, 174

sacramental, the 20, 21, 30, 38, 83, 153, 154f, 211
 – in sexuality 30
sacro egoismo 64
Salāt 21
Salisbury 104
salvation 215
Samaria 62, 79, 125
Samaritans 64, 82, 119
Samson 58
Samuel, Book 66, 89
Sangha 110
Sanhedrin 121
Sarajevo 49
Satan (Shaitan) 36, 43, 103
scepticism 48, 93, 182f, 197, 208
Scholem, Gershom 194, 229
Scriptures 6, 7, 10, 16, 38, 53f, 59, 65, 96, 99, 107, 108f, 122f, 137, 161, 166, 174, 200, 201
Scythians 56
secularity 5, 11, 39, 164f, 180
Seeley, J. R. 74, 169, 226
Seine, the 44
Seir 55
Semitic mind, the 93, 161f
Sermon on the Mount, the 117, 153, 156, 227
'servant songs,' the 63
sexuality, see also: sacramental 30, 31
Shakespeare, William 32, 72, 105, 106, 122, 128, 151, 177, 212, 220, 222, 225, 230, 233, 235, 236, 238, 241
Shechem 57
shirk 195
Shoah, the 3, 70
Shylock 151
Simon the Zealot 78
'sin of the world' 74f, 215
Sinai 10, 78, 148
sincerity 41
society, 'the just' 43
Socrates 156, 207
Solomon 57, 58, 147, 224
 – Psalms of 67
'Son', the 20, 131, 178, 227
 – 'of God' 112, 114
 – 'of Man' 5, 31, 65, 81, 85, 87, 169
Sonship 75f, 80, 159, 214, 226
 – and unity 213
Sordello 39, 40
sovereignty 2, 4, 8, 30, 36, 39, 44, 48, 51, 65, 67, 79, 89, 134, 139, 178
 – criteria of 105, 106
 – 'of good' 41
speculative theology 12f
Sruti Scriptures 110
statehood 40, 41
Stephen 111
subjectivity see also: Feuerbach 201, 202
'substance' (in Creed) 20, 132, 139, 174, 207
'suffering servant', the 62, 74, 82, 85, 103, 169, 206, 226, 227
Summa contra Gentiles 14, 183
Summa Theologica 14, 183
sunistesin 166, 167, 225
'supernatural', the 210, 211, 239
Sychar 124

symbol 215
synagogue, the 67, 77, 148, 153
 – expulsion from 232

Tacitus 124, 242
Talmud, the 68, 220
Tamerlane 80
Tanakh 6, 126
Tatian 126
Tawhid 38
Te Deum Laudamus 174
teleology 27, 209
Temple, the 12, 37, 57, 59, 60, 63, 78, 83, 98,
 102, 147, 159, 236
 – cleansing of 83, 120
Tennyson, Alfred Lord 49, 223
territorialism 10, 11, 37, 55, 56
theism 28
theologies, folk 15
theophany 34, 37
Thessalonians, First Letter to 96
 – cited:
          1.3–10   97
          5   125
Thomas the Apostle 94, 95, 100, 101
'thorn in the flesh' 58
Thucydides 118, 122, 231
Tigris, the 58
time, nature of 8, 32
 – and space 21, 37, 38
Timothy, First Letter to
 – cited:
          1.15   164, 172
          1.20   111
          3.16   112
 – Second Letter to, cited:
          4.10   111
Titus 122, 231
tolerance 11
Tolstoy, Leo 16, 105, 130, 230, 233
tomb, the empty 13, 93, 95, 98, 99, 100
Torah 2, 7, 65, 66, 67, 68, 148
Toynbee, Arnold 220, 235
traditio 142, 160
Traherne, Thomas 23, 24, 26, 221
 – Centuries of Meditations 23, 24
transcendent, the 2, 4, 8, 9, 11, 16, 18, 28, 37,
 38, 45, 48, 50, 89, 133, 134, 193, 201, 204,
 210, 217
 – unity of 10, 29, 69, 142
tribalism 55, 56
Trilling, Lionel 16
Trinity, the 131

unigenitus 213
universality 69

'unknown god' an 50, 51

Van Gogh, Vincent 24, 45, 200, 201, 221, 223,
 241
Varanasi 212
verification 185, 186, 187, 216
Vermes, Geza 227
violence 40, 44, 55, 88, 89
 – 'men of' 79
Virgin Birth, the 133f, 233, 234
Voices from the Margin 10
Von Hugel, Baron 38, 222
vows 60
vulnerability, divine 4, 43, 44, 65, 131, 137
 – of the Church 145

Waiting for Godot 49
Walton, Isaac 104
Warrior, R. A. 10
Wesley, Charles 34, 127, 198, 222
Wesley, John 127, 198
Whitman, Walt 18, 190, 240
Wiesel, Elie 2, 219
Wilde, Oscar 166, 235, 237
Wiles, Maurice 8
Wiltshire Downs 25
wisdom 14, 27, 35, 37, 39, 45, 49, 101, 137, 163,
 169, 170, 192, 221, 235
Wittgenstein, Ludwig 199, 241
'woes', Messianic 125
 – 'to you' 78
'Word of the Lord', the 6, 165, 219
 – ministry of 152f, 174, 175
'Word made flesh', the 20, 50, 71, 100, 108, 129,
 133, 136, 156, 190, 214
Wordsworth, William 1, 9, 24, 25, 26, 130, 219,
 220, 221, 232, 233
worship 36, 38, 59, 60, 77, 112, 139, 191, 196,
 210, 232
Wrede, W. 226

Yahweh 11, 53, 56, 57, 58, 60, 62, 65, 67, 75,
 76, 80, 146, 166, 179, 187, 189, 234
 – and 'Messiah' 67, 70
Yeats, W. B. 90, 168, 228, 238
Yeshiva 68
'yoke', imagery 75, 76

Zealotism 66, 76, 100
Zebedee 122
Zechariah 64, 67, 224
zenophobia 39
Zephaniah 61
Zerubbabel 64
Zion 57
Zionism 60, 68, 70, 161
zulm 195